The W. R. Banks Library
Prairie View A. & M. College
Prairie View, Texas

Turmoil in Teaching

The W. R. Banks Library
Prairie View A. & M. College
Prairie View, Texas

Turmoil

The predicament of teachers today, without unionism, is not only economic; it is a predicament also of integrity. There is more and more evidence that teachers cannot afford integrity and honesty.

—James B. Carey, President, International Union of Electrical Workers, AFL-CIO, in an address before the annual convention of the National Education Association, Denver, July 3, 1962

You [teachers] are the high servants of the state, but for that very reason you are not the servants of any sect or party or class, and sects and parties and classes must keep their hands off you. You must be free—you of all men and women.

—Walter Hines Page, *The School That Built a Town.* New York: Harper & Row, Publishers, 1952, p. 64

in Teaching

A HISTORY OF THE ORGANIZATIONAL STRUGGLE FOR AMERICA'S TEACHERS

T. M. Stinnett
Visiting Professor of Education
in the Graduate College
Texas A. & M. University

LB 2842
S 86

The Macmillan Company, New York
Collier-Macmillan Limited, London

The W. R. Banks Library
Prairie View A. & M. College
Prairie View, Texas

For Tom and Bob

© Copyright, T. M. Stinnett, 1968

All rights reserved. No part of this book may be reproduced or transmitted in any form or by any means, electronic or mechanical, including photocopying, recording, or by any information storage and retrieval system, without permission in writing from the Publisher.

First Printing

Library of Congress catalog card number: 67-20821

The Macmillan Company, New York
Collier-Macmillan Canada, Ltd., Toronto, Ontario

Printed in the United States of America

121862

PREFACE

The idea for this book was born during the speech by James B. Carey in which he shocked the Denver Convention of the National Education Association on July 3, 1962, by bluntly asserting that "teachers cannot afford integrity" (complete quotation is in Chapter 1). I sensed that his announced raid by big labor on the membership of teachers' professional organizations portended a coming turmoil among public school teachers and in public schools. I sensed also that there were turbulent years ahead for the then somewhat staid teachers' organizations, with violent overthrow of many of their sacrosanct dogmas and procedures.

My reactions were, of course, largely automatic because Carey's expressed philosophy diametrically clashed with that which had dominated my own work for many years of my professional career. Through the TEPS (Teacher Education and Professional Standards) Movement, my work had been to help build teaching into an independent, self-managing, self-directing, proud, and dedicated profession. The philosophy of this movement allows no room for escapism, for leaning on "big brother" or the "man on the horse." Its philosophy demands individual initiative and aggressive group action to solve any and all teachers' problems, including teachers' welfare and economic justice.

There were two things about this scene at Denver that started the wheels turning in my mind. First, the all-out drive of organized labor to proselyte the public-school teachers of this country by invoking the old labor practice of raiding established organizations was, for the first time, brazenly brought into the open. Prior to this scene, there was plenty of evidence that the drive was under way, but it had been a somewhat hush-hush operation. The NEA and its affiliated state and local associations had been such warm admirers and supporters of the great work of the unions in improving the lot of the working man that they could not seem to bring themselves to believe that the AFL-CIO was actually plotting their ruin.

The high regard for organized labor still continues among too many members of education associations, with the result that they feel bound to preface every comment about the deliberate drive to take members away from them by kind and admiring words for their attackers. This situation exists despite the fact that every word of criticism of AFT, however

BAKER & TAYLOR
APR 18 '72

reasonable or considerate, is immediately met with the charge of having an anti-labor or anti-union bias. This is, of course, blatant nonsense, the substitution of slogans for reason.

It would be unfair to leave the matter at this point. I must confess that my own viewpoint has changed radically between 1962 and the present. I now believe that the impact of the teacher-union drive has, on the whole, been fruitful in forcing NEA and its affiliated professional associations to assume a vigorous, dynamic, activist posture. Now, one thing is clear: these professional associations are outstripping the teacher unions in aggressiveness.

The second thing that stirred me at Denver was the expedient course laid out for teachers to save themselves. I don't believe this. Admittedly, there are a few situations in which school conditions have become so callously permeated by politics and public neglect that teachers have no recourse other than tooth-and-claw battles in the streets. But, as a general rule, I believe that such battles are not the best possible way for teachers to seek economic justice.

I make no pretense that this is a wholly objective, impartial document. It is frankly *written from a point of view*. But I have earnestly sought to interpret the facts as honestly and to make it as factual as an admittedly biased man can possibly do. In addition, I have not sought to gloss over or ignore the faults and the weaknesses of my own side. I have labored too long to advance the goals of teachers' professional associations to feel that I now must prove my devotion by blind praise.

Materials used in the writing have been drawn from many sources—union publications, the files and releases of the NEA Urban Project, publications of professional associations, publications of AFT and AFL-CIO, newspapers, news magazines, general magazines, and books.

I express major indebtedness to the staff of the Urban Project. They have been most generous with their time and materials. This is the group closest to the battle with the teacher unions: the group that has come to know the battle plans and tactical maneuvers of the adversary. Their aid and advice have been invaluable. This appreciation extends to my other professional colleagues at NEA—the salary consultants, the members of the staff of the Professional Rights and Responsibilities Commission, and others involved directly or indirectly in the conflict. Several of the state and urban association secretaries have also aided by furnishing materials on the teacher-union tactics they have had to meet in their own associations.

Grateful acknowledgment is due Geraldine Pershing for help in the preparation of the work; and, especially, to Nancy Burger for correcting the manuscript, checking citations for accuracy, compiling bibliographical lists, searching out additional source materials, and for typing and processing the manuscript.

Finally, although I have had extensive help and advice from many of my colleagues at the NEA, I must assume sole responsibility for the publication of this book, for whatever virtues or defects it may have. This is in no sense an NEA publication. In the beginning the writing was done on my own time, when I was not engaged in my NEA duties. The later stages were done after my retirement from the NEA staff on August 1, 1966. But at all times I have felt completely uninhibited by any parochial considerations. The book does not presume at any point to speak for or imply endorsement by NEA of viewpoints expressed herein. No official member or official body of the NEA has endorsed, approved, or condoned the book. In fact, to the best of my knowledge, none of them knew that the book was in preparation. And it is not beyond the bounds of reason that they may not be completely pleased with some of its contents.

In sustained efforts to assure that the volume be made as fair and as objective as possible, the manuscript underwent many revisions.

T. M. S.

CONTENTS

Appendixes

Part One

THE SETTING

1

Big Labor Launches the Big Push

> In the long history of the National Education Association, there have been many occasions when Association policies were under vigorous and even bitter attack. This, however, is the first time in which forces of significant scope and power [AFL-CIO] are considering measures which could destroy the Association. This is the turning point of 1962. This is the convention which must defend or surrender the independence of a profession, with all that this implies for the future of public education and American institutions.
>
> —William G. Carr[1]

Organized labor's decision to launch an all-out raid on the nation's teachers' associations was first publicly proclaimed in loud and dramatic tones at the Denver Convention of the NEA in the summer of 1962.

Those close to the situation knew that the raid was already under way, that the New York City hassles (in 1960 and 1962) really launched the shooting war. But the extent and the commitment of organized labor itself to the raid was first publicized at Denver.

The relatively small American Federation of Teachers, affiliated with AFL-CIO, had been plodding along, nibbling at the huge national potential teacher membership since 1916. But its gains had been small and largely confined to dissident elements among teachers in a few large cities.

It was a steaming hot night in the mile-high city of Denver.

The scene was the Municipal Auditorium, sweltering and not air-conditioned. Denverites say that they don't need air-conditioning at their altitude. Maybe they don't normally, but this particular day was an exception. In fact, the unusual weather continued throughout the entire week of the 1962 Annual Convention of the National Education Association.

That night both the weather and the program seemed to reach a crescendo.

The place was filled to the rafters and the crowd overflowed into the air-conditioned theater adjoining the auditorium, where the program was piped in via closed-circuit TV. Up in the balcony of the auditorium, the giant circular fans were noisily sucking in hot air from the outside and giving little relief to the spectators. As one looked from the stage in the center of the arena, the scene seemed to be one vast ocean of undulating fans in the hands of the 10,000 spectators.

The program was proceeding evenly, if not comfortably. Then it happened. James B. Carey, Vice-President of the AFL-CIO and President of the International Brotherhood of Electrical Workers, AFL-CIO, rose to speak to the teachers, his bushy, curly hair making an impressive contrast to his impeccable white dinner jacket and black tie.

The speaker obviously was accustomed to large audiences and began in a restrained, scholarly way to develop the theme assigned to him, "Public Education Tomorrow." The audience was following him appreciatively.

Then, suddenly, he let the teachers have it. With stepped-up tempo and obvious zest, he took off.

> In these remarks, I intend to be critical of the NEA and critical of the teaching profession . . . and right there is that word *profession* as the best starting point.
>
> One of the prime troubles—if not the chief curse—of the teaching *industry* is precisely that word *profession*. That term, as it is used so frequently here, implies that your *craft* is somewhat above this world of ours; it implies a detachment, a remoteness from the daily battle of the streets, in the neighborhood, and the cities.
>
> Newspapermen learned many years ago what American teachers are learning slowly and painfully; that "professionalism" is too often used as a substitute for economic dignity. . . .
>
> Newspapermen learned the hard way, but they learned comparatively early. They decided in the middle 1930's that they were sick and tired of being "paid off in prestige" . . .
>
> The predicament of teachers today, without unionism, is not only economic; it is a predicament also of integrity. There is more and more evidence *that teachers cannot afford integrity and honesty.* [Italics supplied by author.][2]

Then the explosion occurred. Mr. Carey thundered, "No wonder, therefore, there is unionism in the teaching field. What happened in New York City [teacher strikes in 1960 and 1962 and recognition of the teachers union; see Chapter 2], and you know it deep down in your hearts, is no accident or temporary phenomenon."

At this point there was a brief exchange between a spectator in the balcony and Carey over the amount of money AFL-CIO poured into the campaign to organize teachers in New York City. Later, there were newspaper accounts that Carey was booed and heckled by the audience. There were also rumors that the heckler was a labor plant.

In actual fact, the audience was extremely well behaved; it sat in complete silence throughout Carey's outbursts, and at the conclusion of the speech gave him a polite round of applause. The applause was restrained, of course; it was quite obvious that the audience did not like what they had heard. But at no point did they heckle or boo Carey or in any way express discourtesy to him.

Carey had been invited by the president of the National Education Association to speak on the subject, "Public Education Tomorrow." Obviously he was not invited to discuss the union drive to organize teachers. There could have been no question in Carey's mind about this. He simply took advantage of his invitation to seize the headlines.

A half-dozen newspaper and wire-service reporters were in the balcony. They had been given advance copies of Carey's speech, and they had already filed their stories on it. In fact, one or two reporters from Eastern papers were caught off guard by Carey's off-the-cuff remarks because their stories were already in type, to be carried in their newspapers the next morning. However, with their news instinct, all had surmised that the labor leader might seize the opportunity to exploit the occasion, and several were able to send "overrides" on the stories they had filed earlier.

One observor of Carey's performance before the NEA Convention said:

> This is worth a million dollars to the NEA, for the simple reason that the NEA could have had a hundred books written about the union threat and had a thousand speeches made across the United States on the same subject, but the real import never would have gotten across to the teachers. But here, before 10,000 teachers, a hot-headed labor baron laid it on the line for them and warned them in the bluntest kind of language what they could expect if they ever became involved in the processes of the labor movement. The very boorishness of the man was a dead giveaway of what treatment teachers would receive once they came under the domination of labor leaders.

Carey's concluding remarks put a clincher on his unconventional performance:

> And if I sound shocked because the charwomen in some high schools get a higher rate of pay than the high school teachers, *understand*, it comes from the heart. And if the charwomen in the high schools have more tenure in their jobs and more security than the high school teachers, to me it is a shocking disclosure of the method by which we pay our rewards. *Or if the charwomen in the schools have sense enough to band together and organize and negotiate contracts and the teachers do not, I wonder sometimes who should have the degrees.* [Italics supplied by author.][3]

Obviously, Carey's harsh comments were deliberate. He was not hoping to make any converts with his strongly pro-NEA audience. Again, obviously, his remarks were for news media and for teachers in general, especially non-NEA members (some 600,000 at the time). And of course he made no comments about labor's urgent need to entice teachers into their ranks.

That this was a clever ploy by Carey, there can be little doubt. The very boldness of his attack before an NEA convention would earn him not only the headlines but a sympathetic response from many teachers who were not present.

Many people doubtless were convinced that at long last the mistreated, ignored teachers had found a courageous spokesman with a power structure behind him to rescue teachers from their ignoble state. It is probable that Carey's obvious play for the headlines, his extravagant claims of what union affiliation can do for teachers, caused many new teachers or experienced teachers who were dissatisfied with their economic lot and their working conditions to listen more attentively to the blandishments of the teachers' union.

But for those in attendance at Denver, the reaction was reflected by a delegate, Ernest Groff of California, speaking from the floor of the convention:

> I feel it would be unfortunate if some response were not made to the address presented before our General Assembly by Mr. Carey. I believe integrity is a primary characteristic we, as educators, must uphold and teach. I believe integrity is fundamental to a free democratic society. While I listened to his recruiting address as he departed from his prepared text, Mr. Carey impressed me as one who had little regard for this characteristic so basic to free people.
>
> After his address, I am convinced that union leadership, as represented by Mr. Carey, has little understanding or feeling for our goals in education. Therefore, I do not want to be a member of an organization subject to union direction. [Applause.][4]

The Genesis of the Scene

Carey's onslaught at Denver was an open declaration of war on the NEA and its affiliated state and local associations by organized labor or that portion of it represented by the AFL-CIO and its recruiting and organizing arm—the Industrial Union Department (IUD). It was an overt act in a long-simmering organizational struggle for America's teachers. Now the struggle was out in the open.

In back of this performance at Denver were the two teacher strikes in New York City, one in November 1960 and one in April 1962, sponsored by the United Federation of Teachers, an American Federation of Teachers local and AFL-CIO affiliate. At least that was the backdrop. The immediate spark that set off Carey's explosion, apparently, was the keynote speech delivered by Dr. William G. Carr, NEA Executive Secretary, to the convention delegates the night before. After describing in his address, "The Turning Point," the kaleidoscopic nature of changes taking place in the United States as well as the growth of urbanization and its attendant problems, he hit the threat to unionization of teachers head on:

> It now seems probable that a change may be taking place in the attitude of leaders in organized labor toward education. Some years ago [in 1957], after

some internal controversy, the AFL-CIO condemned the NEA and your state and local associations as "company unions." Within the past year, the AFL-CIO (although I believe differences of opinion continue) has been spending heavily to unionize public school teachers. I believe the resources assigned this year by union labor to achieve its objectives among the teachers of New York City alone amounted to about a half-million dollars. . . . [Carey, in his speech, disputed this amount.]

Why has the AFL-CIO, after decades of cooperation with the NEA, suddenly moved in on the teaching profession? Union membership has been declining since 1956, the average loss being about 140,000 members per year. Many union leaders believe that they must organize the white-collar workers—office employees in the main—in order to serve the labor movement properly. Perhaps they regard teaching as a relatively undefended gateway to this wider objective. I think it is *not* really the gateway, and I am sure it is not defenseless.[5]

Carr's analysis of the *raison d'etre* of the AFL-CIO drive to garner the nation's teachers had been confirmed previously by a labor spokesman.

In 1958, James W. Goodsell wrote:

How do we organize white-collar workers? This is no idle question. It may prove to be a life-or-death question for the American Labor Movement.

If we don't, unions will represent a dwindling minority of American workers, and the influence of unions for economic and social progress will gradually fade away. This is much more easily said than done. The fact is we don't know how to organize white-collar workers. Many an old-time organizer has tried it, with all the skill and dedication at his command, only to come away defeated and shaking his head in genuine puzzlement.

Among other reasons given by Goodsell for the indifference of white-collar workers are these:

Most white-collar workers are snobs. The word *labor* offends their self-esteem. . . . they are glad to accept a title, a pat on the head or a Christmas bonus in lieu of decent wages and working conditions. . . . Employers of white-collar workers are smart . . . they play upon them [employees] as Heifetz plays a violin. But most unions have not yet tumbled to the fact that white-collar workers are a different breed of cats.[6]

It will be remembered that James Carey played this same tune (of snobbery) in his Denver speech.

It seems strange that these highly intelligent labor leaders, knowing the urge of teachers to make themselves into a true profession, should use such contemptuous terms about these efforts. And Carey's poor psychology in using such deliberate designations as "the teaching industry," and "the teaching craft" seems to confirm Goodsell's thesis that the old-line union organizers don't know how to appeal to teachers.

This poor psychology permeates the comments of labor leaders. They seem puzzled by teachers' rejection of the promised land of unionism, by their stubborn determination to solve their own problems, to be in charge of their own business, to regulate their own affairs, in short to be free and unbound to any other group even if this determination means financial loss to them.

The reaction to Carey's reference to charwomen would have elicited more of a yawn than shock if teachers had been familiar with union tactics over the years of rather unsuccessful drives to organize white-collar workers. Organizers' literature, recruitment hand-outs, and speeches have almost invariably used this shopworn argument (of snobbery); it got them nowhere, but they stubbornly continued to use it. Usually the reference is to janitors and to sweepers; when talking to secretarial people in offices attached to factories, organizers may refer to "Sadie at the sewing machine."

The point of this comparison, at least the point union people are trying to make without stating it as such, is simply a reverse snobbery. They imply to white-collar workers: "Surely you are superior and you should be paid much more than the lowly janitor." But somehow they failed to see (or maybe they hoped others would fail to see) that one cannot rail in one breath against white-collar snobs who consider unions beneath them, suited only for the lowly blue-collar workers and then, in the next breath, use snob appeal to sell unionism. Nevertheless, year after year, white-collar drives were founded on this contradictory kind of reasoning. The psychological basis for it may have been that word had gotten around that office workers identified with management rather than with industrial workers or janitors. By arguing that management paid more to lowly people, the conclusion was clear to the unionist that unions made the difference; therefore, white-collar wearers ought to join unions. However, office people simply did not arrive at the same conclusion. They concluded that a good part of their troubles were caused by the unions and their strikes; union demands for more pay for janitors cut into funds management had available for them. And they continued to stay out of unions.

Carey used the very same approach in his speech. In one breath, he attacked the teachers' striving for professional status and assured them they were no better than anyone else; in the next, he appealed to snobbery with the charwoman example.

NEA Action Resulting From Carey's Speech

An immediate result of the Carey blast at the NEA Convention was an arousal to battle, so to speak. His inflamatory speech so aroused the 6,000 voting delegates that they subsequently voted overwhelmingly for two resolutions—professional negotiation and professional sanctions— establishing new and aggressive procedures for the professional associations. The professional-negotiations resolution doubtless would have been adopted even without the labor leader's outburst. But there is some evidence that the one on professional sanctions probably would not have been presented for a vote had

Carey not invited it by his sneering references to the impotence of teachers and their professional organizations in dealing with school boards.

Here is the background of the two resolutions. The staff members of the NEA directly concerned with teachers' working conditions, including salaries, had become convinced in recent years that the NEA and its affiliated associations had to take a more aggressive attitude. Since its decision to go into New York City in 1960 and compete with the United Federation of Teachers for the organizational loyalty of the more than 40,000 teachers there, the NEA had been at great disadvantage at many points. In the first place, there were no officially adopted specific procedures especially designed to settle overt cases of mistreatment or indifference to the salary, welfare, and working conditions of large groups of teachers. NEA had, over the years, developed processes for protecting the individual teacher against mistreatment, but not for mass action.

It should be observed at this point that neither professional negotiation nor professional sanctions was a new process. True, they were new as officially adopted procedures of NEA. But both had been used before. The principle of professional negotiation had been used by the Connecticut Education Association, for example, which had in the early 1950's developed a process usually termed *cooperative determination.* The prior use of sanctions is described in Chapter 6.

The Coming Struggle

Thus was the battle joined at Denver. The NEA moved with new procedures to meet the threat to teachers of being inextricably enmeshed in labor legislation and labor machinery. The issue was to be professional negotiations versus collective bargaining; professional sanctions versus strikes. *But*, in the struggle for America's teachers, the issue was much broader. The issue, in fact, was whether teaching would seek to be an independent profession unaffiliated with any other segment of society.

To be a profession means that the group involved must be so firmly in charge of the management of its own internal affairs that it is enabled largely to determine the conditions under which its members work, without recourse to outside power structures to enforce these conditions.

This means that a profession solves its own problems and does not expect other groups to do so. Under this concept, the teaching profession seeks the rights, *de jure* or *de facto*, of setting the standards for admission to preparation for teaching; for determining the nature and length of preparation; of setting the standards for admission to practice through legal licensure; of setting standards and procedures for ousting those members who do not measure up.

These rights are all aimed at guaranteeing to society the competence of members admitted to a profession and permitted to continue in practice. Moreover, this means the guaranteeing of professional working conditions of the profession's members. These are inescapable roles of a profession, which the broad programs of the professional teachers' associations seek to fulfill. The basic issue, therefore, is much more that the bread-and-butter issue, much more than salaries and fringe benefits.

The paramount issue is who will control and direct our public schools. The kind of organization with which teachers affiliate has great bearing on this issue. The traditional belief in the United States is that the public schools belong to all people. A corollary is that the people therefore control and direct these schools through their legally elected or designated representatives to the end that the welfare of all is served. This principle could easily break down by public indifference or plain inertia. The schools could be captured be vested-interest groups, by pressure groups, or by any one segment of our society. This has happened in many school districts, to the extreme detriment of the education programs, because of the imposition of the dogma of certain groups. Should any of these eventualities come to pass, the public schools of America, one of the dynamos of our free society, could be on the way to a steady loss of importance. Thus this is no small issue. It is, in fact, a crucial issue which transcends a mere struggle between two organizations for members.

The current flow of events, along with the trend toward greater and greater financial support by states and the Federal Government, will inevitably tend to alter the ideal of local control. What this trend may eventually mean is not yet clear.

It may be, in time, that Federal legislation mandating the collective right of teachers to negotiate salaries and working conditions will be enacted and declared Constitutional. It is no secret that organized labor is covertly advocating this development, and that the AFT leaders are pressing the United States Office of Education to propose such legislation to Congress, the justification being tied to the Federal funds involved in the support of public schools. Apparently, organized labor feels that Federal legislation can be more easily secured and enforced to labor's liking than can state legislation. Whether such a development will be considered constitutional in the courts remains to be seen.

The American people are not likely to concern themselves unduly with a jurisdictional fight between two teachers' organizations—a mere fight over members.

"A plague on both your houses" is likely to be the public's attitude about such a struggle for teachers' organizational loyalties. But once the nature and import of the struggle is clear, the public will be concerned. The public will be concerned about retaining control of its schools in fact as well as in name. It will be concerned that teachers not be bound to any one segment of the population and beholden to the economic, political, and idealogical commitments of that segment—whether that segment be big government, big business, big agriculture, big church, big extremist groups, big labor, or even big and selfish education groups.

In other words, the public must be concerned that teachers can serve fairly, honestly, and faithfully the children of all the people, without reservation or possible encroachment. It must be concerned that teachers have and hold academic freedom and exercise academic authority.

The public must be concerned over whether teachers solve their own problems through educational channels, in partnership with the public's chosen representatives, or by outsiders who may have an ax to grind.

The public must be concerned about whether teachers are free and competent professionals, capable and willing, able to participate in the ongoing development of our system of popular education; or whether they are scared hired hands, mere menials who are bossed by pressure groups.

Meanings of Denver

In short, the public must be concerned about how teachers are organized and what the policies and controls of their organizations are.

The scenes at Denver were symptomatic of multiple meanings. First, they symbolized, of course, the open declaration of war by organized labor upon the NEA and its affiliated professional associations—a declaration aimed at organizing teachers under the labor banner.

But this aspect is coincidental. The second, deeper, meaning is that the Denver incidents simply marked the coalescing of events which had been slowly emerging for a decade or more.

A new set of mores in school-staff relationships had emerged, if not in full flower, at least clearly and discernibly. The events at Denver marked the end of an era and the beginning of a new one in such relationships.

A new climate had emerged for public employees. After Denver public opinion regarding the rights of public employees underwent a change. This was the end of the beginning to make first-class citizens of public employees. Conversely, it was the end of the traditional view that those who subsist upon tax monies are really parasites and incompetents, existing upon public sufference. The Denver Convention clearly trumpeted the idea that, henceforth, teachers were to be accorded the rights, privileges, and dignity of other respected professions. The vastness and significance of this revolutionary reality can be easily missed. Obviously, school boards, as represented by official pronouncements of their national organization, the National School Boards Association, missed the point. They seem to continue to miss the point. They continue with pronouncements angrily demanding a return to the *status quo ante*. The whole revolution has, momentarily at least, passed them by. The movement is forward—and no force can stop it. Of course, there will be here and there a clinging to the old mores of board and staff relationships. Only time will ameliorate the encrusted, outmoded climate in which teachers have been frozen into a subservient posture.

On this changed climate, James E. Allen, Jr., New York State Commissioner of Education, said to a meeting of school-board members in his state:

> In the formulation of educational policies, boards of education should make specific provision for the full and active participation of the teaching staff. The *enactment* of policy is a single act and responsibility of the board. But the formulation of policy should be a cooperative process utilizing the intellectual resources of the whole school staff. This participation in the development of policy should not be thought of as a favor granted by the board of education or the administration but rather as a right and an obligation.

And on the focal point of NSBA's objections to staff involvment in policy formulation—the threat to local control—Commissioner Allen commented in the same address:

> Local control is a principle of fundamental importance to education. . . . But local control is also a privilege. . . . Its preservation depends on the demonstration of good education resulting from local control. If local control does not produce good education, the state must act. The state's responsibility is direct and inescapable.[7]

BELEAGURED SCHOOL SUPERINTENDENTS AND BOARDS. In defense of superintendents and boards at this point, because much of what is to follow will be critical of superintendents and school boards, it seems only fair to look sympathetically at their side of the turmoil in which they now find themselves as a result of the deeper meanings of the Denver scene.

Superintendents, as a group, are a highly competent, dedicated lot. Moreover, the vast majority of them firmly believe in and practice democratic administration. They strongly believe in the dignity and competence of classroom teachers, and they as firmly practice this belief. They do not view themselves as unfeeling martinets, demanding a demeaning obeisance. They truly have at heart the interests of teachers who work with them. Here is where the current conflict between the professional associations and the teachers' unions hurt them most deeply. The superintendents have been made villains in a simulated melodrama. They are the stereotyped characters teachers are invited to hate. That this is the ultimate in unfairness is obvious, but who cares about the facts when the search is on for a scapegoat?

The superintendent is the man in the middle in the often artificially stimulated battle between teachers and school board. Moreover, he is the man in the middle between the public and the numerous pressure groups which are often not concerned with the facts or with fairness in their head-long drive to impose their wills upon whole school systems. The superintendent, in short, is the man to blame for every failure, every community headache even remotely related to the schools. It is doubtful that there is a tougher job in American life today than being superintendent of schools in a large community.

Of course, not all superintendents are paragons of wisdom and fairness. Not all are devoted to democratic staff relationships or to the search for dignity and recognition for members of their school staffs. Of course there are many insecure school administrators whose chief sense of security arises from unilateral authority, from arbitrary decision-making. These give them a sense of power without which all the joys of their position would evaporate.

Of course there are incompetent superintendents, as there are teachers, and one would suppose in about the same proportion. By the same token, there are as many decent, dedicated ones as there are decent, dedicated teachers.

One of the disturbing stereotypes that have been implanted in this country in the last generation is that of the school administrator as a callous, unscrupulous, inept opportunist who stands up with courage and conviction only when his own salary is being determined. According to this stereotype, he vacillates with every wind that blows. He is pictured as the natural enemy of those who work for him or with him. All of this arises, one supposes, because he is in authority.

How did this stereotype come to be imbedded in so many minds? There is a complex of causes. The union drive to caricature management as demons doubtless is a factor. The mass mind and its sometimes distorted concept of freedom is another. The popular new eagerness to throw off all restraints and to hate all authority is still another. All of this has slowly seeped into education, beginning at the college level and feeding down to the lower schools. Although not universal among college faculties, the contempt for administrators is often deep, widespread, and frightening. This bitterness is focused primarily upon presidents and deans. One quipster has observed that where, in the past, college boys were notorious for chasing girls, now they are chasing presidents and deans. One gets the impression from conversations with individual faculty members, from passages in public speeches at educational conferences, and from writings in educational journals, that anarchy is greatly to be desired in the management of institutions of higher education. One can only speculate about the causes for the enmity toward college administrators. Perhaps it has something to do with the political choice of college presidents, which has beeen especially noticeable and irritating in the state teachers' colleges, state colleges, and in a few state universities. The trend is definitely and discernibly away from this practice, but the practice still exists.

Perhaps this enmity goes back to the first universities, which were collections of scholars and students in informal relationships held together by the personal loyalties of clusters of students to given teachers. This was an ideal teaching-learning climate, untrammeled by the minutia of entrance processes, grades, credits, class schedules, formalized tests, registrars, presidents, deans, department heads, and computers.

Perhaps, too, as institutions grew in size and enrollments, and as formal machinery grew more complex, the positional classifications, rank and salary, promotional criteria, and all the other status symbols fostered frustration and rebellion among the unrecognized faculty members. These college practices are often held up as shining contrasts to the single-salary schedules and lack of graduated positional ranks in the lower schools. There is mixed evidence on this point. Many assert that the college system is ideal and recommend it for the lower schools. But one wonders if the system is as perfect as it is depicted to be.

At any rate, whatever the causes, the administrator of anything, but especially of the schools, currently tends to be a much maligned character in American life.

The same holds true of most school-board members. They are, as a rule, community-minded, unselfish citizens who generally serve without pay. They give of their time and energies in service to a cause they believe to be in the public interest. Often they receive in return the vilest kind of abuse, especially from the tax haters and the dogmatists who want to fasten their peculiar ideologies on the school system. To be sure, as among teachers and superintendents, there are exceptions. There are on school boards some members with axes to grind, some devoted to self-interest and not public interest. And there are board members dedicated to holding down tax rates and public spending for schools; this is observable and undeniable. But the number of such people is relatively small. All in all, it is a pleasing fact of American life that so many able people serve as school superintendents and so many capable and unselfish people serve on school boards.

There are at least two other important implications of the emerging new climate of school-staff relationships.

First, the programs of preparation for school administrators must undergo a drastic overhaul, especially in the aspects of personnel policies and staff relationships. School boards and administrators simply have not caught up with management in private industry in enlightened practices in personnel relationships. Perhaps this is attributable in large measure to pressures of the labor unions and to the failures of teachers' associations to exert enough pressure.

Second, the program of school administration must be greatly expanded to prepare competent people for a cluster of new responsibilities in negotiation, in employer-employee relationships, in defining rules and administering elections. In short, the need for such preparation arises from the obvious fact that few such experts now exist in school administration, for these are new fields, and from the other obvious fact that school boards simply do not have either the time or the expertness to carry on these delicate relationships.

There is indeed a new turmoil in teachers' organizational matters.

The significance of this, however, lies in the fact that it points up the deeper significance of changing personnel relationships in the public schools.

The inevitable reaction by school boards, administrators, and laymen to the rising turmoil among teachers was that the teachers had turned "radical." New words began to be applied to teachers, such as *militant, aggressive,* and *activist.* Evidence of use of these designations is plentiful.

Actually, the basic meaning of the teacher upsurge is grounded in idealism rather than selfishness.

This idealism came to the surface in the form of resentment that educational facilities and conditions had been permitted to deteriorate alarmingly while the American people increased in wealth. Teachers interpreted this to mean that the American people were suffering from a sad case of mistaken attitudes, a muddled system of values.

The basic idealism of teachers in their search for quality education, the equal chance for all children, burst into rebellion and activism. It is as simple as that.

Moreover, this idealism spilled over into the realm of staff relationships. Again idealism was at the base of this revolt. Teachers simply began insisting that the concept of equal human beings living under democratic laws—laws which they participate in writing—permeate the whole of Western culture. They began insisting upon their rights to such participation.

Turmoil among teachers will continue in the organizational fight.

But the intense area of the turmoil will be in the struggle for teacher status.

Meanings for Teachers' Organizations

Finally, the meaning of the events at the Denver NEA Convention in the summer of 1962 is simply that general teachers' organizations—of all types—have in large measure become irrelevant to the needs of teachers and of education. This is a harsh indictment, but the evidence is overwhelming. In fact, education itself is suffering from the same lag in relevancy.

The nation is now involved in an educational revolution, in a desperate effort to escape the trap of history and to emerge into the reality of modern life. The unprecedented Federal legislation of 1965 is precise evidence of this struggle and of the impending revolution in education.

By the same token, there is an emerging revolution in the concepts, status, roles, working conditions, and personnel relationships of teachers in the lower schools. All of these must change drastically, and they are in the process of change.

Teachers' organizations, likewise, must change or die. The revolution that is to come for them, to make them relevant, will be no less drastic. The organizations that take the middle road of complacency or seek to retain the comfortable mores of the past are not likely to survive.

The struggle for America's teachers thus takes on characteristics of a race for survival.

Involved too, but easily obscured, in the Denver scenes was the impact of other forces, some already visible, some imperceptible but dimly emerging.

Urbanization of the United States was in full flower, but the full implications of urbanization were yet to be unfolded. Already the even tempo of a predominantly rural society had given way to a migration unparalleled in the nation's history—a migration that was changing power structures, motivations, values, and human relationships. The vast tides of people migrating to cities brought with them new concerns, puzzling problems, and staggering frustrations. Loyalties of people changed from one community to clusters of neighbors or shopping centers. People were losing their sense of civic responsibility, at least in the old meaning of the term; they were becoming consumers of public services without any great sense of participating in the founding and management of the services. They were compelled to seek a sense of security in group rather than in individual action. Likewise, teachers, to get recognition, found themselves caught up in the necessity for mass action.

Activism became a necessity to attract public attention and to get public action. Redress of grievances replaced the quiet of individual negotiation; the simple application of individual fairness changed to the grab for group power. The philosophy that groups must take power from society, not ask for it and wait for that which never comes, was on the upsurge. The Civil Rights Movement was based on this pragmatic approach. The rise of unionism, when farmers began to migrate to cities in about the middle of the nineteenth century under the impact of the Industrial Revolution, was grounded in the same pragmatism.

It was inevitable that teachers and other public employees would be involved in such a readjustment. It was inevitable that many teachers would conclude that they, too, must fight to get for themselves economic justice and fair working conditions.

Organized labor sensed these changed conditions, and, by inducing President Kennedy to issue Executive Order Number 10988 in January 1962 authorizing collective negotiation for Federal employees, got in position to make a drive for state legislation conferring the same rights on all public employees.

The great danger is that teachers' organizations will seek to outdemand each other until, like some of the civil-rights groups, they stand not for solid achievements but for Samuel Gompers' cry for more and more—until the balance of reason and responsibility give way to turmoil, riot, and rebellion, the end of which is chaos.

2

Evolution of the Organizational Struggle

Oklahoma's Education War
The Lesson It Can Teach a Nation

Micawber Schoolhouse, standing alone in high weeds, is a casualty of revolution. It was built about 1907, the year Oklahoma became the 46th state. A year ago last July, its doors closed for the last time. Students and three busy teachers filled it once. Hay bales fill it now.

The slow death of country schoolhouses like Micawber—and the rural communities they serve— is revolutionizing education everywhere. In this revolution, a new teacher has stepped into the classrooms of America. The old country schoolmarm—bookish, unobtrusive and so dedicated to teaching children that she asks for little money in return—is fading. The new breed—college-trained, younger, with kids of his own to support—is replacing her. But the old idea dies hard. Wherever it is kept alive, the new teacher must beat it down with a political militancy strange to his profession. Ever since the Second World War ended, his voice has been heard with increasing force across the United States.

—Shawn Kalkstein, *Look*, January 25, 1966

Why in the particular year 1962 should the giant NEA and the small AFT clash so loudly as to attract national attention?

For almost a half-century the two national organizations of teachers had existed side by side with little public acrimony. The American Federation of Teachers in this period had grown at a snail's pace and, outside of the heavily unionized large cities, had made only small gains in membership. The giant

National Education Association, on the other hand, had skyrocketed in membership to include more than half of the nation's public school teachers.

Why the clash now?

Obviously, a cluster of casual factors came together in 1962. Among the basic causes, stated in Chapter 1 and elaborated upon later in this chapter, were the skidding membership figures of AFL-CIO, the decrease in the nation's number of blue-collar workers, and the increase in the number of white-collar workers—all of which pinpointed the necessity of labor's launching an all-out drive on white-collar workers. Also, the President's Executive Order Number 10988, labor believes, was made to order for AFL-CIO to raid established white-collar organizations of public employees.

As a matter of fact, the current infighting is not the first overt clash between NEA and teachers' unions.

In 1902, the American Federation of Labor chartered the Chicago Federation of Teachers (organized in 1897 as an independent or unaffiliated federation). There was at that time no national teachers' union. From 1902 to 1916, when the American Federation of Teachers came into being, the AFL chartered some 20 local teachers' groups.

But the San Antonio Teachers Association was the first to receive a charter from the AFL a few months before the formal affiliation of the Chicago Federation of Teachers. The latter had affiliated with the local labor body—the Chicago Trades Federation—prior to the San Antonio tie-in with the AFL.

In June 1915, three Chicago federations (Chicago Federation of Teachers, Chicago Federation of Women High School Teachers, and Chicago Federation of Men Teachers) issued a call to form a national organization. These three federations and the Gary (Indiana) Federation met on April 15, 1916 and formed the American Federation of Teachers. Within a month the Teachers Union of New York, the Oklahoma Teachers Federation, the Scranton Teachers Association, and the High School Teachers Union of Washington, D.C. joined. Thus these eight federations formed the nucleus of the AFT.

But, in contrast to the present situation, there was apparently no concerted drive on the part of organized labor to enroll teachers in its ranks.

Actually, prior to 1960 the initiative for affiliation with labor came largely from the teachers themselves. The motivation of teachers in seeking labor affiliation in the early years was to find a powerful ally in fighting for economic justice against conservative or reactionary business interests. The movement began in the early years of this century in Chicago, where the teachers had been shabbily treated and where, through a combination of political control and the power of commercial interests, tax rates for school support were kept at a disgracefully low level. The result was poor schools and impoverished teachers.

The recourse of the teachers was to turn to a sympathetic segment of the community power structure—organized labor—for help; and it got such effective help that significant gains were won. Teachers in other communities, facing similar conditions and similar problems in getting justice from the existing power structures, turned to labor for help. This movement eventually resulted in binding together these widely dispersed units, all of which had voluntarily sought affiliation with the American Federation of Labor, into the American Federation of Teachers in 1916.

The drive of teachers themselves to affiliate with organized labor is set forth in a publication of the AFT:

> The story of the American Federation of Teachers makes one thing clear. The movement to get teachers to unite with organized labor was from the beginning a grass-roots movement. It was a movement of and for teachers, and it grew out of their own felt needs—personal, professional, and social. Teachers joined labor not as a result of outside propaganda and promotion, but because they believed it provided the best promise for the satisfaction of their own life interests and aspirations. As the record shows, the national organization followed—it did not precede—the organization of locals in communities widely separated.[1]

The second major effort to bring the teachers of the United States into affiliation with labor occurred in the period 1918–21. This was an effort to take over the National Education Association structure or to reshape its policies along the lines of AFT philosophy. The backbone of the effort was the Chicago Federation of Teachers under the leadership of Margaret Haley, a veteran, militant, effective battler for teachers' economic rights. The point of division was the same, essentially, as it is now. Miss Haley and the core of her support (members of the Chicago Federation of Teachers) insisted upon rather exclusive emphasis upon teachers' salaries, tenure, and pensions. The NEA members wanted these things too, but they insisted upon a balanced program of professional development and provisions to improve education all along the line.

The climax of this internecine warfare was reached at the Milwaukee Convention of the NEA in 1919. There was at that time no representative assembly of the NEA with voting confined to elected delegates from affiliated state and local associations. There was instead an annual meeting where any member could attend and vote. Because of the proximity of the annual meeting to Chicago, Miss Haley caused to be registered as NEA members a relatively large delegation from the Chicago Federation of Teachers, which undertook to dominate the convention and push their policies to adoption. The convention reached a deadlock and had to be dissolved by a song period featuring the "Star Spangled Banner" to break the negative posture of the union members. Successive efforts to dominate the deliberations were made at the NEA conventions of 1920, at Salt Lake City, and of 1921, at Des Moines.

But by then the Representative Assembly was functioning to the extent that the union delegates were in a decided minority.

The late Dr. Frederick M. Hunter, NEA President in 1920–21 and a Life Director of the Association, in an address to the NEA Board of Directors at Detroit on July 6, 1963 delineated his version of the early attempts of the teachers' unions to infiltrate NEA membership and take over its structure:

> I am bearing witness personally concerning three meetings that happened back in what I think might well be called the critical period in NEA—1919 at Milwaukee, 1920 at Salt Lake City, 1921 at Des Moines. The relation of organized labor to those meetings is wholly misunderstood by those who ought to be well informed and have the history at easy disposal. That is my reason for coming before you at this time and submitting a statement. . . .
>
> The critical period began when a group rose up [in NEA] and took the leadership by electing Ella Flag Young of Chicago [in 1910] president. She came in as a herald of the classroom teacher and a grassroots regime, and for ten years there was a real battle.
>
> The great element that created the [modern] NEA was the classroom teachers, and their uprising was exactly what labor unions counted on. The assaults on the three meetings were not by people who were at that time members of labor unions because the Chicago Board of Education had passed a rule expelling them if they did not leave the union. So, naturally, they were the emissaries who were representing in the field their classroom teachers group. There were hundreds all over the country—school women's clubs and various classroom clubs—that included no administrators, principals, or supervisors. They were the grassroots insurgents. *They were the ones that the labor unions were seeking to set up as an independent national organization, ultimately to become a part of the union structure of the nation.*
>
> The assault upon the NEA at the three critical meetings, Milwaukee in 1919, Salt Lake City in 1920, and Des Moines in 1921, was aimed at the disruption of the delegate assembly plan of operation. The adoption of this operative instrument would turn over to the classroom teachers the basic overall control of the nation's teaching organization. The union plan was to capitalize fully upon the movement among classroom teachers to set up units exclusive of members such as principals, supervisors, and superintendents. Already in major cities these exclusive classroom teacher groups were active, effective, and powerful.
>
> The AFT, founded in 1916 in Milwaukee, was the tool to be used. The leaders who attempted to coerce the 1919, 1920, and 1921 meetings [of NEA] had been forced out of union ranks by the Chicago Board of Education forbidding membership in unions.
>
> The current propaganda attempts to show that the whole procedure at the three crucial conventions had no relationship to the AFT and the union courtship of the NEA. On the contrary, the spearhead of the movement sought to separate the new vigorous organization of classroom teachers from the integrated professional NEA. These "school women's clubs" and the like were to become a nationwide organization of their own. Their program would parallel and finally join the AFT.[2]

Despite this testimony from a former NEA president, the evidence seems to indicate that these early efforts to overhaul the NEA structure arose from union-minded teachers rather than from direct and vigorous efforts of organized labor as such.

Apparently, the NEA began (in 1857) with a restrictive concept. Women were excluded until 1866. From 1857 to about 1920 the dominant elements were college presidents, normal-school presidents, and school superintendents. The break-up of this hierarchial leadership and the charting of new directions for the NEA has been described as follows:

> Unfortunately, the period of the "great names" on committees directing the country's educational policy was relatively short. It ended about 1905. The pressure of new problems apparently scattered the small groups of national leaders; partly also these problems were of a kind for which the old guard was no longer competent. As a matter of fact, even before the period of the great committees, issues appeared far beyond the orbit of education, if understood in the merely scholastic sense of the word. Women, admitted in 1866, entered the NEA in larger numbers and asked for equal rights; there was the desire for the discussion of teachers' salaries; the relation between education and the government became increasingly complicated. Labor tried to increase its influence on the public school system; the assimilation of minorities became more and more urgent; there was the conflict between nationalism and internationalism; various reform movements asked for consideration; the new technological society in America was no longer satisfied with schools dating from earlier times.[3]

So strong became the tension that some observers doubted whether the NEA could survive. William T. Harris, who in many respects had shown admirable qualities of intellectual and administrative leadership, was blind to the understandable and necessary demands of the teachers for better living conditions. Nicholas Murray Butler, president of Columbia University, who thus far had played a most active part in the NEA as well as in education generally, described the situation in 1905 in the following words:

> Then that organization [NEA], from being a body of genuine educational leaders who were dealing with ideas and institutions, degenerated into a large popular assembly which quickly fell into the hands of a very inferior class of teachers and school officials whose main object appeared to be personal glorification and personal advancement.

Out of this long hassle, however, came significant changes in the NEA structure in 1919–21. Some of the changes produced by this controversy were establishment of the *NEA Journal*; formation of the Research Division; establishment of the Representative Assembly based upon proportionate representation; provision for all-inclusive membership; and creation of a commission to press for national legislation in education, the forerunner of the NEA Legislative Commission and the Division of Federal Relations. Out of the current clash with the teachers' unions doubtless will come other needed reforms in NEA structure and procedures. By the very nature of its size, clientele, and democratic structure, the NEA is admittedly a slow-moving, often ultraconservative organization. However, without exception significant reforms have arisen from successive crises.

The Skidding Union Membership

Another crucial reason for the struggle between NEA and AFT was the skidding membership of the AFL-CIO. The labor leaders apparently were getting panicky at standing still, or even losing ground, in a burgeoning labor market.

TABLE 2-1

Make-up of Total Labor Force in the United States for the Years 1960 and 1962, and Union Membership

Total Force and Classification of Workers	Year	
	1960	1962
Total civilian labor force	70,156,000	71,315,000
White-collar workers	29,466,000	30,808,000
Blue-collar workers	26,309,000	26,244,000
Total union membership	17,100,000*	16,586,000*
Total union membership, white-collar workers	2,200,000	2,285,000

* Does not include 1,044,000 Canadian members.
Source: U.S. Department of Labor, Bureau of Labor Statistics, April 1964.

The peak year in union membership was 1956, with a total for all unions of 17.5 million. By 1962, this total had dropped by about 900,000.

The total union membership in 1960 for all types of unions, including the AFL-CIO, was 17.1 million; 14.9 million (87 per cent) of the union members were blue-collar workers; only 7 per cent of the nation's white-collar group were union members; union membership included only about 24 per cent of the total work force. It also should be noted that there was a net loss of 65,000 in the total number of blue-collar workers between 1960 and 1962.

Why has organized labor declared war on the professional associations of teachers? Why did the Industrial Union Department (IUD) pour money into the coffers of the United Federation of Teachers in New York City and provide many of its top organizers to man the drive to win the New York City fight to bring the city's 40,000 teachers into the ranks of organized labor? Why has IUD continued to pour money (estimated to amount to $360,000 in 1964–65) and to furnish hordes of organizers to raid the professional organizations' membership? Why did Walter Reuther, at the 1962 AFT

Convention in Detroit, urge the teachers' union to go out after 1 million new members from the teachers' ranks?

The reasons appear to be simple and clear-cut. Labor was then losing membership despite significant increases in the labor force. It not only was losing members, but it was losing ground in the proportion of the total labor force belonging to unions. In 1956, organized labor enrolled nearly 25 per cent of the nation's work force; in 1962, this percentage had dropped to slightly over 22 per cent. And, significantly, elections to choose bargaining agents, which were push-overs for the unions in the 1930's and 1940's, were won in only 56 per cent of the cases by 1961.

The complexion of the labor force was changing. Where it once was predominantly blue-collar, it was in 1962 predominantly white-collar. In the preceding five years (1957–62), the former category declined by 1 million while the latter increased by 3 million. In 1962, there were 26,244,000 blue-collar workers in the total labor force and 30,808,000 white-collar workers. White-collar workers constitute 55 per cent of the total labor force now (1966), but only 7 per cent are union members. Labor's paramount problem, therefore, is to organize the unorganized; in other words, to go after the white-collar workers.

James Carey himself is quoted as saying:

> Without membership strength, all our past gains might as well be written on water.... Like the free-enterprise economy itself, the labor movement must maintain a process of dynamic development, or it will decay. There is no middle ground where we can sit back and brood over our navels and contemplate the blessings of the status quo.... We must advance, or we must retreat. Our numbers and our influence must expand, or they must crumble.[4]

In November 1963 the United States Department of Labor reported losses in union membership, blaming the change on the increased number of white-collar workers, who do not seem to recognize the need to be represented by unions.

According to the Bureau of Labor Statistics report, the AFL-CIO, with more than 14 million members in the United States and Canada, lost 222,000 members from 1960 to 1962. Total union membership declined from 1960 to 1962 by 487,000. In emphasizing the job loss in certain industries, the bureau reported that 545,000 members were lost in the metal, machinery, and transportation-equipment industries. The only major union gains were in California and Michigan, about 50,000 in each state. More than half the AFL–CIO membership is in New York, California, Illinois, Pennsylvania, and Ohio. In Massachusetts, the union membership loss was 250,000 and in Wisconsin 136,000. The bureau bluntly predicted that labor had to make gains among white-collar workers if any gains were to be realized.

To present a balanced picture of the membership plight of organized labor, it should be pointed out that some observers view the skidding membership in recent years as temporary, until the unions can readjust to transitional conditions. All concede that the one chance organized labor has to recoup lies in the white-collar field.

In 1964, according to the Department of Labor, the 189 labor unions with headquarters in the United States had a total membership of 17.9 million, in contrast to 17.6 million in 1962. AFL–CIO in 1964 had 15.1 million members, with but 14 million of the members in the United States.

Between 1956 and 1961, a net loss of 1.2 million in union membership had occurred. By 1964 about half of this loss had been recovered. The percentage of union members in the labor force declined from 24.8 per cent in 1956 to 21.9 per cent in 1964.

Between 1962 and 1964, the unions showed a significant upturn in the number of white-collar workers organized. The number of organized white-collar workers in 1964 was 2.6 million or 14.4 per cent of total union members.

Indeed, the *Monthly Labor Review* for May 1964 reported that in 1962 there was a gain in union membership of 300,000, the most significant gain since the peak year of 1956, and that this may foreshadow a reversal in union-membership trends. This gain is largely attributable to enrollment of Federal employees as a result of President Kennedy's Executive Order.[6] By Labor Day 1965, AFL–CIO claimed that it had enrolled 1 million employees of the Federal Government. Also, AFL–CIO had checked its numerical loss, but its percentage of membership among the total labor force was still declining. Also, the Johnson Administration is indebted to labor and may, indeed, be instrumental in reversing the deteriorating membership situation of the unions. The effort to repeal Section 14 *b* of the Taft-Hartley Act in 1965, backed by the administration and another effort in the second session of the Eighty-ninth Congress in 1966, could have been the harbinger of a great resurgence in union membership. The 1965 and 1966 efforts at repeal failed, but new efforts will be made. This repeal would nullify the right-to-work laws in 19 states.

That organized labor had, prior to 1962, come upon dog days of enthusiasm among working people seems evident. How serious and sustained those bad times were remains to be seen. The great dynamic, pulse-accelerating expectations of the labor movement of the New Deal days has somehow lost significant momentum. The old slogans and battle cries have lost some of their rousing effects.

In other words, it appears that big labor has momentarily at least, become a victim of its own success.

Not only is the refrigerator full for the employed, but generally speaking there is a car (or two) in every garage and two chickens in every pot. Enlightened management in recent years often has stolen the thunder of the labor leaders by beating them to the punch. Income-tax regulations have enabled corporations to increase real wages through fringe benefits not subject to income taxes. More and more workers, with, figuratively, arms akimbo and chins jutting out, are asking of labor, "What have you done for me lately?"

The strike, the one giant, frightening weapon which labor could wave about, seems to be gradually heading for some degree of obsolesence. Here and there big labor continues to flex its muscles, to assert its courage and aggressiveness by calling strikes.

But the strike is becoming too costly to be tolerated, all too often forcing upon industry the alternative of further automation. Consequently, labor must now find alternatives to offset the job losses caused by automation, particularly to offset the shortened work week that resulted in order to stretch out the number of workers needed. Too, the Federal Government's interference in the longshoremen's tie-up of shipping in 1963, in the threatened nation-wide rail strikes in 1963, 1964, and 1967, and in the threatened steel strike in 1965, was an omen of great significance. Also, the public bitterness over the New York City Transit strike of January 1966 and the machinists' strike against the major airlines in the summer of 1966 stirred demands for Federal legislation to curb the power of unions. These are indicators of the decline of the concept of free collective bargaining in the classic, purest sense.

The Drive to Organize Teachers

The New York City teachers' strikes in 1960 and 1962 marked not the beginning but the intensification of sporadic efforts by organized labor to gain a foothold among the teachers of the United States. It did mark the beginning of a well-financed drive by IUD to assist AFT and its local to organize teachers. Down through the years since 1916, when it was organized and affiliated with the AFL (later merging with CIO, when AFL-CIO became one organization), the American Federation of Teachers struggled to attract teachers into the union, but with little success. By the time of the first strike in New York City in December 1960, the AFT had acquired only about 60,000 members. In 1918, the AFT and NEA memberships were about the same: less than 10,000. Over the years, the NEA has grown to about 1 million (in 1966), gaining membership increases in most years in excess of the total membership of the AFT. By 1966, the AFT membership was as shown in Table 2–2. NEA membership in 1967 exceeded 1 million.

AFT made considerable gains in membership in the period 1961–1966, that is, significant in comparison to its previous annual growth rate which, between 1956 and 1961, ranged from a loss of 318 in 1957 to a gain of 4,364 in 1960.

In 1961–62 its membership increased by 10,109, and in 1962–63 the increase was 10,977 (almost exclusively due to New York City membership growth).

The W. R. Banks Library
Prairie View A. & M. College
Prairie View, Texas

TABLE 2-2

Estimated AFT Membership, 1956 to 1966

Year	Total Membership	Net Gain or Loss	Percent Gain in Total Membership	Total Number of Locals
1956	50,535	+3,952	—	418
1957	50,217	−318	—	421
1958	53,025	+2,808	5.591	410
1959	54,817	+1,792	3.379	416
1960	59,181	+4,364	7.961	426
1961	60,712	+1,531	2.586	433
1962	70,821	+10,109	16.650	454
1963	81,798	+10,977	15.499	476
1964	100,109	+18,311	22.385	502
1965	110,500	+10,391	10.379	574
1966	125,421	+14,921	13.5	634

Source: Some figures on AFT membership in this chapter and elsewhere in this book are estimates gathered from several sources, since certain official figures are not available from the AFT. The total membership and the total number of locals are generally released at the annual AFT convention each year, but the membership of its locals is generally not released.

In fact, the AFT appears to be quite touchy about its local membership figures. During 1962–63 its attorney implied a threat, in a letter to the NEA Executive Secretary, to sue NEA for circulating false statistics on its local membership.

This touchiness, AFT has attributed to the tendency of school boards and administrators to fire teachers who join the teachers' union. There is no question that such incidents have happened in the past. But whether they have happened to such an extent that the AFT is justified in keeping secret the size of its membership is questionable. Actually, some observers believe that this is a gimmick to embellish its underdog role and to gain sympathy as well as to cover up AFT's small membership in most situations.

For example, AFT began in 1958 to copyright its membership figures, thus effectively limiting the publication of state and local memberships.

In 1963–64, the gain was 18,311. In 1964–65, the gain was 10,391, and in 1965–66 the gain was 14,921.

Of the 10,109 increase in 1961–62, about 8,000 came from New York City and the remaining 2,000 came from gains in St. Louis, Chicago, Detroit, and Los Angeles. Outside of the large cities, there was generally a decline in membership. Of the AFT's 1963 growth of 10,977, almost exactly 10,000 came from the following cities: New York City 4,206; Chicago, 3,225; Detroit, 939; Boston, 540; St. Louis, 455; Gary, 317; Milwaukee, 210; and Minneapolis, 113. The AFT in 1962–63 generally lost membership in the

South, Southwest, and the West. (See Appendix B for 1964–65 state-by-state memberships of the NEA and AFT.)

More than half of AFT's increase in membership in 1964–65 occurred in four cities: New York, with 4,900; Chicago, 400; New Orleans, 550; and Detroit, 510. Actually, more than 40 per cent of the growth came from the New York City increase. In fact, of the increase of about 50,000 in AFT membership from 1961 to 1966, fully 60 per cent has resulted from growth of the UFT in New York City in 1965–66; in 1965–66, AFT gained 14,921 members, an increase of 13.5 per cent over the previous year. Four states (Illinois, Michigan, New York, and Pennsylvania) contributed about 87 per cent of this gain; New York City alone provided more than half the total gain.

But the significance of AFT gains since 1960, when IUD began to pour money and organizers into the drive to organize teachers, cannot be obscured.

As shown in Table 2–3, NEA membership increased between 1959–60 and 1965–66 by 318,993, an average annual growth of 45,570. AFT's growth in the same period was 70,604, an average annual growth of 10,086.

TABLE 2-3

Percent of all Public School Instructional Staff Members of AFT and NEA, 1959–1966

Year Ending May of	Total Instructional Staff	Total AFT Members	Percent of Total Instructional Staff	Total NEA Members	Percent of Instructional Staff
1959	1,419,881	54,817	3.8	667,120	47.0
1960	1,453,816	59,181	4.1	713,994	49.0
1961	1,545,549	60,712	3.9	765,616	50.0
1962	1,590,000+	70,821	4.4+	812,497	51.0+
1963	1,665,065	81,798	4.9	859,505	52.0
1964	1,718,435	100,109	5.8	903,384	52.6
1965	1,807,466	110,500	6.1	943,581	52.0
1966	1,866,273	125,421	6.7	986,113*	52.3

* NEA's total membership in 1965–66, if members of the Student National Education Association (124,257) are added, was 1,110,370.

Source: Figures for AFT are estimates, gathered from several sources, since some official figures, except total national membership, are not available from the AFT. Figures on NEA membership are taken from *NEA Handbook* (for local, state, and national associations), for the years listed. Or see *NEA Handbook* for 1966–67, Tables 1 and 2, pp. 369–70.

But in terms of percentage increase in membership over the previous year, AFT grew faster than NEA in the years 1962, 1963, 1964, 1965, and 1966.

The percentage increases for NEA for each of these five years were 6.1, 5.8, 5.1, 4.4, and 4.4; for AFT the percentage increases were 16.6, 15.5, 22.4, 10.3 and 13.5. It appears also that the 1964 AFT gain included significant gains in smaller locals, rather than being confined to a few large cities, although the large cities continue to furnish the big gains.

In 1963–64, some 93 per cent of the AFT membership was in 14 states (California, Connecticut, Illinois, Indiana, Massachusetts, Michigan, Minnesota, Missouri, New Jersey, New York, Ohio, Pennsylvania, Rhode Island, and Wisconsin). Twenty-five per cent of the AFT membership was in New York City; 38 per cent was in two cities: New York and Chicago; and nearly 70 per cent was in five states: California, Illinois, Michigan, Minnesota, and New York. No AFT membership was reported in eight states: Arkansas, Mississippi, Nebraska, North Carolina, Oklahoma, South Carolina, South Dakota, and Texas. In 1964, among AFT locals, 11 had 1,000 or more members; 12 had from 500 to 999 members; 105 had from 100 to 499 members; and 358 had less than 100 members, of which 189 had 25 or fewer.

In 1962–63 AFT had no members in ten states (Arkansas, Nebraska, North Carolina, Oklahoma, South Carolina, Utah, Vermont, Virginia, West Virginia, and Wyoming). By 1965–66 Oklahoma and West Virginia showed some AFT membership, while teachers in Mississippi, and South Dakota dropped completely from the AFT ranks.

Between 1962–63 and 1965–66 NEA membership grew by 126,608, or nearly 15 per cent. But the proportion of its membership of the total public-school employees remained constant at 52 per cent. In this same period AFT membership increased from 81,680 to 125,421, and increase of nearly 54 per cent.

In 1965–66 more than one third of AFT membership was in New York State; almost one half was in two states. New York and Illinois; and almost three fourths was in six states: New York, Illinois, Michigan, California, Minnesota, and Ohio.

Of the 634 AFT locals in 1965–66, 12 had memberships of 1,000 or more; 17 had from 500 to 999 members; 122 had from 100 to 499 members; and 483 had 100 or fewer members, of which 230 had 25 or fewer members. The largest AFT was, of course, New York City, with more than 37,000 members, followed by Chicago with about 11,700; Detroit, about 5,800; Cleveland, about 2,200; and Philadelphia, about 2,800. The ten AFT locals with a membership of 1,000 or more were Los Angeles, 2,327; San Francisco, 1,132; Chicago, 11,685; Gary, 1,678; New Orleans, 1,100; Boston, 1,657; St. Louis, 1,003; New York, 37,291; Cleveland, 2,200; and Philadelphia, 2,770.

What was in back of the labor drive in New York City to recruit teachers? Many things. Chief among these, as has been pointed out, was a decided loss of membership by the AFL-CIO in recent years. Automation, reducing craft jobs in industry, probably is the major reason why the AFL-CIO was losing membership at the rate of over 100,000 a year. Naturally in such a situation labor organizations had but one thing to do and that was to make an all-out effort to organize the white-collar workers of the United States, who number somewhere in the neighborhood of 32 million people and heretofore had little or no union affiliation.

The decision to start this drive to secure a break-through with teachers may have been happenstance. But on the other hand, it may have been psychologically and realistically sound. If labor could crack the professional shell with which teachers have surrounded themselves this could have a tremendous impact on other white-collar workers who either did not constitute a recognized professional group or did not have the status and prestige that teachers presumably have with the American public.

The drive to get teachers was probably realistically sound because it is a well-known fact that the pay of teachers has always been well below that of other professional groups and has lagged in an advancing economy, particularly in terms of fringe benefits, behind most other occupations, even the skilled workers. The NEA and the respective state education associations have struggled manfully with this problem for a hundred years, and, although they have made significant gains, there has been less than a dramatic break-through to a satisfactory economic status for teachers. The average salary of teachers in the United States in 1965–66 was $6,792; in Alaska, $8,550; New York, $8,400.

Of course, involved in this is much more than the alleged ineptness of the NEA and the state education associations. Certain segments of the public vociferously contend that these associations have become too powerful, have raided governmental treasuries alarmingly, and have obtained abnormal tenure and economic rights for teachers. At base, public apathy regarding adequate support for public education was the root of the evil. But the failure of the NEA and the state associations to get the Federal Government to meet its responsibility for adequate general support of the public schools soured thousands of teachers. In 1964–65, significant break-throughs were secured under the leadership of President Johnson, with massive infusion of Federal funds presaging a new climate in the financing of public education but not relating directly to teachers' salaries.

But prior to the Johnson Administration, there was a vast unrest among public-school people over the backing and filling of the Federal Government. There were, it seemed to teachers, some strange means of ducking responsibility for adequate support of the public schools. This unrest doubtless aided the teachers' union cause.

Politics does, indeed, make strange bedfellows rallying around the same slogan. Business groups have consistently supported specific, or categorical, aid programs which were either tied to the sacred name of national defense or to corporate advantages—fat contracts which promised jobs and profits.

Thus we had prior to the Johnson Administration a Federal Government spending some $2 billion for highly specialized aspects of education. Most of these programs were loaded with Federal controls; yet general Federal support for public education was opposed on the basis of fear of Federal control of education. We had appropriations of hundreds of millions of dollars each year for support of schools in the impacted areas, those school districts wherein employees of the Federal Government are presumed to have put an unusual burden on the school district.

The aid to impacted areas was, until 1964–65, allocated on a formula requiring a minimum of 3 per cent in small schools and 6 per cent in large districts of the children who come from homes of Federal employees. Yet, in the capital city of the nation, where perhaps as many as half the school-age population are children of Federal employees, impacted-area aid to the schools was denied until 1964–65. And just across the Potomac, the Arlington County (Virginia) School District, where thousands of the government's highly paid professional employees live and where per capita income is among the highest in the nation, received annual grants of some $7 million.

Also, the nearly 200,000 children in the Overseas Dependents Schools, children whose fathers are in the armed services of the United States in foreign countries, were and still are denied the impacted-area aid as well as the surplus-commodity programs for school lunches. These schools are supported, at inferior levels, by funds appropriated for the Department of Defense.

Congressmen have wholeheartedly supported impacted-area aid and categorical aid, but many of these same congressmen have aggressively opposed general aid to the lower schools on the grounds that it would lead to Federal control. Teachers would observe, to their disgust, the Federal Government pouring out billions of dollars all over the world to aid other countries and the children of other countries but doing little or nothing to aid the education of most of America's children.

This continuing sham battle in Congress prior to 1964–65 over Federal aid to education, the obvious pussyfooting, plus similar ducking and dodging in many state legislatures and by many local school boards, had filled the teachers with a dangerous sense of unrest. This was part of the setting for the New York City organizational fight to launch its raid on teachers organizations.

The Elementary and Secondary Education Act of 1965 (Public Law 89–10) was predicated upon the impacted-area principle as applied to children of poor families.

The New York City school situation was made to order for one overt and heavy drive by labor to launch the raid on the teachers' organizations. Here more than 40,000 teachers had been mistreated, abused, ignored, and neglected for years. The whole school system had become one vast, unwieldly bureaucracy, with politics rearing its ugly head in almost every aspect of the administration of these schools.

Emerging New Climate Regarding Public Employees

In recent years the public has come to have a new concept of public employees and their rights, and teachers have begun to demand a new concept.

Calvin Coolidge's somber pronouncement regarding a strike of the Boston police in 1919 for adequate pay—"There is no right to strike against the public safety by anybody, anywhere, at any time"—was considered for a generation as sacrosanct. The statement still is generally accepted, but the absolute nature of it is no longer universally tenable. Time alters circumstances and concepts. Thoughtful analyses have searched out the fact that not all public employees are vitally involved in the public welfare and safety to an extent remotely approximating the role of the police and the military. Moreover, at the time of Coolidge's pronouncement public employees were generally considered as holders of gratuitous sinecures, as relative incompetents supported by public largesse, and as something of parasites on the body politic, This is no longer true.

The number of such employees has proliferated (some estimates are that they make up one sixth of all workers) into an extraordinary array performing essential services to society. Also, the nature of the extended services has moved away from the almost wholly political to largely professional, automatically upgrading the caliber and the preparation of the people involved. Presently, the Federal, state, and municipal governments find themselves in intense competition with industry and private institutions, hospitals, schools, colleges, and universities for highly competent professional personnel.

For example, the *Chicago Tribune* indignantly charged the United States Civil Service Commission with leading us into socialism because of governmental competition with industry for top college graduates. An article in the *Washington Star* of May 14, 1963 with reference to an editorial from the *Chicago Tribune,* was inserted into the *Congressional Record* by Congressman Alger of Texas and reads:

> The *Tribune's* ire was aroused when it discovered that Robert Mello, chief of the Civil Service Commission's college recruitment division, had invaded Chicago to announce at a press conference that the Government is looking for 16,300 engineers as well as scientists and other professional people and hoped to find them among the various college graduates.
>
> Mr. Mello also said the Government had been raising its pay and improving fringe benefits to meet the competition of private industry in the recruitment of top college graduates. Mr. Mello stressed the "challenge and opportunity" of Government work.

All this angered the *Tribune*, whose editorial on the subject concluded:
"Don't go into private industry," say the Washington Socialists. "The future lies with us!"

Representative Alger, in inserting the editorial, declared:

If there is any doubt as to where the social planners of the Kennedy Administration are heading this Nation, the hiring practices of the federal government should make it plain.

They are using taxpayers' money to hire college graduates away from private industry and this is a straight road to socialism.

Civil Service Commission officials are a bit bewildered by the attack.

They point out that the Government has no desire to deprive industry of top college talent—all it wants is its rightful share.

Because, like it or not, Government's responsibilities are increasing, not decreasing. And especially in such vital competition with the Russians in the fields of weapons, aeronautics, rockets, missiles and thermo-nuclear devices, it's essential that the Federal Government have the best scientists and engineers it can get. The country's future and very life depends on this, officials point out.

The day of the concept of the public employees as something of indentured servants or second- and third-class citizens is fading. More and more, these employees are being made full-fledged partners in a creative enterprise. Evidence of this is the tenure and personal considerations of municipal, state, and federal civil service laws. The chief evidence is President Kennedy's Executive Order Number 10988 of January 17, 1962 on "Employee-Management Cooperation in the Federal Service" directing the recognition of employee organizations and the consultation with these organizations in the formulation and implementation of personnel policies and practices and matters affecting working conditions. The order expressly prohibits recognition of employee organizations which (1) assert the right to strike against the Government of the United States, (2) advocate the overthrow of the constitutional form of the Government of the United States, or (3) discriminate with regard to the terms of conditions of membership because of race, color, creed, or national origin.

NEW CLIMATE AMONG PROFESSIONAL PEOPLE. Another significant symptom of the upgrading of public employees is the unrest and aggressiveness, even militancy, among professional people, including teachers. The strike of 1,000 medical doctors in Saskatchewan in 1963 and of 12,000 doctors in Mexico in January of 1964, a similar strike in Italy, one threatened in New Jersey, and the strike of 3,000 nurses in San Fancisco in August, 1966 shocked people everywhere. A medicare plan also resulted in a three-week strike of 12,000 doctors and dentists in Belgium in April 1964. All these events served to alert the public to a new climate of behavior among professional people, especially those in public practice. The teacher strikes in New York City in 1960 and

1962 are well known. These events in New York City are generally shrugged off as "Well, of course, in New York . . . " the import being that with radicalism there and the well-nigh intolerable conditions in the schools ". . . what else could one expect?".

Generally overlooked is the burgeoning restiveness among teachers which has been mounting in this country perceptibly since World War II. There were 105 strikes by teachers between 1941 and 1961.[7] In one school year of 1946–47 there was a series of strikes in 12 states involving some 5,000 teachers, doubtless reflecting the impatience of teachers with the failure in getting their salaries adjusted to those of other workers during the war and the apparent indifference of the public to doing so after the war had ended. The largest of these strikes was in Buffalo, involving 2,400 teachers; the smallest was in Sabattus, Maine, involving only one teacher who got tired of being the teacher and the janitor too.[8]

In the spring of 1963, a state's entire public-school staff refused to sign contracts for the ensuing school year. In March of that year the 10,500 teachers in Utah voted to withhold contract negotiations until and unless the state provided funds to improve the school program. (The actual vote, in a special convention attended by nearly 8,000 of the state teachers, found only 189 against the action.) Here is a case where militant action was prompted not by dissatisfaction with salaries alone, but by what the teachers felt were intolerably inadequate facilities, equipment, and personnel to provide high-quality educational services for the state's children.

The legislature had appropriated money for substantial raises in teachers' salaries. But it appropriated less than half of the amount proposed for improvement of the total school program by a coalition of public-spirited organizations—a coalition consisting of the Utah Education Association, the Utah Society of School Superintendents, the Utah School Boards Association, the State Board of Education, and the Utah Congress of Parents and Teachers.

If we attempt to explain the New York City teacher strikes by the catchword *radicalism,* as many do, what is the explanation of the Utah situation?

Utah is one of the most conservative states in the union, with a population predominantly of hard-working, thrifty, devout Mormons, where the conservative influence of the Mormon Church is paramount. Presumably the teachers of Utah are a part of that conservative climate and predominantly members of that faith. Yet the teachers' impatience was with what they considered a reactionary climate toward adequate support for the schools, and this impatience apparently included impatience with the position of their church.

They were especially bitter about the failure of the Utah Legislature to let the proposed legislation come out of the sifting committee for full discussion on the floors of the two houses, where votes would be taken and noses counted. To them, this meant that the hidden hands of the state's economic power structure were functioning in a way to protect the identity of the supporting legislators.

Causes of New Militancy Among Teachers

It is doubtful that anyone can give a definitive, all-inclusive analysis of the recent and continuing upsurge of teacher aggressiveness. Recent events suggest three possible causes, one tangible and obvious, the others intangible and not clearly perceptible. There are probably others.

The first and obvious causal factor is the mounting anger of teachers with economic injustice specifically and with the relative economic neglect of schools generally.

Teachers have simply become irritated beyond the point of tolerance with the failure of the American people to demand the right of teachers to share equitably in the fruits of an affluent society. Teachers are, one surmises, weary of hearing grandiloquent lip service to the importance of education and of teachers while they are getting what seems to them to be the run-around from the movers and shakers of the local economy, the big national business and industrial groups whose great influence reaches into the state legislatures and into the Congress of the United States. In certain New England and Middle Atlantic states several teacher strikes—or threatened strikes or the invoking of sanctions—have occurred in recent years because of the fiscal dependence of school boards on other local authorities such as a city council, city finance committee, or mayor.

In one case, the school board had sought for several years to raise teachers' salaries, and every year its proposal would be vetoed by the town council. In another case, the mayor exercised the veto.

Teachers behold the spectacle of national groups plugging for ever growing Federal appropriations for military hardware but consistently fighting general grants for the schools. They see the most menial kind of laborers being rewarded far beyond teachers. They know that some 40 per cent of the young men in teaching, those who want to make a career of their profession—and up to 75 per cent of the married men—have to moonlight in one, two, three, and even four extra jobs to support their families. The general public rationale for teachers' moonlighting often is not that salaries are inadequate but that teachers want to keep up with the Joneses.

The second causal factor in the upsurge of teacher restiveness is the changed working conditions and the changed fabric of the teaching profession.

Some of the obvious changes are as follows.

1. *The rapid decrease in the number of school districts, with a consequent enlargement of the size of the average school district.* This is a factor of considerable import. In 1931–32, for example, there were in the United

States a total of 127,422 districts. By 1965–66, this total had dwindled to about 27,000 with as many as 2,500 not operating schools.

The significance of this decline is that, as districts grow larger, paternalism in staff relations declines in appeal; also, staffs are better prepared.

The enlarged size of school districts, of course, tends to impersonalize staff relationships, as well as to make more complex and difficult effective communications between the administration and staff. Often the result is staff dissatisfaction and frustration, and a rebellious attitude tends to develop among segments of the staff.

2. *A recent and steady increase in the number of young people, especially men, in the teaching force.* In 1955–56, about 26 per cent of the public-school teaching staff was men; in 1963–64 this per cent had increased to 32. In 1955–56, the median age of all teachers in the public schools was 42.9; in 1963–63 this median had dropped to 39.9. In the latter year, the median age of men was 34; of women, 44.3. In 1963–64, about one third of all men were under 30 years of age.

These are factors of great significance. The new college graduates entering teaching are a new breed. They have grown up in a new social and economic milieu. Their preparation for teaching is different, more comprehensive, more realistic. They have a different concept of the roles and rights of teachers. The traditional image—an image held by society generally and too often by teachers themselves—of the teacher as a sort of indentured servant or timid hired hand, something of a third-class citizen, inept and bumbling, who must be told by his betters what to do and when to do it, is not acceptable to this new breed. In short, it is not acceptable to teachers in general any more. This has been a subtle, almost imperceptible change in the teaching profession. Its impact is profound and cannot be ignored in the future.

3. *A fact closely allied to the infusion of new blood into the teaching ranks: the increasingly higher levels of preparation and, thus, of competence of any given total teaching staff.*

In the short span of a decade and a half, the requirements for preparation and licensure of beginning elementary-school teachers have risen drastically. From little or no requirement of college work in many states the minimum requirement of the bachelor's degree is now almost universal. Preparation for high-school teachers is rapidly climbing toward the master's degree. In 1955–56, the per cent of public-school teachers with preparation below the bachelor's degree was 22.2. By 1965–66, it had dropped to 7.0.

For high-school teachers the preparation levels are, of course, still higher. In 1955–56, about 97 per cent of high-school teachers held bachelor's degrees or had higher preparation; by 1965–66 the per cent had increased to about 99.4. Perhaps the most significant factor of all is that elementary-school teachers are rapidly closing the gap between their preparation and that of their high-school colleagues. In 1955–56, only 62.9 per cent of elementary teachers had bachelors' degrees or higher preparation; in 1965–66 the per cent had increased to 87.1. In 1955–56, about 34 per cent of elementary-school teachers had no degree; by 1965–66 this had dropped to 12.9 per cent. The significance here is that, as this gap in perparation is closed, staff attitudes become more uniform and perhaps on the more aggressive side.

These figures point up clearly that the era of the typical teacher as a normal-school graduate, equipped only with meager general and liberal education and a bag of tricks, has ended. Typically, the new teacher now is well educated, competent, and confident. The profile of the nation's public-school teaching staff has changed. So has its outlook and its posture. Yesterday's paternalistic treatment of teachers is likewise outmoded.

The third causal factor, which obviously is at the heart of the new and aggressive climate among teachers, is the hunger to be a real part of a creative enterprise, not cogs in a well-oiled machine.

Here, it appears, is the big challenge of the future to administrative leadership. The challenge may be summarized in this manner: How can administrative leadership achieve an effective, constructive relationship among the staff, the administrators, and the school board toward the common goal of better educational services to children?

This means participation of the staff in the decision-making regarding policies under which teachers work. There seems to be an automatic assumption that the term *professional negotiations* applies exclusively to salaries. This is erroneous. Salary policy is only one among many problems. The process has to do with conditions of work, teacher load, personnel policies, grievances, conditions of employment, promotion, tenure and dismissal, academic freedom, textbook selection, curriculum determination, and a whole cluster of related policies.

The National School Boards Association, although endorsing in its policy statements the principle of teachers' participation in policy formation, rejects the implementation of such participation. It reacted negatively to the teachers' union and professional-association procedures in a resolution passed at its Denver Convention in April 1963.

However generous and benevolent unilateral decision-making may be, it still falls short of the stimulative power of involvement. It still has something of the debilitating effect of a kind of paternalism.

As an analogy we can consider the status of a nation whose conditions under an enlightened colonialism might be very good but whose people yearn to be free and to have a measure of self-government. Here is the reason for the emerging of the world's new nations. They doubtless will make many mistakes; it may be, in fact, a long time before they will be able to create new conditions as good as the ones they enjoyed under colonialism. But the free spirit can never be free so long as it is directed from the outside; it must be directed from the inside. This is a law of life, and the generosity of others can never provide this life-giving ingredient. A profession also is independent, free, and self-directing, or it is nothing.

Dr. John H. Fischer, President of Columbia University Teachers College, recently suggested two alternatives in teacher-school board relations:

> We can look on the relation between the school board and its teaching staff as a typical employee-employer relation in which the logical action to set salaries at the lowest level is consistent with maintaining an adequate staff. In such a situation management emphasizes production efficiency or its educational analogy, and the effort is made to see that supervision produces results. . . .
>
> We can, on the other hand, view the relationship between a school board and its staff as a unique situation in which a body of licensed professionals who happen to be public employees participate with the agency that employs them to arrive at mutually agreeable understandings about salaries, working conditions, professional duties, administration, supervision, and program development.[9]

Fischer suggests that the first alternative inevitably results in treatment of the teacher as just another employee engaged in a sort of mass production. The inevitable concomitant of this concept is to rest salary and welfare negotiation in an outside agency, which represents a threat to the academic authority and academic freedom of the individual teacher.

The second alternative, of viewing the teacher as a professional first and an employee second, implies the desire to utilize his experience, professional wisdom, and advice through participation in policy-making. This second alternative must ultimately depend upon the quality of administrative leadership as far as board attitudes and policies and creative staff participation are concerned.

To put the matter bluntly, the period of the old line-staff relationship, of the benevolent despot or the benevolent paternalist, of the hierarchial concept in administration is rapidly fading from the American scene. There are still some pockets left where there are such attitudes on the part of both school boards and school administrations, but they are on their way out.

The American Association of School Administrators went through a sustained period of soul-searching apprehension (as the National School Boards Association, it appears, still is) regarding the upsurge of determination of teachers to be accorded a real part in policy decisions. This now is the viewpoint of the association as written in a recent policy statement of its Executive Committee:

> Creating and sustaining a professional climate and operational procedures that call forth and use the full creative capacities of all employees in the attainment of educational goals is a prime responsibility of school administration. By its very nature this calls for common understanding, mutual respect, and a full measure of confidence among all who work in the schools and all who serve on the school board, the agency to which the people have delegated so large a measure of responsibility for their children's education. There is no place in this mutual responsibility for authoritarian methods of selfish advantage-seeking.

> If democracy, with its fundamental emphasis on the worth, dignity, and importance of each individual, has taught the people of this country anything, it is that on the whole the capacities of people are used more fruitfully, results are more rewarding, and the job is better done when the individuals who are directly involved in any common endeavour participate freely in setting goals, developing operational procedures, and establishing general working conditions. . . . This is the kind of school personnel administration that thoughtful people seek.[10]

In 1966, AASA, in its publication *School Administrators View Professional Negotiation,* came round to a rather categorical endorsement of the *use* of professional negotiation and sanctions.

The conditions which impelled some teachers' organizations to seek an alliance with labor in the first two dedades of this century were described in "A Call to Action," a pamphlet issued by AFT, as follows:

> Long before the great war teachers in all parts of the United States were restless under the conditions of their employment. . . . With few exceptions, American public schools are autocratically administered by officials chosen by and subservient to school boards representing business and politics.
>
> Teachers' salaries have been kept down to the level of the most poorly paid unskilled laborer, and this in the face of higher standards and the soaring cost of living. Their tenure of position is insecure and they are without provision for sickness and old age. Everywhere we find the great mass of public school teachers exhausted by overwork; harrassed by the petty tyranny of supervising officers, and struggling against the handicap of unsanitary, overcrowded, poorly equipped schools. Is it any wonder that submitting to such conditions, teachers have been unable to take their proper place of dignity and influence in the community—that they are gibed at as forming "a third sex"?[11]

The accuracy of this description can be challenged only on the minutest points. Remember, this was an appraisal of conditions in the formative years of teachers' and unions' alliance, from 1902 to 1920. This was the period in which NEA continued to be largely dominated by college and university presidents and, to a lesser degree, by school administrators. It was before the reorganization and democratization of NEA in the early 1920's. It was before the creation of the NEA Representative Assembly and was to no small degree influenced by the militancy of Margaret Haley and her colleagues from the Chicago Federation of Teachers. After the creation of the NEA Representative Assembly, which was based on proportional representation, the voice of the classroom teachers began to emerge as a powerful one. That voice began to demand greater participation in educational affairs and greater attention to the economic and status conditions of the rank and file.

Of course great progress has been made in the conditions described above in the years since. But too many of the conditions remain true for a comfortable contemplation of the past, for satisfaction with the present, or for complacency about the future.

It will be recalled that many of the unfavorable conditions for teachers, especially the economic ones, recurred or still obtained during and after World War II, resulting in a rash of teacher strikes. With the upsurge of the country's economy in the 1950's, and a new burgeoning in the 1960's, the economic condition of teachers, while vastly improved, still continues to be a source of deep unrest. It is this new wave of unrest which explains in large part the new upsurge of teacher unions.

To ignore this unrest, in part an expression of the hunger of teachers for recognition, in part dissatisfaction with the economic returns of teaching, is to invite overt action. For the professional organizations to discuss the upsurge of the teachers' union appeal with contempt or by resort to clichés and slogans in lieu of vigorous action to satisfy the real aspirations of teachers, is to invite disaster. The future of the organizational struggle hinges precisely on this point.

Future of the Struggle

This is, in vignette, the history of the evolution of the struggle for the organizational loyalties of American public-school teachers. There are, of course, other factors involved in this struggle.

Essentially it is a fight on the one hand to move teaching forward, on all fronts, to professional status. This is the challenge to the professional organizations. To do this, these organizations are compelled to broaden their programs and to provide services which heretofore they have been reluctant or timid in doing. Involved in this goal, also, is the imperative of a new attitude on the part of the public about the status of teaching and what constitutes adequate support of the schools.

On the other hand it is a fight by organized labor to enlist America's teachers in close alliance with America's organized workers, with all that such an alliance implies for the status of teaching and the future operation of our system of universal free education.

Organized labor could win this fight; there should be no mistake about that.

The struggle has just begun—in earnest.

3

Battleground: The Big Cities

Students will be proud of their teachers who have the courage to violate the law.

—Charles Cogen, President, United Federation of Teachers, New York City Local, No. 2, American Federation of Teachers

For the big drive to organize teachers, labor wisely chose the big cities, where it was strong and where the NEA and its affiliates were weak.

The kick-off of the struggle—and the showcase—was to be New York City.

Hindsight is, of course, always 20/20.

In retrospect, many observers, including many NEA members and doubtless some members of the NEA staff, question the wisdom of the association's becoming involved in the New York City school situation in 1960.

And those with a critical view of the decision to do so have a strong case.

In the first place, these critics contend, NEA by becoming visible in the New York City contest made the wrong move at the wrong time in the wrong place. Moreover, they contend, NEA effort was too little and too late.

According to this view, NEA's direct and visible entrance into the internecine struggle of local organizations gave the UFT a perfect outside target to shoot at, thus relieving UFT of the difficult and complex task of dealing with New York City issues.

In short, these critics contend, NEA could have won the big city contest had it stayed in the background and made resources available (as did IUD) for a carefully selected and developed local organization to wage the battle against UFT. The battle was essentially one between local groups. And this should have been the focus of the fight. But when NEA became visible it presented a choice target for an outsider.

In addition, critics hold that NEA was woefully unprepared for the battle that was precipitated by its entrance into the big city. By intervening, it asked for the image of defeat. UFT probably would have won anyway, but an NEA defeat could have been avoided. For example, UFT was enabled to concentrate upon this outside target and obscure the really bitter issues for which it had no real answers. UFT's slighting of the elementary-school teachers to gain its victory did not come to light during the campaign. This slight was exposed only with the conclusion of its first bargaining agreement with the School Board. The professional differential gave the high-school teachers the salary advantage for which they had been fighting since 1947. Presumably this was in keeping with a campaign pledge to the high-school teachers. The High School Teachers Association had been bitter toward NEA since the single-salary schedule was adopted in 1947.

None of the critics of NEA's involvement in the New York City fight is critical of the involvement *per se,* only the visibility and directness of the involvement. They readily admit that NEA had to be involved. At any rate, the complexity of the problems of the schools and teachers there were such as to defy precise analysis and evaluation. Even now, it is virtually impossible for the outsider, however objective and impartial, to assess fairly all of the factors involved.

The Eroding Climate

It is relatively easy to identify the deteriorating nature of the New York City school system in 1960, the eroding influences of political interference, the stifling anticreativeness of the huge administrative bureaucracy, and the harassed and frustrated teaching staff. But it would be less than fair to sketch only this part of the picture.

New York State and New York City were among the early leaders in setting high standards for their schools both in terms of preparation and certification requirements for teachers and in terms of per capita expenditures.

Among New York City teachers, too, was doubtless a deep feeling that their problems were unique, as indeed many of them were and are. It would logically follow, therefore, that they should question whether any outside organization could really be of much help to them. Especially would this skeptical attitude apply to a general organization (NEA) which had the image of serving teachers in small cities and in predominantly rural areas.

In addition, a feeling of resentment toward so-called state equalization programs, which had generally been growing in large cities throughout the nation, probably existed to a high degree among New York City teachers. This problem was highlighted by the decision of the United States Supreme Court on reapportionment of state legislatures. This decision, of course, was aimed at correcting the imbalance in representation between rural and urban areas. It is well known that with the rapid upsurge of urbanization, over-representation of rural areas in state law-making bodies and a consequent under-representation of cities obtained almost everywhere in the United States. During the last half-century, the rurally dominated legislatures sought a perfectly reasonable goal of equalizing education by closing the gap in school expenditures between the relatively poor rural areas and the relatively rich urban centers. But it stands to reason that, because of the rural over-representations, the cities were often penalized.

There was an especial bitterness toward Albany, it appears, on the part of New York City teachers concerning the allocation of the school funds. They felt that the deep differences between upper New York State and New York City on economic, social, and many other issues was reflected in an unfair amount of school funds going upstate. The fact that upper New York State was predominantly Republican and New York City predominantly Democratic heightened the bitterness toward the state legislature.

During the 1920's—in fact until the great postwar exodus to the suburbs and the influx of the economically and culturally deprived—New York City schools were among the best; experimentation and frontier practices were notable, and teachers felt themselves to be among the professional elite of the nation. Their salary schedules during this period of great prestige reflected this status. Then, with the emergence of the factors mentioned above and others a steady deterioration set in with the inevitable consequence of steadily declining teacher morale.

The long-simmering bitterness between high-school and elementary-school teachers was a factor that deserves further elaboration. The adoption of the single salary schedule in 1947 really precipitated open warfare between the two groups, resulting in threatened strikes by the high-school group and in one actual work stoppage.

Involved in this bitterness was the fact that a high-school teacher was required to hold a master's degree as minimum preparation whereas the minimum requirement for an elementary-school teacher was the bachelor's degree. In addition, there still was a large group of elementary school teachers who had entered teaching in the city as normal-school graduates. These non-degree teachers comprised the older group. Their number was rapidly diminishing, but this did not prevent the high-school group from feeling that it was grossly discriminated against by the single salary schedule. Of course, a single salary schedule makes allowance for differences in preparation and experience. But apparently the high-school teachers in New York City still felt that they ought to be given pay preferment for their superior preparation and specialized expertise in given subjects or fields. Too, for many years high-school teachers had been in a separate department in the Board of Education and on a separate salary schedule. Such preferred status is not easily relinquished.

Too, New York City has had a great proliferation of professional organizations of teachers. Its 40,000 or so teachers at that time—perhaps as many as 50,000 if all types of educational workers were included—belonged to some

90 different organizations. Most of these were special-interest associations dealing with the professional positions or teaching fields or area interests of teachers. Only a handful of these 70 or so organizations were general in nature and concerned themselves with teachers' welfare.

Such a proliferation of interest groups among the city's teachers has always been difficult for outsiders to understand. The extreme size of the city doubtless is a large factor in contributing to the great diversity of interests and viewpoints of its teachers. Such diversity does not necessarily negate the development of a community of interests, but it doubtless does tend to make it more difficult.

Too, a hard-core feeling of self-sufficiency existed in the big cities. Teachers of large cities seem to have a firm conviction that no outside organization can possibly understand or be helpful in solving their complex problems—in any large city, not New York alone. They assume that their problems are unique, that there are no common goals or problems that justify their organizational affiliation with colleagues in the small cities or small urban areas.

In the large cities status consciousness was pronounced. Assignment to a good neighborhood school or a slum school had overtones of prestige or the lack of it, creating symbols of division, especially if these assignments were suspected of being connected with administrative favoritism or discrimination. In such a climate, efforts at unity are generally sneered at, personalities often clash in meetings, and verbal exchanges tend to be intense.

Significant, too, is the fact that neither the NEA nor its state affiliate, the New York State Teachers Association (NYSTA) had ever developed any great strength in New York City. Perhaps it would be fairer to say neither ever developed the kind of meaningful program that would attract and hold considerable numbers of teachers as members in New York City. The maximum membership that NEA was ever able to attract was 10,214 members in 1938.

There is an interesting causal factor back of this peak membership. NEA held its annual convention in New York City in the summer of 1938. This fact probably brought about the increase in memberships in the city from a total of 2,758 on December 31, 1937 to 10,214 on May 31, 1938. By May 31, 1940 membership had dropped to 2,744. Thereafter the New York City membership of NEA steadily declined, with slight fluctuation upward or downward through the 1950's. By 1960, when NEA decided to go into the city and make a fresh start, its membership was only 700, less than 2 per cent of the New York City teachers. In all probability, the actual percentage of the city's teachers who were members of NEA was lower since this membership included college people and others not connected with the city's schools.

Why this low membership in NEA and NYSTA?

Obviously, one major factor was the failure of the two to develop realistic and significant programs from the viewpoint of the teachers. Had NEA sought vigorously to build on the 1938 membership after its New York Convention, there might have been a different climate in 1960.

The very climate of New York City, with its heavy concentration and political power of labor, and with its labor ties to city hall, certainly did not hurt the teachers' union. Relativively few New York City teachers knew anything about NEA. Probably its predominant image among these teachers was of a sort of national organization concerned solely with research and curriculum, an inept kind of organization to compete in a tooth-and-claw battle. Of course, the teachers' union belabored this image of impotence. To be frank, NEA had done little to present to New York teachers an image of vigorous orangization battling for teachers' right. It seems unfair to belabor the New York City teachers for their unfavorable attitude toward NEA.

Actually the showdown in New York City in 1960 and 1961 was not essentially one between the teachers' union and the professional organizations It was, rather, the culmination of years of growing discontent ending in bitterness, years of weak or politically dominated administration. The City's administration seemed deliberately to use the divisiveness among teachers' organizations, playing differing salary groups and interest groups against each other, with the excuse that until the groups could agree among themselves there was nothing anyone else could do. The storm, gaining momentum over the years with increasing political meddling in the schools, the exposure of alleged corruption, and the deterioration of administrative effectiveness and teacher morale, had to explode sooner or later. The explosion came in 1960 and 1961.

The Entrance of NEA into the Fight

In 1958, the few New York City organizations which had maintained affiliation with the NEA formed the NEA Council, supplementing the existing NYC-NEA Committee. These organizations were concerned with salary and other matters. The AFT local affiliate was the United Federation of Teachers, which had come into existence from defections from the old Teachers Guild and the High School Teachers Association. But at this time (1958) the UFT was making no great inroads on teacher membership. It was then just one among many organizations trying to gain headway. At that time the NEA affiliates were not greatly impressed or greatly concerned by UFT. In May 1960, the leaders of five organizations of the NEA Council and four other influential organizations agreed to meet and discuss their problems with NEA officials in Washington. The problem of collective bargaining was on the agenda, but not in the union context. These leaders were seeking help in fighting a situation of general deterioration in the city schools. These organizations felt that they had to support collective bargaining because of their belief that a substantial majority of the city's teachers favored collective bargaining (although at this time NEA itself had no policy regarding collective bargaining, for or against).

Actually, the showdown in 1960 and 1961 was not essentially a battle between professional associations and the teachers' union; therefore, NEA involvement did not stem initially from the union threat. The showdown was the result of the culmination of mounting frustration and bitterness among the teachers over factors which have already been enumerated.

Resulting from the May 1960 meeting was a request to the NEA for assistance. Specific assistance was requested in the form of establishment of an NEA regional office and staff to coordinate the work of these organizations. Such a request had been made before, but NEA did not respond until 1960 when it was beginning to be evident that IUD was prepared to pour money and organizing help into the organizational struggle. The 1960 request was transmitted to the NEA Executive Committee meeting in connection with the annual NEA Convention in St. Louis. It was decided that an NEA regional office would be established on September 1, 1960 to conform to a pattern already in the process of development. (Prior to the New York teachers' request, NEA regional offices were already in operation in Burlingame, California, St. Paul, and Boston and additional ones have been established subsequently in Minneapolis, Indianapolis, Atlanta, Dallas, Denver and Trenton.) The New York office was to serve, in addition to New York City, the remainder of New York State, New Jersey, and eastern Pennsylvania.

The magnitude of the problems in New York City quickly was apparent to the staff of the regional office. There were an incredible number of teachers' organizations, many of which had once been vigorous but were now moribund, classed by the union as paper organizations. There were, because of old differences and competition for members, incessant squabbling and bickering among the various organizations, who were dissipating their energies either in attacking one another or defending against attacks. At the outset of NEA's work in the city, many leaders of the various organizations refused even to to meet with the leaders of the other groups. There was continuing internecine warfare over salary matters, with the high-school teachers demanding a higher pay schedule and the elementary-school teachers as vigorously defending the single salary schedule adopted in 1947. There were some bias images built up against the NEA by charges of anti-Semitism relating to NEA permitting travel tours to countries barring admission of Jewish teachers; doubtless many Catholic teachers felt unkindly about NEA because of its stand against public support for private and parochial schools; and Negro teachers and their sympathisers resented the existence of segregated NEA locals in the South. And of course the high-school teachers were bitter toward NEA's long-time advocacy of the single-salary scale. But these were old charges and probably did not enter very significantly into the situation in 1962. Other factors were of greater importance.

Two other conditions of the local climate were powerful obstacles to the NEA:

1. Organized labor had great political power in New York City because organized labor was heavily represented in the population with something like 1 million votes.

2. There was a close tie-in between the city administration and organized labor; in other words, the political power structure was stacked against the NEA. This, of course, was simply the pragmatic realism of where the votes were. Many indications of this tie-in came to light during the course of the struggle between the union and NEA.

The mayor put pressure on the board of education, the members of which were his selectees, to give in to the union for a collective-bargaining election. Furthermore, he personally intervened (as he did again in April 1962 and September 1963) to save face for the union in its abortive one-day strike in November 1960 by failing to invoke the Condin-Wadlin Act and by granting amnesty to the strikers. He appointed a fact-finding committee consisting of labor leaders to mediate between the teachers' union and the board of education. He had the city's labor department conduct the collective-bargaining election.

Progress was slow in such a climate. The NEA office acted as mediator in slowly bringing the teachers' groups together, representing these organizations in hearings before the board of education, before the city government, and with the press. During 1960–61, the number of organizations affiliated with the NEA grew from 12 to 19, including the five borough teachers' organizations, the Elementary School Teachers Association, and the Secondary School Teachers Association. During that year the difficult problem of getting consensus on a proposed salary schedule was finally consummated with a compromise agreement. The union reacted with attacks on the organizations and the NEA and with some weird interpretations of the salary plan.

In June 1961 the New York City teachers voted 27,000 to 9,000 for holding a bargaining election, which on its face was a union victory. It was apparent to the NEA at this point that the odds were greatly against NEA success in the city. It faced the dilemma of whether to continue, facing almost certain defeat, or to withdraw, leaving to their own resources the teachers who desired to remain independent of the union. There were insistent appeals from teachers and officers of existing organizations, for whom unionization was distasteful, not to forsake them. But in any case the union would claim a decisive victory over the NEA.

The decision was made to stay and fight. The union still had only about 5,000 members, leaving some 35,000 teachers as yet unaffiliated with any national teachers' organization. This unaffiliated majority still provided grounds for hope that an alternative organization would be chosen as the bargaining agent. After sustained consideration, the nonunion organizations formed the Teachers Bargaining Organization (TBO) as an affiliate of NEA.

The Defeat and Its Lessons

The campaign that followed to secure votes in the bargaining election to be held in November was again one against great odds for NEA. The campaign required contacts in 840 schools, and since meetings could be held only at lunch hour and after school, the NEA central staff, assisted by field workers on loan from several nearby state association staffs, had a virtually impossible job. But in the end, over 10,000 signatures supporting the TBO listing on the ballot were secured, with a minimum of 4,300 required.

Some of the difficulties encountered by the TBO were political influence at city hall to speed up the election date, which was to the advantage of the teachers' union; official directives from the board of education forbidding principals and other administrators from taking any part in the campaign; pressures on the New York City Labor Department to rule the TBO's petition form invalid; the decision of the city labor department to have ballotting by mail instead of in each school, which, it is believed, substantially reduced the vote for TBO; the ruling that several classes of nonsupervisory personnel, who represented substantial NEA support, were ineligible to vote; entrenched union personnel, especially chairmen of organizational activities, making it difficult for TBO representatives to gain access to many schools; TBO materials being withheld from teachers in some buildings; and the old anti-NEA bias charges—ethnic and religious—that were being widely distributed via the grapevine.

In addition, to be starkly frank about it, NEA staff members came up against tactics which in their relatively cloistered world they had never encountered before. After it was all over, they discovered that copies of every bit of correspondence from the NEA office reached the UFT headquarters before being received by the addressees. Mimeographed materials from the NEA office, processed by trade-union members, reached the UFT office before NEA personnel saw them. Members of the NEA task force scheduled to speak at one of the city schools often were notified by telephone that their schedules had been changed only to find when they showed up that school was out and teachers had long since departed for home, or the addresses given them were not schools but vacant lots. One UFT advocate reported that he dropped by the NEA office one day to check on some NEA research data. He went from the NEA office to the UFT office and was questioned about his loyalty. Word of his visit to the NEA office had been reported by an office worker to the union before he could reach the UFT office.

The election to select a bargaining agent for the teachers on December 15, 1961 resulted in a solid victory for the union. Of the estimated 43,500 eligible voters, approximately 20,000 voted for UFT, 10,000 for TBO, and 2,500 for the Teachers Union (an independent group affiliated neither with organized labor nor with the NEA), with some 12,000 to 13,000 teachers not voting.

There is no question of the smashing victory which UFT won in New York City in this election. The odds were in its favor, to be sure. But this did not obscure the magnitude of the victory, and NEA officials made no efforts to discount it.

Was the entrance of NEA into the New York City fracas a great mistake, a complete fiasco? Opinions are mixed.

Some of the results of the battle in the big city were clear.

1. The New York City hassle gave clear evidence that both the NEA and its affiliated state associations could no longer continue their passive or defensive position toward the union threat or toward the very real problems of urban teachers. It became clear that this fight was no longer a scrap with a rather inept AFT; it was now a fight with organized labor as such for the teachers' organizational loyalties. Instead of having to fend off the weak and ineffective efforts of AFT, NEA now must repulse an all-out campaign of the AFL–CIO (through the structure of the Industrial Union Department), with all its money, power, and votes. This realization had to come sooner or later. The New York City battle underscored this fact for those close to the situation, although IUD's participation was not trumpeted until the Denver NEA Convention.

2. The UFT garnered less than half the votes of all New York City teachers. When it won preferred status to become a recognized bargaining agent, its membership was only about 5,000 (or roughly one eighth of the total number of teachers), and it grew to only 25,000 in 1964 (little more than one half of the total); by 1965 the UFT membership had reached 30,355 and in 1966, 37,291. Thus, there are presently (1966) some 15,000 teachers who have affiliated with neither national group.

3. The establishment of the Urban Project by the NEA was a partial outgrowth of the New York City battle. The rapid strengthening of the project, at least, was influenced by the New York City battle although the project had been established prior to the battle. This project originated from the realization that, with the rapid urbanization of the nation, an increasing proportion of teachers would be in the urban areas. Here is where organized labor is strongest and teachers' problems most severe. Here also is where, at least up until 1962, local accociations were generally weak and where few had full-time staff members. The New York City battle speeded up the resolve of the NEA to slug it out with the teachers' unions in the big city, a field in which NEA had previously made only token efforts. This resolve would have

come in time, but maybe too late, had the NEA not been involved in the New York City fight.

The Background of What Happened

The story of the big battle in the big city includes two strikes and several threatened ones sponsored by the United Federation of Teachers, which was formed in the spring of 1960 by an announced merger of the New York Teachers Guild and a group of teachers of the secondary School Teachers Association. Actually this was not a merger; only a few of the leaders of the association joined with the guild at that time. It is difficult to ascertain how many defected from the Secondary School Teachers Association. Prior to this projected merger, the guild had claimed 6,000 members (with the record showing only 2,400 for whom they had paid national dues), and it claimed 1,500 new members as a result of the "merger." However, in subsequent press releases it claimed a membership of 10,000.

In May 1960 the UFT learned that Dr. John J. Theobald, Superintendent of Schools, was planning to recommend certain improvements for teachers which had long been advocated by many organizations in the city. These included sick leave for permanent substitute teachers, the equalizing of salary increments, and lengthened lunch periods for elementary-school teachers. The UFT immediately demanded, in loud voice and big headlines, that these things be done, presumably to claim a great victory concerning things that had already been decided upon. It added to its demands a collective-bargaining election, payroll deduction of dues, and a promotional increment designed to attract more high-school teachers into the union. And to add a great show of force and muscle-flexing, for the benefit of the 30,000 to 40,000 New York City teachers who were not yet affiliated with it, the UFT threatened a strike.

There were some conditions existing in New York that made these demands seem very attractive to the city's teachers—a loss of confidence in the board of education, lack of communication between board of education or administration and the teacher, exposure of corruption, poor buildings, inept and inadequate supervision, and growing numbers of difficult children.

Thus was inaugerated by UFT a pattern of bluster, intimidation, and showy demands which were to produce two actual strikes in which the law was flouted. Three strikes were threatened: in May 1960, in September 1963, and again in 1965 at the opening of the schools. The two actual strikes occurred on November 6, 1960 and on April 11, 1962. (Another strike in 1967.)

A thread of coincidences ran throughout all these threats. It was as if a precise scenario had been written in advance, as indeed many people believe had been the case. Perhaps there was not actually a written script, but one agreed upon verbally in advance.

The sequence ran like this: A series of demands were made upon the New

York City Board of Education involving concessions either already decided upon by the board or impossible of attainment by the board alone. Then came the strike threat, always accompanied by denunciation of the board. Next were sustained negotiation, more threats and bluster, and denunciation of the law against strikes. Somewhere along the line, at the appointed time, the New York City Central Labor Council would join in to reinforce UFT's demands and to announce its unequivocal support of the demands.

Things would get dark, indeed everyone would be quaking at the prospect of closed schools. But the hero would gallop in at the last minute to rescue the teacher's union.

The hero? Who but Mayor Robert F. Wagner. Here came what was then generally referred to in New York as the Mike Quill-Mayor Wagner routine. The transit workers, being public employees, had found an invariable friend and last-minute protector of the public interest in the person of the mayor, who not only mysteriously could come up with the money, but who could keep the workers just inside the bounds of the law. Somewhere in this script, maybe, were the more than 1 million votes supposedly controlled by the labor unions in the city.

It must be acknowledged that a careful following of the prepared script has paid off for the UFT, which has been able to build a paper-tiger image into that of a powerful lion and has been able to make some solid gains for the teachers.

After delivering its demands in the spring of 1960, the UFT threatened work stoppage to be scheduled in May in support of these demands, a strike which the UFT claimed would involve 10,000 teachers. This threat being properly delivered with the usual public fanfare, the next step (here is that script again) was to get a conference with the superintendent, Mayor Robert F. Wagner, and representatives of some of the city's trade unions.

The superintendent, as he had previously promised, reiterated his plans to make various improvements for teachers. Also, if 30 per cent of the teachers requested it and if it were legal, he agreed to recommend to the board of education a collective-bargaining election, including provision for dues check-off. The appeasing approach of the superintendent proved to be anything but that. The UFT immediately claimed a great victory and the surrender of the superintendent and the board. Therefore, said the UFT, the strike was called off. The superintendent began preparing his recommendations to the board. No other teachers' organization representatives were present, so UFT could and did loudly proclaim victory, although the gains had been the product of the work of many teachers' groups.

The board of education then set up a subcommittee to study collective bargaining. The first act of the committee was to request the opinion of the New York City Corporation Counsel regarding the legality of a collective-bargaining election, In the meantime, the UFT pressed a vigorous campaign

Beyond the Horizon of the Law

for signatures on a petition requesting a collective-bargaining election, obtaining 12,000 signatures which it claimed represented 30 per cent of the classroom teachers of the city.

During the summer of 1960, while the Corporation Counsel continued to study the legal question of the election, teachers began to ask questions about the UFT's great victory and when the fruits of that victory would be obtained. The UFT, finding itself in a corner because of its extravagant claims, began to prepare for another threat of work stoppage by referring to a double cross and began to talk of the necessity for a strike in the fall.

The First Strike

The UFT Executive Committee did in fact, recommend a strike for November 7, 1960. In back of this action were several developments.

When the board did not act quickly enough on the petition to test the teachers' sentiment on whether or not they desired collective-bargaining,

UFT delivered an ultimatum setting forth six demands. The board, incidentally, had already agreed to the election if the legal council ruled that collective bargaining was legal. The six demands were

1. An election to decide if teachers wanted collective-bargaining.
2. The equalizing of salary increments.
3. Sick leave for permanent substitutes.
4. Adoption of the promotional increment.
5. Full lunch periods for elementary-school teachers.
6. Dues check-off.

After voting to recommend a strike, and before calling for a vote on the strike by its membership, the UFT Executive Committee sent a telegram to Superintendent of Schools Theobald demanding to know what he was doing about these six issues.

With the threat of a strike over his head, the superintendent replied that the board had not received the opinion as to the legality of collective bargaining for teachers, but that this opinion was expected momentarily; that the board was instituting six days of sick leave per year for permanent substitutes (one day more than the UFT demanded); that changes had been ordered in assignments to lengthen the lunch period of elementary-school teachers; that the board's new budget would provide increased funds to equalize increments and to hire aides in elementary schools to help lengthen lunch periods of teachers; that the dues check-off was being studied by a committee of the board. Only on the matter of promotional increments was the union flatly turned down, being advised that the superintendent would make no recommendation on this until the elementary and high-school teachers were able to agree on a plan.

Yet with practically every demand already met or promised to be met, the UFT Executive Committee called for a strike vote. Ostensibly, the reasoning was that, with virtually every point over which they were contending already conceded, what had the union to lose? Besides, an impressive show of having won a great victory could then be trumpeted to the teachers as a recruiting device. The vote of the membership was 2,896 for the strike and 117 against—out of a claimed membership of 10,000 and a total teaching force of over 40,000.

Superintendent Theobald went on TV and denounced the proposed strike as a "shameless power grab" by the UFT to force itself into the position of bargaining agent for all teachers. All other teachers' organizations opposed the strike on the grounds that it was, first, senseless, since all points save one were already in the bag and second, illegal under state law.

The UFT claims were extravagant. First, this was proclaimed as a strike by the teachers rather than by the UFT. The UFT claimed that 15,000 to 20,000 teachers would strike and that a majority of the 840 schools would be closed. It claimed that the strike would have the full support of organized labor.

Finally, the UFT proclaimed that only a signed agreement with the superintendent and the board could end the strike.

What were the actual outcomes?

The board of education had full access to the records, with reports made throughout the day from all schools. The results as announced by the board were these:

1. A total of 5,900 teachers were absent from their classrooms. Allowing for the normal rate of absences for illness, about 4,600 of the 5,900 appeared to be on strike. How many of the 4,600 were actually on strike and how many simply respected picket lines is not known. At any rate, the number away from their teaching jobs on November 7 was strikingly short of the UFT claim that 15,000 to 20,000 would walk out.
2. No schools were closed. In a few junior high schools, where UFT was strongest in membership, classes were consolidated in auditoriums.
3. Only in about two dozen schools (out of 840) were a majority of the teachers absent and the schools at a virtual standstill. In the other approximately 820 schools a normal day's routine occurred.
4. About 2,000 teachers picketed some 220 schools.
5. The predicted all-out support by organized labor did not materialize. The fact is that labor leaders were embarrassed by the trigger-happy UFT and its illegal strike. The President of the Central Labor Council, Harry Von Arsdale said, "The announcement by the UFT is extremely regrettable."
6. The one-day strike actually was abandoned at the insistence of labor leaders.
7. No new gains were made by the strike and no signed agreement with the superintendent and the board was obtained. Assurance was given that the striking teachers could return to their jobs with the loss of one day's pay.

The aftermath of the one-day strike occurred on November 8, Election Day, a school holiday. Mayor Wagner met with the superintendent, the president of the board of education, and a group of labor leaders. At this meeting, UFT president Charles Cogen agreed to call off the strike. The mayor then appointed David Dubinsky, President of the International Ladies Garment Workers Union, Harry Van Arsdale, President of the Central Labor Council, and Jacob Patotsky, President of the Amalgamated Clothing Workers, as a fact-finding committee to evaluate the circumstances of the dispute and deliver a report to the mayor.

The debacle came into real focus when the UFT Executive Committee reported Mayor Wagner's meeting and the agreement to call off the strike to a meeting of its delegate assembly. This was a bitter, acrimonious three-hour session. The wrangling ended in grudging acquiescence with the decision. The delegates were partially mollified with some more grandoise claims such as that the mayors' committee of labor leaders was mediating the controversy.

There was loud talk of winning the strike (in fact, the AFT ran an article in *The American Teacher* on how the AFT won its strike), and delegates were told to watch for the report of the fact-finding committee, with the implication that they would then really see something important.

On the other, less glamorous side of the coin, was the hard, unmentioned reality of the situation. The fact-finding committee never said or claimed it was mediating or negotiating. UFT was generally recognized as having over-played its hand. By its strike action it had stripped itself of the extravagant membership claims. Instead of the 10,000 the UFT had claimed, the actual membership was revealed to be perhaps half that. After the unsuccessful strike, the leaders referred to 6,000 members, a figure which, judging from the past record, was probably still somewhat inflated.

The fact-finding committee report further deflated the UFT. The report was simply a fact-finding one, no more, no less, and contained facts already well known even before the abortive strike: that the superintendent and board were already taking steps to grant the sick-leave demand, to equalize increments, and to extend lunch periods; that the collective-bargaining election would be held after the board finished studying the legality of the matter and appropriate procedures for conducting the election: and that dues check-off was being studied. The report also stated that the matter of the promotional increment could best be solved by the teachers themselves, which was precisely the view that Superintendent Theobald had taken.

THE COLLECTIVE BARGAINING ELECTION. In October 1961 the city's corporation council ruled that an election to select a bargaining agent for the teachers of New York City was legal. Rules were then established by City Labor Commissioner Harold Felix: each organization which aspired to be selected to represent the teachers must file a petition signed by at least 10 per cent (4,500) of the teachers qualified to vote; the vote would be by mail; November 27 was the final date set for the filing of petitions and December 15 the date for all ballots to be in the hands of the Labor Commissioner. Three organizations qualified to be on the ballot: the Teachers Bargaining Organization (NEA-sponsored), with more than 11,000 signatures; the United Federation of Teachers, with about 15,000 signatures; and the Teachers Union (independent), with about 5,000 signatures.

In the election, UFT won overwhelmingly as has been stated. Of the approximately 32,500 votes cast, the UFT received about 20,000, the TBO received about 10,000, and the Teachers Union about 2,500.

There is no possible way to deny the fact that the NEA took a drubbing in this election. Here is where the 20/20 hindsight began to question in earnest the wisdom of the NEA's choosing this particular battleground. In this hindsight the stacked cards were now visible: the alliance of the UFT both with the great power of organized labor in the big city and with the political hierarchy that controls the purse strings for New York schools.

The NEA's justification for entering the contest is that it was requested to do so by teachers' organizations not affiliated with the teachers' union. Also, there was the fact that almost 40,000 teachers were as yet unattached to any national teachers' organization.

The NEA at the time had only a handful of members in New York City. There was certainly little possibility of damaging its own membership situation there by going in. And there seemed to be a fighting chance to pulling the quarrelling groups together and, if this could be done, a good chance of reversing the situation. The number of signatures the NEA-sponsored group was able to secure on the petition to hold a collective bargaining-election seemed to be evidence of substantial progress. Too, the vote it polled in the election to select a bargaining agent was substantial. The election itself found more than half the teachers opposed to the UFT as their agent. Even after the two strikes, the new contract negotiated by the UFT, and the threatened strike in September 1963, UFT had still been able to enroll less than half the teachers in the city.

An ironic sidelight on the UFT's victory in being selected the bargaining agent partly by denouncing the NEA as an inept organization, particularly in the salary and welfare field, was that it was compelled to request data on teachers' salaries from the NEA Research Division simply because neither it nor its parent organization, the AFT, had any research material of their own.

Naturally, the UFT victory in New York City set off a lot of editoralizing as well as a resurgence of AFT locals which suddenly began to think that an easy victory could be theirs for the plucking.

Impact of the New York City Election

On the heels of the New York victory, the California Federation of Teachers announced a renewed drive to face local school boards with demands for collective-bargaining elections.

Likewise, the Colorado Federation of Teachers (then representing about 5 per cent of Colorado's teachers) began an all-out campaign to establish collective bargaining for teachers throughout that state.

In Minneapolis, Detroit, Chicago, Los Angeles, and elsewhere AFT locals hailed the "great victory" in New York as the harbinger of the coming unionization of teachers throughout the United States. Los Angeles was judged to be ripe for the picking.

One recalls the shock and anger of the NEA staff at the extreme criticism leveled at it by certain publications and individuals during the New York City crisis.

NEA friends were shocked at the number of slick magazines and intellectuals who joined in to denounce NEA during the New York City campaign or joined in gleeful expressions afterwards at the UFT victory.

The newspapers, however, concerned themselves very little with the union-NEA struggle. In general, the New York City papers dealt kindly with the striking teachers. But newspapers generally condemned the strike in vigorous editorials. The *New York World Telegram* said:

> A number of observers have pointed out that the illegal strike called by the United Federation of Teachers may have an adverse effect on the fate of the teachers' labor movement throughout the country.
>
> We agree. And we think the way the strike is apparently being settled will have a profound effect on public-employee unions generally. . . .
>
> The zealots in the UFT . . . don't seem to know the difference between collective bargaining with industry and collective bargaining with government.
>
> Somewhere along the way they forgot, if they ever knew, that their boss is the public. . . .
>
> In over-promising its members, over-threatening the public and finally inciting a strike, the UFT's hotheads have grievously and shamefully abused a privilege long sought and only lately won by New York teachers—the privilege of collective bargaining.[1]

Of course organized labor also jumped to the conclusion that it was in, boasting of the victory of the IUD and teachers and of contributing $25,000 and organizers to the campaign. As one writer said: "For AFL–CIO, the vistas were even wider. 'How long will the file clerk go on thinking a union is below her dignity,' asked an official, 'when the teacher next door belongs?"[2]

Events Leading to the UFT Strike of April 11, 1962

The winning of the collective-bargaining election by UFT in December 1961 shot new life into the traditionally moribund AFT. *There can be no doubt that this was a life-saver for the national teachers' union.* The resurgence of demands by AFT locals across the country has already been cited.

In February 1962, the AFT affiliated with the Industrial Union Department (IUD) of the AFL–CIO. This is a federation of CIO unions within the combined organizations, known for its aggressive organizing and political activities. IUD had put $25,000 plus extensive organizing and press-relations personel into the collective-bargaining election. Prior to this time AFT had maintained affiliation only with the AFL wing.

The UFT moved immediately to be made the exclusive bargaining agent for all New York City teachers. This move was opposed by the Secondary

School Teachers Association and the Teachers Bargaining Organization. The Secondary School Teachers Association (SSTA) threatened a strike if UFT was permitted to get a dictator's control of the city's 40,000 teachers. Its president said, "SSTA will unalterably fight any greedy grasp by labor politicians to create a dictatorship which clearly abrogates the well-established right of every teacher involved in a grievance case to select his own spokesman to safeguard his interest."

Charles Cogen, the UFT President, retorted that "the UFT policy is the same as in all collective bargaining agreements, which gives the bargaining agency jurisdiction over all employees covered under a contract. It would be ridiculous to allow organizations which were rejected by the teachers to assume the responsibility for grievance disputes."

Thus, teachers began to find that the seemingly innocuous act of selecting a bargaining agent had thrust them all the way into the full labor machinery.

AFT President Megel called upon all locals to press vigorously for collective-bargaining rights from their school boards.

The AFT and IUD seized upon the New York City bargaining election to map a national campaign. The AFT was made a full-fledged member of IUD at a meeting in Washington in early 1962. At this meeting, Walter Reuther announced that the AFT victory in New York was one of the most important events occurring in the labor movement in the last twenty years. Some have compared it to the historic break-through by the United Automobile Workers at River Rouge in 1933.

In the meantime, while collective bargaining between the UFT and the New York City Board of Education continued, ten AFL–CIO organizers augmented the AFT staff in New York to enroll a majority of the city's teachers in the union.

With the bargaining not going well, UFT became increasingly bellicose, throwing strike threats about repeatedly.

On March 3, 1962, at the spring conference of the UFT, Secretary of Labor Arthur J. Goldberg (later to become Associate Justice of the United States Supreme Court and Ambassador to the United Nations) was presented the annual John Dewey Award. Mr. Goldberg, prior to his government positions, was legal counsel of AFL–CIO, had consistently supported the union organization of teachers and had rendered valuable service to the UFT. He had also served as Chairman of President Kennedy's Task Force, the report of which led to the Presidents' Executive Order Number 10988 establishing collective negotiation for Federal employees. In his address to the conference, however, Mr. Goldberg bluntly opposed teacher strikes:

> We have made it clear that the union shop and the closed shop are inappropriate to the Federal service, despite our own belief that the union shop is an entirely legitimate device in the private economy.... The public interest involved many things in the area of employee-management relations with the Government, but

clearly the first requirement, and indeed the essence of the relations of a Government union such as yours and the Government, is that there be no interruption of Government service.

You must resolve your differences by means other than strikes, which are inadmissable in the new responsibility you now exercise as the bargaining representative for the people.

The truculent attitude of UFT President Charles Cogen, in his response to Goldberg's admonitions, was a tip-off on subsequent events. He said: "We will take seriously any advice Mr. Goldberg cares to give. However, in the case of extreme urgency we will reserve the right to take whatever action we deem necessary."

The negotiations between the UFT and the board of education became snarled in late March 1962. The UFT demanded $53 million for increased salaries. The board offered $33.8 million (Final settlement was $30.8 million). The UFT then voted to strike on April 10, unless the board increased its offer. The vote was 7,255 for and 240 against the proposed strike. The UFT then demanded $53 million in increased salaries to sustain a proposed salary scale ranging from $5,400 to $9,500 and provisions for promotional increments of $700 for specialized training (largely for high-school teachers). This contrasted with the existing scale of $4,800 to $8,650, with two $400 differentials for extra training.

Looming large in the impasse between the teachers' union and the board of education was the fiscal dependence of the board upon city hall and the government of New York State. This dependence for funds inevitably, in the language of the *New York Times*, made the schools a dueling ground between Mayor Wagner, Democrat, and Governor Rockefeller, a Republican. The school system is the largest division of the city government, with an annual budget in 1962 of $650 million, of which $196 million came from the state. The mayor charged, as had his predecessors, that the city was being shortchanged in allotment of state funds to school districts. The governor denied this and pointed out that under the new state formula, the city schools would receive an increase of $48.2 million, for a total of $244.2 million for the ensuing year. The mayor immediately charged that by the changed formula the city schools were, in fact, losing $48.2 million still due for the current fiscal year. Under the new formula there was a shift from a deferred to a current basis. In prior years, the city schools received in October funds to pay for the operation of the schools from April to June in the preceding school year. It had been borrowing from banks to finance this portion of the school year, pending receipt of state funds in October. But the new formula provided that state money received after July 1 could be used only for debts incurred after that date.

The mayor demanded a new interpretation of the formula to permit payment for the April–June period and a special session of the legislature to rectify the matter. Governor Rockefeller responded, accusing Mayor Wagner of "political fakery" because the state budget director had ruled that under the new law state money to be received on September 15 could be used to pay school expenses in the April–June period.

While this jockeying for political position was going on, the bargaining situation deteriorated. The board still could offer only $27 million for increased salaries, because that was all the money in sight for this purpose. The UFT insisted on $53 million. The board's offer was tentative, since it could not make a firm commitment until its full budget picture was known.

Faced with this financial-political tangle, the UFT called a strike meeting of its membership on Tuesday, April 10. The strike order for April 10 was postponed by the 1,000-member delegate assembly. During the day of April 9 a court order was issued directing the UFT to show cause why it should not be permanently enjoined from striking, and barring a strike for 24 hours from issuance of the order. The order could not be served because the UFT officials were behind locked doors debating whether to accept the mayors' plan to continue negotiations.

The strike meeting on April 10 overrode recommendations of the UFT Executive Board and voted to strike on Wednesday, April 11 rather than wait until Monday, April 16. The vote was 2,544 for and 2,231 against. The meeting was attended by only a third of the UFT's claimed membership of 15,000.

The strike meeting was the focus of political maneuvering among the officers of the UFT. Elections of new officers were to be held on May 15. It required President Cogen 40 minutes to still the demonstrators and restore order to proceed with the business of the meeting. He was repeatedly booed when he called for delayed action and repeated the executive board's recommendation to postpone strike action to allow time for Mayor Wagner to come up with a plan. Shouts of "sell-out" and "strike" rolled through the hall.

Despite its illegality under the Condin-Wadlin Act, the strike went on, with teachers picketing. Superintendent Theobald declared the strike illegal and voiced determination of the board of education to invoke legal penalties.

About half (20,558) the city's 40,000 teachers remained off the job. How many of these were actual strikers and how many simply respected picket lines is not known.

Also, just how many schools were actually closed seems obscure. The board early in the day claimed that only one school was closed, but later admitted to ten closings. Policemen contended that about 25 schools had been forced to close during the day because of too few teachers. In at least two schools disorders occurred. At Evander Childs High School, 2,000 students left without permission, with egg-throwing and car-rocking taking place. At Seward Park High School, window panes were smashed, desks overturned, and bric-a-brac thrown from windows into the street, and some fist fights occurred.

In general, however, students were well behaved. Where the UFT's membership was highest, the schools were hardest hit. This was in the junior and senior high schools. In the junior high schools, about 7,000 of the 9,500 teachers stayed off the job. In the vocational high schools, about 5,000 of the 8,000 teachers did not report for duty. In sharp contrast, only 7,200 of the nearly 20,000 elementary-school teachers were absent. In a normal day in New York City approximately 1,400 teachers (about 3.5 per cent) are absent because of illness.

Some schools were dismissed early; in others pupils without teachers gathered in auditoriums and lunchrooms for study assignments or singing and group games. Many schools were relatively untouched by the strike and maintained normal schedules.

ENDING OF THE STRIKE. While the strike was in progress, the New York Supreme Court issued an injunction against it under terms of the Condin-Wadlin Act at the request of the board of education. The UFT Executive Board, faced with contempt of court and possible jail terms, called off the strike in a heated, seven-hour session on the night of April 11 by a vote of 32 to 12. UFT President Charles Cogen called the court order "a slave labor injunction." The School Board announced an amnesty policy, stating that all would be forgiven to teachers returning to their jobs.

Behind the UFT one-day strike in April 11, 1962 in New York City was a jungle of confusion, charges and counter charges, political maneuvering, and bluster by the union. As an aftermath of the unnecessary strike of November 7, 1960—a strike called to force a bargaining election (which the board of education had already promised if found legal)—leaders of organized labor had promised that a teacher strike would not happen again. But the UFT leaders had found the magic formula to intimidate politicians and win converts among teachers who had heretofore felt helpless. UFT leaders learned that city hall would go to any lengths to woo the votes of more than 1 million union members in the city. These leaders had learned that the leaderless, frustrated city teachers hungered for a show of power, for someone or something to beat down the ruling (and to them unfeeling) administrative hierarchy. They badly wanted recognition, status, consideration as a group. (Interestingly this same hunger was reflected by many of the Utah delegates to the NEA Convention at Detroit in July 1963. Their vehemence, however, was not so much over winning the battle with Utah's governor as compelling the governor to respect them and deal with them in a considerate way.)

REACTIONS TO THE APRIL 11 STRIKE. Some UFT officials declared the strike had a wholesome effect on the pupils. One expressed the view that "the children should like to see their own teachers acting in a spirit that is courageous." There were other, and far from favorable reactions.

Max J. Rubin, President of the Board of Education, termed the union's action as reckless, irresponsible, and immoral, and charged that the strike violated a pledge given in November 1960 by responsible union leaders.

EDITORIAL REACTION TO THE STRIKE. Paul Woodring, Editor of the "Education Supplement" of the *Saturday Review*, wrote of the New York City strike:

> It was a strike nobody really wanted. Even in a moment of desperation only 6 per cent of the city's teachers voted for it. But when it came 20,000 teachers, half of those in the New York school system, refused to cross picket lines and, on April 11, the situation in many schools was chaotic.
>
> Most of the elementary [school] teachers stayed on the job, but in several junior and senior high schools education came to a standstill. Newspaper reports that in one school "a thousand students went on a wild rampage, throwing eggs and rocks," and that in another they "tossed chairs and other school property from schoolhouse windows" may have been exaggerated, but the truth was bad enough. . . .
>
> But the strike was only a symptom. When teachers have confidence in the administration, they work hard for higher salaries but do not walk out on their students. The decision to strike revealed bad teacher morale of long standing, resulting from deep-seated maladies in the school system and in the body politic. On the surface the issue was the demand for more money, but, in a deeper sense, the strike was a protest against ineffective administration, public apathy, a bumbling city government which places education low on its list of priorities, and a disgraceful political squabble between City Hall and Albany. . . .
>
> Teachers cannot have it both ways. They cannot expect professional status and the respect and security that goes with it, and at the same time demand the right to exercise the ultimate economic weapon of a labor union. Professional ethics are of a higher order, and the great majority of the nation's teachers, including those who join the NEA and other professional organizations, always have denied themselves the right to strike, however great the provocation. . . .
>
> It appears to have been demonstrated that in New York an illegal strike can be made to pay off. But New York is not a typical American city and citizens in other cities have viewed the New York strike with deep concern. A wave of teacher strikes across the nation would have a disastrous effect on public respect for the teaching profession and public support for the schools. A firm "no strike" pledge from all teacher organizations would do much to restore public confidence. We believe that teachers can best contribute to the advancement of education, and in the long run to their own welfare, by demanding such a pledge of whatever organizations they choose to represent them.[3]

In the same issue of the *Saturday Review*, Fred Heckinger, the Education Editor of the *New York Times* analyzed the April 11 strike as a power play by UFT:

> The key to the answers is not primarily a salary scale. The key word is *power*. The power of the UFT in New York was clearly established after the 1960 one-day strike. . . .

> Overnight the UFT not only emerged as a power in New York; it became the potential showcase for the American Federation of Teachers in its nationwide recruiting drive. If the UFT could demonstrate the effectiveness of collective bargaining, the AFT with fewer than 80,000 members throughout the country could hope to begin competing more aggressively with the vast (780,000 members) National Education Association and its network of state and local affiliates. The conflict is sharpened by the fact that the NEA strongly condemns the strike as a weapon and calls for "professional negotiation." It uses as its ultimate threat the strike-like refusal by its members to sign contracts, which it calls not a strike but an impasse. . . .

Mr. Hechinger also commented upon what generally happens when a group sets out upon the road of extremism:

> Within the UFT a different kind of power play was acted out. The moderate leadership, represented by Mr. Cogen, from the start appeared driven to outlandish demands by the more extreme leaders and members. And when the moment of decision came, the Cogen faction found itself technically out of control. It argued. It explained. But it could not reassert itself. In violation of good bargaining practice, it had burned the bridges of honorable retreat. It also knew that, within a month, it would have to defend its stewardship in an election of officers at which the less moderate wing would try to take over and might succeed. It is quite likely that the more militant members of the leadership group actually made Mr. Cogen fall into the trap of asking so much that a settlement which would normally have made him appear as the hero would turn him into the loser in the eyes of the members.[4]

The September 1963 Fiasco

But the power-hungry UFT was driven still further by the momentum of its two strike victories in 1960 and 1962.

Another "overwhelming victory" (to use the usual language of the AFT) was chalked up in September 1963.

Early in the spring of that year, the UFT began singing the song of "no contract, no work." But this time the walls didn't come tumbling down. All along, the board of education had insisted that no raises in teachers' salaries were possible in 1963–64. The money simply was not there. The board did concede that a raise was possible for the school year 1964–65. The UFT kept shouting for a raise in 1963–64, repeated time and again its litany "no contract, no work", and on this principle voted to strike in September. The strike was called off. The teachers did not get the demanded raise. And they worked from September 1963 to January 1964 without a contract.

The publicity claimed that UFT had wangled a raise of $580 each for the New York City teachers. Actually, that was not the case. Those on the level of Step 2, effective April 1, 1964, got a raise of $8.35 per month for the months of April, May, June and 1964—a total raise of $25.05 for the year. Those above Step 2 got a raise of $10.85 for each of the three months, or a total of

Teachers Should Use All the Procedures of Trade Unions

$32.55 for the year. Those on Step 1 got nothing in the way of a raise for the school year 1963–64, and they got nothing in the way of a raise in 1964–65.

This was a great victory?

For the school year 1964–65, if anticipated revenues held up, teachers on the schedule at all levels, except for first-year teachers, were to get a raise of $330. True, a promotional increment did accrue, largely to high-school teachers, in January 1965; the maximum of this increment for the year was $124 (one half of the $250 increment proposed).

The maximum raise that any teacher in the New York City system got for the two-year period, 1963–65, was $487.50 ($32.50 for 1963–64, plus $330, plus the promotional increment of $125), or a two year average raise of $243.75 per year. The bulk of the elementary-school teachers averaged a $362.50 raise for the two years, or $181.25 per year. For beginning teachers, there was no raise at all during the two-year period.

UFT said this was a great victory, but some of its own officers and members dissented. A member of the UFT who voted against the contract said:

> My particular vote of "no" was based on the fact that both the Board of Education and the UFT negotiators have cheated the children of our city and duped the teachers into believing that progress has been made. . . . The children will be cheated in the future of their seats in a classroom due to the many loopholes in the article dealing with class size. The teachers have been duped into believing that additional sick-pay considerations were granted.[5]

With the failure of the UFT to get a teacher raise for 1963–64, the two-year contract was developed as a face-saving gimmick with IUD's brilliant Jack Conway engineering the deal from the shadows. The loudly heralded $580 (which applied only to a few) will simply make it harder to get public support when new contracts are negotiated. For publicity purposes, this was hailed as a great victory. Ida Klaus, the board's negotiator, said: "It was all done with mirrors."

One of UFT's strong emphases in its justification of the 1964–65 contract was the emphasis it gave to agreements about limiting class size. David Selden stressed this in an article in March 1964.[6] In late April, the New York City School Board announced that it could not activate the agreement about class size in 1964–65 (which was qualified by the words *insofar as possible*) because of lack of funds resulting from the mayor's cut of $45 million in the school budget.

The *Washington Star* paid its editorial respects to the September 1963 fiasco:

> If it had happened anywhere else, the shocking conduct of the strike-happy New York teachers' union during the last few days would have been beyond belief.
>
> Not in New York. For the United Federation of Teachers, which claims to speak for that city's 43,000 teachers, obviously thinks it is immune from the law. And why not? Back in 1960, the UFT thumbed its nose at the state law which makes it a crime for public employees to strike—and walked away without a scratch. It repeated the same performance in another walkout last year, once again drawing nothing more than a tardy, innocuous rebuke from Mayor Wagner. . . .
>
> The open and deliberate contempt which Mr. Cogen and his followers have shown for the law is a matter which goes beyond the disruption of children's education, and beyond a strike by public servants against their government. For if a labor union, or any other group, is permitted to put itself above the law—and to get away with it—this country is in real trouble. This same thought recurred with nagging persistency during recent months—when, in the emotionalism of civil rights demonstrations, local laws were violated in what the

violators considered to be a just cause. The wretched performance in New York, however, is an example of the chaos to which this sort of thing, unchecked, can lead.[7]

The UFT did come up with a clear cut-undoubted victory in its 1965–66 contract after again threatening a strike. The New York City teachers got raises.

Also of great significance was the UFT's securing a provision for a welfare fund, with $100 per teacher assigned to UFT for administration. The 1966–67 allotment will amount to $140 per teacher. This is a significant breakthrough. Although there are legal grounds for questioning the legality of union administration of public funds for public employees, NEA backed off from contesting this legal question.

4

The Campaign Shapes Up

> The Milwaukee election, won by the NEA after a wicked battle, may turn out to be the most significant of the recent series, in which the AFT won only four out of eleven (there is one stalemate) but got representation rights for nearly 11,000 teachers, including 10,000 in Detroit, to the NEA's total of 7,000. Milwaukee is significant because it proved the wealthy AFL-CIO Industrial Union Department to be relatively ineffective in influencing teachers. The IUD poured money and men (including Walter Reuther) into the campaign, but only about 200 teachers switched to the union camp.
>
> Milwaukee suggests that the NEA can, if it continues to accelerate its current program, eliminate the AFT except in the largest cities where unionism is a way of life. There is little doubt that the NEA means to do just that.
>
> —Stanley Elam[1]

When the battle of New York City had clearly been won, teacher unions proclaimed that an irreversible tide had set in, that American teachers would flow in an unchecked flood to the AFT and away from the professional associations. It is true that there were some grounds for such optimism.

The NEA seemed to be floundering, at least momentarily. The NEA was confronted with a totally new set of circumstances—new to it, that is. True, a few of its affiliated state associations had been fighting this battle with the teacher unions for some time and were learning fast about the tactics and strategy of the union approach and how to combat them.

The aftermath of the New York City battle was a moment of rout for the NEA. There is no denying that fact. But NEA began to exhibit what is always extremely difficult for a large and comparatively comfortable and rich organization—the will and the ingenuity to refine its structure and to revitalize its procedures to fit new conditions.

In the face of expected and often bitter resistance by a significant portion of its membership the NEA began to launch drastic plans for self-renewal. The decision of Executive Secretary William G. Carr and the official bodies to drive forward aggressively to meet these new conditions must be labeled as courageous, to say the least. They well knew that most of the NEA state affiliates and a vast majority of NEA members had not encountered competition with the teacher unions in any meaningful way. They well knew that many of those state affiliates looked to the state legislatures for improvements in the economic status of their teachers and that any gestures of militancy that might be interpreted as emulating the tactics of the unions would meet with adverse reactions in those state legislatures.

They were also well aware that any proposed procedures that implied significant changes in the traditional administration-board-staff relationship would arouse apprehension among most superintendents and local boards of education and indignation among many. It was clear that many of the affiliated independent departments of NEA would be disturbed over these changes.

But Carr and other officers also knew that public education had come upon new times, times that demanded appropriate adjustments and new procedures. They were aware that there was a new restiveness among teachers which, if not dealt with by reasonable approaches, would rapidly deteriorate into overt aggressiveness and perhaps a destructive militancy. This abrupt change of direction, tactics, and procedures in the face of head-shaking and powerful resistance required a high type of courage, the courage to risk failure and the attritions which easily might occur as a result of internecine warfare among NEA members and groups.

Following is a brief sequence of developments stemming directly or indirectly from the New York City battle.

Creation of NEA Urban Project

The NEA Urban Project was established on March 15, 1962, with a director and staff. For the first four fiscal years of its operation it had substantial budget appropriations: 1962–63, $216,500; 1963–64, $385,000; 1964–65, $442,000; and 1965–66, $557,000. In addition, a special appropriation from the emergency fund was set aside for strengthening local association programs, including urban areas, of which $437,990 was spent in 1964–65. In 1965–66, another $362,000 was spent from this special appropriation. Regular budgeted funds of about $1 million were spent by this division, and emergency funds approximating $800,000 were spent in this period.

It is a reasonable guess that other NEA units have expended on urban services in terms of staff time, travel, publications, and other services, a total equal to double the amount of the funds ($1.6 million) regularly budgeted for the Urban Project; that is, a total of 3.2 million was spent by all NEA units. Thus in the four-year fiscal period 1962 throu gh 1966 (school years

1962–63, 1963–64, 1964–65, and 1965–66) this would represent a total probable expenditure, from regular budgets of all NEA units, of nearly $5 million; or, when the expenditures of special appropriations are added, something like $5.8 million, which have been poured into the effort to upgrade local urban associations.

It would be inaccurate to ascribe all or even a major portion of these expenditures to the competition with the teachers' unions. The purposes are much broader. It would be reasonably accurate to say, however that the extraordinary expenditures were influenced directly and significantly by the union upsurge.

In order to give the Urban Project clear priority and visibility, it was originally attached directly to the office of the NEA executive secretary rather than to an existing NEA unit (see results of Norton Study on following pages). Beginning with the 1964–65 school year, the project was placed under the administration of the NEA assistant executive secretary for field operations and urban services; in the summer of 1965, the name of the project was changed to the Urban Services Division.

The over-all assignment of the Urban Project was to assist urban education associations to develop dynamic programs to meet the peculiar problems of teachers in large cities. A parallel function was to create a unit to coordinate all NEA services in order to fight the teachers' union onslaught on local NEA affiliates. Thus for the first time the NEA moved on a broad front to contest directly and vigorously the drive of the AFT upon its membership.

The movement for special attention to the problems of big-city associations, associations which had many problems not common to smaller or rural areas, actually began at the NEA Convention in Atlantic City in 1961 with the adoption of a resolution authorizing a study of the organizational needs of big-city associations and an initial appropriation of $50,000 to underwrite the study. Dr. John Norton, retired Professor of Education from Teachers College, Columbia University, was engaged to direct it.

The Norton Study indicated that a large cluster of problems peculiar to urban centers had emerged in recent years and that the NEA had given relatively little attention to providing direct services to the urban associations. Moreover, the study found that the existing NEA structure and organization would have to be modified to provide effectively the needed services. The establishment of a new unit (the Urban Project) was recommended to provide direct services and to coordinate the work of all existing NEA units to serve better the urban areas.

The study found demands for several services specifically aimed at the specialized problems of the urban associations:

1. Research concerning urban problems such as the education of the culturally deprived, personnel policies in large cities, assistance to urban areas caught in the throes of conflicting local governments, and so on.

2. Special NEA consultive services—more consultants and field representatives, one or more new regional offices.
3. NEA service as a clearing house and coordinating center for exchange of ideas and programs of urban associations. Better intercommunication among urban associations and between the NEA and urban associations; also, and very important, better communication between local associations and their state associations, and between state associations and the NEA.
4. Help in selection and training of executive secretaries. Help in big-city professional-organization problems.
5. New and specialized help on salaries.
6. Help on retirement housing.
7. Special publications and materials for local organization publications; help in distribution and implementation of publications.
8. New types of research studies with findings graphically presented.
9. Financial help in special cases—help which would be worked out in a co-operative arrangement between the NEA, the state, and the local association.
10. More useful information for building representatives.[2]

Obviously, NEA had delayed beyond the danger point the establishment of a unit directly charged with dealing with the peculiar and, in many cases, unique problems of large-city associations. If the rapid urbanization of the United States after World War II caught the nation as a whole unprepared for and unoriented to the vast and complex new problems inevitably created by the hordes of rural migrants coming into the large cities, as it doubtless did, this was certainly true of the NEA and its state affiliates.

It is not unfair to say that both NEA and its state affiliates proceeded throughout the decade 1950–1960 in the even-paced routine of a predominantly rural economy. They continued through this decade, not universally, but in large measure, to do business at the same old stand and in the same old way while all about them the world was changing at a dizzying pace.

The fact is that the local association had been the Achilles heel of teachers' professional organizations—and still is. Here at the grass roots the local association program has tended typically to be weak, confined largely to social functions and to routine organizational matters. Many of these associations are little more than paper organizations, providing the opportunity for the holding of offices, the selection of delegates, and petty politicking for state and national offices. Contrary to conditions in many other professions such as medicine and law, where the local association is the heart of professional endeavor, local teachers' associations have tended to be rather ineffective. Of course there are many exceptions, but that is the general rule.

This is one aspect of the program of teachers' professional organizations which must be reversed. Obviously, neither the NEA nor its state association affiliates can ever solve the problems of the thousands of local units (there are nearly 9,000 NEA-affiliated locals alone). These problems, in large part, must be solved at home. Both the NEA and the state associations can provide indispensable help, but neither can carry the full burden; they can never secure the resources or the staffs to do so. And if they could, this would be a negation of the philosophy that the members of a profession seek to solve their own problems.

The Urban Project began an immediate attack upon the problem of strengthening the programs of large-city associations. At the time of its inception only 32 such associations had full-time executive secretaries; as of January 12, 1966 a total of 78 urban associations had employed executive officers (see Appendix B). Thus the NEA and its state affiliates sought rapidly to get into the position of being able to counteract the teachers' union activities in urban areas.

The assumption of the AFT and its adherents that the UFT victories in New York City marked the beginning of an irreversible trend probably was in part based upon the notion that the NEA would remain silent, inept, and inured to change; that the union's extravagent claims, based upon one unique and isolated case, would go marching across the landscape uncountered.

What are the facts?

After New York City, the AFT had two quick, easy, and small victories: in Plainview, New York and in the Milwaukee Vocational School, in January and June of 1963 respectively. Since then, NEA affiliates have won 19 elections as indicated in Table 4–1. Thus, since the New York City debacle and through June 1965, the NEA won 23 of 37 elections. (Table 4–1.)

A total of 52,232 teachers were involved in these elections. In the aggregate, NEA affiliates received 22,477 votes and AFT, 21,641. (Table 4–2.)

It is significant that the AFT has won three of the big ones (Detroit, Cleveland, and Philadelphia), while the NEA won in Milwaukee, Rochester, and Newark. (Boston, Chicago, Rochester, Washington, D.C. and Baltimore have been added since to AFT victories.)

It is estimated that about 1,000 school districts have recognized local education associations and entered into professional-negotiation agreements with them between September 1, 1965 and January 1, 1966. The 1965–66 and 1966–67 box scores will be found in Chapter 13.

In these 37 elections between January 1, 1963 and June 1, 1965 certain significant points have become clear. (1) The uncommitted teachers, the groups which do not belong to either (or any) affiliate, tend to have the balance of power. Considering the size of its membership, the AFT affiliate tends to attract the vote of a disproportionate number of the uncommitted teachers. There are several possible explanations of this phenomenon: (a) these groups may often consist of the disaffected or disgruntled teachers who naturally turn to the more radical appeal; (b) these groups may be convinced that the teachers' union has the muscle for quick settlement of their grievances; (c) the middle-of-the-road conservative organizations obviously do

TABLE 4-1

Representative Elections, January 1, 1963–June 1, 1965. Summary Data for the Nation

National Overview			Association Victories			Union Victories		
Number of Elections	Number of Locations	Number of Teachers	Number of Elections	Number of Locations	Number of Teachers	Number of Elections	Number of Locations	Number of Teachers
37*	34*	52,232	23	23*	21,483	13*	11*	30,749

* The smaller number of election locations is due to the fact that three elections were held in Plainview, N.Y., one each year since 1963 (1/4/63, 6/9/64, 5/14/65) ; and two elections were held in Yonkers, N.Y., the first of which (5/11/64) resulted in no winner since neither side won the required 51 percent majority of eligible voters. The union won all three times in Plainview and the second time in Yonkers (5/14/66). The lack of a winner in the 1964 election in Yonkers also accounts for the fact that there were 36 victories in the 37 elections conducted.

Source: National Education Association, Urban Services Division (Mimeographed).

TABLE 4-2

Box Score Teacher Representation Elections, January 1, 1963–June 1, 1965. Data by School Districts

Date of Election	School District	Number of Teachers Eligible to Vote	Affiliated Organization Votes Received	
			NEA	AFT
January 4, 1963	Plainview (L.I.) N.Y.	549	196	235
June 3, 1963	Milwaukee (Voc. Sch.)	263	99	149
September 25, 1963	Meriden, Conn.	443	277	130
November 26, 1963	E. Hartford, Conn.	510	381	103
December 10, 1963	Wethersfield, Conn.	253	161	83
January 28, 1964	Groton, Conn.	410	244	148
February 12, 1964	Milwaukee, Wisc.	4,318	2,249	1,645
February 28, 1964	Bremerton, Wash.	382	241	106
March 20, 1964	New Rochelle, N.Y.	632	317	274
April 9, 1964	Janesville, Wisc.	366	235	—[1]
April 14, 1964	West Allis–West Milwaukee, Wisc.	532	320	189
May 6, 1964	S. Kitsap, Wash.	180	150	28
May 11, 1964	Detroit, Mich.	11,000	3,848	5,739
May 19, 1964	Superior, Wisc.	272	88	161
May 25, 1964	Port Angeles, Wash.	217	139	—[2]
May 26, 1964	Two Rivers, Wisc.	77	38	36
June 4, 1964	Madison, Wisc.	1,115	342	—[3]
June 8, 1964	Cleveland, Ohio	5,500	2,026	2,701
June 9, 1964	Plainview, (L.I.) N.Y.	571	231	240
June 18, 1964	Berlin, Conn.	133	79	51
September 22, 1964	Cherry Hill, Mich.	159	133	16
October 14, 1964	Bellingham, Wash.	341	183	5
November 18, 1964	Minot, North Dakota	409	154	250
December 2, 1964	Rochester, N.Y.	2,134	1,185	692
December 15, 1964	Newark, N.J.	3,200	1,466	1,446
January 28, 1965	Tulsa, Oklahoma	2,758	1,841	—[4]
February 1, 1965	Philadelphia, Pa.	10,670	4,671	5,403
February 3, 1965	Kenosha, Wisc.	700	364	309
February 5, 1965	Taylor, Michigan	614	175	378
March 19, 1965	Menosha, Wisc.	105	38	58
April 8, 1965	Racine, Wisc.	1,054	700	—[5]
April 29, 1965	Shirley-Mastic, (LI) N.Y.	122	55	60
May 4, 1965	New Haven, Conn.	1,075	627	—[6]
May 14, 1965	Plainview, (L.I.) N.Y.	571	249	265
May 17, 1965	Yonkers, N.Y.	1,223	449	733
May 8, 1965	Manchester, Conn.	494	367	8
	Totals of Elections	50,593	22,477	21,641

[1] No active union. [2] Union withdrew. [3] Union withdrew.

[4] Union did not appear on ballot, but it had challenged the Tulsa Education Association. Thus, the vote was on the representation by the TEA.

[5] No contestant on ballot.

[6] New Haven High School Association received 125 votes; union withdrew and campaigned against the election.

not appeal to many teachers who want action now. (2) The AFT group, usually in the minority, generally are dedicated, vocal, and aggressive. They tend to be aggressive in the election campaign and tend to vote. The local members of the NEA affiliate are more inclined to indifference, many often not bothering to vote. (3) The fact that a majority of local teachers are members of the local association is not necessarily an indication of victory. The most surprising aspect of these elections has been the numbers of association members who have voted for the teachers' union. This suggests either that something is wrong with these local associations or that a new format is needed. (4) Putting these factors together tends to show that the AFT chances of victory are increased by a small vote; that is, the lower the percentage of eligible voters actually casting votes, the greater the chance of an AFT victory. (5) A most significant factor appears to be that typically the associations have held a majority membership. Teachers dissatisfied with prevailing conditions tend to blame the associations for not having rectified these conditions. They reason that the logical thing to do is to give the union a chance to do so. (6) In virtually every election the AFT has attracted many more votes than its own membership. As a general rule, the associations have attracted fewer. In part, the reason for the latter is the exclusion of association members who are in supervisory or administrative positions. In Philadelphia for example, nearly 1,000 members of the association were ruled ineligible to vote in the election.

Perhaps the biggest factor of all has been that the entrenched associations tend to be viewed as representing the *status quo,* while the teachers' unions tend to be viewed as representing the future.

THE MILWAUKEE ELECTION. The largest election immediately following the one in New York City was that held in the Milwaukee, Wisconsin, School District in February 1964. The AFT, since New York City, had been trying to force collective-bargaining elections in Detroit, Dearborn, and Chicago, cities where they have a majority of the teachers in their membership or where their membership exceeds that of the NEA affiliate. But the laws in Michigan and Illinois did not at that time mandate such elections (Michigan now does) and the respective school boards resisted demands to call elections. Both the Detroit and Chicago boards later authorized elections. Milwaukee, therefore, was the second opportunity for the AFT and IUD to pull out all the stops and to pour in organizers and money to carry the election. The AFT brought in the big guns—IUD's Nicholas Zonarich and Franz Daniel—to run the campaign. Walter Reuther was brought in to speak to an election-eve rally (attended by only 325 persons). The Milwaukee Federation of Teachers (MFT) emphasized the essential importance of ties with organized labor and its national leadership. The Milwaukee Teachers Education Association (MTEA) on the contrary, stressed self-reliance and local-association responsibility and pledged an aggressive campaign to represent local teachers. In keeping with this emphasis, the MTEA refused to accept more than token aid from the NEA, insisting on running its own campaign in conjunction with the Wisconsin Education Association. The MTEA won the election by a vote of 2,249 to 1,645.

The truth is that NEA did, behind the scenes, provide considerable help and would have provided more, but the MTEA insisted on running its own campaign. The fact may have some significant meanings.

THE BREMERTON ELECTION. In some ways the Bremerton, Washington election on February 28, 1964 was an essentially significant collective-bargaining election. Brumerton is a ship-building center, highly industrialized and unionized. The bulk of school revenue of the district has for years come from Federal impacted-area funds and state school funds, with a steadily declining portion coming from local taxes. The Bremerton teachers had been represented by the local teachers' union, an AFT affiliate, since 1945. The Bremerton Education Association won the election by a vote of 241 to 106. The Bremerton teachers had become disenchanted with union representation and its lack of effectiveness in securing salary gains comparable to other Washington communities. The Bremerton Education Association based its campaign on the assertion: " . . . that teaching is a profession whose first concern is for the youth it serves. While we have the highest regard for skilled laborers and we fully recognize their vital role in our society, we know also that teaching is not a clocked task, nor is it simply folded up at the end of the day to be unfolded in the morning. Teaching is a life-time commitment as is medicine, the ministry, or the law. Professional teachers cannot consider their future along industrial lines."

Bremerton marked the seventeenth community in Washington to adopt professional-negotiation agreements up to 1965, when a new professional-negotiation law accelerated the number of such agreements.

THE DETROIT ELECTION. The second major victory (after New York City) of the AFT was that of its affiliate, the Detroit Federation of Teachers (DFT), in May 1964, by a vote of 5,739 to 3,848.

The AFT local, knowing that it had a majority of the Detroit teachers in its membership, had been demanding a bargaining election of the Detroit Board of Education ever since the UFT victory in New York City. The board had denied this demand on the grounds that its legal authority to bargain exclusively with one group was doubtful. The DFT had repeatedly threatened strike action because of this refusal and several times picketed school board meetings in protest. It is significant that AFT locals in several instances, by these tactics, have been able to intimidate school boards and public officials, forcing them to retreat or to find legal authorization for such elections. The Detroit School Board had sought to maintain a balance by recognizing both DFT and the local NEA affiliate, the Detroit Education Association (DEA). But the DFT would have none of this and continued its picketing and strike threats.

On March 4, 1964 the Detroit Board of Education adopted a proportional representation plan. It established an 11-member Teacher Representation Committee to be made up of members of the two organizations and called for an election to determine how many members of each organization were to serve on the committee.

On March 19 the Michigan Attorney General ruled that school boards could negotiate and bargain with an organization acting as agent for the teachers. Subsequent to this opinion, the board circulated a questionnaire among teachers asking for their preference as to how an agent be chosen. A majority of the teachers favored an election to choose an exclusive agent. This the board called an election for May 11.

The DFT won with 5,739 votes out of a total of 9,646 cast, 59 votes being voided. At the time of the election the DEA had 3,886 members and the DFT 5,100. But 514 of the DEA members were in supervisory positions and declared ineligible to vote. Thus the DEA picked up some 500 votes from nonmembers and DFT over 600. The DFT ranks among the strongest of the AFT locals after New York and Chicago. Detroit is, of course, Walter Reuther's home town and a well-known stronghold of labor-union strength.

In back of the growth of the Detroit local, however, at least in part, is a fact of great significance to NEA and its affiliated state and urban associations. There had been in recent years a steady decline of Detroit teachers in the membership in the DEA and the Michigan Education Association. For example, in 1954–55, the DEA had 5,537 members, 2,463 of whom belonged to the MEA and 1,459 to the NEA. By 1963– 64, these totals had declined as follows: DEA, 3,886; MEA, 1,141; NEA, 1,062. One must assume that the DEA program had not kept pace with new needs, and its adaptations were too slow. Obviously the MEA and NEA had not been too effective in providing help to the DEA in overhauling its program. Prior to 1945 the DEA did not have an executive secretary and paid staff.

There were other factors involved, of course. Among the teachers polled by a reporter after the election, such words as *dynamism, action, more militancy,* were attributed to the DFT by those voting for it.

THE CLEVELAND ELECTION. Involved in the Cleveland election was what some observers have called the "New York City pattern." This refers to the obvious tie-in between the AFL-CIO and certain influential members of the Cleveland Board of Education.

Thus on June, 1 1964 the board called for an election to be held on June 8—one week's notice. It is alleged that the resolution of the board was written in the office of the president of the Cleveland Teachers Union (CTU), or was it the AFL-CIO office? It was alleged that the teachers' union campaign literature was prepared in advance, printed, and ready for distribution the day after the boards' announcement of the election.

It was further alleged that the board wanted the election held before the publication of the report of the investigation of the Cleveland schools by NEA's Commission on Professional Rights and Responsibilities. This investigation had been requested by the CEA shortly after the Cleveland Superintendent of Schools, William B. Levenson, submitted his resignation to the board of Education on February 13, 1964. On February 21, the Executive Committee of the Ohio Education Association endorsed the CEA request for the investigation by the Commission on Professional Rights and Responsibilities.

Levenson's was the second resignation of a Cleveland superintendent in three years. Behind these resignations, it was charged, were generally unsatisfactory conditions in the Cleveland schools, particularly board interference in administration of the schools.

The commission began its investigation on April 26. Its report, issued in June 1964, condemned board interference with administration as well as the triple-headed administrative set-up with divided authority and divided administrative loyalties. The report severely criticized the partisan nature of the boards' procedures. Especially severe was criticism of the activities of the board president. The report, in short, strongly recommended that administrative direction of the schools be restored to the new superintendent when appointed.

It seems probable that NEA damaged its case by speeding up the issuance of the PR and R Commisison report in an obvious effort to affect the outcome of the election. The report was exactly the same as it would have been if the established procedure had been followed of awaiting formal publication of the report before making public its contents. But announcing the contents before publication was a departure from normal procedure. The integrity of the studies and reports of the Commission on Professional Rights and Responsibilities has been carefully safeguarded throughout the 25-year history of the commission. The deviation in procedure in the Cleveland case, the PR and R Committee contends, was in order to bring an end to the divided administrative set-up before a new superintendent was employed. But NEA should not repeat this procedure. Like Caesar's wife the professional associations must avoid not only evil but the appearance of evil. Absolute integrity is their major strength. They cannot afford to resort to expediency.

There were other factors involved in the Cleveland election. The civil-rights issue had reached extreme tension in the city. There had been boycotts, riots, and violence in connection with efforts to end *de facto* segregation. The CEA had aligned itself vigorously and publicly with the United Freedom

Movement (UFM). The UFM had stirred up deep resentment in some segments of the Cleveland population by demonstrations seeking to halt construction of some school buildings because of the fear of freezing *de facto* segregation. Doubtless this alignment with the UFM cost the CEA many votes in some schools in the city.

Of course, another factor is that the AFL-CIO was powerful in Cleveland.

The results of the election were as follows: CEA, 2,026; CTU, 2,701; about 86 per cent of the city's 5,500 eligible teachers voted. The CEA received about 400 more votes than its membership total, while CTU received about 500 more. The preponderance of the CTU vote came from the high schools. This was one election the NEA affiliate could have won. Since the election, the CTU has been helpless because the board has ruled that under the law it does not have to bargain with the winning unit. So nebulous was this relationship of board to winner under Ohio law that the CEA refused to enter into the election called in the summer of 1966.

THE PHILADELPHIA STORY. Perhaps the greatest blow to NEA to date (through 1965–66) was the loss of the election in Philadelphia. The loss of elections in District of Columbia and Baltimore in the spring of 1967 certainly were severe setbacks.

In Philadelphia both its local-association affiliate, the Philadelphia Teachers Association (PTA), and the NEA were highly confident of winning. All the factors seemed to be overwhelmingly in their favor—membership, program, and aggressive leadership.

As to membership, PTA had at the time of the election (February 1, 1965) 4,400 members; the PFT had, 3,400 members. The PTA was, in a real sense, a showcase local association of the NEA, especially in terms of its record in areas where AFT had been able to direct highly effective propaganda against NEA. In the area of integration of membership, the PTA had an impeccable record. The association was completely integrated, always had been and had a clear record of fighting vigorously for fully integrated schools. Yet, ironically enough, the integration issue, because of NEA's separate affiliates in the South, provided a telling campaign issue for the union. The leadership of the PTA was intelligent and vigorous. Its program was among the most effective in the nation.

The Philadelphia campaign is generally considered to have been the dirtiest in all the clashes between the NEA and AFT affiliates. Both NEA and AFT made all-out efforts in this election. NEA sent several staff members from its Urban Services Division to work full-time in the campaign. In addition, it brought in several staff members of nearby state education associations. It provided generous funds for campaign materials and public-relations work.

AFT sent in a horde of organizers from IUD (the Chief one was the organizer for the Brewery Workers Union) and poured in money from its own budget and from IUD coffers. The entire 29-member Executive Council of AFT came into the city for the closing week of the campaign. There is no way to derive an accurate estimate of the cost of this election. But the cost was obviously high on both sides. All in all, it was the kind of a no-holds-barred campaign that was foreign to the dignity and status of teaching. It was a campaign largely based on bigotry and racism.

Charges of anti-Semitism and anti-Catholicism were subtly injected into the campaign. The PTA issued a signed leaflet identifying IUD as the power behind the campaign. This leaflet was cleverly altered—by whom is not known—by changing the I to a J and adding an E to make the leaflet read JUDE, thus giving an anti-Semitic suggestion to a leaflet bearing the PTA imprint. Moreover, this altered leaflet was pushed under the apartment doors of Jewish teachers. This was a repetition of a tactic used in the New York City campaign.

This incident, in addition to persistent anti-Catholic and anti-Semitic rumors circulated widely among Philadelphia teachers, impelled the Executive Secretary of PTA to announce publicly that he was a Roman Catholic and that his wife was Jewish and impelled the president of PTA to state publicly that both she and her husband were members of the Catholic faith. But the apogee of this campaign of vilification and filth was yet to come. It occured about a week before the election when AFT staged a rally on the integration and civil-rights issues. This program obviously was staged to enable AFT to capitalize upon organized labor's identification with the Civil Rights Movement and, by inference, to assail again NEA's toleration of segregated affiliates in the South. A letter (later discovered to be unauthorized) was read from Dr. Martin Luther King endorsing collective bargaining and lauding organized labor, thus by implication endorsing the teachers' union.

Suspecting that this letter was a hoax, PTA leaders got in touch with Dr. King's headquarters in Atlanta, where knowledge of the letter was denied by an associate of Dr. King. At one point, it appeared that the letter would by repudiated. Finally, Dr. King issued a statement denying that he intended to interfere in the Philadelphia election but praising organized labor and collective bargaining. All of which doubtless had the effect of influencing the votes of many teachers.

However the really sickening aspect of this rally was the distribution of a leaflet attacking the featured speaker of the evening, a well-known leader of the Civil Rights Movement. The leaflet was an allegedly verbatim reproduction of a San Diego, California police report of the arrest of the speaker on a morals charge. Police discovered that distribution of the leaflet to the assembling audience was taking place before the program started and stopped the distribution.

It was never made clear who was responsible for the distribution of these handbills. The only plausible explanation given was that the sponsor was a reactionary women's group in Philadelphia. Certainly neither PTA nor the teachers' union had any connection with the incident.

Perhaps the moral of this dirty campaign, assuming complete innocence on the part of the contesting groups in the election, is that the bitter collective-bargaining elections, with all the characteristics of all-out industrial warfare, inevitably lead to incidents and procedures that have no place in the public schools, or among teachers.

In the election, the PFT received 5,403 votes and the PTA received 4,671.

This was a bitter, unexpected defeat for NEA and its Philadelphia affiliate, so bitter, in fact, that NEA employed a polling firm to analyze the causes of the defeat. While several factors were uncovered, the major one was the union campaign. The union's slogan, which proved to be extremely effective, was in effect, "The PTA has been in charge 100 years and has done nothing to improve the terrible conditions in the schools. Now they are asking to be continued—to do nothing. Give the union a chance to show what it can do!"

This plea made sense to enough teachers to swing the election for the PFT. Considering the desperate plight of the schools, the erosion of the inner city, the dingy, obsolete school buildings and equipment, the *de facto* segregation existing all about, and the flight of the well-to-do to the suburbs, where excellent, modern buildings were predominant, the result makes a lot of sense —at least from the standpoint of the teachers.

Conditions Favorable to Teacher Unions

The explosive upsurge of the teacher-union movement in New York City and elsewhere doubtless came as a surprise, if not a real shock, to the older and somewhat sedate established teachers' professional associations. Even more taken aback by the vehemence and strength of the movement were boards of education and superintendents.

The associations and school officials were aware of the existence of the teachers' unions, but they had tended to look upon them as ineffective catch-alls for the malcontents among teachers, a group that is expected to exist in some size in all lines of work. As such, the teachers' unions were viewed as petty irritants to be shrugged off with amused tolerance or dismissed with contempt. To be blunt, neither the professional associations nor school officials generally were aware of the extent to which personnel relationships within the schools had been allowed to deteriorate or lag behind economic and sociological changes in society. Also, they obviously were not aware of the extent to which the great power and wealth of the AFL-CIO had been thrown behind the teachers' union drive.

From the vantage point of hindsight, several conditions can now be identified that were veritable assurances for union growth. These conditions should have been obvious, but apparently they were not. Even now, many school boards and a few administrators obstinately refuse to recognize these conditions as causes for unrest among teachers and continue to denounce NEA for moving to correct unwholesome conditions with the assertion that it is hell-bent to "outunion the unions." They prefer, instead to dismiss the defections of teachers to unions as the flight of radicals. This is an easy answer and a gross oversimplification. Some radicalism exists, of course, but there are deeper, more compelling motivations.

What are the conditions that contribute significantly to the appeal of teachers' unions?

1. Autocratic school administrations and paternalistic board policies invite teacher unionism. The new breed of teachers is demanding the dignity of recognition as competent, creative professionals. The violation of the dignity of teachers can no longer be practiced without an explosion. Teachers are demanding a partnership in the development of school programs. They are demanding the right of participation in policy formation. The longer these demands are ignored, the greater will be the defection to unions and the greater will be the pressures upon the professional associations to fight for these demands.

At this point, there is much evidence that the chief sinners are school boards rather than superintendents. School superintendents, as a rule, are highly intelligent, highly competent, and highly sophisticated professionals. They know their jobs and they know the abilities of their staffs. For the most part, they are fully aware of the changed nature of the teaching staffs and the need for a new teaching climate. But all too often their inclinations to modernize and liberalize staff relationships are vetoed or frowned upon by their boards. There is too often the defensive cry of "our legal authority."

2. Poor communication between the boards and administration on the one hand and the staffs on the other is a prime cause of teacher unrest. When the administration of a school district becomes so routine, so mechanized, that teachers can only guess at what official policy is, in many instances initiative and creativeness are dulled. In many places, teachers have turned to unions in the hope that they can blast loose the encrusted bureaucracy.

3. A prime reason for teacher defections to the unions is the ineffective, do-nothing programs of some local professional associations. Too many of these programs are incredibly weak. Some exist only as social organizations, as an excuse for office-holding by a few leaders. Perceptive members, especially the young teachers, observe these local leaders playing the game of musical chairs, passing the offices around among the members of a small clique, and shake their heads in frustration. Or they observe this office-holding as a career. In some local associations, one or more strong characters can reign for years.

The weaker the association, the longer the tenure. Also, quite often office in a local association is used as a stepping-stone to regional, state, or national offices or appointments to choice committees and commissions.

4. The crisis school district is another seedbed for union recruitment. By *crisis district* is meant the relatively leaderless school system where there is persistent confusion and lack of direction. This may be the fault of the administration or it may be the fault of a weak local association. Amid such confusion, the perceptive teacher who cares about his work will welcome any possibility of constructive leadership.

In such situations, many teachers reluctantly turn to the unions. The unions may not be able to do any better, but they are untried, and "Why not give them a chance?" is the rationale.

5. The unbalanced school staff is a fertile source of more teachers for the union. An imbalance of men to women can work two ways. First, if there is a preponderance of women and relatively few men on the staff, the tendency is for the men to become disgruntled and seek affiliation (to gain recognition) with the teachers' union. Second—and this is almost a sure-fire recruiting help for the unions—is the staff which is made up preponderantly of men. Many superintendents deliberately plan to develop such staffs for very good reasons. But there is trouble ahead. The minute this imbalance becomes too great, the superintendent is confronted with a new staff climate with which he has not previously had occasion to deal. Any superintendent embarking upon this course had better be prepared to alter the old mores of staff relationships—even though as previously indicated, there are good arguments for it. Otherwise, sooner or later he will find a teachers' union firmly supported by his staff. This development is not inevitable, but it is common. This is peculiarly true where there are weak, inept local professional associations—where in other words, the only alternative is to turn to the unions. Professional associations must refine themselves to the point of being able to compete.

The Union Appeal to Individuals

It is time to consider some of the causes and symptons of the unions' appeal to teachers, at least in the early stages of the union drive.

What are the characteristics of teachers who somewhere along the way seek union affiliation? Some of these characteristics are easily identified. Of course it would be unfair to ascribe to any and all members of teachers' unions these classifications or motivations. Basic to many, however, are two factors: (1) the parochial hope that teachers' unions represent exclusively the interests of classroom teachers and (2) the belief that unions can do more for the welfare of teachers than the professional associations can do. But these are specialized motivations.

Among the more obvious types of teachers attracted to the unions are the following as reported by seasoned observers among state association staffs:

THE TRUE BELIEVERS IN UNIONISM. In large degree, the true believers in unionism are teachers such as vocational, trade, and industrial teachers who come into teaching through indirect routes and already are members of trade unions. Such teachers had to go the union route to get apprentice training. They have naturally a strong devotion to organized labor and the union philosophy. It is no accident that the nucleus of many small AFT locals are teachers in the vocational, technical, and trade schools. This does not apply to all teachers in such schools, but it does apply with great force to the teachers who have been certified largely on the basis of apprenticeship training in the trades and experience in industry rather than upon college preparation.

Then there are the academic teachers who meet the degree requirements for certification but are compelled to moonlight to supplement their income from teaching. In many instances, membership in a trade union is required. Examples are teachers of music who add to their pay by playing in orchestras, by truck-driving, or by bartending. They firmly believe that teacher unions can gain for teachers the economic rewards that the trade unions have gained for workers in private industry.

JUNIOR HIGH SCHOOL TEACHERS. Junior high school teachers are a prime source of union membership, especially young men who, for one reason or another, failed to gain coveted promotions to teaching in high schools, or to positions as administrators. They tend to become embittered and a source of loud and raucous protest. There is perhaps another factor here. The junior high schools, especially in the large cities, are notoriously the citadels of unrest and rebellion on the part of students. This is a puzzling aspect of our educational system, the reasons for which are not all clear. Partly it is because this is the rebellious age of youth for some well-known physiological and psychological reasons.

The junior high school, too, is the moment of truth. It is the period in which the college-headed youth are usually identified, and those who don't quite have it academically become aware that they are probably destined for inferior positions in society. So frustration and rebellion tend to be rampant here, more so than at any other school level. Such a climate cannot help but have its impact upon teachers. Often the climate elicits a like response from teachers. There is no accurate information on the point, but simple observation leads one to believe that the hard core of teachers' unions are certain vocational teachers and men teachers in the junior high schools.

THE FRUSTRATED. A solid source of potential material for the union recruitment is a group of teachers which some observers have dubbed "the frustrated." These are preponderantly men who started out in teaching with high hopes and enthusiasm. Their high hopes and enthusiasm abounded for the first several years of teaching. Somewhere along the route, they acquired wives and children—a perfectly desirable and laudable goal for any normal male. But income did not keep pace with the needs. Hoped-for advancement to administrative positions, which might have yielded adequate income, did not materialize. With affluence all about in their society, the fact of such teachers becoming disgruntled with things as they are was inevitable.

The first mile in teaching, so to speak, was thrilling and filled with glamour. Now these teachers find themselves pursuing the route of the second mile. The glamour is gone, the road ahead is pedestrian, filled with the dust of common days. Frustration piles upon frustration until rebellion is the logical result. The teachers' union offers surcease from the heightening sense of failure. The union offers a scapegoat—the administration and the school board. It offers vocal and other forms of protest. And, human nature being what it is, these appeals to the frustrated are often irresistible.

THE WOMEN. The characteristics and motivations identified above apply almost wholly to male teachers. The appeal of the teachers' unions is not nearly so potent to women as it is to men. But for some women the appeal is for a very simple reason: here is a cause, a militant cause, an exciting cause, the adherents of which are set apart by their very militancy. The cause itself provides unusual opportunity for association with men, who form the vast majority of membership of the teachers' unions. This is, to be sure, a form of escapism. But it is a powerful magnet for some women teachers. Of course, it would be inaccurate and foolish to assert or to imply that this is the sole motivation of women in joining teachers' unions. But it is a motivation significant enough to be noticeable.

A teacher, a young man, after witnessing one of the big-city elections, was horrified at the emotions aroused. He wrote:

> A new breed of teacher is coming to the fore in our urban schools. He is a young male teacher who sees himself as an aggressive, militant, liberal mover of destiny. He is surrounded by the young attractive female teacher who wants to be with and where the young male is. He is not too thoughtful and not given to introspection. He espouses causes and loves slogans and resents being asked to take time to investigate, study and think. He is prone to arrive at conclusions by a simple black and white kind of logic which goes something like this—I am educated, therefore I am smart. Smart people know that what is right is right and what is wrong is wrong. Liberalism is right—therefore, I am a liberal; liberals are for civil rights—therefore, I am for civil rights; liberals are for labor—therefore, I am for labor. NEA is against unionism for teachers—therefore, NEA is anti-labor, anti-civil rights and anti-liberalism—therefore, NEA is against me, the new breed of smart teachers.

Part Two

THE WEAPONS

5

Collective Bargaining and Strikes

> It seems to me that there is a very simple lesson to be learned by American teachers. You will never shed your second-class status as second-class economic citizens until you have access to collective bargaining, but you cannot have access to collective bargaining in the absence of having a strong union, because a strong union provides the essential tool with which collective bargaining is made possible.
>
> —Walter Reuther in an address before the AFT Convention, Detroit, August 23, 1962

> The strike, as a weapon for attaining economic and professional ends by teachers, is first, inappropriate; second, unprofessional; third, illegal; fourth, outmoded; and fifth, ineffective.
>
> —Arthur Corey[1]

Collective bargaining and the strike, in the labor-management context of private industry, are the weapons of the teachers' union.

The appeal of the teachers' union to teachers is the fact that the union has muscle—the raw power to subdue the administration and the school board. In addition, its approach is blunt, direct, quick-acting, and dynamic.

To admire power is a very human trait; the more ruthless the power the better if that power can be used to get something the individual or group wants desperately. Generally, the rawer the power and the quicker the action, the greater the appeal.

This image of the teachers' union has great appeal for many teachers. And, having recourse to the teachers' union, these teachers easily become impatient with the deliberate, slower process of the professional associations.

Too, human beings are often easily persuaded to let somebody else handle their vexing problems for them. How else can we explain the appeal of authoritarianism during the 1930's? It must be remembered that almost the first, if indeed not *the* first, group to succumb to this philosophy in Germany were the intellectuals—the university professors.

Without question, the appeal of the teachers' union will be accelerated as teachers are thrown together in increasingly large groups, as urbanization of the country increases, as individual teachers and even local groups of teachers tend to be swamped by the bigness of the school systems in which they work.

One of the easiest things in American life, or any other free society for that matter, is to organize a group or groups around their biases and to start screaming for their rights. That there are other viewpoints, other considerations, other rights which should be respected—well, there tends to be impatience with such restraints.

One of the most difficult things in American life is for a professional group to pursue the democratic process in obtaining economic justice for its members, eschewing the ruthless power play and using the studied, careful building of a case based on facts, comparative data, and fair play. This is much too slow, too involved, and too difficult for many people, including some teachers.

The democratic form of government is doubtless the most difficult of all political organizations to make work. The reason is simple: This form of government is based upon the concept of fair consideration of the rights of all, fair treatment of minorities, the curbing of the selfish, the seeking of true balance among interest groups.

Just at this point is where the professional associations are most vulnerable, where they face their most dangerous problem: whether power in a complex, densely populated, highly industrialized society can be earned by competence and dedication and superior service to society or whether it must be taken by force. There is much evidence on both sides. But probably the preponderance is in favor of the latter.

So the extraordinary appeal of the teachers' union is that it has a magic formula—quick and easy—for forcing actions favorable to teachers. Another circumstance enhancing the appeal of the unions is the rapidly changing background of teachers now entering the profession. The great lure of the unions is to the younger teachers, particularly young men. There are several possible explanations for this. In the first place, to young men seeking to establish families the inadequate incomes of teachers are most galling. Second, new teachers are increasingly coming from urban backgrounds rather than from rural areas as was the case earlier in this century; therefore, they are not bothered by more aggressive group action.

Too, it must be admitted (at least at the moment) that the teachers' unions are more sophisticated in dealing with the political power structures in the urban communities. They have a built-in advantage, politically speaking, with the political organization of the AFL–CIO.

The professional teachers' associations are vulnerable, in the minds of some teachers, precisely because they seek to persuade, not drive; they seek the gentle pressure of facts, not the overt pressure of force, although this posture is changing rapidly. Thus, this difference in appeal of the two types of teachers' organizations comes to focus, in significant measure, in the strike threat.

The NEA and its affiliates have traditionally sought to avoid the use of the strike or the threat of strike. Always in the background of the AFT appeal, spoken or not, is the use of the short strike to pound out a quick victory for teachers.

There is need to examine collective bargaining and its close ally, the strike, in the labor context and their applicability to a public profession such as teaching.

Collective Bargaining for Teachers

Arguments regarding appropriate negotiation processes for teachers who are public employees revolve around existing law dealing with employee rights. For organized labor, these rights are spelled out in the National Labor Relations Act of 1935 and the Taft-Hartley Act of 1947 (with some restrictions of these rights in the Landrum-Griffin Act of 1959). The latter was aimed at correcting certain weaknesses in the Taft-Hartley Act. These laws and subsequent court decisions clearly established the rights of employees in private industry to collective bargaining and to the use of the strike in impasses.

Both laws exclude public employees, and teachers in public schools are public employees. The laws of 13 states (Florida, Georgia, Hawaii, Michigan, Minnesota, Nebraska, New York, Ohio, Oregon, Pennsylvania, Texas, Virginia, and Wisconsin) specifically deny the use of the strike to public employees; and the laws of not a single state specifically grant this right.

It can, of course, be argued that, in the absence of state legislation forbidding teacher strikes, such strikes are legal. But this is a legal question yet to be determined. The fact that the courts of four states not having no-strike legislation have ruled them illegal would seem to argue against this conclusion.

A lower court in Minnesota, in a case involving noncertificated school personnel, held that "The right to strike is rooted in the freedom of man, and he may not be denied the right except by clear, unequivocal language embodied in a constitution, statute, ordinance, rule, or contract." The Minnesota Supreme Court upheld this decision.[2]

This decision, plus a similar one in New Hampshire, would seem to state the principle that if teachers are to be given the right to strike, it must be done by state laws, not court decisions.

Collective bargaining and *professional negotiation* are quite commonly used as interchangeable terms. In fact, because of the similarities, the term *collective negotiation* has come into widespread use to describe both.

It is contended by many that there is no fundamental difference between collective bargaining and professional negotiation, the latter being the procedure adopted by the NEA and the teaching profession in general. The Taft-Hartley Act defines collective bargaining as follows:

> Collective bargaining is . . . the performance of the mutual obligation of the employer and the representatives of the employees to meet at reasonable times and confer in good faith with respect to wages, hours, and other terms and conditions of employment, or the negotiation of any agreement, or any question arising thereunder, and the execution of a written contract incorporating any agreement reached if requested by either party, but such obligation does not compel either party to agree to a proposal or require the making of a concession.

Professional negotiation, as defined by the NEA, is "a set of procedures to provide an orderly method for teacher associations and school boards, through professional channels, to negotiate on matters of common concern, to reach mutually satisfactory agreement on these matters, and to establish educational channels for mediation, and appeal in the event of impasse."[3]

The similarity in the phraseology of the two definitions is obvious. What are the differences, if any?

The differences are that collective bargaining

1. Is designed for private employees, and its use is mandatory under law.
2. Uses procedures that are subject to Federal and state laws and interpretations of the courts. Administration of collective bargaining is under jurisdiction of Federal and state labor departments or agencies.
3. Employs, in cases of impasse, the strike, which is recognized under the laws as the weapon of the employee.

In contrast, professional negotiation

1. Is designed for public employees (teachers).
2. Requires that all processes are to be through professional channels, that is, through education personnel and agencies.
3. Must use educational channels for appeals or mediation of impasse.
4. Does not advocate or consider legal the use of the strike as a weapon.

In short, professional negotiation seeks to keep public employees (teachers) out of labor techniques as defined in labor laws. The rationale is that schools and factories are not analogous; schools are not profit-making enterprises, and management and employees are not natural enemies fighting over division of profits.

The assumption that the paraphernalia of collective bargaining can be applied *en toto* to public employees inevitably collides with the concept of state sovereignty. Perhaps some aspects are applicable, but not all.

President Franklin D. Roosevelt once defined the obstacles:

> ... the process of collective bargaining, as usually understood, cannot be transplanted into the public service. It has its distinct and insurmountable limitations when applied to public personnel management. The very nature and purposes of government make it impossible for administrative officials to represent fully or bind the employer in mutual discussions with Government organizations.
>
> The employer is the whole people, who speak by means of laws enacted by their representatives in Congress. Accordingly, administrative officials and employees alike are governed and guided, and in many instances restricted, by laws which establish policies, procedures, or rules in personnel matters.[4]

The National Labor Relations Act, commonly called the Wagner Act, specifically excluded the United States and any state or political subdivision as employer. Thus the act would not apply to public employees. Also, the Wagner Act declares it unlawful for any individual employed by the United States to participate in any strike; penalties for violation of this restriction are immediate discharge, forfeiture of civil-service status if (any), and ineligibility for re-employment for a period of three years, plus possible fines and even prison terms.

State legislation regarding rights of public employees to collective bargaining or collective negotiation varies widely. By 1965, 10 states had enacted such laws (Alaska, California, Connecticut, Florida, Massachusetts, Michigan, New Hampshire, Oregon, Washington, and Wisconsin). New statutes have since been enacted in Massachusetts and Rhode Island; and the Michigan law has been amended. Also New York passed a new law in 1967 superseding the old Condin-Wadlin Act. And Texas in 1967 enacted a mild, permissive board-teacher Consultation Act. Nebraska also enacted a law in 1967.

In Alaska, legislation permits governmental units to bargain with employee organizations and to enter into contracts. In California, governmental units must meet and confer with employee organizations. In Connecticut, boards of education must negotiate with exclusive representatives of employee organizations. In Florida, committees of the teaching profession may be involved in policy determination and in reaching agreements affecting certificated personnel. In Massachusetts, municipal governments and schools must bargain with employee organizations. In Michigan, school boards are mandated to bargain with the exclusive representatives of public employees. In New Hampshire, towns are permitted to enter into collective-bargaining contracts with public-employee organizations. In New Jersey (under the constitution), school boards must discuss matters of mutual concern with employees or recognized organizations. In Oregon, boards of education are mandated to meet, discuss, and confer with elected representatives of certificated employees. In Washington, law mandates that school boards negotiate with the elected majority organization. In Wisconsin, it is permissible for governing boards to negotiate with employee organizations, and agreements reached must be put in writing. In at least three states (North Carolina, Texas, and Virginia) bargaining with public employees is prohibited by law. In several states public employees may present grievances to governing bodies. Public employees are not mentioned at all in the labor legislation of some 25 states. Restrictive legislation regarding collective bargaining or negotiation has been enacted by seven states, and at least two states (Alabama and North Carolina) prohibit public employees from joining labor organizations. Nineteen states have enacted right-to-work laws specifying that the right to work shall not be abridged or denied because of membership or nonmembership in labor organizations.

Such legislation was sanctioned by Section 14*b* of the Taft-Hartley Act. The Democratic Platform of 1964 pledged to repeal this section, and the Johnson Administration was pledged to support its repeal in the Eighty-ninth Congress. The repeal was not acted on in both sessions of that Congress. The transit strike in New York City in early January 1966, created such public indignation that a severe setback was given to the effort to repeal Section 14*b*.

The rights of public employees in negotiation with their employers appear to be in somewhat the same muddle as were those of labor in private industry prior to the passage of the National Labor Relations Act in 1935. It seems reasonable to assume that a major break-through in public attitudes and consequent legislation in establishing more enlightened procedures for public employees are imminent. President Kennedy's Executive Order Number 10988 issued in January 1962, establishing the right of organization and negotiation for Federal Government employees, is indicative of the trend.

The nature of this legislation is going to be all-important—at least to existing professional associations. It is apparent that state legislation spelling out the rights and procedures of public employees as to the type of organization and negotiation will become increasingly common. Whether such legislation is to be sponsored by organized labor or the professions is the key consideration. Virtually all such legislation in existence had prior (to 1965) been enacted at the behest of organized labor. The professional associations were compelled to seek appropriate legislation reflecting their philosophy of employer-employee relationships. The alternative would have been a steady erosion of their present position of strength and ultimate surrender to organized labor. Some kind of legislation must protect the sovereignty of the state, and a substitute for the strike must be found. Thus, as has been previously stated, five state professional negotiation laws were enacted in 1965 (in California, Connecticut, Florida, Oregon, and Washington). Such legislation in 1965 in Minnesota and New Jersey was vetoed.

COLLECTIVE BARGAINING NOT FOR PUBLIC EMPLOYEES. As has been pointed out several times, collective bargaining is a term which by law has been specifically applied to employer-employee relationships in private industry, and its companion piece legally is the strike. In this context, public employees are specifically excluded from the provisions of such Federal and state laws. Professional employees in private industry are expressly excluded by Federal law from collective-bargaining procedures dominated by nonprofessional employees. For example, the President's directive of 1962, establishing employee-management relationship in the Federal Government, avoided use of the term *collective bargaining.*

The President's Task Force Report, upon which the directive was based, stated that there are fundamental differences between public and private employment. The obvious dissimilarities are such that it would be neither desirable nor possible to fashion a Federal system of employee-management relations directly upon the system which has grown up in the private economy. Thus, the report said, professional and supervisory employees should be free to establish organizations of their own.

To spell out further that public employment is different and that collective bargaining, as applied to private industry and as generally interpreted, is inappropriate for public employees, the President's directive enunciated the following principles:

1. Federal employees do not have the right to strike.
2. Public interest must be paramount.
3. The union shop and the closed shop are inappropriate for the Government.
4. Labor arbitration as in private industry is not appropriate for Federal Government use.
5. Where Congress fixes salaries and other conditions of employment, these are not subject to negotiation.
6. All negotiations and agreements must conform to civil-service regulations.

To summarize, the President's directive specified a decidedly different pattern of negotiation from that of collective bargaining, although the directive was designed to help blue-collar workers, too, thousands of whom are employed by the Government or by Government-connected agencies and installations. Moreover, professional employees are identified as a special group with unique interests and requirements.

Roughly the same limitations apply in such cities as Philadelphia and New York. In 1957, Philadelphia became the first major city to recognize an exclusive bargaining agent for municipal employees—the American Federation of State, County, and Municipal Employees, an AFL–CIO union. Cities as a general rule recognize several bargaining agencies. Some provision of the Philadelphia agreement are:

1. Professional employees (including teachers) and supervisors above the foreman level, employees of the police, fire departments, and district attorney's office are excluded.
2. Strikes are banned.

3. Wages are determined by the pay plan adopted by the Civil Service Commission and the administrative board of the city.
4. The legal authorities are not bound by the decisions of a mediation board that was established with advisory powers in cases of impasse.

The "Little Wagner Act" of 1958 was adopted for employees of New York City after a comprehensive survey by the New York City Labor Department to find ways of granting to employees the fullest possible collective-bargaining rights. This report parallels almost precisely the report of the President's Task Force—the Kennedy Task Force—referred to above. The necessity of an employer-employee relationship agreement different from collective bargaining is spelled out. The United Federation of Teachers secured a limited version of this plan in 1962, although clearly the act was not intended to apply to teachers.

Although many aspects of the continued dispute over whether there is any difference between collective bargaining and professional negotiation is a play on semantics, these differences are valid:

1. Federal labor legislation has consistently excluded Government employees. This was true of the National Labor Relations Act of 1933, the Fair Labor Standards Act of 1938 (wages and hours bill), the War Labor Disputes Act of 1943, and the Labor-Management Relations Act of 1947.

2. In Federal, state, or municipal provisions for employer-employee relationship processes, whatever they may be called, professional employees without exception are identified as a special group.

3. Professional employees are also singled out as a special group in private industry, where collective bargaining is specifically designated by law as the appropriate procedure. The National Labor Relations Act, which first established collective bargaining for industrial employees, specified professional employees as a special group and as free to determine their own procedures in employee-management relations. The Act specifies that professional employees may not be bound by a majority vote of nonprofessional employees regarding adoption or nonadoption of collective bargaining and are not bound to accept representation by a nonprofessional bargaining agent.

Federal employees themselves reacted adversely when the Clark Bill, a bill designed to extend possible areas of collective bargaining, was pending in Congress in 1958–59. It sought to reduce the scope and powers of the Civil Service Commission and to transfer many of the commission's personnel-administration functions to a new agency attached to the President's office. Federal employees opposed the bill, largely on the grounds that they were satisfied with the treatment accorded by the Civil Service Commission and were apprehensive about what might or could happen to their rights under the proposed plan. This opposition, in effect, was a rejection of collective bargaining in the private-industry context.

It is valid to point out that teachers may subject themselves to unknown and unforseen adversities if they turn to collective bargaining for broader rights and rewards and away from provisions in the law. If their privileges are to be renegotiated in collective-bargaining contracts every year or so, certain rights which they now have in the law could conceivably be sloughed away.

The so-called UFT collective-bargaining contract in New York City is not so viewed by the New York City Board of Education. The board contends that it is not a contract but an agreement. The board claims that the agreement lacks legal force and that the employees do not have the right to go into court over and what they consider violations of it.[5]

SWEETHEART CONTRACT IN DENVER. The Denver Classroom Teachers Association completed a Level II professional-negotiation agreement with the Denver Board of Education in February 1963. The AFT vehemently ridiculed this agreement as a "sweetheart contract." Apparently the teachers' union tends to operate on the philosophy that if no loud threats are made, if no violent charges of mistreatment of teachers by the school board accompany the negotiations, then something is wrong and somebody apparently has been outsmarted.

As pointed out elsewhere, the President of the Denver Federation of Teachers appeared before the board of education and complained that collective bargaining had been rejected. When advised by the board that collective bargaining was illegal, the teachers' union leader replied that the DFT would have been happy to represent Denver teachers under the professional-negotiation agreement.

Let's look at this sweetheart contract in Denver. For the 1962–63 school year, Denver teachers received salary increases ranging from $450 to $725. Actually, these increases were determined by the board before the professional-negotiation agreement was in full operation, but of course the Denver Teachers Association participated in the discussions. Then for the 1964–65 school year, the teachers and the board negotiated additional increases ranging from $200 to $715. Thus, in a two-year period the Denver teachers received raises ranging from $650 to $1,440, with top salaries exceeding $10,000.

Obviously, this is quite a good deal. And it wasn't done with magic labor formulas. It was done without fuss and feathers; without picketing, without the threat of strike, without denunciation of management, callous school boards, and dictatorial administrators. It was done by calm, reasonable, and fair consideration of all factors involved.

The 1964–65 Denver scale provided higher minimums, higher maximums, immediate recognition of the master's degree, increased increments at the tenth step and beyond, and a greater increase in the maximums than in the minimums, thus rewarding the career teacher.

The Denver schedule range (according to years of experience) will be for bachelor's degree teachers, from $5,100 to $8,325; for master's degree teachers, from $5,325 to $8,925; for the master's degree plus 30 semester hours, from $8,880 to $9,240; for the master's degree plus 60 semester hours, from $9,185 to $9,550; for the doctor's degree, from $9,435 to $9,825, with a special increment for 17 years of service, taking the maximum to about $10,200.

In the three-year period 1962–65, the Denver teachers got raises exceeding those of the New York teachers. The total raise in the bachelor's degree minimums were Denver, $525; New York, $500. The totals for increases in the top maximums were Denver, $1,825; New York, $1,575.

In addition to the new salary schedules, the Denver Board of Education approved certain other recommendations of the teachers, including principles of salary scheduling in the future, the development of joint studies, and criteria for payment for assignments outside school hours. The assumption that either collective bargaining or professional negotiation is a sure-fire gimmick which can invariably produce instant results in pay increases is far-fetched. Actually, the NEA advocates professional negotiation as a part of a continuing, many-faceted approach to economic justice; professional working conditions; and recognition and participation for teachers in respected national research, effective public relations, cooperation with key lay groups, and strong legislative leadership at both state and national levels.

The pursuit of a single procedure, in the long run, is bound to be illusory.

Commitment of the AFT to Teachers' Strikes

After the New York City teacher strikes, with the striking teachers getting away with two violations of the Condon-Wadlin law, and with a threatened third strike by the UFT on September 9, 1963, the August 1963 AFT Convention came full circle in its strike policy.

For example, in 1951 the AFT Executive Council adopted this statement:

1. The statement of policy in regard to strikes adopted at the Boston Convention [a no-strike policy], August 21, 1947, is affirmed as the policy of the Executive Council of the American Federation of Teachers.

2. The American Federation of Teachers does not assert (and hereby expressly disclaims) the right to strike against the Government of the United States or any agency thereof.

3. The use of the strike is rejected as an instrument of policy of the American Federation of Teachers. The Executive Council and its national officers will not call a strike either nationally or in any local area or jurisdiction, nor in any way advise a local to strike. The funds and facilities of the National Organization will not be used to support a strike.

4. The facilities of the National Office are available to all locals for the negotiation, adjustment, mediation, and redress of problems and grievances.
5. Locals should be instructed in the dangers and problems of the strike and of the national policy with respect thereto.
6. When it appears that a local may be involved in a strike situation, the area vice-president, secretary-treasurer, and other national officers and employees whose services may be available will make every effort to adjust the grievances and to avert the strike. If any strike is called, it must be made clear that the national officers have taken no part in the decision to call the strike. However, the existence of a strike or work stoppage will not terminate the efforts of the national officers to adjust the grievances and effect the resumption of the educational process. In any such situation it will be the aim of the national officers to promote the education of the children by eliminating the causes that have led to interruption of classes.[6]

In 1958, the AFT Convention adopted the following resolution:

> That the American Federation of Teachers urge the repeal of no-strike legislation. That legislation be enacted or existing anti-injunction legislation be amended to guarantee public employees protection against injunction in labor disputes.

The following quoted amendments (No. 23 and No. 79 of 1963) contain much ambiguity. But in 1963 the AFT was faced with the dilemma of either adhering to its previous policies and being put in the position of not backing up its largest local, or modifying its previous policies to conform to the New York situation.

It is clear from reading the two 1963 resolutions that the AFT made a valiant effort to preserve some aspects of its former no-strike policy while giving support to the strike under "certain circumstances."

Here are the two resolutions adopted at the Forty-Seventh Annual Convention of the American Federation of Teachers in New York, August 19–23, 1963.

Resolution No. 23
Support of Strike Action

Whereas, the United Federation of Teachers, Local 2, American Federation of Teachers, has pioneered in securing collective bargaining status for the 40,000 New York City teachers, and

Whereas, the United Federation of Teachers has adopted a policy of "no contract-no work", and

Whereas, the membership of the United Federation has rejected the offer of the New York City Board of Education, and

Whereas, a strike has been called by the membership of the United Federation of Teachers to commence September 9;

NOW THEREFORE BE IT

RESOLVED: that the American Federation of Teachers strongly supports the strike action of Local 2, and BE IT FURTHER

RESOLVED: that the American Federation of Teachers recommends similar support on the part of the leadership of the AFL-CIO.

Resolution No. 79
Collective Bargaining

Whereas, the American Federation of Teachers has pioneered in the establishment of collective bargaining for teachers, and

Whereas, collective bargaining is recognized as the best technique for the realization of economic democracy and the peaceful resolution of conflicts, and

Whereas, numerous boards of education have refused to grant the right to a representation election in accordance with established policy, procedure and practice in other areas of employment, and

Whereas, even after the establishment of collective bargaining school boards often fail to bargain in good faith,

THEREFORE BE IT

RESOLVED: that the AFT recognize the *right of locals to strike under certain circumstances*, and BE IT FURTHER

RESOLVED: that the AFT urge the AFL-CIO and affiliated international unions to support such strikes when they occur.

NEA's Position on Teacher Strikes

NEA has often been criticized for not having adopted a direct, categorical no-strike ban.

Myron Lieberman often made this charge. He has repeatedly chided the NEA for not having adopted a no-strike position and at the same time has praised the AFT for having done so.[7]

Lieberman was technically correct. No resolution had ever been voted by the NEA Representative Assembly to this effect.

The matter of a no-strike policy was rarely if ever discussed at NEA meetings. Apparently it was taken for granted that the no-strike principle was not even debatable. Actually the old NEA Code of Ethics (adopted in 1952) and the new Code of Ethics for the Education Profession (adopted in 1963) imply strike prohibitions (as do similar statements in codes dating back to 1929).

Principle IV of the old code stated:

> The members of the teaching profession have inescapable obligations with respect to employment. These obligations are nearly always shared employer-employee responsibilities based upon mutual respect and good faith. In fulfilling the obligations of this fourth principle, the teacher will . . . *adhere to the conditions of a contract until service thereunder has been performed, the contract terminated by mutual consent, or the contract has otherwise been legally terminated.*

Principle IV of the new code states:

> We regard the employment agreement as a solemn pledge to be executed in spirit and in fact in a manner consistent with the highest ideals of professional service. Sound professional personnel relationships with governing boards are built upon personal integrity, dignity, and mutual respect. In fulfilling our

obligations to professional employment practices we . . . *adhere to the conditions of a contract or to the terms of an appointment until either has been terminated legally or by mutual consent. . . .*

Obviously a teachers' strike is a violation of contract and is clearly prohibited by the NEA Code of Ethics, although the ban is aimed at the conduct of the individual teacher. Whether it was intended to affect concerted action by a group of teachers is not so clear.

But of course this is not a direct and categorical declaration of a no-strike policy. Lieberman's repeated criticisms of NEA, it appears, are on the grounds that NEA has not declared a clear-cut policy either for or against the strike, while AFT has—at one time against and now for the strike.

Several AFT conventions did disclaim the use of the strike by teachers, finally incorporating a no-strike policy in the AFT constitution. In 1958, the categorical no-strike statement was amended by the annual AFT convention to an ambiguous one. And the AFT 1963 resolution clearly shifted to an endorsement of strikes, "under certain circumstances."

It is difficult to explain why the NEA Representative Assembly has never adopted a clear-cut policy against strikes by teachers. There is no question of the attitude of NEA members in the past: they have been, and remain, preponderantly against the use of the strike by teachers. This traditional opinion is so ingrained, one supposes, that NEA members have never really felt the need to state the obvious. But times and circumstances and perspectives change, and it may be that NEA may eventually embrace the strike-under-certain-circumstances position of AFT. This assertion is based on the fact that in several recent cases, NEA by silence of its officials has been put in the position of condoning strikes.

Actually, the only official NEA reference to the inappropriateness of teacher strikes, except for possible references by speakers before the annual conventions, editorials in the *NEA Journal*, and the implied ban in the codes of ethics, was a public statement issued in 1948 by Dr. Willard E. Givens, who at that time was executive secretary of the NEA. The year 1946–47, it will be recalled, was one in which a rash of teacher strikes occurred.

The peculiar conditions which impelled public-school teachers to resort to this radical weapon (in 1946–47) were an accumulation of grievances growing out of World War II conditions. As with most wars in our history, the American people tended to neglect everything not obviously and directly connected with the war effort. It has been said that the people of the United States (at least through World War II) traditionally have fought wars somewhat in the manner of the operation of a volunteer fire department—dropping everything else when the conflagration starts, putting out the fire, and then picking up the threads of every-day life again.

This neglect of the public schools during the years of World War II reached alarming proportions. Thousands of teachers, unable to meet the skyrocketing cost of living on their meager salaries, were compelled to leave teaching for higher-paying jobs in defense industries. Instead of adjusting teachers' salaries to rising industrial wages, the American people, as reflected in the actions of their official representatives—the state and local school boards—simply lowered standards and employed unqualified teachers who for one reason or another could not or did not seek other employment. At the height of the war, one in every six teaching positions was filled by a holder of an emergency certificate. The result of this public indifference was an unprecedented outflow of teachers from the schools. It has been estimated that in excess of 600,000 came into and left teaching between 1939, when preparation for war began to gather momentum, and the war's termination in 1945. This has been aptly described as the greatest professional migration in history.

The war's end brought no amelioration of the teachers' plight. The adjustment of tax rates and state appropriations can be an exasperatingly slow business, especially if there are no overt pressures exerted upon the public to do so. Prices and wages kept going up under the impact of accumulated shortages of consumer goods during the war years. Business and industry boomed. The loss of teachers resumed. Such unrest existed in the ranks of those who elected to remain in the profession that strikes by teachers occurred in many school districts in 1946–47. For the most part, these were actions by teachers in local situations where conditions had simply become intolerable. These strikes were not sponsored or inspired by the NEA or AFT. There were, however, both NEA and AFT affiliates among the striking groups. The teacher strikes were spontaneous outbursts of indignation at public neglect and indifference.

As a result of this rash of teacher strikes, Willard Givens, then NEA Executive Secretary, issued a public statement disclaiming the strike as an appropriate weapon for use by teachers and asserting that there were effective procedures available which did not involve interruption of services to children.

While this position obviously reflected the over-all sentiment of NEA members, it was not an official position of that body. That it was generally accepted is indicated by the fact that it did not arouse discussion in the next annual meeting of the Representative Assembly.

Future of the Strike in Private Industry

The strike as a weapon of organized labor may become increasingly obsolescent.

There is some evidence that strikes in major industries are on the way out. Basically, the irritation of the public over the impact of these strikes, often for petty reasons and often over power struggles or jurisdictional disputes within the labor hierarchy, has resulted in the widespread conviction that there is a better way of handling labor-industry impasses.

Of course there will continue to be work stoppages here and there in the economy. But these will tend to be minor irritants the public can tolerate.

Basically, the reason for the probable decline in use of the strike is that the public is developing the conviction that there should be, and can be, better means of settling labor grievances.

But in back of this basic cause are other important factors which contribute to public impatience.

What are the evidences of this trend toward making strikes obsolete?

The intercession of the Congress of the United States in the threatened nation-wide rail tie-up in 1963 and 1964 is one tip-off. Congress, for the first time in recent history and by a nearly unanimous vote, passed a compulsory arbitration law. This is indisputable evidence of public wrath. And if the 180-day truce decreed by this law does not bring peace, perhaps another more drastic law will be enacted. In April 1964, at the end of the truce period, when another nation-wide strike threatened, President Johnson called negotiators for the railroads and labor to the White House and told them to settle the issues "or else." The issues were settled and the strike averted. But not by the free operation of collective bargaining, although there were involved some characteristics of compulsory bargaining. Again in 1967 Congress interceded to head off the strike.

Federal intervention in the longshoreman's strike and the steel strike is evidence that the nation is not going to tolerate much longer large-scale work stoppages that threaten the economy. The disastrous airline strike in July 1966, was an added irritant to the public.

According to A. H. Raskin there are four major factors involved in the trend away from strikes: automation, the growing inability of labor to hurt the big employers without bringing greater hurts to itself, chronic unemployment and surplus plant capacity, and the growing intolerance of the public with strikes that hurt the community.[8]

The New York City transit-workers strike on January 1, 1966, which devastated that city for a week, is ample evidence that a solution must be found for strikes of public employees when vital services to the people are involved. Here the biennial Mayor Wagner-Mike Quill routine failed to work with incoming Mayor Lindsay. For a week a great city of 8 million people was immobilized by two factors: the arrogance of the union leaders and the inability of law and order to meet and solve the dilemma. That such defiance of society can and will lead to chaotic conditions, if remedies cannot be found in fair and progressive legislation, seems obvious. By this strike organized labor itself was hurt and hurt badly.

Perhaps to these should be added the fact that some industrial leaders are taking the play away from the big-labor leaders by voluntary long-range planning that gives employees as much or more than unions or strikes can get, but without the hazards of lost pay and the attendant strains of work stoppage. Of course it must be said that such generous action would probably not result without the constant pressures of labor unions and the implied threat of the strike.

As examples of the failure of strikes to materially cripple the big industries, A. H. Raskin cites the giant telephone companies and the electric utilities so automated now as to be virtually invulnerable to strikes. He mentions the Shell Oil Company in Houston, which, in 1962 when about 2,000 union employees walked out, maintained normal operations for a year. More and more, with automation and the use of nonunion supervisory personnel, the big companies will survive work stoppages and continue full-scale operations. Moreover, labor is beginning to realize that every strike now is a stimulant to industry to seek greater automation, thus eliminating an increasing number of jobs.

The American Newspaper Guild, which James Carey in his Denver speech pictured as the near-perfect example of the professional union, is learning that the strike is far less than the near-perfect weapon. With almost every big city newspaper strike in recent years (excepting the Baltimore strike and the *New York Times* strike in 1965), papers have gone out of business through financial failure or mergers, throwing thousands of editorial employees out of work. To make matters worse, the remaining papers are automating operations to the extent that thousands of workers—allies of the guild members such as linotypists, compositors, and printers, the groups that often pull editorial people into sympathy strikes—are being displaced. The *New York Mirror,* which had the nation's second largest circulation, is a good example. This paper closed down after the sustained New York City newspaper strike in 1962–63, displacing 1,400 employees. In the summer of 1966, the famed *Herald Tribune* succumbed as a result of still another strike.

The 1966 strike forcing the merger of the *World-Telegram and Sun,* the *Herald-Tribune*, and the *Journal-American* into a single paper, the *World Journal Tribune,* hinged in part on seniority demands of the unions involved. Agreement on this aspect was reached only after a large number of editorial workers voluntarily agreed to resign. The *World Journal Tribune* management charged that excessive demands of the 10 unions involved, plus their insistence on virtual veto power over plans of the management to improve efficiency, made the situation impossible. The merged paper lasted only 236 days, closing down in May 1967, losing in that period more than $10 million. Some 2,500 employees lost their jobs in the paper's closing down. The head of the typographical union was reported in the press as saying . . . "All they (the *World Journal Tribune*) can do is pay or shut down."

Thus, New York City, which once had a dozen top-flight daily papers, now has been reduced to three major ones. The chief victims among the employees were the members of ANG. The printers could readily find other employment in New York City since it is the major center of the printing industry. In a bitter column on the forced shut-down of the *World Journal Tribune*, syndicated columnist Bob Considine wrote:

> The WJT may become the classic example of how union leaders can succeed in putting their members out of work by striving to ingratiate themselves with those very same members . . . Lichty . . . put it all in a single panel drawing and a caption some time ago. His cartoon showed the head of the union confronting the boss of the organization and saying to him something like: "Okay, you've given us a guarantee of an annual income, a guarantee of three weeks vacation and triple-time overtime, and health and accident coverage to the third cousinship. We want one more guarantee from you—a guarantee you won't go broke!"

Considine adds about the union's arrogance: "Infuriating? Sure, but fundamentally we're all too chicken to do anything about it."

Eastern Airlines kept its planes flying in the face of a sustained flight engineers' strike by using full-fledged pilots in their places. An example of industrial leadership in outmoding the strike is the Kaiser Steel contract, an employee profit-sharing plan which bans the strike for a four-year period. There are other such plans, and this seems to be the trend of the future.

The continuing factor of some 3 to 4 million unemployed, many of whom are desperate enough to take strikers' jobs, cannot help but worry the union leaders. The key to future labor-industry relations, it appears, is not to be exclusive reliance upon the combination of collective bargaining backed up by the strike, but the cooperative approach and long-range planning of government, industry, and labor, each earnestly seeking a fair balance of justice for all sides. The success of labor courts in Australia is often cited as an alternative.

In view of all this, the cooperative plan of the teaching profession (professional negotiation) seems not so naive after all. Actually, considerable documentation for the NEA's procedures can be found in labor literature written by labor leaders.

The magnitude of the deep trouble which organized labor is in is indicated by the defection of many of the nation's outstanding liberals who once gave militant support to labor's philosophy and tactics. Max Lerner, who certainly qualifies as one of the able and articulate liberals who has given enthusiastic support to labor in the past, expresses the new disaffection. He writes:

> Up to now, the liberal has not questioned the moral right of a union to use whatever power it can muster to protect its men against the greater wealth and power of the corporations. It has made sense for the liberal to identify with labor as the underdog. And it has made sense to believe in unions because they have helped the worker to organize, to bargain collectively, to increase his wages and, therefore, his purchasing power and living standards, to cut down on his working day and control his job conditions and thus to become a human being rather than a victim. All this has helped society as well, and humanized it. But the liberal today is caught between his old loyalty to the cause of the unions

and a new social realism that makes him ask whether the paralyzing power exerted by a few unions is good for society as a whole. He is driven to ask whether there is not a way out of the whole mess that will protect the rights and the living standards of the workers, but also protect the larger society.[9]

The losses of the 114-day New York City newspaper strike in 1962–63, one of 27 such strikes in 1962, were staggering. The estimated cost of the strike was $200 million. Some $100 million of this was in sales and advertising. The 20,000 workers lost $47 million in wages. Loss of taxes to the Federal and state governments totaled $11 million. City news dealers lost a similar amount. Restaurants lost $16 million; department stores, $6.5 million; hotels and railroads, $2 million each.

Total daily circulation of the struck papers dropped by 1 million, or ten per cent, and the evidence indicates that this will not be regained, not soon anyway.

There was another American Newspaper Guild strike in New York City in 1965, settled in about 25 days. Observers predicted that at least one of the city's daily papers would go out of business as a result. They were wrong but evidently the paper came very close to the end.

As a result of the 1966 New York City strike three papers merged and one closed.

There is some evidence that organized labor, as represented by the AFL–CIO, has grown fat and torpid. The old crusading zeal, momentarily at least, is gone out of the house of labor.

At least one observer thinks so.

Even if the alliance (merger of the AFL-CIO) were not torn by jurisdictional feuding—and it is torn almost to the point of paralysis—it would be creaking under the strain of holding together those labor leaders who believe in more bread and butter plus a few social platitudes and those who want labor to be the vanguard of enlightenment and reform from here to Tibet.

On the surface the latter group, mostly from the old CIO, has about given up. The merged federation's political, social, and economic policies are geared to the lowest common denominator, and there is no question that the body as a whole is much more conservative than the hosts that followed Lewis in the 1930's, Phillip Murray in the 1940's and Reuther in the 1950's. Resolutions still pour forth at conventions, but they are perfunctory compromises, watered down in advance to avoid debate and to arouse no alarm in the most Republican member of the Building Trades. Pro-labor congressmen complain that except when strictly trade-union matters are at issue, they have to call up union headquarters and urge them to send their lobbyists around to support bills in the general interest.[10]

A. H. Raskin has written of the malaise of the labor movement:

Suddenly they all are gone—the pioneers who gave fresh direction to the American labor movement in the first feverish thrust of the New Deal. In the marbled palaces they erected as monuments to labor's new found eminence sits a new breed of union civil servants. It is a corps of organization men, bland,

Strikes Last One Or Two Days. . . . They Are Just Unscheduled Vacations for the Children

faithful, uninspired, drifting into an era of limitless technological change with compass points set in the Great Depression. In a society confident of everything except what reason it has for being, no element is more serene, more complacent, more satisfied of the eternal rectitude of its ancestral policies and practices.[11]

Strikes or Sanctions for Teachers?

What is a strike? And how long is it?

Myron Lieberman has pointed out the controversy over a satisfactory definition of *strike*. He suggests the definition of the Bureau of Labor Statistics as a generally acceptable one: "a temporary stoppage of work by a group of employees in order to express a grievance or enforce a demand."[12] The definition of a strike becomes important when eligibility for unemployment compensation or loss of tenure, retirement benefits, and placement on the teachers' salary schedule may be threatened.

The AFT, which until the UFT strikes in New York in 1960 and 1962 championed a no-strike policy, now seems to favor short strikes according to statements of some of the union officials.

"Strikes last one or two days . . . they're just unscheduled vacations for the children," says one.

"It would hurt children far less [than sanctions] to have teachers on strike for one day as in New York City," another suggests.

"Which is worse, a short strike of all teachers—one day in New York City—or professional sanctions which would permit the long, dragged-out continuance of poor conditions?" adds a third.

Are all teachers' strikes short and all sanctions applications long and drawn out? The picture is mixed.

A strike in St. Paul by an AFT Local in 1946 lasted 33 days.

A strike in Pawtucket, Rhode Island, in 1946 by an AFT affiliate also lasted 33 days, ending then only because the school year ended.

A strike in Minneapolis in 1948 by an AFT unit lasted 27 days.

It should be pointed out that the short strikes (one day each) in New York City were ended by court injunctions, not by settlement of the controversies. Also, it should be pointed out that strikes tend to recur. The 33-day Pawtucket strike was preceded by a shorter one and followed by four others in later years. There have now been six strikes of Pawtucket teachers, two in 1964–65; the 27-day strike in Minneapolis was followed three years later by a 23-day strike; the one-day illegal strike in New York City in 1960 was followed by another one-day illegal strike in 1962, and a three week strike in 1967.

Too, it should be pointed out that the Pawtucket strike resulted in state legislation barring teachers' strikes. Also, the threat of a teachers' strike in Buffalo in 1948 triggered the passage of the Condin-Wadlin Act by the New York Legislature. The New York City strike of 1960 stimulated the revision of that act, with another proposed revision in 1966, and a new really drastic law in 1967.

Parallels for the adverse effects of professional sanctions are difficult to find. None of the case examples described in Chapter 6 resulted in work stoppage by teachers or interruption of services to children. It is true that the elementary-school children in North College Hill, Ohio, did strike and stay out for two months, and that the high-school students of the same town were prevented at first from striking only by pleas of the aggrieved superintendent of schools; even then many did strike for a month during the agonizing period of settling the controversy. But sanctions were not in effect, and the strike resulted from conditions that ultimately brought about the invoking of sanctions. In the other sanctions cases, the matters were relatively long and drawn out, but were resolved to the satisfaction of the professional staffs without interruption of educational services to the children.

In Little Lake, California, a case settled early in 1964, the controversy extended over a two-year period. But school services were not interrupted, and the teachers won their major grievance points.

Whether the overt act of a teachers' strike, even though it is illegal, is more effective than the application of the sanction of withdrawal of services is a moot question.

We can be rather certain, however, that the threat of sanctions is now, and in the future will become more so, an effective device for curing teachers' grievances. The basic reason why this is so is exactly the same reason as why sanctions cannot be a weapon of the teachers' unions, which must resort to the illegal strike. That reason is the broad, comprehensive program of the professional associations in the areas that bear most effectively upon the enforcement of sanctions, the areas in which the teachers' unions have virtually no programs at all. These areas are a code of ethics and its effective enforcement: a program of professional certification, constantly refined to assure competence of those admitted to practice; a program of professional accreditation to assure high-quality programs of teacher preparation; NEA teacher-position listing service; programs of professional teacher-placement services in state education associations, state departments of education, and colleges and universities; machinery in the NEA and state education associations for protecting and disciplining members; and organizational strengths and loyalties, from the local association to the national, embracing approximately 90 per cent of public-school personnel.

Relative Effectiveness of Processes

How about the relative effectiveness of the two sets of procedures—professional negotiation versus collective bargaining, and professional sanctions versus strikes?

It is at the moment difficult if not impossible to make a fair, reasoned assessment. The professional procedures (negotiation and sanctions) are relatively new and untried processes. Collective bargaining and strikes, on the other hand, have had a generation, in terms of legal recognition, of trial and error. There is for collective bargaining and strikes a mountain of precedents built up and buttressed by experience, law and court decisions.

The professional procedures are yet to yield, in significant measure, the perspective of experience and the power of precedent. It was to be expected that NEA and its affiliates would flounder at many points, err at others, be uncertain and ineffective at others.

Thus in a few places the teachers' unions can point with vigor to their quick successes with the strike while hooting at the ineffectiveness of professional negotiation and sanctions. But the real picture actually is not so conclusive.

As for professional negotiation, the Denver agreement, achieved without strike and fanfare, has worked with mutual satisfaction, although there have been inevitable irritations. There are several hundred other agreements throughout the country—and the number is growing daily—working with varying effectiveness. Some are working superbly, some gropingly, and some poorly. Allowed time for experience, adjustment, and adaptation, these agreements probably will result in growing acceptance and satisfaction with the procedure. In contrast, AFT has perhaps two score or so effective collective-bargaining contracts.

As for sanctions compared with a few notable cases of teachers' strikes, it can easily be concluded that strikes are by all odds the more effective. At least they appear to be quick, dramatic, and sure-fire. But this is the short-range view. Sanctions certainly do not work so quickly or dramatically, but they do work, and there are reasons for believing that they are more effective and more lasting.

Some examples follow.

Sanctions in North College Hill, Ohio in 1949 got complete results within 24 hours after they were invoked.

In Waterbury, Connecticut, the threat of sanctions was instrumental in getting a completely satisfactory settlement within a period of two months.

In Little Lake, California partial sanctions took two years to work, but they resulted in correction of the conditions about which teachers were dissatisfied and in the defeat of all offending school-board members.

The Duval Teachers Association, Duval County, Florida on October 21, 1965, declared five sanctions against the Duval County Budget Commission, which had consistently cut back the budget request of the board of education. The action of the DTA so aroused citizens of the county that virtually every civic and tax-payer group joined forces with the teachers. Within a month the voters had approved an extra 10-mill levy for the schools, and the budget commission reversed its position, restoring almost all the things previously cut.

Similar dramatic results were secured by the Dade County (Miami) Classroom Teachers Association by invoking sanctions against the county board of education in the spring of 1965.

In Utah, partial sanctions (applied only to teachers outside the state accepting employment in Utah) had no immediately discernible effect. The teachers had to go to the polls to assure victory for sanctions after 400 days of application. However, quietly and behind the scenes, sanctions were hurting. It is reliably reported that many industries refused to consider locating factories in the state while sanctions were outstanding. The extent of the impact is implied in the threat of the Utah Chamber of Commerce to go to the courts to compel NEA to lift the sanctions. The governor of Oklahoma in August 1965 voiced a similar threat. In the Oklahoma case some 150 days were required to win the case for teachers.

Frankly, not enough time has elapsed to demonstrate the real power of sanctions. On the basis of the evidence at hand at the moment, the impartial observer would have to conclude that the strike appears to be the better weapon. But from the long-range view, there is stronger evidence on the other side. The so-called short strike is effective, sometimes, as one day's expedient settlement. But generally it results in no real and lasting solutions.

Scars and bitterness are the inevitable aftermath of strikes and alter the search for solid, continuing curative answers. This is indicated by the fact that strikes recur and recur, and with each recurrence gulfs are widened and real solutions fade into bitterness and recrimination. In time, school districts will come to fear sanctions a great deal more. Why? Because the invoking of sanctions, with deliberation and calmness, after exhaustive, objective, and fair studies, says to the world that a great profession has judged the educational conditions of a given district as woefully inadequate and a cheating of children. No community wants such censure. The district can withstand the overt often unilateral bias of a summarily called strike. Often in such cases public opinion is on the side of the school board. However, sanctions, if invoked only after deliberation and study, will win virtually without exception. They will win because they will appeal to the good conscience of good people. That is really the great power of sanctions. But it is a power to be reckoned with.

The President of AFT, has used the examples of Utah, in which NEA invoked sanctions, and East St. Louis, in which the AFT local used the strike, to demonstrate the alleged superiority of union tactics. (See *Phi Delta Kappan,* September 1964.)

He refers to a four-day strike of the East St. Louis teachers in May 1964 which resulted in a 6 per cent raise in salary for the 1964–65 school year. Subsequently, the school board granted (without the threat of a strike) a 10 per cent raise to nonteaching personnel (janitors, cafeteria workers, and so on). Incensed by this more liberal treatment of the nonteaching group, the local AFT unit demanded that their increase be raised to 10 per cent. The Board refused, so in September 1964 the local staged another strike which also lasted four days. The board agreed to increase the raise an additional 4 per cent—to the 10 per cent granted nonteaching personnel— "if funds are available."

Then the union demanded that the striking teachers be paid for the four days they were out in May and the four days they were out in September. The board refused.

Next, presumably in an effort to assure that funds would be available from state aid for the raise, the AFT local demanded that the board record that the children of the district had been in attendance during the eight days the schools were closed because of the strike. This plea was made, the union said, to preserve the perfect attendance records of many children. The board, of course, refused to falsify the records.

Let's look at this "overwhelming victory" of the East St. Louis local. Assuming that the average salary in that district was $6,000 (about the national average), the 6 per cent raise gained by the first strike there added $360 to the year's salary. The second four-day strike added another $240, making a total of $600 for the year. But the eight days' pay the teachers lost while on strike cost them $266, leaving a net gain for the year of $334 or $1.85 per day, for the 180-day school year, "if funds are available."

This is another example of the questionable logic of the union's claim, "After all, what is a short strike? The children get an unexpected holiday, it's all over after a day or two, with a great victory in the bag for the union." But, as has been pointed out, not all teachers' strikes are short strikes, and whether short or not they are usually followed by subsequent strikes—as in the case of East St. Louis. Apparently, the strike gets to be a heady wine, with a taste of power which some teachers' union leaders cannot resist.

There is good evidence that, in the long-range view, sanctions are the most powerful weapon any profession has. And for so sensitive an institution as public education, the effectiveness of sanctions is much greater than the effectiveness of the strike, for the basic reason that the power of sanctions resides in public opinion and public action. So powerful are sanctions that they should be used by the teaching profession with the greatest of care.

To safeguard the use of sanctions against hasty, ill considered, unfair or arbitrary use, the teaching profession should seek to invoke them as the expression of the total profession, not as the expression of a small segment so close to a given local situation that it cannot separate itself from biased considerations.

Myron Lieberman has provided an interesting rationalization of the "short strike philosophy":

> Actually, students can (and do) learn as much or more when we reduce the amount of time they normally spend in class or in school. The amount of time many students spend in school is more a reflection of custodial than the educational functions of our schools.[13]

In summary, the teachers' unions have to use the strike, though it is illegal, because there simply is no other weapon to which they can resort. The professional associations can use the traditional weapon of professions (sanctions) because they possess the cluster of essential ingredients. The teachers unions do not.

6

Professional Negotiation and Sanctions

> The California Teachers Association has lifted professional sanctions against the Little Lake City School District. . . . The reason is that the new school board has re-established good personnel relationship with the teachers of the district. . . .
>
> We, at the time, editorially took exception to this means (sanctions) of coercing an elected school board into altering its personnel policies.
>
> However, in retrospect, it seems that such a means of settling a long-standing problem is preferable to relying on a strike, which is advocated by one teachers' organization.
>
> No schools were closed, no educations were interrupted. Instead, the voters of the district, made aware of the differences between the board and the teachers, elected new board members who have worked to evolve a more understanding personnel policy with the employees.
>
> We feel that the responsibility of curriculum and employment rests with the board. But we also believe that professional teachers must have some recourse if they have a board that is dictatorial and not amenable to discussing differences.
>
> —*San Gabriel Valley Tribune*[1]

Any general organization of teachers must have the will and the processes to protect its members from mistreatment and to further their welfare.

Concurrently, there must be the will and the machinery to further the professional growth of the members and to contribute to the continual improvement of education.

In connection with the first, the NEA has sometimes been pictured as a paper tiger, and AFT a fearsome lion.

What is the true picture?

The answers depend upon many factors, but mostly upon what each has at its disposal—especially what the power-obsessed would call the weapons, the firepower.

AFT and its affiliates have chosen a close alliance with organized labor as represented by AFL–CIO. NEA and its affiliates have chosen to retain their independent status, rejecting all outside alliances.

The AFT has chosen collective bargaining, in the labor connotation, as the means of dealing with teacher-school board relationships. Although until the New York strikes it had not deliberately chosen the use of the strike as a weapon for teachers, this is the one weapon the AFT has at hand in case of an impasse over collective bargaining. After the New York experiences it openly condoned the strike, and its 1963 convention openly advocated use of the strike "under certain circumstances." And in 1966 AFT was apparently calling for more and more strikes to improve its image of bold militancy.

The NEA has deliberately rejected both collective bargaining and strikes and has stood for professional negotiation to determine teacher-school board relationships and the settlement of impasses through educational channels. As a weapon in extreme circumstances, professional sanctions were chosen as official policy, not the strike.

That confusion and argument have ensued regarding the full meaning of each set of procedures is natural. It is also natural that the two are equated in the minds of many. Newspaper reporters and editors (especially editors) profess to see no difference between collective bargaining and professional negotiation. They are even more adamant in insisting that there is no real difference between a teachers' strike and the withdrawal of services contemplated as the ultimate form of sanctions. Likewise, many, perhaps most, school-board members have been led to believe that the differences are marginal and that the NEA is simply trying to "outunion the unions." It will be helpful to examine some of the facts in the origin and development of professional negotiation and examine also the realistic differences.

What are the differences, if any?

Arthur Corey, Executive Secretary of the California Teachers Association, in a speech at the NEA Denver Convention in 1962 attacked both collective bargaining and the strike as inappropriate for use by teachers:

> To strike or not to strike is no longer an academic question. . . .
>
> An added fact which emphasizes the importance of this issue is the inescapable connection between collective bargaining and the strike as an ultimate weapon. The term *collective bargaining* is being used very loosely by people who are either ignorant of the facts or who deliberately seek to confuse the public and the teaching profession through misrepresentation. Those who piously say that they are for "collective bargaining" but against the strike are engaging in legalistic double talk. A large body of law, both statute and precedential, has given the term *collective bargaining* a legal meaning which inescapably ties the strike into the process. No matter how much sheep's clothing we wrap around the wolf, the fangs are still present under the masquerade. The present widespread discussion of collective bargaining for teachers, if honest and forthright, finally turns on the question: Should teachers strike? The strike, as a weapon

> for attaining economic and professional ends by teachers, is first, inappropriate; second, unprofessional; third, illegal; fourth, outmoded; and fifth, ineffective.
> ... to strike is unprofessional. Oliver Wendell Holmes, speaking to a group of young doctors in 1858, said: "A physician's first duty is to his patient; his second, only to himself. All quackery reverses this principle as its fundamental axiom. Every practitioner who reverses it is a quack."[2]

If these instrumentalities of collective bargaining and the strike are to be rejected by teachers, what recourse do they have to improve their working conditions or to correct conditions which have become intolerable?

On this question Corey stated:

> The relinquishment of the strike does not mean that teachers will tolerate a continuation of the *status quo* in many communities in which they come to the board of education as mendicants and, like beggars, give humble thanks for the largesse of their superiors. Teachers no longer accept the concept that those who serve children must be subservient or that devotion demands obsequiousness. It should be stipulated that if employer-employee relations in a school system are to rise above the concept of beggar and king, the employing body must voluntarily limit its own authority by adoption of procedures which grant dignity and stature to teacher organizations.[3]

Here Corey is obviously referring to professional negotiation, although he does not use the term. Subsequently, he suggested professional sanctions as the recourse for teachers in cases of unacceptable or intolerable conditions.

Corey's speech at Denver gave rise (without his intending it) to the notion that the NEA was, sheeplike, following the promptings of the California Teachers Association. *Time* magazine so stated in an article about the Denver Convention; several newspapers, including some in California, have drawn this inference; and some executives of state education associations have grumbled about this alleged fact. It would, of course, be naive to contend that any procedures of its largest affiliate have no impact on NEA policies. In fact, of course, they do, but not to the extent that the UFT in New York City has affected the AFT. The truth is that the process had been evolving for some time.

As early as 1947 the annual meeting of the National Association of Secretaries of State Teachers Associations (NASSTA) had considered a resolution on professional negotiation.

Actually, the NEA Representative Assembly considered a proposed resolution on what later came to be known as professional negotiation at its Los Angeles Convention in 1957. But the delegates were not at that time ready for so drastic a step. Too, there had been several formal agreements during the 1950's, notably in Connecticut, entered into between school boards and professional associations.

Furthermore, the basic statement on professional negotiation, a statement which a subcommittee of the board had worked on for two years, was adopted by the NEA Board of Directors in 1960. The only significant changes made in that statement at Denver were (1) categorical rejection of the use of labor techniques for settlement of school-staff problems, (2) a demand for the legal right of teachers to negotiate with boards of education regarding development of policies under which they work, and (3) a demand for an appeals procedure in case of an impasse. The statement on professional negotiation adopted at Denver was a revision of the board's original statement. In fact, certain NEA staff members began work on suggestions for revision after the first New York City strike. It had become clear that there was abroad in the land a new climate of restiveness among teachers, and that they were not going to be satisfied with the philosophical statement of the board.

Definition of Professional Negotiation

Almost immediately after adoption of the resolution on professional negotiation by the NEA Representative Assembly at the Denver Convention in the summer of 1962, there was a widespread assumption that this was NEA's counterpart for collective bargaining. There were charges that the NEA was trying to emulate the unions. Cries of anguish and lament arose particularly from school boards and administrators. Newspapers delighted in equating collective bargaining and professional negotiation as precisely the same thing, with the exception that the NEA had adopted a softer name for its process. Teachers' unions sneeringly called the process collective begging. These reactions generally ignored President Kennedy's directive assuring negotiation rights to Federal employees. In retrospect, it is probable that had some other term been used, such as *cooperative determination*, the union connotation could have been avoided or ameliorated. Perhaps not.

Are the two the same?

Decidedly not. But there are, of course, obvious similarities, and obvious borrowings from the older, established process of collective bargaining.

Professional negotiation is not, basically, a new process, except perhaps in name. Enlightened school districts have for years involved their total professional staffs in the determination of personnel policies and other conditions of work. Not only has the NEA advocated this, but so have the American Association of School Administrators and the National School Boards Association, as reflected in official statements of these bodies.

Simply defined, professional negotiation is an orderly process by which a school board and staff enter into an agreement to meet and discuss mutual problems and policies, put their agreements in writing, and provide for an appeals procedure in cases of impasse.

As has been previously stated, certain members of the NEA staff and many members of the association had become convinced during the period 1960–62, partly as the result of the New York City teacher strikes but largely as the result of changed conditions and changed teacher attitudes in the urban areas, that the NEA had to assume a more aggressive posture if it hoped to serve effectively the organizational needs of teachers. The first effort in this direction was the appointment of a special committee by the NEA Board of Directors in 1960 to develop a position statement for submission to the 1961 NEA Representative Assembly in Atlantic City. The substantive portions of the resolution, adopted by the assembly in 1961, state;

> The National Education Association believes, therefore, that professional education associations should be accorded the right, through democratically selected representatives using appropriate professional channels, to participate in the determination of policies of common concern, including salary and other conditions for professional service.
>
> The seeking of consensus and mutual agreement on a professional basis should *preclude the arbitrary exercise of unilateral authority by boards of education and the use of the strike by teachers as a means for enforcing economic demands.*

This has been called a weasel statement. It has been said that the phraseology is ambiguous; perhaps the real meaning is: ". . . *should* preclude the arbitrary exercise of unilateral authority by school boards and the use of the strike by the teachers for economic reasons." (The phrase *use of the strike*, was deleted at the New York Convention in July 1965.)

During the 1961–62 school year, many NEA members in the urban centers and staff members directly concerned with salary and working conditions became convinced that the 1961 resolution was inadequate. Consequently, the staffs of the NEA Office of Professional Development and Welfare and the newly established Urban Project worked out a proposed resolution for the 1962 NEA Representative Assembly. This proposed resolution was submitted to the NEA Resolutions Committee at Denver. Proposed resolutions from individual NEA members and affiliated associations were also submitted for consideration. The committee developed from the several proposals the following resolution for submission to the representative assembly:

> The teaching profession has the ultimate aim of providing the best possible education for all the people. It is a professional calling and a public trust. Boards of education have the same aim and share this trust.
>
> The National Education Association calls upon boards of education in all school districts to recognize their identity of interest with the teaching profession.
>
> The National Education Association insists on the right of professional associations, through democratically selected representatives using professional channels, to participate with boards of education in the determination of policies of common concern, including salary and other conditions of professional service.
>
> Recognizing both the legal authority of boards of education and the educational competencies of the teaching profession, the two groups should view the consideration of matters of mutual concern as a joint responsibility.
>
> The seeking of consensus and mutual agreement on a professional basis

should preclude the arbitrary exercise of unilateral authority by boards of education and the use of the strike by teachers.

The Association believes that procedures should be established which provide an orderly method for professional education associations and boards of education to reach mutually satisfactory agreements. These procedures should include provisions for appeal through designated educational channels when agreement cannot be reached.

Under no circumstances should the resolution of differences between professional associations and boards of education be sought through channels set up for handling industrial disputes. The teacher's situation is completely unlike that of an industrial employee. A board of education is not a private employer, and a teacher is not a private employee. Both are public servants. Both are committed to serve the common, indivisible interest of all persons and groups in the community in the best possible education for their children. Teachers and boards of education can perform their indispensable functions only if they act in terms of their identity of purpose in carrying out this commitment. Industrial-disputes conciliation machinery, which assumes a conflict of interest and a diversity of purpose between persons and groups, is not appropriate to professional negotiation in public education.

The National Education Association calls upon its members and upon boards of education to seek state legislation and local board action which clearly and firmly establishes these rights for the teaching profession.[4]

This was a clear rejection of collective bargaining as defined by labor and an adoption of negotiation as an alternative; yet it is not a no-strike declaration except as implied in the rejection of collective bargaining. The big difference in this and the 1961 resolution is the demand that the legal right of teachers to negotiate with school boards regarding salaries and other working conditions be established by state legislation and local board action.

The adoption of the resolution on professional sanctions was unexpected. The NEA staff had presented this proposal to its resolutions committee, but the proposal did not clear that committee. Only after Carey's explosive speech was it decided to introduce the sanctions proposal from the floor. The sponsors had correctly gauged the temper of the convention, and the resolution was adopted virtually without dissent. Without Carey's needling, it is doubtful that it would even have been introduced.

The sanctions resolution, involving enforcement weapons in intolerable situations, reads as follows:

The National Education Association believes that, as a means for preventing unethical or arbitrary policies or practices that have a deleterious effect on the welfare of the schools, professional sanctions should be invoked. These sanctions would provide for appropriate disciplinary action by the organized profession.

The National Education Association calls upon its affiliated state associations to cooperate in developing guidelines which would define, organize, and definitely specify procedural steps for invoking sanctions by the teaching profession.

The demand for legal rights to professional negotiation stemmed from the threat of AFL–CIO-sponsored laws in several states (notably in Michigan,

Minnesota, and Wisconsin) which, in one way or another, in one degree or another, made it possible for teachers to become embroiled in labor processes and machinery. While the preponderence of professional negotiation agreements doubtless will be made legal by action of local school boards rather than by state legislation, the NEA did develop a proposed model law to be used by state education associations as they saw fit in attempting to secure state-wide legislation. In 1965, the move for state legislation by professional associations began to emerge. Such a move was inevitable under pressures of the drive of AFL–CIO to enact laws that will mandate or make permissible teacher participation in labor-sponsored processes.

The National School Boards Association and the American Association of School Administrators (an independent department of the NEA), both long-time, staunch allies of teachers' professional associations, were unhappy over these developments. The first reactions were angry charges that the NEA and its affiliated state and local associations were aping the unions. But the fact was that, by the pressures of events and the evolutionary process of human rights, a new era in school-staff relationships had come into being. No individual or group had wilfully planned it this way. It all came to pass in the sequence of time.

The American Association of School Administrators has adopted the following resolution:

> We believe that there are common goals and interests among teachers, school boards, and administrators. We further believe that the development of school policies and programs and the solution of school problems can best be accomplished by these groups working in unison and with respect for the unique roles of each.
>
> Efforts to superimpose a pattern of staff relations borrowed from another segment of society, whether through legislative fiat or staff election, will do major harm to the basic unity of our profession and should be resisted vigorously. We therefore support the concept that shared responsibility for policy development and program development is a professional concept requiring a uniquely professional approach.[5]

The National School Boards Association adopted in 1963 this resolution:

> The efforts of teacher unions to obtain collective bargaining rights and the activities and programs of professional teacher organizations calling for professional negotiations and sanctions will have significant effect upon the operation of our public schools in the years ahead. The National School Boards Association is opposed to sanctions, boycotts, strikes, or mandated mediation against school districts and does not consider them to be proper remedies for use in problem situations. The authority of the board of education is established by law and this authority may not be delegated to others. . . .[6]

The remainder of this resolution simply restated NSBA's determination to retain the *status quo* in staff relationships, calling upon its member boards to fight enactment of state legislation that would alter existing procedures.

The NSBA resolution was a flat rejection of both collective bargaining and professional negotiation as well as their means of enforcement, strikes and sanctions. This categorical and negative position of NSBA was not changed until 1966.

Apprehension over the 1962 NEA professional-negotiation resolution arose because of two new ingredients: the demand for the legal right of teachers to negotiate and the demand for means of resolving impasses. Of course the adoption of the resolution on professional sanctions really inflamed the apprehension. Coming upon the heels of the New York City strikes and the aggressive drive for collective bargaining by teachers' unions, the negotiation and sanctions resolutions which were passed in Denver clinched the notion in the minds of many that the NEA had come up with a package which simulated the labor approach.

Why was the legal right of teachers to negotiate demanded in the resolution?

It may be surmised that this arose from two considerations: first, that the process already in operation informally in many school districts needed only to be formalized and adopted by local boards to make it legal. Second, that the impact of the New York City situation and the inroads of labor-sponsored legislation forced teachers into the labor machinery to some degree in at least three states. These, plus the threat of still further inroads of such legislation as a part of the announced drive by labor to organize teachers, forced the NEA and the state associations to advocate legal means of keeping negotiations within educational channels.

There were other considerations: if teachers were to renounce the strike, there had to be legal recognition of their right to negotiate. Moreover, there had to be legal recourse when an impasse with a school board developed.

Subsequent to the 1962 NEA convention, efforts of labor in several states[7] to push for collective bargaining legislation for all public employees made it obvious that if the NEA hoped to keep teachers' problems within educational channels and out of labor laws and machinery, legal alternatives had to be the answer. A negative posture was not enough; positive response was indicated.

Laws sponsored by the AFL–CIO for public employees, including teachers, were passed in Massachusetts and Rhode Island in 1966, and the existing legislation in Michigan was amended in 1965, pushing teachers farther into labor procedures.

However, in 1965 state education associations in California, Connecticut, Florida, Minnesota, New Jersey, Oregon, and Washingtom secured passage of professional-negotiation laws for teachers. The acts for such laws passed by the legislatures of Minnesota and New Jersey were vetoed by their governors. As previously pointed out, New York, Nebraska and Texas enacted legislation in 1967.

The denunciation of sanctions as just the strike under another name is less than realistic. Sanctions, as officially endorsed by NEA in 1962 , were neither new nor radical.

The NEA had been involved, prior to Denver, in three cases of sanctions in the school districts of North College Hill, Ohio; Kelso, Washington; and Polson, Montana. Also, there has been several cases in which state associations invoked sanctions. In all, these cases of sanctions had been extremely effective. Professional sanctions have been effective (1) because they have been applied rarely, only in extreme situations, (2) because they have been applied only after careful investigations have revealed subminimal educational conditions, (3) because virtually without exception the people of the community involved have been shocked by the revealed conditions and have demanded a housecleaning, and (4) because members of the profession have supported the ban.

Actually, sanctions of one type or another have been applied and supported informally by the state education associations and the NEA for years. And in higher education, sanctions of one kind or another have been widely used for many years.

Principles of Professional Negotiation

The basic principles involved in professional negotiation are these:

1. That the board of education recognize teaching as a profession and the local teachers' organization as the representative of its members.
2. That education associations are professional channels to discuss matters of common concern.
3. That education-association representatives and boards of education meet and exchange views.
4. That each in good faith listen to the views of the other and take the other's views into consideration in coming to a decision, and that both negotiate matters on which they do not at first agree.
5. That a procedure be set up to deal with an impasse.
6. That decisions leading to adoption of policy be jointly determined by the association representatives and the school board with, when necessary, the assistance of other educational agencies.

The notion of an appeals procedure upset school-board members on the grounds that this would rob them of their legal authority to make final decisions affecting the operation of schools. Some superintendents were apprehensive that the legalizing of teachers' participation in the development of policies would infringe upon the superintendents' prerogatives.

There are complex problems involved in providing such participation of teachers. What is the role of the superintendent? He is a member of the professional staff and a professional adviser of the board. While he wears two hats, he is neither the board's man exclusively nor the professional staff's man exclusively. He is in the middle, and this is a difficult role. It is still to be determined whether he can, in fact, serve both roles. Quite naturally, some superintendents saw in the professional-negotiation concept an effort to bypass them. It is still to be determined what the role of the superintendent is to be. Many school-board members contend that he is exclusively the board's man. This viewpoint—which is precisely the AFT viewpoint in the private industry-labor context—if fully implemented, will tend to drive superintendents out of the general professional associations or take from them the right to vote, at least at the local level. After the Utah impasse in May 1964, editorials in Utah papers demanded that superintendents and principals withdraw from the UEA. But they did not. In Michigan, in 1966, the superintendents association withdrew from affiliation with the Michigan Education Association.

What is the role of the board of education? It has the legal authority for decision-making. And it is obvious that some boards interpret this authority in such an arbitrary way as to deny participation of the staff in policy-making. The assumption that staff participation would mean a surrendering of the board's legal authority is a little far-fetched. Professional negotiation is participation in policy development. It is not policy adoption. That is the function of the board. It is not policy administration. That is the function of the superintendent. But arbitrary and unilateral exercise of either the board's powers or the superintendent's powers is unwise and unwarranted.

One is compelled to put this problem of negotiation within the context of what a profession is and what the rights of a profession are. In other words, the problem must be placed in the context of the true meaning of professional autonomy—the right of a profession to manage its own concerns.

The controls of a profession are aimed at better service to society through enforcement of standards which will guarantee the competence and ethical performance of its members. There can never be a profession in the real sense until society is willing to grant to a professional group the right largely to manage its own affairs, set and enforce standards for admission and continued service in it, and to discipline its own membership.

With such rights a profession is obligated to guarantee to society the competence of those permitted to begin practice. But this is not enough. It must also guarantee a work climate that will keep them in practice and functioning at the highest possible level. Professional autonomy, therefore, would imply also the right to participate in prescribing the standards or policies with reference to working conditions. Professional negotiation, then, properly conceived, is at the heart of professional autonomy. The fact that teaching is a public profession in large degree does not alter the principle. But the fact does mandate that there be close checks and balances, and it does mandate withdrawing or reducing such rights if they are abused or used in a selfish, monopolistic manner.

George Bernard Shaw once defined a profession as "a conspiracy against the laity." This harsh appraisal could be true if adequate checks and balances are not imposed by society. Doubtless, there have been cases in which exploitation of the public has occurred.

There is another and perhaps more significant reason for teacher participation in policy development. This has to do with the increased effectiveness with which people perform when they are accorded such participation. Not only do they tend to assume responsibility for making policies work, but each individual tends to perform at a higher level of productivity.

There is considerable evidence that teacher morale is dependent to a greater degree upon enlightened personnel policies than upon salaries. Frederick Redefer has made available the conclusions of several doctoral dissertations and other studies made over a period of seven years by 50 graduate students, involving 50 school systems and 10,000 teachers. His study confirms the thesis that personnel policies are the primary determinant of good or poor relations between teachers and their school boards and administrators. He states that most school boards and administrators, unlike leaders of industry, have largely ignored staff relations and communications. With respect to the role of the administrators, Redefer's study concludes that "unless personnel administration releases the potential of a staff to achieve the goals of education, it is neither efficient nor effective in the education of students."[8]

Summary of Distinctions

The Minnesota Education Association, plagued with confusions about collective bargaining and professional negotiation, distributed to teachers the following analysis of conditions and law in that state:

1. Collective bargaining operates under labor law and is administered, when necessary, by the labor department of government. Also, collective bargaining is a specific labor term that has a statutory meaning developed through the years of legislative implementation.
2. Collective bargaining determines the organization which will represent the employees on the basis of an election rather than on the basis of membership. In Minnesota, the State Labor Conciliator has already tried to make such determinations in local elections involving teachers. The Minnesota State Supreme Court has held that he may not do so for teachers.
3. Collective bargaining assumes monopoly of representation within a bargaining unit. The Minnesota Supreme Court has held that exclusive representation for teachers is illegal.
4. Collective bargaining recognizes the right of any group of employees with

similar interest and similar duties to bargain separately with the employer. The Minnesota Supreme Court upheld the position of the MEA in the Richfield case that a school district is a single unit and cannot be fragmented. The teachers union supported fragmentation which is contrary to effective unified negotiations for salary on the part of the teachers.

5. Collective bargaining bars all administrative and supervisory personnel from participation in the bargaining procedures. Principals, supervisors, guidance people, and anyone other than a classroom teacher would be barred from any participation in salary negotiation affecting themselves. This is part of the fragmentation.
6. Collective bargaining bypasses the normal administrative machinery of the enterprise involved. This means that teachers would no longer have the assistance of their superintendent and other administrative personnel in promoting a satisfactory salary climate in the school system.
7. Collective bargaining assumes the right of employees to strike and picket as an inherent part of the process. Any attempt to suggest a collective bargaining procedure without the strike is double talk. Teachers may not strike by law, and this is true of all public employees.
8. Collective bargaining assumes that a written contract covering all items negotiated and a specific period of time will be entered into by the employer and the representatives of the employees. This arrangement is specifically prohibited by Minnesota law.

Most teachers have no interest in the collective bargaining process. They would be deeply disturbed if labor at the state or national level were to begin to administer school policies or establish regulations for teachers. What is sometimes not understood by teachers is the fact that the terminology of labor bargaining is used out of context and confused with professional salary negotiation procedures.

Professional Negotiation Contrasted with Collective Bargaining

Professional negotiation uses education channels for appeals where an impasse occurs; collective bargaining uses labor channels.

Professional negotiation includes all members of the professional staff and does not distinguish between superintendents and teachers; collective bargaining assumes an inevitable conflict of interest.

Professional negotiation removes the teacher from the operation of labor laws and precedents; collective bargaining uses labor law and precedents.

Professional negotiation permits all personnel to negotiate as one unit; collective bargaining fragments; schools might need a special official or department of labor relations to handle the red tape.

Professional negotiation maintains the school administrator in his dual role of teacher and board executive; collective bargaining makes him an agent of management thereby blocking a channel of communication. If the superintendent remains strictly on the sidelines, he is abdicating his leadership in the profession.

The reasons why collective bargaining in the labor sense is not appropriate for public-school teachers, and why new procedures must be evolved has been described by the chairman of the American Bar Association Committee on Law of Government Employee Relations.

> One of the essentials of bargaining in private industry is that management have power to make binding commitments in respect to economic and other matters affecting the terms and conditions of employment, and having made such commitments, the ability to make them good. The management of governmental enterprise frequently lacks such authority. Its financial resources are determined by some other organ of government and, since it is not marketing a service or producing a product, the price of which it may adjust in order to increase revenues, bargaining over many matters may be an illusory exercise.[9]

Professional Sanctions

The use of sanctions, too, is an integral part of the drive for professional autonomy. Within the framework of the law, but in addition to direct and specific legal prescriptions—because the law generally assumes that profession themselves must, in large part, enforce certain requirements to assure maximum services to society—all professions must have a weapon to carry out policy consensus of their membership. This weapon is professional sanctions. It really is not a weapon but the moral force of unanimity or near-unanimity of conviction. Webster's New Collegiate Dictionary defines the term *sanction* as "a means, often in the form of a declaration, which induces observance of law or custom by impelling its object toward moral action through imposition of a detriment, loss of reward, or other intervention."

As applied to education, sanctions may be used to bring about the improvement of undesirable conditions, to assure fair treatment of staff members, and to provide an adequate educational program. Sanctions do not always require positive action. More often their power derives from the mere possibility or threat of concerted action. In any event, sanctions seek to reflect the will of the total profession. Sometimes this will is imposed by intense influencing of opinion within the profession, which has the effect of a strongly held set of mores in a community. Sometimes more direct, positive action is essential.

From the floor of the NEA Representative Assembly at Denver, when the resolution on professional sanctions was being debated, the following uses or purposes of sanctions were suggested:

1. They can express the profession's serious disapproval of unsatisfactory conditions.
2. They can attract the community's attention to specific problems which make quality education difficult or impossible.

3. They can be used to withhold further professional service or support when service or support would be used to continue unacceptable conditions.
4. They are a process through which the corporate profession can protect children from unacceptable educational practices.
5. They are a process through which the profession can protect its members from being forced to contract their services under conditions that are demeaning, compromising, or otherwise intolerable.
6. They are a process through which the profession can protect the public from unknowingly condoning and financing indefensible programs or unacceptable practices in education.
7. They are a process for exerting the profession's influence in areas where it has expertness and should have autonomy.
8. They can be used to protect the public and children against incompetent or unethical practices by members of the profession.
9. They are a device which makes forced acquiescence unnecessary and the strike obsolete.

TYPES OF PROFESSIONAL SANCTIONS. A discussion of the evolution of the idea of sanctions is essential to an understanding of their meaning. Generally speaking, when the term is used or heard, we think of only one kind of sanction—withdrawal of services, which many equate with the strike. There are, in fact, several types of sanctions that can be used by the teaching profession.

Among the first, if not indeed *the* first, type of sanction is accreditation or disaccreditation of schools and colleges. Accreditation, as the term is used in the United States, is the act by a voluntary group or association of putting its stamp of approval on the quality of the educational program of a given school or college. This would not be, or could not be, the case scarcely anywhere else in the world, since central ministries of education would dictate standards leaving nothing to the action of the profession or to voluntary associations.

Accreditation is said to be unique to the United States for this reason. To place the enforcement of standards in a profession or voluntary groups within a profession is one of the marks and one of the great strengths of a free society in which pluralism is cherished. Thus, when a high school, college, or university fails to become accredited, a sanction has been negatively applied, in effect denying transfer of credit or validation for licensure. On the other hand, when accreditation is granted, a powerful positive sanction has been set in motion resulting in the recognition of the quality of an educational program and the validation of credentials from the particular institution for transfer, graduate work, or licensure.

Disaccreditation, therefore, is one of the most powerful sanctions a professional group can employ. A popular argument is that no outside agency has any right to interfere in the affairs of a school district, the schools of a state, or of a college or cluster of colleges. These, it is argued, should be under local control. This argument ignores the possibility of violation by local authorities of normal procedures which often become intolerable and which often only an outside power can rectify.

For example, about two decades ago in Georgia and Mississippi the incumbent governors made political footballs of the state university systems, violating every vestige of academic freedom, hiring and firing professors on a political basis. The citizens of the two states were powerless (at least until the next election) to institute remedial measures because the action of the governors were within the limits of state laws.

The Southern Association of Colleges and Secondary Schools invoked the sanction of disaccreditation on the university systems of the two states. When it dawned upon the people that their children could not transfer credit, that they were the victims of cynical partisan politics, they were shocked into action. In Georgia, in the subsequent race for the governorship, the candidate who pledged to restore accreditation and to refrain from interference with the state's higher education institutions was elected.

Similar cases also developed in Oklahoma and North Dakota, where the North Central Association of Colleges and Secondary Schools had jurisdiction. These were cases in which an outside influence gave the people of each state a powerful recourse for rectifying unsatisfactory conditions.

A second type of sanction has to do with the disciplining of the professions' own membership. A profession that seeks autonomy must guarantee competence of its members. But it must do more than this—it must guarantee ethical conduct of its members. There are two steps in such a guarantee. One is the creation of a code of ethics and the acceptance of that code as a condition of membership. The second step is to provide machinery for disciplining those few members who violate the code. The penalties for violation are censure or reprimand, suspension for a period of at least one year, and expulsion (permanent unless the offender is reinstated).

A "Code of Ethics for the Education Profession" was developed by the NEA Ethics Committee and approved by the NEA Representative Assembly in Detroit in 1963. By 1965, all of the state education associations had adopted the code and it is expected that in time this will be the universally accepted code of the teaching profession. In the past there has been a multitude of ethical codes. Virtually every teachers' association had developed its own; hence there was no one code to which all subscribed and were subject to. Acceptance of this code has been made a prerequisite to NEA membership.

It is frequently charged that NEA has never disciplined its members, the expulsion from membership of the superintendent of the Chicago schools in 1940 being the only such case on record. With adherence to the one code, however, this inaction is ending. A member was expelled in 1962, and three were disciplined by the NEA Executive Committee at Detroit in 1963. The

NEA Ethics Committee is now vigorously following up cases of alleged violations referred to it. And the committee and the NEA Commission on Professional Rights and Responsibilities are pressing vigorously for enforcement machinery in state and local associations.

Also in 1965 an amendment to the NEA by-laws was adopted shifting responsibility from the NEA Executive Committee to the Ethics Committee for holding hearings on code violations and fixing the punishment of violators. The former will review decisions of the Ethics Committee and serve to hear appeals. This change should expedite cases involving alleged violations of the code.

A third cluster of sanctions is suggested in the New Horizons Project report,[10] which recommends that professional and legal sanctions, based upon graduation from an institution accredited by the National Council for Accreditation of Teacher Education (NCATE), be used as a basis for interstate reciprocity in teacher certification. This principle has been adopted by about 30 states.

The significance of this sanction is often missed. Without some such yardstick the free movement of teachers across state lines is fraught with many minor obstacles and petty irritations. Each state has its own certification requirements, often in rather precise terms of specific courses and hours. Thus a well-qualified teacher in one state, a graduate of a superior college or university, might be denied certification in another state or at best be accepted with deficiences to be made up by completing additional courses simply because the precise requirements of the receiving state were not met. The sanction of NCATE accreditation enables such deficiencies to be waived on the assumption that the migrating teacher has met superior standards of preparation regardless of the variations in courses completed from the prescriptions of the receiving state.

Another sanction advocated for the future is that priority in licensure and employment be given to graduates of NCATE-accredited institutions. A proposed sanction of great import is that, in time, admission to membership in professional associations be based upon this prerequisite. This priority for graduates of NCATE-accredited institutions is already a prerequisite for membership in the American Association of School Administrators.

These sanctions are powerful weapons, and many in education recoil from contemplation of such powers being vested in the teaching profession. Yet these powers are exercised by virtually all other professions. Some abuse of them has resulted, but in general they are accepted by the public as valid and reasonable, as means of guaranteeing competent practitioners and improved service to society.[11]

WITHHOLDING THE SERVICES OF TEACHERS. A fourth type of sanction—the one that is often mistakenly equated with the strike—is the withdrawal of service by teachers to a given school district. There are several steps or degrees involved in this sanction.

The first and mildest is the publicizing by the professional association of a current dispute between presently employed teachers and the district or the publicizing of unsatisfactory conditions which tend to prevent teaching services of professional caliber. This is simply an advisement to local and state associations, to teachers and to placement agencies (such as the notice sent out by the NEA in February and November 1963 regarding conditions in the Overseas Dependents' Schools) by which teachers can be alerted to true conditions and can make their own decisions as to whether they would like to seek employment in the district. NEA called this procedure an "Urgent Advisory."

The second step is for the association to request its members employed elsewhere not to seek or accept positions in the offending school district (or state) until and unless the indicated conditions are removed; no such request, however, is made to the teachers presently employed in the district. The next step would be for the association to request both the employed staff and outsiders to boycott the school district. The ultimate step, of course, would be to declare it unethical for either outsiders or current members of the staff, or both, to accept employment in the offending school district. The Connecticut Education Association voted to employ this extreme process in two cases—West Haven in 1958 and Waterbury in 1963—but settlements of the issues occurred before it had to be invoked.

Also, NEA specified in its sanctions against Oklahoma in 1965 that teachers from outside the state *might* be judged guilty of unethical conduct if they accepted positions in the state and *might* be subjected to expulsion from membership.

As a prerequisite to NEA's invoking the sanction of boycotting a school district either by the employed staff or by those teaching elsewhere, a definite procedure must be followed whereby an impartial investigation of the facts reveals conditions of gross injustice to teachers or general conditions which clearly preclude the achievement of adequate educational services to children. The invoking of sanctions is an extremely serious step and utmost care must be taken to avoid hasty or unjustified action or action based on inadequate grounds. Irresponsible use will inevitably destroy the process and emasculate sanctions as a weapon. The procedure must have such integrity that public support will be enlisted when sanctions are invoked.[12]

A question often asked is: What is the difference between the strike and the sanction of withdrawing services? There are several differences. Sanctions do not violate a contract. Services to children are not interrupted. Teachers serve out their contracts for the current school year. Under sanctions, there are no picket lines. Under sanctions, school districts are given several months' notice and told that existing conditions make possible only inferior programs for children, that professional people cannot, under the existing conditions, provide first-rate services. As a general rule, sanctions are made effective in the succeeding school year except in the case of withdrawing extracurricular services. If the people of the district, by their indifference or by direct action, support the inferior conditions, they can doubtless continue some kind of inferior school services. The choice of such inadequate services is theirs, not the profession's.

The Origin and Use of Sanctions

The origin of the idea and initial use of professional sanctions (that is, the withdrawal of services) has been widely attributed to the California Teachers Association. This erroneous concept arose of course from Corey's Denver speech and his description of sanctions invoked by the CTA against the Little Lake School District in September 1961. (The sanctions were, incidentally lifted in February 1964 after the CTA affiliate had won its demands). Also, of course, there was the fact that the term *sanctions* was a new one to most teachers.

Actually, the NEA had invoked sanctions officially in one case and had participated in the invoking of sanctions by state associations in two or three other cases a decade or more before the adoption of the resolution at Denver. Several state associations (Connecticut, Colorado, Washington, Montana, and Ohio, for example) had previously used sanctions against school districts where unsatisfactory conditions were persistent.

Examples of Sanctions

NORTH COLLEGE HILL, OHIO. The first case in which the NEA participated in the invoking of sanctions against a school district was that of the North College Hill, Ohio District in June 1947. This was a joint application of the sanction of withdrawal of members' services by the NEA and the Ohio Education Association.

After a thorough investigation of the turbulent situation in the North College Hill school system, the executive committees of the Ohio Education Association and the NEA issued on June 17, 1947 the following joint statement invoking sanctions against that system:

1. We declare that the attitude of the three majority members of the Board of Education, North College Hill, Ohio, makes that school system one in which no professional teacher can carry on his work efficiently and happily.
2. We call upon all worthy members of the teaching profession to refuse to accept a position in the North College Hill System as long as it remains

under the domination of the present Board of Education majority and until it is clearly evident that it is under the administration of a board of education that observes its primary responsibility for the public schools of the community.

3. We urge that school administrators give preference to applications for positions to the teachers from North College Hill who have set such a fine example of high professional conduct.[13]

On the same day as the declaration of joint sanctions by the OEA and NEA the entire five members of the North College Hill Board of Education resigned. Although the investigation and the sanction declaration condemned only the three majority members, the two minority members offered to resign also in an effort to restore harmony in the school district. Upon the resignation of the board and in accordance with Ohio law the school system came under the control of the probate court until a board election could be held. The court immediately renewed the three-year contract of the school superintendent, who had been dismissed by the board and whose dismissal brought to a head public dissatisfaction with the handling of the school district's affairs by the board. Following this action of the court, the OEA and the NEA immediately lifted the sanctions against the district.

This is believed to be the first application of the sanction of withdrawal of teaching services imposed on a school district by a professional association or associations of teachers.

Dr. Richard B. Kennan, Executive Secretary of the Defense Commission (at that time the NEA investigating body in such cases, now known as the Commission on Professional Rights and Responsibilities) has stated that the sanctions idea came to him while he was wrestling with the problem of taking drastic remedial action to save the school system from disintegration. His belief is that the idea was probably borrowed from the American Association of University Professors as a modification of their "censure of administration" procedure.

Behind the North College Hill case was the sordid injection of sectarian considerations in the management of the affairs of the school district. The problem began with the incorporation of a private school within the public-school system, with the public school leasing the private-school building and placing the religious teachers on the public school payroll. This procedure was declared legal by the state's attorney general. In fact, there were several such examples in Ohio. Although there was serious division in the community over this arrangement, the people apparently were accepting it.

Trouble began in earnest with the election of a majority (three of five) on the board of education who set out upon a course of making decisions along sectarian lines. Gradually, this majority began to usurp the powers of the superintendent in the nomination, selection, and assignment of teachers, ostensibly to give preference to members of their faith. A principal who had been demoted by the superintendent for cause and who was reassigned as a teacher was reinstated as principal by the board (by a vote of three to two), and the superintendent's selection of a replacement was overruled. These actions were protested by the superintendent as a clear usurpation of his legal prerogatives. The board majority pursued the tactic of rejecting the superintendent's nominations, compelling him to make such nominations as they desired, again apparently to select teachers of their faith. Finally the board majority declared that no nominations would be approved until the superintendent submitted all applications to the board for review. The superintendent refused, offering to furnish the board with a list of all applicants by age, preparation, and experience but to reveal nothing else about them. This impasse continued and grew worse as makeshift arrangements had to be made to fill vacancies at the last minute before the opening of school in the fall. The three majority board members finally charged the superintendent with insubordination, and in February 1947, by a vote of three to two, the board declared the superintendent's position vacant as of July 31, 1947 (the termination of the incumbent's contract).

With this board action, rebellion broke loose in the community. Accumulated grievances, suspicions, and animosities became much greater, and resentment against the board majority reached a boiling point. A petition signed by 28 teachers protested the dismissal of the superintendent. High-school students immediately threatened a strike, but were dissuaded by the superintendent.

In March, when the board of education ignored pleas to reinstate the superintendent, some 90 per cent of the students did strike. The high-school students remained out of school for a month, and 400 elementary-school pupils did not return until May 29. There was daily mass picketing of the schools, supported by parents. The teachers and the superintendent, however, remained faithfully at their posts. A petition was circulated among parents requesting reinstatement of the superintendent, and more than 1,100 signed it. The Schools Improvement Association vigorously supported the superintendent. From February on, until the blow-up with the sanction declaration of June 17, school-board meetings were attended by steadily increasing numbers of citizens, reaching about 1,000. Bitterness grew and violence erupted at one meeting when two of the board majority were physically attacked. At the subsequent board meeting, twenty policemen were in attendance to preserve order.

The 28 teachers who in February had sent a petition to the board for reinstatement of the superintendent submitted their resignations, effective at the end of the school year, following the March meeting at which the board refused their request.

Richard Kennan has written his impression of the intolerable situation which had developed in the school district:

> The teachers were going to school each day, but hardly a pupil attended since the parents had arranged for them to be taught in the churches or basement recreation areas. Most of the seniors had been transferred to other nearby high schools, but there was a great deal of worry over whether or not this action would interfere with their being certified for college entrance. At one emotion-packed board meeting, all of the teachers but one had walked to the front of the room and placed their resignations before the President of the Board, the action to take effect at the end of the school year. At another meeting, which had been moved from its usual place to the school gymnasium because of the number of persons in attendance, the board majority had obstinately refused to listen or to accede to requests of parents and citizens. One young man, a veteran of World War II, who was in the group, took two high school girls, who were crying about the situation, by the arm and led them up to the President of the Board and said: "See what you are doing to our students. Why don't you listen to us and change your ways?" The Board President replied: "All I can see is that you are not going to have your way"; whereupon the young veteran vaulted upon the stage and floored the President with one punch. A general riot ensued, requiring police intervention to restore order.[14]

Here is the case of the first invoking of professional sanctions—a case based upon six detailed charges against a disruptive and inflexible board—by the NEA Defense Commission (now the Commission on Professional Rights and Responsibilities). The sanctions were invoked not to enforce teachers' salary demands, as some critics contend is always the case, but because of an intolerable teaching and learning climate in the offending school district.

Thus the belief that the California Teachers Association originated the sanctions idea in the Little Lake School District in 1961 is not well founded. It is true that the NEA Representative Assembly did not officially adopt the technique of sanctions until the summer of 1962, after the Little Lake action. Too, the CTA was probably first in withdrawing placement services to a school district and in seeking to influence other placement agencies to refrain from supplying applicants.

KELSO, WASHINGTON. The second sanctions case in which the NEA was involved was in the Kelso, Washington School District in 1950. The story of the Kelso case in brief was this: A worsening school situation came to a head in March 1950 when 17 teachers and the principals of all five schools in the district (out of a total faculty of 120) were threatened with dismissal, all without cause, due process, or proper notice. Immediately the town was in an uproar, with hundreds of citizens joining the teachers to protest against what they considered an unwarranted attack on teacher morale—and the welfare of education.

The local teachers' association requested an investigation by the Washington Education Association and the NEA Defense Commission. After a careful study of the situation, the joint WEA-NEA investigating committee recommended:

1. The immediate issuance of contracts to teachers and principals.
2. The immediate removal of the superintendent of schools by a leave of absence or otherwise.
3. The employment of a temporary superintendent and the initiation of procedures to secure a permanent successor.
4. The development of programs to improve the educational climate and to secure more cooperative relationships between the board and school personnel.

The board apparently paid little attention to the investigating committee's recommendations. As a result of the apparent indifference of the board, a mass meeting of citizens on April 18 developed petitions requesting reinstatement of the threatened teachers and principals and the resignation of three board members within 72 hours. Furthermore, the Washington Education Association issued a statement declaring that the conditions in the Kelso district were such that no sincere professional person would want to seek employment there.

The School of Education of the State College of Washington (now Washington State University) issued an unprecedented statement on April 25 as follows:

> Since the school board, in general, has seen fit to disregard this fully accredited professional investigating committee, we of the School of Education have taken the position that if requested by the school board, under existing conditions, to recommend a superintendent, we will inform them that until the situation has been cleared by the investigating committee, we cannot make any recommendations for superintendent. . . . [Moreover] the School of Education requests that each candidate who requests his papers to be sent to Kelso be notified of the report of the WEA-NEA Investigating Committee.

This, incidentally, is believed to be the first action taken by a school of education to withhold placement services to a school district under ban of a teachers' professional organization.

On April 4 members of the Kelso Education Association, returned their signed contracts to the school board with a resolution stating reservations under which the contracts were signed. They demanded (1) that the board pledge its adherence to the code of ethics of the State School Directors Association, (b) that the board adopt and put into effect recommendations of the joint WEA-NEA investigating committee, and (3) that the members of the Kelso Education Association reserve the right, if these conditions were not met, to resign at any date prior to July 15, 1950.

Faced with these ultimatums, which had wide support in the community, the school board on April 22, 1950 accepted the recommendations of the joint investigating committee and gave an immediate leave of absence to the superintendent. Thereafter the situation cleared up rapidly. Thus the sanction, merely a mild one, got almost immediate results.[15]

POLSON, MONTANA. The Polson, Montana case was the first in which procedural steps to be followed in applying sanctions to a school district and the criteria for removal of the sanctions were carefully spelled out by a professional teachers' association. The case arose over the summary dismissal of the superintendent, who had served the district for seven years. The board was clearly within its legal right. Under Montana law a superintendent does not have tenure, but he must be notified in writing on or before February 1 of the year in which his contract expires that the contract will not be renewed. This notice was given by the board on January 23. But the unusual circumstances of the dismissal created immediate unrest in the community and apprehension among the teachers. The local teachers' association and the state-wide Congress of Parents and Teachers requested a joint investigation by the Montana Education Association and the NEA.

The investigation resulted in a declaration by the MEA that the board, in dismissing the superintendent, had "created a school crisis wherein doubt and uncertainty are evident among pupils, parents, and teachers of the community. Such an atmosphere makes good teaching difficult if not impossible. Many competent Polson teachers are already planning to seek positions elsewhere. Competent, professional teachers who value their professional futures will not be attracted to Polson."

In today's language this would be probably called an advisory. But it was, in effect, a declaration of application of a sanction. The major significance of this declaration, however, lies in its spelling out of sequential steps in invoking and enforcing sanctions through adoption by the MEA of the following recommendations of the investigating committee:

1. The Montana Education Association should at once make clear to the Board of Education in Polson that they are convinced that until there is a clear improvement in the Board of Education policies and practices resulting in a much better relationship between the Board and the school faculty, the Montana Education Association must conclude that the Polson school system is not a desirable place for competent members of the teaching profession to seek positions.

2. The Montana Education Association should make known immediately to all its own members, to the Montana State Department of Public Instruction, the North Central and Northwest Accrediting Associations, and should alert the state education associations and state departments of education and teacher training institutions of nearby states to the unsatisfactory conditions existing in Polson; and should continue to so alert the profession at regular intervals until the situation is cleared.

3. The criteria for determining the improvement of the Polson situation might include the following tangible evidence . . . [These included such things as the offer of renewal of the superintendent's contract, adoption of a better salary schedule, the opening of board meetings to the public, and replacement of the incumbent members of the board of education.]

Although gradual improvement occurred in Polson, the significance of the situation is not to be found in the improvement but in the spelling out of procedures for disseminating information about the invoking of sanctions against the district and about the existing unsatisfactory conditions. Further, the spelling out indicated to the people of the community the conditions to be met for the lifting of the sanctions.

WEST HAVEN, CONNECTICUT. In the spring of 1958, the Connecticut Education Association invoked what is believed to be the first application of the ultimate form of the sanction: withdrawal of service. In its action, the CEA Executive Committee requested members not already employed there not to apply for or to accept positions in the West Haven School District; furthermore, it declared such actions would be a violation of professional ethics. This type of sanction is generally termed *ultimate* because it implies the possible expulsion from membership in the state education association. Actually, the ultimate action would be to apply this threat to teacher members currently employed in the district as well as to those currently employed elsewhere. It is believed that there is no record of so drastic a case.

In back of this action of the CEA were several years of frustration in adjusting teachers' salaries because of dual control of school-district finances. Or, to state it more definitively, the West Haven Board of Education was not financially independent. It could propose annual budgets subject to the approval or veto of the board of finance of the town. For each of the three years preceding the CEA's invoking of sanctions, the board of education submitted budgets providing substantial increases in teachers' salaries only to have these requests reduced drastically.

In 1957, for example, the board of education proposed a $500 salary increase for each teacher; the board of finance reduced this to $200. In 1958 the school board proposed a $600 increase for each teacher, and the board of finance cut the school budget to the extent that only a $200 raise could be given. At this point, the West Haven teachers considered submitting mass resignations but decided instead to withhold signatures to salary agreements for the ensuing school year. Under Connecticut law, teachers may achieve tenure after three years of service and sign permanent contracts. Tenure teachers are required only to sign annual salary agreements. At the time they voted not to sign the salary agreements, the teachers requested the CEA to boycott the school district by withdrawing services of CEA members not already employed in West Haven. Also, they voted to request the NEA Defense Commission to conduct an investigation of the situation there.

At this point, 14 teachers had resigned, 91 had signed the salary agreement, and 233 had refused to sign, submitting instead written notice of their intention to return to their positions in the fall with the understanding that salary negotiations were still open. The board of education then made the mistake of getting tough by voting to notify the 233 teachers that unless they returned signed salary agreements by a specified date they would receive no salary increases at all. This drastic action of the board precipitated the CEA boycott of the district.

Subsequent meetings, which included the board of education, the teachers, the CEA, and the Connecticut commissioner of education, resulted in adjudication of conditions. The board agreed to accept substitute forms signed by the teachers instead of the salary agreement and to rescind its action denying raises to teachers who refused to sign the agreement. In return the CEA lifted its sanctions declaration against the district.

STUDENTS' SANCTIONS. Another first in the area of sanctions was the action of the Student Education Association of Connecticut (SEAC), an affiliate of the CEA and the NEA, in the case of the Bridgeport and Groten School districts. The SEAC is an affiliated unit of the Student National Education Association, which has about 1,000 chapters on college and university campuses throughout the United States. The members of these chapters are studying to be teachers. In the Connecticut case the sanctions voted by the SEAC had the effect of shutting off to the offending school districts the supply within the state of newly graduated teachers. This may become a potent weapon in the future, since there are more than 130,000 members of the Student National Education Association, most of whom presumably are college seniors. Should this source of supply be cut off from a given school district or series of districts, the impact would be great.

In effect, the SEAC came to the support of the Bridgeport Education Association. The SEAC resolution was the result of impasses in Bridgeport and Groton between the teachers and boards of education over salary schedules. The text of the SEAC resolution is as follows:

> Resolved that the Student Education Association of Connecticut take appropriate steps to advise all SEAC members of teacher preparing institutions in Connecticut, who will be graduating in June 1962, of those communities in the state where local teachers associations have rejected salary schedules offered by the Board of Education for 1962–63, and where annual salary agreements for the coming year have not been signed by a majority of the teachers.
>
> Resolved further that the executive board of the SEAC caution SEAC members about the advisability of signing contracts of employment at this time in these towns, and suggest that applicants for positions in communities such as Bridgeport and Groton consider holding their acceptances in abeyance until

satisfactory salary schedules have been agreed upon by the local teachers group and the Board of Education.

The CEA and SEAC resolutions were instrumental in influencing the Bridgeport Board of Education to meet with the teachers leaders in mid-May. Salaries and other matters were adjusted, and the teachers voted to sign salary agreements.

Also, the Michigan Student Education Association, in the spring of 1965, adopted a resolution calling upon its members not to seek or accept positions in school districts with beginning salaries below $5,000.

WATERBURY, CONNECTICUT. The teachers in Waterbury, Connecticut had for years pleaded with the school board and board of alderman for adequate financial support for the Waterbury schools. Despite the fact that Waterbury is a relatively wealthy community, teachers' salaries were the lowest in the state, buildings were in a condition of notorious disrepair, facilities were deteriorating, classes were crowded, and special school services were inadequate. After years of teachers' appeals to the board and the community, nothing happened because the mayor and the board of alderman had a veto on the school board's budget request.

In the fall of 1963, the Waterbury Education Association requested the Connecticut Education Association and the NEA to make studies of the situation—looking toward the possibility of invoking sanctions. In September 1963, the teachers sanctioned the withdrawal of all extracurricular services for which they were paid. Moreover, they carried their fight to the people by actively campaigning, as a group, against the incumbent mayor. They employed a skilled public-relations man for the campaign.

They campaigned openly and vigorously, won the support of the community and defeated the incumbent mayor by some 400 votes out of a total of 17,000. Subsequent to the election, the lame-duck mayor and aldermen again rejected the school board's budget increases (except for a raise for teachers) which would have been adequate to do all the things the teachers requested. The teachers immediately asked the Connecticut Education Association and the NEA to invoke sanctions. In the meantime, the new mayor, whom the teachers had supported, requested that the invoking of sanctions be delayed until January 15 to give him time to mobilize community forces behind the school board's requested budget. This was done. The mayor then formed a committee of the city's leading citizens which recommended an increase of 1.75 mills in the tax rate, enough money to meet the requested budget of the school board. This proposed tax increase was ratified by the board of alderman, the school board's full budget request was approved, and the invoking of sanctions was dropped.

A number of local associations have invoked or threatened to invoke sanctions on their own, usually by withdrawing extracurricular services.

Examples are Waterbury and Dade County and Duval County, both in Florida, in 1965.

The two other notable and highly publicized cases involving the invoking of sanctions against entire states—Utah and Oklahoma—are dealt with in detail in Chapter 12. In June 1967, state-wide sanctions against the state of Florida were voted by the Florida Education Association and NEA. In July 1967, NEA invoked sanctions against the Baltimore school district.

So the weapons have been chosen. The teachers' union believes that the labor process of collective bargaining backed up by the strike is the most effective weapon in the interest of teachers.

The NEA has rejected both collective bargaining and the strike, choosing to keep disputes between teachers and school boards within educational channels. The NEA has chosen professional negotiation as its means of providing teachers with the legal right to participate (1) in policy-making, (2) in having a real role in setting educational policy, and (3) in developing the school program.

The NEA has chosen professional sanctions to rectify unsatisfactory conditions.

During the school year 1965–66, a rash of sanctions applications occurred. This is discussed in Chapter 13.

7

A Comparative Analysis

> The labor story of 1964 is going to be unionization of teachers. So predicts an AFL-CIO insider. Your city may face trouble.
>
> The American Federation of Teachers aims for quick organization of big systems. Prime targets this year are Chicago, Detroit, Philadelphia, Boston, Los Angeles. The Union has already won representation in New York, lost in Milwaukee. [Later it won in Detroit, Cleveland, Philadelphia, Chicago, and Boston.]
>
> Walter Reuther, the United Auto Workers' chief, also masterminds AFT strategy. He sends organizers to shore up local union forces [and] calls the rival National Education Association, the company union.
>
> In search of a bargaining weapon, union men press for changes in laws barring strikes by employees of local governments—including teachers. They argue the late President Kennedy's encouragement of unions for federal employees amounted to endorsement of unions of teachers.
>
> Labor's aims go beyond mere bargaining rights. AFL-CIO President Meany complains schools downgrade the importance of unions; so unions demand role in curriculum-making to get their line across. Strategists figure teacher unionization would speed organization of other white-collar groups which now shun big labor.
>
> —*Nation's Business*, April 1964

What of the chosen weapons and procedures? Do they constitute a clear dichotomy, or only "sound and fury signifying nothing"?

Is the embracing of trade unionism by teachers inevitable? Can NEA sustain its so-called professional approach? Are there any differences between collective bargaining and professional negotiation? Is unionism necessarily unprofessional? Are strikes unprofessional? Are sanctions the same as strikes? Are sanctions legal?

These are vital questions for which there are, at the moment, only confused and confusing answers. And the viewpoints of the protagonists of the competing organizations tend to be doctrinaire, and not too helpful. There is great need for searching analysis by competent outsiders, by unbiased knowledgeable experts in employer-employee relationships.

This writer cannot pretend to be a detached observer. There are, however, certain aspects of the above questions which appear to be clearly discernible regardless of parochial attachments.

There appears, for example, to be no clear-cut dichotomy, in terms of official pronouncements of NEA and AFT. In terms of actions and outcomes, however, there are clearly drawn divisions of policy.

Collective Bargaining and Professional Negotiation

There can be little question that there are great similarities between collective bargaining, as practiced in private industry and espoused by AFT for the schools, and professional negotiation, as advocated by the professional associations—NEA and its affiliated state and local education associations. As a matter of fact, the latter is, in large measure, an adaptation of the former to fit a uniquely different situation and a uniquely different set of circumstances.

This adaptation is logical and natural, since virtually the only precedent with a generation or more of experience and trial and error, established and refined as a developmental process by law and court and administrative agency decisions, is collective bargaining. But in the view of the professional associations, there must be definitive, clear-cut adaptations geared to the uniqueness of the school as a governmental, social institution. Some compelling factors in the desired adaptations, as visualized by the professional associations are (1) the recognition of common goals by the school board (the employer), the administration (the management), and the teachers (the workers), (2) the rejection of the categorical, inevitable dichotomy between management and workers by the professional staff of a school system, (3) the amelioration, if not blanket rejection, of the concept that all differences must be viewed and resolved on the basis that both sides are sworn adversaries forever, (4) The rejection of the strike as the means of winning an impasse situation, and (5) the rejection of what Wildman and Perry[1] have termed "the power relationship and a process of power accommodation," as practiced in industry.

In summary, the professional associations seek, through professional negotiation, the development of a unique process appropriate to a unique institution.

Of course, these associations recognize that there are, and at some points must be, conflicts. There will be at points adversary relationships.

Conflicts and adversary relationships are inevitable in a free society, even in the family unit. But these conflicts can be and are reconciled without violence. Such reconcilement is essential to the functioning of any public institution serving the interest of the whole society.

To deny that there is not a large measure of ambivalence in the convictions and practices of the professional associations would be to deny the obvious. Such ambivalence, resulting in groping and confusion of direction, is inevitable in the development of any complex new process.

Indeed, it is a simple matter to seek to transplant to the schools, as AFT has done, a process already tried in industry. This can be done with few mistakes and a clear sense of direction, because mistakes have already been made and the process refined accordingly. A body of procedure that works not perfectly, but well and effectively, has already been worked out.

For this reason, many superintendents of schools report that they prefer to deal with the teachers' unions because the unions know and state clearly what they want and how they will go about getting it. They also have a clearly defined effective weapon for enforcing their demands. These same superintendents assert that the teachers' associations, on the other hand, are not categorical in their demands, frequently appear to be confused about what their membership really wants, and seem often not to know the facts of life about their school systems, financially and otherwise, thus lacking a realistic view of what is attainable. Moreover, these superintendents claim that often the representatives of the teachers' associations have only superficial understanding of the art of negotiation, with its refinements of compromise and retreat. Teachers groups tend, according to these assessments, to demand all or nothing, and grow highly emotional when they meet opposition.

Assuming the accuracy of these assertions, such deficiences are explainable by the teachers virtually complete lack of experience with, to them, a wholly new and confusing process. Hopefully time and experience will rectify these alleged errors of knowledge, judgment, and behavior.

On the other side of the coin, it is perhaps fair to point out that much of the conflict can be ascribed to inept administration and to the inexperience of school boards in the the process of negotiation. Too, each person involved has a different view of his own and the other people's responsibilities.

The ambivalence and confusion of the professional associations in regard to an appropriate process for collective action by school staffs appears in a number of ways. The first edition of *Guidelines for Professional Negotiation*[2], published by NEA, advocated procedures which sought to preserve, generally intact, the participation of its entire membership. It sought to provide as negotiators units made up of many groups. It was vague on exclusive recognition for negotiation purposes in a given school district. And it sought to propose three levels or kinds of acceptable agreements (Levels I, II, and III). The second edition[3] of *Guidelines,* by advocating exclusive recognition, by categorically endorsing the Level III agreement as the only full-fledged negotiation agreement, and by suggesting that a school superintendent probably should not participate as a member of the negotiating unit, tacitly admitted the lack of sophistication evidenced in the first edition.

Too, the ambivalence of the professional associations with regard to collective staff action was indicated in the reaction to a little-known proposal of NEA to its state associations. This proposal (1962) was in the form of a model bill to establish negotiation procedures by legislation in each state. NEA staff members involved in this area of professional negotiation thought they clearly saw that legislation sponsored by the professional associations was the only realistic way to counteract the drive of AFL-CIO for legislation mandating collective-bargaining rights for public employees, including teachers. Consequently, an outstanding law firm specializing in labor relations was retained. This legal firm was asked to draft a model bill stressing professional negotiation instead of collective bargaining. But this proposal was too far ahead of its time for the state associations to accept at that time. The proposed bill was virtually universally rejected by the state affiliates. By 1965, however, the climate had changed and about a dozen state associations sought professional negotiation legislation. None, however, used the model bill but adapted proposed legislation to local conditions. Thus, in 1965 state associations were able to secure passage of such legislation in six states: Connecticut, California, Minnesota, New Jersey, Oregon, and Washington. Florida also passed a law, but of a superficial nature. The legislation in Minnesota and New Jersey was vetoed by the governors. In the meantime, AFL-CIO succeeded in passing legislation—the type that would apply to labor—for public employees, including teachers, in Alaska, New Hampshire, Oregon, Wisconsin, Michigan, and Massachusetts. The Oregon law was superceded by the professional negotiation law passed in that state in 1965.[4]

The ambivalence of the professional associations towards means of collective action is most clearly discernible in the professional-negotiation legislation passed. The provisions vary significantly. This analysis will deal with the statutes in five states—California, Connecticut, Florida, Oregon, and Washington.

CALIFORNIA. California law specifies that parties "meet and confer" rather than negotiate in the usual sense of the term. Membership verification is required. Exclusive recognition is not provided, but when there is only one teachers' organization there is exclusive negotiation. If there is more than one teachers' organization in a district, a joint negotiation council, with proportional representation is provided.

CONNECTICUT. In Connecticut the negotiation unit has exclusive representation either by one all-inclusive organization or through separate representatives as determined by a ballot election. All members of the professional staff below the rank of superintendent may vote in this election. The provisions are mandatory and teachers' strikes are prohibited. Impasses are settled by mediation by the secretary of the state board of education or by three arbitrators.

FLORIDA. Florida legislation states that a board of education may appoint or recognize committees of a school's professional staff in the formulation of policies; such committees are to include instructional and administrative personnel.

OREGON. In Oregon employees or their elected representatives have the right to confer, consult, and discuss with the board of education on salaries and other economic policies. The state requires that boards establish election procedures for determining representatives. Mediation is vested in three impartial representatives, but their recommendations are not binding.

WASHINGTON. Election by secret ballot is required in Washington. Superintendents are barred from participation in these elections. The designated organization has the right to negotiate with the school board on school policies. Negotiable items fairly well cover the range of school policy. Rights are extended to public junior colleges. Mediation is provided through a committee of educators appointed by the state superintendent. Their recommendations are advisory only (see description of 1967 New York Law, Chapter 13).

There is great diversity in these laws. The right to strike is denied. Exclusive representation is provided, but the negotiating units are diverse. Mediation is a common element, but in most instances is not binding.

Further evidence of the ambivalence of the professional association is the fact that in the states with AFL-CIO legislation (notably Michigan, Wisconsin, and Massachusetts) the state associations seem to live very well with the type of legislation keyed to labor. Perhaps an important factor in this situation is the fact that in all these situations, the state associations were able to amend the AFL-CIO bills to include some key professional provisions. The notable exception is the law in Michigan as amended in 1965. Although the MEA-NEA affiliates are winning overwhelmingly in elections, the incidence of teacher strikes is pronounced.

To summarize: There are great similarities in collective-bargaining legislation and professional-negotiation legislation for teachers. In general, the professional-negotiation legislation seeks to assure a process that works through educational channels and seeks to involve all professional staff members except the superintendent.

Strikes and Professional Sanctions

According to the Bureau of Labor Statistics[5], there were 110 teacher strikes between 1940 and 1962. Ninety-one of these strikes were by public-school teachers and 19 by teachers in private schools. (In addition, it has been estimated, although not by the Bureau of Labor Statistics, that there were about 20 teacher strikes between 1880 and 1940.) Some 49,000 teachers were involved in these 110 strikes between 1940 and 1962. About two-thirds of the 110 strikes occurred in the postwar period 1945–1952. Only 20 strikes occurred between 1953 and 1962.

Of the 110 strikes, in 58 the teachers involved were represented by unions; in 22 the teachers were represented by professional associations; and in 30 the teachers were represented by no organization. Thus in the 110 teacher strikes in the 22-year period 1940–1962 about 53 per cent were by union-affiliated teacher groups; 27 per cent by independent teachers' groups; and 20 per cent by professional-association affiliates. Of the 80 strikes by union and association-affiliated groups, 72.5 per cent were by union groups, and 27.5 per cent by association groups. Thus the incidence of strikes by union affiliates was 2.6 times as great as among the association affiliates. In terms of the relative total numbers of association affiliates and union-affiliated locals (assumed to approximate the ratio of 20 to 1 during this period, based on the estimated average of 400 AFT locals to 8,000 NEA locals), the incidence of strikes by union affiliates was roughly 60 times as great as by association affiliates. In the decade 1953–1962, of the 20 strikes 14 were by locals represented by teachers' unions and none by the professional associations.

The major issues or causes involved in the 110 strikes were wages and hours in 62 strikes; determination of organization to represent teachers (to gain recognition of a union or professional association, to protest discrimination against union membership, and so on) in 16; and other working conditions, 32.[6]

The Bureau of labor Statistics listed 17 of the strikes in the 1940-1962 period as major work stoppages. An adaptation of the bureau's table appears in Table 7–1.

An analysis of the data in Table 7–1 reveals some interesting facts. All except three strikes were under the exclusive aegis of the AFT. The Norwalk strike was by the Norwalk Teachers Association, at that time an unaffiliated organization. The Patterson, New Jersey strike was apparently a joint venture of the AFT affiliate and the Patterson Teachers Association, presumably affiliated with the New Jersey Education Association and thus with NEA. The Buffalo strike involved the Buffalo Federation of Teachers. It is not indicated that this federation was affiliated with any national organization.

Involved in these 17 major strikes were approximately 40,000 of the total of 49,000 teachers involved in the 110 strikes between 1940–1962.

TABLE 7-1

Major Work Stoppages By Teachers 1940–1962

Year	School System	Teachers' Organization Involved	Number of Workers Involved	Duration of Work Stoppage (Days)
1944	Pontiac, Michigan	AFT	500	6
1944	Flint, Michigan	AFT	1100	4
1946	Paterson, New Jersey	AFT		
		PTA	600	1
1946	Norwalk, Connecticut	NTA	200	9
1946	St. Paul, Minnesota	AFT	1200	33
1946	Pawtucket, Rhode Island	AFT	450	2
1947	Buffalo, New York	BTF	2900	5
1947	Dover, Wilmington, and New Castle County, Delaware	AFT	600	1
1947	New Britain, Connecticut	AFT	400	3
1948	Minneapolis, Minnesota	AFT	3000	27
1948	Providence, Rhode Island	AFT	1000	2
1951	Minneapolis, Minnesota	AFT	3600	23
1951	Pawtucket, Rhode Island	AFT	460	33
1952	Providence, Rhode Island	AFT	1100	8
1957	Pawtucket, Rhode Island	AFT	500	10
1960	New York City	AFT	5000	1
1962	New York City	AFT	20,000	1

Source: Ibid. Bureau of Labor Statistics, Table 4, pp. 6–8. "Work Stoppages Involving Teachers, 1940–1962," Summary Release U.S. Department of Labor, Bureau of Labor Statistics, November 1963, 8.

The average length of the strikes was 9.9 days; the median was 5 days; the range was from 1 to 33 days; and the mode was 1 day (4 of the 17 strikes).

The Bureau of Labor Statistics lists 16 work stoppages by teachers since 1962 (see Table 7–2), eleven of which were by AFT affiliates and four by NEA affiliates, with one, Hoboken, unidentified as to affiliation. The bureau's classification of *work stoppage* is unquestionably accurate. The Utah teachers as described in Chapter 12, contended that their 2-day professional recess was not a strike in the usual meaning of the term; *work stoppage* might define it better. The same is true of the Louisville walk-out, which was by a small group and was not a planned, concerted action. But, of course, the public viewed these work stoppages as strikes.

The Jersey City and Lakeview, Georgia work stoppages, on the other hand, were clearly planned, concerted-action strikes.

Thus there have been between 1940 and 1965 a total of 126 work stoppages by teachers. (See Chapter 13 for a discussion of teachers' strikes from January 1 to June 1, 1966.)

TABLE 7-2

Work Stoppages Involving Teachers in Public Schools, 1963–65*

Beginning date	Approximate Duration (calendar days)	School System (Board of Education) involved
1963: May 2	5	Anderson, Indiana (AFT)
1963: May 28	1	Gary, Indiana (AFT)
1964: March 4	1	Jersey City, New Jersey (NEA)
1964: May 18	5	E. St. Louis, Illinois (AFT)
1964: May 18	2	Utah (State-wide) (NEA)
1964: June 2	1	Hoboken, New Jersey (NEA)
1964: June 8	1	New York, New York (AFT)
1964: September 8	5	E. St. Louis, Illinois (AFT)
1964: October 5	9	Pawtucket, Rhode Island (AFT)
1964: November 2	7	Lakeview, Georgia (NEA)
1964: November 4	12	Louisville, Kentucky (NEA)
1965: March 25	13	Pawtucket, Rhode Island (AFT)
1965: Apirl 26	4	Hamtramck, Michigan (AFT)
1965: May 11	6	South Bend, Indiana (AFT)
1965: November 1	12	Perth Amboy, New Jersey (AFT)
1965: December 2	4	Newark, New Jersey (AFT)

* Data for 1965 are preliminary, and thus may be incomplete.
Source: United States Department of Labor, Bureau of Labor Statistics, March 1966.

In 1966, there was a strike by the NEA affiliate in Newark in February and a one-day "professional day" work stoppage in Kentucky by a state-wide NEA affiliate on February 3. In New Orleans a four-day strike by an AFT affiliate took place in March. Also in 1966, there was a one-day teachers' strike in the Plainview-Old Bethpage, New York School District by an AFT affiliate. A sustained strike by a college affiliate of AFT took place at St. John's University, New York City. Also, several strikes in Michigan among both NEA and AFT affiliates occurred at the end of the school year. See Chapter 13.

An interesting comparison to the strikes is the number of school districts against which sanctions were invoked by NEA, its state or local affiliates, or by these professional organizations in joint action.

TABLE 7-3

Professional Sanctions Imposed by Professional Association
(Against School Districts—State, County, and Local) 1962–1966*

Place	Date	Invoking Association
Overseas Dependents Schools: "Urgent Advisory" issued	February 1963	NEA
Waterbury: Sanction against extra-curricular duties	September 1963 Lifted Feburary 6, 1964	Waterbury Education Association
Waterbury (CTA)	November 1963	Connecticut Education Association
Waterbury: Sanction called but postponed	December 1963 Lifted Feburary 6, 1964	
Little Lake, California	April 1962 Lifted January 28, 1964	California Teachers Association
Springer, New Mexico	Fall 1965 Lifted May 1966	New Mexico Education Association
Overseas Dependents Schools: Second "Urgent Advisory" issued	November 1963 Lifted October 1966	NEA
Pleasantville, Iowa	February 1964 Lifted	Iowa State Education Association
Utah	May 19, 1964 Lifted March 15, 1965	Utah Education Association and NEA
Utah: 2-day recess	May 18–19, 1964	Utah Education Association
Cauley, Wyoming	December 4, 1965 Lifted April 27, 1965	Wyoming Education Association
Oklahoma	March 6, 1965 Lifted September 18, 1965	Oklahoma Education Association
Oklahoma	May 11, 1965 Lifted September 24, 1965	NEA
Dade County, Florida	May 5, 1965 Lifted May 20, 1965	Dade County Teachers Association
Washington School District, Ohio	July 29, 1965	Ohio Education Association
Box Elder County, Utah	September 7, 1965 Lifted October 29, 1965	Utah Education Association
Duval County, Florida	October 1965 Lifted November 1965	Duval County Teachers Association
Nantucket, Massachusetts		Massachusetts Teachers Association
Springfield, Massachusetts		Massachusetts Teachers Association

Place	Date	Invoking Association
Newark, New Jersey	January 1966 Settled by strike February 1966	New Jersey Education Association and Newark Teachers Association
Finely, North Dakota	March 1966 Lifted April 1966	North Dakota Education Association
Portland, Maine	April 1966 Lifted June 1966	Maine Teachers Association
Herman, Maine	April 1966 Lifted June 1966	Maine Teachers Association
Baltimore, Maryland	June 1966	Baltimore Public School Teachers Association and Maryland State Teachers Association
Hillsborough County, Florida	June 1965 to January 1966	Local Association
Volusia County, Florida	June 1965 to September 1965	Local Association
Haysville (S.D. 261), Kansas	February 1966 to February 1966	Kansas State Teachers Association
Knoxville, Tennessee	March 1966	Knoxville Teachers League
Warren, Michigan	July 1966	Michigan Education Association
Jersey City, New Jersey	Spring 1966	New Jersey Education Association
Asbury Park, New Jersey	1964	Asbury Park Teachers Association
Ecorse, Michigan	July 1966	Michigan Education Association
Flint, Michigan	May 1966	Michigan Education Association
Southgate, Michigan	June 1966	Michigan Education Association
Crestwood, Michigan	June 1966	Michigan Education Association

* This list necessarily must be considered as a partial one, since doubtless there have been cases of sanctions imposed by local or state associations not reported to NEA.

Strikes Versus Sanctions

As to the respective policies of the AFT and NEA, it was pointed out in Chapter 5 that AFT's policy has evolved from a categorical no-strike policy to a "right to strike under certain circumstances." NEA has never had a categorical, direct and unequivocal no-strike policy. It is true that its members generally think it has or that its policy is tantamount to a universal ban. As will be shown, NEA's somewhat ambiguous position has been a demonstrable deterrent to strikes, while AFT's policy of stated tolerance or advocacy has encouraged strikes.

An analysis of NEA's position reveals no adoption of an official no-strike ban. NEA has, in effect, relied upon its code of ethics to forbid or deter strikes by demanding observance of teachers' contracts, and has relied upon professional sanctions as a recourse in cases of impasses between boards and teachers.

A history of the statements in the several revisions of the code is as follows:

CODE OF ETHICS OF THE NEA (1929)

> Article III, Section 7:
> A contract, once signed, should be faithfully adhered to until it is dissolved by mutual consent. In case of emergency, the thoughtful consideration which business sanction demands should be given by both parties to the contract.

CODE OF ETHICS OF THE NEA (1941)

> Principle III, Section 9:
> A contract, once signed, should be faithfully adhered to until it is dissolved by mutual consent. Ample notification should be given both by school officials and teachers in case a change in position is to be made.

NEA CODE OF ETHICS (1952)

> Principle IV, Section 6:
> Adhere to the conditions of a contract until service thereunder has been performed, the contract has been terminated by mutual consent, or the contract has otherwise been legally terminated.

CODE OF ETHICS OF THE EDUCATION PROFESSION (1963)

> Principle IV, Section 4:
> Adhere to the conditions of a contract or to the terms of an appointment until either has been terminated legally or by mutual consent.

These provisions clearly declare that a strike which violates an existing contract (and presumably this would cover virtually every work stoppage during a given school year) is a violation. A confusing consideration is that the excerpts from various codes obviously refer to individual teachers. (The 1963 code incidentally, has been universally adopted by NEA state association affiliates.) The rub occurs in the enforcement. If the code of ethics is violated by an individual or a few individuals, enforcement would be simple. Violation by a substantial group would make a difficult, if not impossible, problem. What is the solution when a large group, or the whole group, in a given situation walk out? Is this a violation of the code?

Where in the code of ethics is the restraining force? Of course, the realistic answer is that there is no over-all, universal, unfailing restraint. Strikes have occurred among NEA affiliates without subsequent disciplinary action by NEA.

But there are restraints, and powerful ones at that. Perhaps the greatest restraint is the fact that NEA does not advocate teacher strikes as a means of settling disputes in school districts.

Just here, it appears, is the reason why a positive pro-strike policy of NEA would not only be unwise and unjustified, but also could do irreparable damage to the public-school system of this country. It would seem, in the eyes of nearly 9,000 local associations (not to mention the sizeable numbers of NEA members in additional thousands of other school districts where there are no NEA affiliates) to condone a walk-out on the slightest of provocations. In virtually every good-sized group of teachers, as in any group of human beings, there are some who are afflicted with chronic dissatisfaction with things as they are. Within limits, this is good, a propellant to progress. But there should be effective outlets for their dissatisfaction. The NEA policy, it would appear, tacitly recognizes that occasional teachers' strikes will occur among its affiliates. There is no realistic way for NEA always to prevent this from happening. But while NEA may accept this as inevitable and seek to live with the fact, NEA does not embrace the concept that a strike is inevitable in every disagreement or indeed that such action is defensible except in situations that have become intolerable. But it does not advocate strikes to settle issues. The NEA Code of Ethics for the Education Profession adopted in 1963, which has now been adopted by all affiliated state associations, thus involving about 1.7 million teachers, sets forth the obligation to observe faithfully the terms of a contract until that contract is completed or is terminated by mutual consent.

The bylaw on NEA membership now specifies that a pledge of adherence to the code is prerequisite to membership. To be sure, this provision realistically might not be enforced, or indeed, might not be enforceable in the case of several thousand teachers of a local affiliated association engaging in a strike. But the very fact of subscribing to the code is, among members in general, a great deterrent to engaging in such action.

The NEA, like all professions, has difficulty in enforcing vigorously and universally its code of ethics. But the power of that code is profound because it is based in great measure upon the will of professional people—as with good citizens in the observance of the law—and upon self-discipline. Lord Moulton's comments in Parliament upon the magnificent behavior of the men aboard the sinking *Titanic* are germane to this point. He named three areas of human behavior: the domain of the enforceable, the domain of freedom of choice, and the domain of obedience to the unenforceable. Obviously, the indispensable catalyst that holds together a free society is the last. This is not a philosophy that sneers that authorities can't fire 1,000 or 10,000 or any other number of teachers who have either violated the law or public morality. Such a philosphy with its cynical scoffing at the domain of obedience to the unenforceable, paves the road to civil disobedience and, ultimately, to anarchy. Teachers above all ought to be wary of such a philosohpy, however fetchingly it may be clothed in pleasing sophistries.

Even if a temporary victory is won by a teachers' strike, the aftermath is a divided, strife-torn community where bitterness may linger for years.

It would appear that AFT's advocacy of strikes under certain circumstances is more realistic than NEA's position. But the weakness is in the failure to spell out the circumstances. As the policy stands, it would appear to be even more ambiguous than NEA's position because it is unqualified and becomes, in effect, an open endorsement of the teachers' strikes anywhere and under whatever circumstances.

NEA has been and is currently wrestling with the problem of spelling out circumstances which invite strikes, regardless of whether it condones or condemns them. It is doubtful that its present ambiguous position can be maintained. (See the statement of the NEA Executive Secretary to the 1966 NEA Convention, Chapter 14.)

An example of NEA ambiguity is the statement of the NEA Ethics Committee in 1946, when teacher strikes were popping up all over.

> The NEA Ethics Committee recommends a cost of living adjustment in teachers salaries. It reaffirms its position regarding the sanctity of teachers contracts. The Ethics Committee does not endorse breaking contracts by striking. However, the Ethics Committee warns that immediate consideration must be given to upward salary adjustments in countless communities in order to avert a wholesale withdrawal of trained teachers from the profession.
>
> The NEA Code of Ethics for teachers provides that "a contract once signed should be faithfully adhered to until it is dissolved by mutual consent," but it also provides that "teachers should insist upon a salary scale commensurate with the social demands laid upon them by society."
>
> With several hundred teachers on strike at the present and several thousand pupils out of classrooms because of strikes in school systems over the nation, the Ethics Committee expresses deep concern over the outlook for education as living costs skyrocket and as the antiquated school tax structures collapse.
>
> The Committee urges administrators and local and state leaders to bring to the attention of their communities, school boards, and legislatures the gravity of the situation and the distressing implications for American democracy.

Another example is the tentative draft of a proposed statement (still a working paper) developed by the NEA Ethics Committee in 1965:

> The school program in district A had been deteriorating seriously for some time. The School Board was dominated by a politically opportunistic majority. Important teacher grievances had been piling up over a period of years. All efforts to induce the Board to meet with officers of the local association to seek solution jointly to these grievances had been frustrated. The community had

> been alerted in a variety of ways to the deleterious effects on the children's education of the growing controversy, but showed no disposition to intervene. At a turbulent mass meeting in April, the teachers unanimously voted an immediate two-day recess to commence the following Monday. The local executive committee was empowered to develop more severe sanctions if this action failed to induce the Board to meet with association leaders and constructively seek solution to major differences.

A plea against a categorical no-strike ban was made to the NEA Convention as early as 1947 by a delegate, a Miss McGough from St. Paul, a city where there had been a bitter, extended teachers' strike. The delegate was pleading against rigidly interpretating the code of ethics as saying that a strike is always violation of contract provision.

> I should have no objection at all to the inclusion of the idea that we condemn violation of contracts if it were in a different setting from this particular paragraph, because I feel that ordinarily certainly there is nobody who is [more] particular about observing a contract than the teacher would be.
>
> I submit, however, that sometimes you find a national crisis that seems to call for methods that do away with all preconceived ideas of procedure. I would point out that if that had not been true this country of ours would not be existing as an independent nation. Certainly when the American Revolution took place, the people whom we now call patriots and who at the time were called rebels and traitors by those they opposed forsook all their preconceived ideas of loyalty, even to government, in order to establish this country of ours.
>
> I quote that simply to point out that in great crises we do certain things that ordinarily we would not accept at all. Now, in this particular sentence, the Association seems to be sitting in judgment upon teachers who have resorted to the strike. As one who has gone through the strike, I can tell you, first of all, ladies and gentlemen, that it takes more backbone than most of us in the profession have been in the habit of showing in the past. If we had done so in regard to our loads and the public's support, perhaps we would not be in the position of having our schools understaffed and staffed by poorly qualified teachers in many places and this country facing one of the greatest crises in its history at a time when we should be ready to step out and assume leadership of the world. We are not equipped for it because we cannot educate for it and we cannot educate for it because we don't have the teachers to do it. We cannot support education as we should.
>
> In the minds of some of us there is a crisis today as great as this country has ever faced—the crisis that will determine our place in world leadership.
>
> In some of our localities, it was not just teachers, it was the citizen, by and large, who found to his astonishment, he was not ruling his community. That was our situation in St. Paul. There is not a thing you advocate here as to procedure that was not followed by us step-by-step in communion with over-all city groups, hard working men and women from the ministry, from the law, from the PTA groups, from the League of Women Voters, College Women's Clubs, and they were humiliated and embarrassed to find in the last analysis how little they counted in the process of government of the city.
>
> Curiously enough, it was from some of them that the request that the teachers must create a crisis came. Do you know where it was first said? I happen to be a member of the PTA Council Board of the city of St. Paul and it was said

around our council table, with our superintendent of schools there. I was directed by the mothers that the teachers must create a crisis.

There are situations that have to be examined on their integral value before we can pull our skirts around as and say that "The Association condemns violation of contracts."

You know, there is only one terrible thing about a school strike and that is the fact that children are kept out of school. There is not a great deal of difference [between] saying to the teachers of America, "Don't start school in the fall"—and we have said that from our National Headquarters—[and] "Don't open school in the fall unless you get the contracts you want."

You are keeping children out of school then and that is the real crux of the matter as to whether or not a school strike is any more serious than any other stoppage of work. The only difference I can see is whether you are keeping a child out of school in September, or whether you are keeping him out in January. The parents become more conscious of the fact that the child is a person to be dealt with and dealt with by a competent person. The important thing is to get your public aroused.[7]

The strikes in Perth Amboy and Newark by the AFT locals to force collective-bargaining elections, and a strike by the Newark Teachers Association to force the board to negotiate under terms of the agreement won in an election in 1965, impelled the New Jersey State Board of Education to adopt in March 1966 a resolution requiring local boards to adopt written policies regarding relationships with school staffs. This action resulted from the courts declaring illegal collective-bargaining elections and strikes by teachers.

The resolution reads (in part):

> Therefore, be it resolved that the New Jersey State Board of Education require each local public school board of education to formulate and adopt written policies setting forth the procedures to be followed for the presentation, consideration, and resolution of grievances and proposals of its employees. . . .

As a result of the disastrous New York City transit strike in January 1966, New York State began seeking a workable substitute for the Condon-Wadlin Act to give the public protection against strikes in vital services. The subsequent closing of child-health centers in the city by a walk-out of nurses in a dispute over salaries added to the demands for a new law. Governor Rockefeller appointed a five-member panel of nationally known experts in industrial relations to recommend the basic elements of a professional approach to the problem of dealing with public employees.

Recommendations which were incorporated in a bill sponsored by Governor Rockefeller included (1) establishment of a Public Employment Relations Board to certify organizations as spokesmen for public employees, to mediate when direct negotiations break down, and to designate impartial fact-finders when mediation fails to propose peace terms, (2) provisions for working out wage agreements ahead of the adoption of budgets, and (3) recourse, if fact-finding fails, to local and state legislative bodies. The bill also requires specific declaration by every organization certified to represent government employees that it does not assert the right to strike. This provision is in the President's Executive Order Number 10988 for Federal employees. Penalties under the proposed law for violation of its provisions are restricted to fines against the organization and loss of representation rights. This plan seeks to provide greater recourses to means of fair treatment without use of the strike. The need for a public policy on these basic essentials is indicated by the continuing violation of existing law by public employees, including teachers. Walter Reuther himself shocked his colleagues by proposing after the Transit Workers Union Strike in New York City that some formula be found to prevent strikes by public employees. It would perhaps be optimistic to assume that such legislation will prevent all strikes, but it is a general preventive step in the direction of democratic processes that would be violated only in the most extreme cases.

Strikes and Sanctions

Which of the weapons—the strike or sanction—is most effective?

There is no definitive means of answering this question. Generally, teachers' strikes have been extremely effective, but not universally. In most cases they have been of short duration, but some have been long-drawn-out affairs.

NEA and its affiliates have won in virtually all cases where sanctions have been invoked. But, unlike strikes, most sanctions have required a relatively long time to win. In Utah 300 days and in Oklahoma 133 days were required to get satisfactory settlements.

The time required to make them effective is perhaps the greatest weakness of sanctions. When an emergency arises, when teachers are frustrated and angry, the quick, dramatic action is most appealing. Pent-up emotions want an outlet *now,* not next month or next year.

It is obvious that the professional associations must create companion procedures, quick-acting and effective, to enhance the effectiveness of sanctions as effective alternatives to the strike.

Finally, NEA at its 1967 convention felt compelled to clarify its position on strikes among its affiliates. The resolution, in part, read: "The NEA recommends that every effort be made to avoid the strike. The NEA recognizes that under conditions of severe stress strikes have occurred and may occur in the future. In such instances, the NEA will offer all of the services at its command to help resolve the impasse."

Immediately, this statement was widely interpreted to mean that NEA had endorsed strikes. Charges of "me-tooism" were made, that NEA had endorsed AFT's position of supporting strikes under certain circumstances.

Part Three

THE STRATEGIES AND THE TACTICS

8

Conflicting Rationales

> I am persuaded that the following are categorical imperatives for the teaching profession. It cannot properly join forces with any other exclusive groups within the body politic. It cannot properly make common cause with labor or capital, with Democrats or Republicans, with any sect or religious body, or with any other collection of citizens organized for purposes that lie outside the purposes of the teaching profession itself. To further its own interests it cannot even make offensive and defensive alliances with any of these groups in the hope of enlisting their support. Its allegiance must be to the whole public, never to some partisan body within the state.
>
> —Samuel P. Capen[1]

Every organ and order of society operates under a rationale which is its *raison d' etre.*

People and organizations must be sustained by a purpose, a system of values to which they adhere, something in which they believe, to justify their existence.

Always the rationale stems from a philosophy, sometimes altruistic, sometimes pragmatic. But there is a philosophy. There must be to validate behavior.

This is true of the competing national teachers' organizations. Each has a rationale for its existence and its actions. Each is inclined to view its purpose and its actions as the noblest, its motivations as pure and unselfish, and its means as above criticism. Each can do these things in utmost sincerity and dedication. And each can be wrong at many points.

The respective philosophies, rationales, and behavior come to focus in the tactics and the strategy of a particular organization. That there will be some propaganda, some clever attempts at public-relations gimmickery, some exaggerations, some overgeneralizations, some oversimplifications, some synthetic liberalism, some breast-beating, self-righteousness, pomposity, bluster, and bombast is inevitable in the competition for teachers' organizational loyalties.

This section attempts to set forth some of the nuances of the rationales of both NEA and AFT. In this attempt will be included the valid and the invalid, the defensible and the questionable claims of both organizations. Each has its strengths and its weaknesses. Each has made mistakes. Each has postures that are sometimes sublime, sometimes ludicrous. The reader must balance them and judge.

This chapter will be devoted to the endless debate, the propaganda war over the professional approach versus the craft approach. The two succeeding chapters are specialized stories of the teachers unions and the professional associations—with the foibles and the strengths of each delineated.

The manner of waging campaigns to elevate the status of teachers and teaching, the choice of weapons, the strategy, and the tactics employed all come somewhere from the underlying philosophies of competing organizations. The professional associations stoutly defend the concept that teaching is, or ought to be and can be, a profession. Teachers' unions lean toward the craft concept of teaching.

What is a profession and what is a craft?

This question has been raised by some union leaders. They have repeatedly charged that teaching is not a profession but a craft, that teachers' organizations are nothing more than trade unions. Charles Cogen, 1966 AFT President, has said: "I hope to use all the devices available to trade unions because after all, we are a trade union. These include strikes if necessary, picketing, and rallies."

It will be recalled that in his speech before the NEA Convention in Denver (Chap. 1), James Carey went out of his way to express a dim view of teachers' aspirations for professional status. Two or three times he referred to the "teaching industry" and "your craft."

Bluntly, he said that the word *profession* is perhaps the chief curse of the teaching profession, implying that the hope of calling teaching a profession is sheer pretension. He demeaned the teachers for implying by the use of the word profession that they held themselves to be better than the working man, that their "craft" is above the grubby street battle for better conditions for all labor.

This is about as nasty as a speaker can get with an audience. It would be difficult to contrive a more gratuitous insult. It was doubtless intended as such, and it certainly was taken that way by his audience.

Teachers view themselves not as better, but as different. If Mr. Carey wanted to dig for evidence of this alleged snobbery, he could find it in the history of the teachers' unions.

Not until the New York City crisis, for example, did the AFT affiliate with the Industrial Union Department, the recruiting and organizing unit, really, of CIO, but supported, somewhat reluctantly, by the combined AFL-CIO. The first affiliation of teachers' unions was with the American Federation of Labor—a cluster of skilled-workers' unions, each with a membership representing a speciality. These were the aristocrats of labor, because each union represented a highly skilled homogenous group of craftsmen (such as railroad engineers, for example, or machinists), each member proud of his mastery of a given specialized vocation. The CIO, on the other hand, is a mass organization with membership in each union representing all the workers in a given industry, such as the United Automobile Workers. Here was the rabble, the mob, the great unwashed—in the view of the labor aristocracies. With the merger of the AFL-CIO in 1954, the AFT affiliation with AFL was absorbed into the merged group. But the AFT still refrained from direct affiliation with the IUD until the need for all-out help in New York City arose. The IUD is, of course, the creation of some 66 CIO mass unions.

Carl Megel, the President of AFT, in an address to students at Iowa State College on May 14, 1962 also renounced professional status for teachers. He said:

> When a representative of the National Education Association equates professionalism he equates the matter of doctors and lawyers with teachers. This again is erroneous. A doctor or a lawyer is a businessman. . . . A teacher is a worker. You are a day laborer.

In fairness to James Carey and Carl Megel, it should be said that disparaging references to the aspirations of public-school teachers to gain recognition as members of a profession didn't originate with them, nor are such references confined to the ranks of labor. This disdainful attitude has been quite common in higher education. The adherents of one discipline tend to look down their noses at the adherents of another. A professor of chemistry, let us say, or of history, is aware that there are other disciplines and scholars devoted to them, but he finds it difficult to understand why. He revels in the old saying, "A college professor is one who thinks otherwise." And for the lowly teacher in the public schools, all too often he has only contempt.

This attitude, moreover, is not unknown in the lower schools. The high-school teacher in some places often feels innately superior to the elementary school teacher, and, like the college professor, the specialist in a given high-school academic field often counts as inferior the teachers in some other fields. Maybe the psychologists or the Greeks have a word for it, but *perverseness* will do. Perhaps it is a strange streak of human nature that people must find some individual or group to whom they can feel superior, else they will have an unexplainable sense of debasement, a loss of an essential sense of self-confidence.

Indeed, part of the disdain for the NEA by some college professors arises from the fact that it symbolizes the drive for professional status by teachers and administrators in the lower schools, which to the college personnel is presumptuous. College people with this opinion like to think of and describe the NEA as a social-political organization and not a professional association. The college professor who rarely refers to his calling as a profession and almost never to himself as a professional generally views professional status as simply the mastery of his discipline. Thus, he is likely to join only a scholarly society of his field and not a general association. The American Association of University Professors, for example, has a smaller proportion of all college teachers in its membership than the NEA has of all public-school personnel.

In fairness, too, it might be said that the teaching profession in the public schools still has a long way to go in achieving full stature as such. Despite rather remarkable progress in recent years to raise preparation and licensing standards for teachers, too many teachers below acceptable levels of competence are still being admitted as measured in terms of preparation standards; furthermore, too many (about 90,000 a year) are coming into teaching through the back door of emergency certification unsponsored by any organized teachers' group. (In 1964, NEA instituted the requirement of the bachelors' degree as a minimum prerequisite for membership). Teaching is still too much of an in-and-out occupation. It is still plagued with huge turnovers in personnel. Despite substantial progress in disciplining its own members and policing its own ranks, the teaching profession still has too many members who get away with flagrant violations of the teaching code of ethics.

And despite solid progress in economic rewards, salaries generally are still at subprofessional levels, and working conditions often are not what they ought to be. Teachers in the lower schools still have not been accorded the degree of participation in policy development which should be accorded any really professional group. Also, it is true that the word *profession* has been used in many places and under many circumstances as a sort of palliative or substitute for other forms of recognition to which teachers should be entitled.

The meaning of *craft* can be rather easily defined. A craft is a skill—an occupation for which workers acquire their skills through an apprenticeship, a preparation learned on the job with relatively little academic study. A craft possesses, to be sure, some characteristics of a profession. Its members are highly competent possessors of great skills with great pride in their powers to perform unique services to society. And, like members of the professions, they are vitally concerned with the end product of their labors. Craft organizations are concerned almost wholly with welfare matters and working conditions.

A profession is not so quickly or so easily defined.

DEFINITION OF A PROFESSION. The word *profession* in modern society has been so loosely applied, so misused, so debased as to become almost a meaningless term. From the original three (law, medicine, and the ministry), the number of professions has proliferated with the growing complexity of life and with the need for specialized services until there are at least 25 recognized ones today, with half a hundred or more skilled occupational groups having some grounds for claiming the designation. This proliferation of professions, each asserting the right to recognition, will most certainly continue.

The United States Census Bureau, for example, apparently has abandoned its efforts at precise designation of the professions by listing "professional, technical, and kindred" occupations together.

How does one define a profession, then?

There is no single, universally accepted definition. There are many generally acceptable criteria or characteristics. It is much easier to identify the characteristics of a profession than to define it.

One definition, perhaps oversimplified, is this: A profession is a group which has equipped itself to provide a specialized service to society, preparation for this group consisting of completion of a prescribed college or university curriculum containing breadth and depth in general, specialized, and professional education.

Obviously this falls far short of an adequate, definitive meaning. In fact, it is virtually impossible to incorporate into a definition all the nuances of the meaning of *profession.* For this reason, A. M. Carr-Saunders, an Englishman who is regarded as a competent scholar in the field of professions, tended to avoid definitions and concentrated instead upon identifying and describing the marks which were common to recognized professions.

To reduce to a minimum the essential criteria of a profession, one may compress a dozen or so of the generally accepted criteria to four:

1. Specialized college and university preparation for the members of the profession to provide them with unique knowledge, insight, and skills not possessed by laymen (or members of other professions). As a general rule, the period of preparation varies from four to eight years of postsecondary-school work.
2. A large measure of autonomy in the management of the affairs of the profession.
3. Designated status in the law.
4. An all-inclusive professional association.

PREPARATION. With respect to the first criterion—college and university preparation—public-school teaching has found it extremely difficult to emerge as a recognized profession because of its peculiar evolution and because of traditional resistance in higher education. Public-school teaching is of relatively recent origin in society. State schools began to be established only after the Reformation. Prior to that time, education was predominantly the function of the church. Preparation for teaching, then, was incidental to preparation for the ministry.

When the medieval universities began to be founded, the general university degrees quickly became *per se* licenses to teach. The university degree became established as the route into college and private-school teaching, and it continues to be the route to such work today.

But the emergence of state schools, supported by public taxation and designed for the children of all the people, dictated a new design. To prevent waste of the taxpayers' money, preparation curricula were established to assure that teachers were competent to guide the learning of all types of children—the gifted, the above-average, the below-average, and the slow. We have seen in almost our own time that this need brought into teacher education courses on the psychology of learning, the history and philosophy of education, and the theoretical concepts of teaching as well as various courses in teaching methods and student teaching. These, with others added from time to time, became the professional courses which many college teachers have viewed with disdain.

Also, to protect children from incompetent teachers and to prevent nepotism, states and governments instituted legal licensure for public-school teachers. Again, from the viewpoint of the traditional practices in their own field, college teachers generally have had little patience with such precautions of the state or the ways in which these precautions have been implemented.

So great was the resistance in higher education to these new departures in the preparation of teachers that governments were compelled, beginning in 1839, to establish and support separate institutions for the education of teachers. These separate schools were the normal schools, founded first in France and Germany and later transplanted to the United States.

In this connection, it is interesting to note that virtually all professions (except the original three) in the beginning have had to establish separate, single-purpose institutions for the preparation of their members. This necessity arose from the resistance of the universities to incorporating professional curricula into their programs.

In the United States, all the professions—after long, sustained, and often bitter struggles—have battled their way into the mainstream of higher education, their specialized schools and colleges becoming integral parts of the universities rather than remaining in isolation. This is a *sine qua non* of professional recognition and status because all professional disciplines are derived ones in the sense that their basic content is drawn from the established liberal-arts disciplines. A profession, in the preparation of its members, must have access to the scholars in these other fields in the universities.

Public-school teaching in the United States has had the longest and hardest and most bitter struggle of all the professions in achieving integration into the universities. In fact, it is just now achieving such integration in significant measure. To illustrate the point: At the turn of the century there were in existence in this country more than 300 normal schools of one kind or another. They were gradually abolished or transformed into degree-granting teachers' colleges, many later evolving into state colleges and more recently into state universities. Consequently, in 1966 only 20 public and private teachers' colleges existed as separate, single-purpose institutions.

Paralleling the drive in the United States for recognition of education as a respected discipline by teachers of higher education has been the effort to upgrade state teacher-licensing requirements to acceptable professional levels.

As late as 1946, only 15 states required the bachelor's degree for initial certification of elementary-school teachers. In 1966, 46 states were enforcing this minimum preparation level.

Both of these drives have been spearheaded by professional organizations (the NEA and its state affiliates) in the public schools. Almost every step of the way, these drives have met vigorous resistance.

The basic resistance stems from the notion that teaching in the lower schools is and can never be more than only a highly developed craft. Dr. James Bryant Conant in his *The Education of American Teachers* seems to embrace this concept, at least in part, by decrying the efforts of teachers in the public schools, through their professional organizations, to upgrade their standards of preparation and licensure to professional levels; and by a rather summary dismissal as worthless of virtually all professional courses except student teaching. He rejects the proposal to require five years (or the master's degree) as a preservice requirement for admission to teaching; yet virtually all other recognized professions require this much or more preparation. He rejects a national professional accrediting process for teaching; yet all other recognized professions are conceded this process with little argument.[2]

It is not surprising, therefore, that public-school teachers are not likely to take kindly to the idea that they constitute a craft rather than a profession. They have fought too long and too hard for the latter to do an about face now and retreat to the craft status.

AUTONOMY. The second of our telescoped criteria of a profession—the right to manage its own affairs—is indispensible to a profession. This is why teachers in the public schools resist, usually as a group, turning over the handling of their tough problems to an outside group.

The free society long ago discovered that the most fruitful way to get competent and dedicated service from a profession was to entrust the regulating of the profession to its members and not directly to government. Of course, the authority to regulate arises with government as the representative of all the people. And of course that governmental authority must always be in the background to prevent abuse of the public interest or flagrantly monopolistic, selfish practices.

Almost always the instant reaction of laymen to this thesis is that autonomy for the teaching profession implies control of education. Not at all. We have, with reference to our public schools, two houses: the House of Education and the House of the Profession.

The House of Education is the province of the public which owns it. The setting of policies and the designating to legal agencies the task of executing those policies is in the interest and welfare of society.

The House of the Profession is the province of the profession, with public sanction to execute the tasks of managing the house. This is true of all the private professions. It must inevitably become true for the public professions.

What does this involve?

It involves the profession's setting standards of selection, preparation, and licensure to assure competence of those admitted to practice and to membership and it involves the profession's seeing to it that these standards are enforced. The first and inescapable obligation of a profession is to guarantee to society the competence of its members. This can be done—and to an increasing degree is being done—in partnership with state legal authorities.

But it is not enough to get competent people in practice.

The profession must set standards for proper working conditions and a climate enabling its members to perform the high quality of service for which they have spent years in preparation, and the profession must see to it that these standards are enforced. This too can be done—and to an increasing degree is being done—in partnership with local legal authorities.

The profession must define ethical conduct and standards of professional service—and see to it that these are enforced. This can be done—and to an increasing degree is being done—by the profession alone.

Finally, the profession must set standards for adequate remuneration for the services of its members and seek persistently and vigorously to obtain and maintain these standards.

What the profession of public-school teaching seeks is, largely, that which college personnel already have and what public-school teachers in many enlightened districts already have; job equity; the enforcement of rigorous standards of preparation and admission; the careful evaluation of programs for the preparation of its members; academic freedom; a real voice in the determination of curriculum and methodology; a manageable teaching load; integrity in teaching and grading; protection from capricious and emotional pressures to conform to the dogmas of power groups in communities; time and conditions of work to let teachers be the scholars that professionals ought to be; time to eat for the harrassed teacher with no free period; time to reflect; time to confer with students; time to study; time for research; and time to write. Above all, teachers want to shed the image of the scared hired-hand and win recognition as professionals with the concomitant right to be listened to and to share in the development of the educational program in which they function. Without these, there is no profession.

LEGAL STATUS. It is essential for a profession that the law grant it virtual monopolies in addition to the right to manage its own business.

A. M. Carr-Saunders has designated this monopoly aspect as *closure*. By this he means that specific responsibilities are reserved to certain professions. For example, the right to represent a client in court is generally reserved to attorneys; the right to sign a death certificate is generally reserved to medical doctors. That occasional exceptions occur does not negate the principle. These rights in the law are almost universally assured by registry or licensure —the maintenance by government of a list of practitioners whose competence has been demonstrated by preparation and examination.

One writer has expressed this thesis as follows:

> No profession can exist without this protection under the law. It alone must have the right to set conditions of entrance. It alone must have the right to set codes of professional conduct. It alone must have the right to determine the values of professional competence. It follows from this that it alone must exercise discipline over its members and, with due regard to basic human rights, remove delinquents from the lists. Doctors are striken from the rolls, lawyers disbarred, priests defrocked.[3]

If these rights are expected, or extended by society, teachers must be prepared to exercise them in the public interest. No one must be denied access to their professional services. This is why teachers as a group have generally—not universally to be sure, but generally—abhorred the strike. Often when they have condoned the strike, it was only where not their welfare but that of the children was involved—where there were unsafe buildings or unsanitary and dangerous facilities, or where the total educational climate had reached such a state of turmoil as to make it impossible to give proper educational services to children.

These legal rights of teachers and other professionals are the most effective middle course between, on the one hand, the threat of human regimentation by governmental bureaucracies and, on the other, the laissez-faire concept of individual freedom rampant a century ago. At either of these two extremes the individual is maltreated—on the one hand, by the stifling power of bureaucracy, on the other hand by the ruthless power of the unchecked, rugged entrepreneur. In fact, perhaps the most serious handicap to the freedom of teachers is the tendency of the state to treat them as civil servants and not as professionals. This attitude is changing somewhat, but the change must be given greater impetus by the concerted efforts of teachers themselves.

PROFESSIONAL ASSOCIATION. If there is to be a profession, there must be a voluntary, free, independent general association as described above for unified efforts (1) to set the standards, (2) to enable the guaranteeing of individual competence, (3) to enforce ethical practice, and (4) to provide the means of continual growth in service.

The Craft Approach and the Professional Approach

The craft approach to organized effort seems inevitably to focus almost exclusively on the economic advancement of the people within the craft. The professional approach has always been to seek a balance in striving to meet the obligations of the profession to society and at the same time advancing the welfare of its members. Of course, to state or to imply that a teacher who elects to affiliate with a teachers' union is not or cannot be a competent professional is to distort the facts. Such a teacher can be, and most often is, a professional in every sense of the word. In fact, many competent observers assert that the militancy evidenced in the strike and union affiliation is prime evidence of professionalism. Many members of the AFT are also members of the NEA and its affiliated state associations. Although there are no definitive data on the matter, one can assume that this is especially true regarding membership at the local or state level.

What happens in such cases is that the member of the professional association in his impatience with the professional group, which is often slow in correcting grievances and, especially, in securing economic justice, turns to the promise of the teachers' unions for quick and drastic action. Such dual affiliation has to do almost completely with welfare matters. The fact that such teachers tend to retain their affiliation with the professional association is indicative of a kind of organizational schizophrenia (perhaps a temporary one). They want the security which each organization seems best able to provide. At the same time, this would seem to indicate a deep and persisting commitment of teachers to the professional concept. It is apparent, therefore, that the national organization which will attract the loyalties of teachers must provide both types of security.

There is here no intent to imply that the AFT is not, or cannot be, a truly professional organization. However, it is not presently so, as its great friend Myron Lieberman has often pointed out:

> Undeniably, the UFT's parent organization, the American Federation of Teachers, is seriously deficient both as a professional organization and as a union. The AFT has no real program in certification, accreditation, or professional ethics. Its journal is nothing but a house organ, and most of its publications are propagandistic in nature. . . .
>
> Nationally, the AFT has been like a desert tribe, devoting most of its energies to a relentless struggle for existence. It has had little surplus energy for more creative tasks.[4]

The AFT could be a professional organization, and if it should develop professional services, the NEA and its affiliates are doubtless going to be in grave trouble in competing for teachers' loyalties. But this does not appear to be likely in view of AFT ties and obligations to organized labor. By virtue of these ties and obligations, the AFT is most likely to continue to concentrate upon the hope of quick economic rewards and improved working conditions for teachers.

The then director of organization for the United Federation of Teachers (New York City local of the AFT) has cogently expressed the difference between the craft concept and the professional concept of teaching in stating the union's position in attempting to negotiate with the new York City board on class size. The board had ruled this subject non-negotiable on the grounds that class size in a matter of educational policy, not of working conditions.

The union's argument at this point is commendable. Here is the argument as stated by David Selden:

> Teachers are professionals, the UFT stated. In this they differ from other employees who work by the hour or on a piece-work basis, because part of the compensation of a professional is the satisfaction he derives from successful use of his skill. A machine operator is paid by the hour to operate his machine and so long as he is not "sweated" and operates his machine under satisfactory working conditions, his only legitimate concern is with his wages and other benefits. . . . If a teacher is to be considered a production worker, the board's position of tolerance limits would be correct. But a teacher is not merely a production worker. He is a professional.[5]

This statement of the contrast between the craftsman and the professional could hardly be improved upon.

William G. Carr, in his Denver speech, spelled out the unique role of the NEA as a professional association in contrast to a trade-union organization:

1. This is a professional association. This means, among other things, that its members place the welfare of students above all other considerations, and that when the Association defends the rights and interests of the members of the profession, as it must and will, it will do so in a manner calculated to improve the quality of the educational service to society.
2. This is an inclusive organization. Teachers and school administrators are colleagues, not opponents. They do not occupy a master-and-servant or boss-and-hired-hand relationship. Each ought to be deeply concerned about the common objective of high-quality education.
3. This is a democratic organization. Issues are settled by informed voting in which each member, no matter what may be his work in the school system, has one voice and one vote—never more and never less.
4. This is an independent organization. The difference between an independent professional organization and a branch of organized labor is not superficial. It goes to the heart of the unique function of public education in American democracy. The public school serves all the children of all the people—laborers, craftsmen, professional people, office workers, farmers, public officials, managers, and businessmen. Its personnel should not be affiliated to any one segment of the population.

The NEA and Teacher Welfare

Every professional association must have two broad purposes. The first is dedication to the nurture of the altruistic, intellectual, and spiritual qualities basic to any profession worthy of the name, in short, advancing the quality of its services to society. The second is the bread-and-butter purpose, the furthering of the economic welfare of its members.

The NEA has often been criticized for its overemphasis on the one purpose and its lack of aggressiveness concerning the other. This is probably a valid criticism. By its charter, granted by a special act of the congress of the United States in 1904 (the NEA having first been established in 1857 as the National Teachers Association), the NEA is dedicated to this purpose: "To elevate the character and advance the interests of the profession of teaching and to promote the cause of popular education in the United States." This purpose would seem to constitute a dichotomy, two intentions that appear to be contradictory. But the NEA has never considered it as such, believing that everything the NEA does to elevate the character and advance the interests of the teaching profession inevitably promotes the cause of popular education, and vice versa.

Thus its teacher-welfare activities have tended to be indirect. Promoting the cause of education has been its major emphasis. But this is not to say that it has not fought vigorously to advance the interests of the profession, although perhaps it has not fought aggressively enough. It has sought this advancement indirectly, by elevating the character of the profession.

This dual purpose, with each part affecting the other, is often misunderstood and sometimes resented. For example, one of the great revolutions in the NEA structure occurred in the early years of this century when the old guard, the college presidents, was ousted from leadership positions because they refused to concern themselves—or let the association concern itself—with teacher-welfare considerations.

Further revolt occurred about 1920 (partly influenced by Margaret Haley and her colleagues in the Chicago Teachers Federation) because of dissatisfaction with the association's lack of emphasis upon teacher welfare. This revolt took the form of providing proportionate representation in the Representative Assembly, making that body representative of the total profession so that the voice of the rank-and-file members could be heard.

Any discussion of the achievements of the NEA in teacher welfare must always be placed in the context of the association's partnership with the affiliated state and local education associations. As a matter of fact, the state associations have spearheaded most of the gains simply because education is a state responsibility and these gains must largely be activated within the states. Here is where the direct action largely takes place.

The role of the NEA has been that of the great originator of ideas and the great stimulator of action. By serving as the focus of policy-making for the profession as a whole, the NEA has influenced the programs of state and local associations. By providing basic and up-to-date research on every phase of the public-school system, it has stimulated a concerted drive among the states to achieve national standards and goals. By providing intense study of every substantive area of education, through its independent departments, the NEA has stimulated constant improvement in curriculum and methodology in every teaching field. A summary of achievements in teacher welfare would include the following points.

TEACHER TENURE. The AFT, in speeches by its officers and numerous articles in its publications, has sometimes implied that it has been the great instigator and promotor of teacher tenure and that the NEA has been uninterested and inept in achieving job equity for teachers.

The fact is that the NEA began work on tenure legislation as early as 1887 with a resolution urging more suitable tenure of office for teachers. In 1908 the first major report on the problem was made by the NEA Committee on Salaries, Tenure, and Pensions. At that time no state had tenure legislation. New Jersey was the first state to pass a tenure law, in 1909, through the efforts of the New Jersey Education Association.

In 1964, largely as the result of the joint efforts of the NEA and the state associations, thirty-seven states had tenure laws with total or partial coverage of teachers. In addition, seven states had continuing contract-legislation. Six states had neither tenure nor continuing-contract legislation. It is estimated that probably 80 per cent of the nation's public-school teachers have some degree of job security under state laws. In at least two states, superintendents and other administrative personnel have tenure in the system but not in the specific job.

That there is not universal coverage of career teachers with tenure provisions is a crucial weakness of the teaching profession, and the NEA and its state affiliates cannot escape valid criticism for this lag.

NEA and its affiliates in states where no form of tenure legislation exists can be justly and severely criticized for not fighting more vigorously for such legislation. As long as 20 per cent (or whatever the precise percentage is) of public-school teachers do not have job security but are subject to the whims of employers and to capricious and arbitrary treatment, there are just grounds for criticism.

The AFT repeatedly claims that unionism is synonymous with high salaries. This claim certainly has some degree of validity in the industrial field. It does not necessarily obtain in public-school teaching.

An examination of the salary schedules for 1963-64 in the nation's 101 highest salary districts reveals some significant facts. (1) Of the 101 districts, 80 had no AFT locals at all in that year; teachers were members solely of professional associations. (2) All 21 union locals to be found among these 101 districts had a total membership of 1,257. (3) In the same 21 districts, the NEA had a total membership of 6,682. Thus for each teacher who joined a union, more than five joined the NEA, and still more joined their local and state NEA affiliates. (4) Only 3 of those 21 systems, all of them in California, are located in the large urban areas for which both state and NEA professional membership information is readily available. In those 3 districts (Long Beach, Sacramento, and San Jose) there were in 1962–63 a total of 6,577 teachers of whom 4,128 belonged to the NEA, 5,580 to the California Teachers Association, and 157 to the AFT. Thus, while about 2 per cent of the urban teachers with highest-level salaries joined the AFT, over 64 per cent of these teachers were NEA members and 85 per cent were state-association members.

An annual study of the NEA Research Division analyzes salary figures in districts enrolling 6,000 or more pupils. The 1965–66 study[6] reports that of the 101 districts with the highest salaries, 66 were from systems with no AFT membership, and in only 1 of these systems did an AFT local hold exclusive negotiation rights.

A multitude of factors, of course, are involved in any raise in teachers' salaries and school funds in general. No association could pretend to be the sole causal factor in such advances. The general economic growth of the country, particularly in given states, as well as inflation, new taxes, and many other influences enter into the picture.

The NEA and the state associations can claim credit for waging a continual program for adequate support of the public schools. They can also claim credit for having available at all times up-to-date national and state statistics and for using these to create public sentiment for increased school funds. Moreover, the NEA and the state associations can claim credit for developing salary formulas acceptable to the total profession. They can claim credit for training thousands of chairmen of local salary committees throughout the country to present effective salary proposals to local boards of education.

Here are some items reflecting progress. Teachers' salaries, in the 11-year period 1951–62, showed a greater increase in percentage than did the salaries of all national employees (78.9 per cent compared to 55.5 per cent), and showed a greater increase in percentage than those of manufacturing employees (78.9 per cent compared to 58.7 per cent).

In the decade 1951–61, teachers' salaries had a 70 per cent increase as compared to a 54.4 per cent increase for nonschool employees of state and local governments.

The 1966 NEA salary resolution calls for beginning salaries of $8,000 and, for teachers with the master's degree and ten years of experience, a range to $16,000 and higher for career teachers. As to salary schedules, the NEA advocates the single schedule based upon preparation and experience and without discrimination as to grade or subject taught, residence, creed, race, sex, marital status, or number of dependents.

For the nation as a whole, in 1965–66 the average salary of classroom teachers was $6,506, ranging from an average of $5,585 in the Southeast to $8,168 in the Far West. The highest state average is that of California, with $8,600, followed by Alaska, with $8,550.

A total of 62 school systems provide maximum teachers' salaries of $10,500 or more. Thirty-two states have mandated by law state-wide minimum salary schedules for teachers. These laws have been sponsored by the respective NEA state affiliates.

TEACHER RETIREMENT. The NEA has, since 1887, worked vigorously for adequate retirement systems for teachers. In 1936, it joined with the executive officers of state and local retirement systems and state education associations to form the National Council on Teacher Retirement to improve retirement provisions for teachers. Today every state has a teacher-retirement system. In addition, 23 cities have separate retirement systems for their teachers. Thirty-eight of the state systems also include their members in the Federal Social Security Program. The benefits to retirees range widely among the states; in some instances the benefits are deplorably low, in others they approach decent levels. The range in any state closely approximates the range of average teachers' salaries in the same state. Another handicap is the lack of reciprocity among most state retirement systems.

FRINGE BENEFITS. The NEA has in recent years sought other rewards than financial ones for teachers, comparable to those benefits in private industry. In 1958, the NEA sought to amend the Internal Revenue Act to make it possible for teachers to deduct educational expenses for further college work and educational travel. The Internal Revenue Service issued a regulation which appeared to grant this right for teachers. In 1959, the NEA sought a clarification of this regulation from the IRS. In order to gain teachers' full rights comparable to those granted businessmen, the NEA has helped finance many court cases of teachers appealing adverse rulings of IRS regional offices. The NEA has a special fund—the DuShane Defense Fund ($100,000)—and an annual appropriation to help in such legal cases and in cases where teachers have been dismissed without due process. In 1967, an amended IRS regulation greatly liberalized teacher deductions for educational expense.

Another area of fringe benefits for which the NEA works is group insurance for teachers, part of the costs to be borne by the local school system. All but a few of the state associations sponsor group insurance. A low-cost term life insurance program, a group accident insurance program, a mutual fund, and a tax-sheltered annuity program for members of state associations and the

NEA are sponsored by the National Education Association. In addition, certain tax credit for retired teachers was obtained in 1954 and extended in 1962.

DEFENSE OF TEACHERS. The National Commission on Professional Rights and Responsibilities is charged with defending teachers who have been illegally or unfairly dismissed from their positions. Since its creation in 1941, when it was known as the Defense Commission, it has made formal investigations in about 60 communities and defended thousands of teachers against unfair treatment. The DuShane Fund makes grants both for legal fees and for subsistence to teachers who are dismissed without due process. Many teachers have been restored to positions by the courts and many have won judgments for back pay during the period when they were suspended from office.

In 1965, the NEA Board of Directors established the NEA Subcommittee on Human Rights and authorized a campaign to raise by voluntary contributions a fund of at least $1 million to come to the aid of Negro teachers displaced in school integration and to expand the work of the DuShane Defense Fund. (The name of this Fund was changed to DuShane Defense Fund for Teacher Rights, in 1966).

In 1965–66, the DuShane Defense Fund gave legal aid or subsistence, or both, to 51 teachers in 30 states. Among these cases were two that resulted in precedential decisions by the Federal courts of great significance. One involved the dismissal of seven Negro teachers in Giles County, Virginia when their school was integrated. The lower court held that the rights of these teachers under the fourteenth Amendment had been violated and ordered the school board to give them priority in subsequent hiring of teachers. On appeal, the Federal circuit court reaffirmed the decision of the lower court and ordered the immediate offering of position to the dismissed teachers.

In the case of Willa Johnson in Halifax County, North Carolina the lower Federal court upheld the school board, but the circuit court reversed the lower court, ordered the teacher reinstated with back pay for two years, and ordered the lower court to assess damages against the board for discrimination against the teacher.

This case involved a Negro teacher of 12 years' teaching experience in the district. She was dismissed on the grounds of incompetence, but there were strong allegations that the dismissal resulted from civil-rights activities of the teacher and her husband. A procedure believed to be a precedent in Federal courts occurred in this case when the Federal court requested NEA to set up a panel of expert teachers to examine the dismissed teacher as to competence and to testify in the court on their findings.

NEA supported this case with subsistence grants and legal fees over a two-year period at a cost of about $6,000.

With its drive for $1 million for the DuShane reserve fund NEA will be in a position to come to the aid of any teacher where unfair treatment or dismissal without due process is alleged. To an appalling extent teachers are still fair game, in all too many places, for extremists and arbitrary school boards.

Thus the NEA and its affiliated state and local associations are no Johnnies-come-lately in the teacher-welfare field. The gains have not been spectacular, but they have been steady and significant.

A forward-moving aspect of teacher welfare that is rarely recognized is the great advance of the teaching profession under the aegis of the TEPS movement to upgrade standards of preparation and licensure for admission to teaching. This movement, spearheaded by the National Commission on Teacher Education and Professional Standards (NCTEPS), established by NEA in 1946, has had a remarkable effect upon the status of teaching, which in turn has raised the economic rewards for teachers.

As a prime result of the efforts of the NCTEPS and its parallel TEPS commissions in all states, a total of 23 states in the 11-year period 1950–1961 changed their requirements so that the bachelor's degree was required for elementary-school teachers. More states (23) adopted the degree requirement for beginning elementary-school teachers in this period than in all our previous history.

The points often missed in this professional development are these: (1) the raising of admission standards to the college-graduate level creates an image of competence and of professional status for teachers; (2) such levels of preparation tend to prevent this image from being obscured and prevent the undercutting of career teachers by the unqualified; and (3) such levels tend to justify in the public mind the concept that teachers are worthy of professional salary levels.

In other words, it is a mistake to assume that approaches to economic rewards for teachers can be accomplished in only one way. The fact is that the broad approach of improving the quality of education through improving the competence and dedication of teachers may be the most effective long-range attack on the problem of economic justice for teachers.

In addition, the TEPS Commission, in collaboration with the PR and R Commission, has advocated professional practices acts for vesting legal authority in boards of the profession for policing professional requirements. Six states by 1965 had enacted such legislation.

Breadth of the Professional Program

The NEA has been sneeringly referred to by the teachers' union advocates as "the nice old lady of Sixteenth Street" (Sixteenth Street being the location of the NEA building in Washington). This image is made to order for the teacher with a local grievence who wants somebody to crush—immediately—the opposition. It is also made to order for the angry young men who want cataclysmic action to remedy alleged injustices in pay and status.

Is the NEA really so inept as this sneering reference implies?

There is just enough truth in it to enable the image to find favorable response among some teachers. There is, at least, enough truth in it about NEA's past to justify this, but things are changing and changing rapidly. No longer is there in NEA the inertia about helping with and meeting the problems of local teachers' groups. No longer is there inertia about putting some muscle into the fight for teachers' rights and status.

But that's another story, told elsewhere in this volume.

NEA contributions to the furthering of the goals of the teaching profession—what Walter Reuther just before the February 1964 Milwaukee election (which the union lost) referred to as the "abstract professionalism of NEA"—have been significant.

Apparently, Mr. Reuther, in using this denigrating phrase, was referring to every NEA activity not somehow tied directly to money or wages, fringe benefits, and working hours.

It is the "other things" that constitute much of the emphases of any professional organization worthy of the name. "Other things" have to do with such abstract professionalism as the teaching profession's obligations to society: the constant improvement of education and educational opportunity; the upgrading of instruction; the inculcation of idealism and good citizenship and standards of integrity and good moral character; the eternal search to find better ways of serving children; a continuing and honest program of public relations; research; professional growth of its members; stimulation of ever improving standards of preparation and licensure; accreditation of teacher-education programs; dissemination of findings of research about new processes in teaching; enforcement of ethical conduct and practice; the valid use of technology in education; means of dealing with the school drop-out problems; protection of members from unfair or capricious treatment; preserving the principles of academic freedom and academic authority; development and adoption of enlightened school personnel policies; professional orientation of preparing teachers; selective recruitment of future teachers; enforcement of appropriate teacher assignments; development of policy-making machinery extending from the local to the national level, providing every member with the opportunity to participate in determining educational policy; sponsorship of legislation for the improvement of education and the welfare of members, and opposition to legislation deemed harmful to educational progress; and preservation of pluralism through dissemination of diverse viewpoints on educational problems and processes.

These things and more, many more, are involved in a professional program for the teachers. To serve only his welfare needs would leave real voids in the aspirations of the individual teacher.

The "nice old lady of Sixteenth Street" seeks to fulfill these aspirations.

The Professional Unions

James Carey's illustration, in his Denver speech, of the American Newspaper Guild as a case of what unionism can do for a profession turns out to be not so rosy as he pictured it.

The guild is not the perfect answer to the economic problems of journalists; *Time* reported that "in their attempt to organize the newspaper business, the unions are now losing ground. After 29 years of trying, the Guild, for example has barely made a dent; although Guildsmen are sprinkled throughout most of the nation's 1,761 dailies, the Guild has contracts with only 171 papers. . . . In 1938 the Guild membership included 13,505 editorial workers; today, although Guild membership is up to 28,000, the editorial worker category has remained about the same, at 13,000."[7]

Two reasons are given by *Time*. The first is that the Guild is being used to support the strikes of other shop unions. The second is the merger or discontinuance of newspapers as a result of excessive demands by strikers.

Here is a lesson and a warning for teachers. The oft-repeated claim that organized labor would not dictate to or use the teachers' union is not borne out in practice. The occasion for the *Time* story was the settlement of the long and bitter strike of the Teamsters Union against the Cowles Minneapolis papers (the *Star* and *Tribune*). The teamsters enlisted the support of other unions, including the guild, drawing them into a costly, disastrous strike with which the other unions were only peripherally concerned. Is there any assurance that teachers' unions will not be used in the same way to present a united labor front, although the teachers' local may have no grievance at all? For example, on the heels of the New York City strike in April 1962, the press carried accounts of UFT members joining the picket lines of strikers in a Brooklyn hospital. The *Time* article, which delineated the mergers and discontinuance of large city newspapers resulting from strikes and the devastating effect of strikes upon the number of editorial jobs and guild membership, commented: "With the number of newspapers in the United States dwindling at a worrisome rate, has labor's ultimate weapon become too dangerous to wield?"

The argument that teachers' unions will not be used by organized labor to support other unions, that teachers will not be subjected to labor discipline, is not supported by the facts.

The strike of teachers in Granite City, Illinois on April 6, 1964 is a case in point. The teachers were not striking, but the teachers' union voted to support a strike of school janitors and cafeteria workers by refusing to cross picket lines, thus closing the city's 19 schools.[8]

Another case in point:

> The United Federation of Teachers today urged its members serving in private schools struck by the Community School Employees Union not to perform duties usually performed by striking non-teaching personnel.
>
> The struck schools are Hawthorne Cedar Knolls School, Pleasantville Cottage School, Linden Hill School, Ittelson Center and the Edenwald School.
>
> The UFT, together with the Empire State Federation of Teachers, asked the teachers in the schools not to perform extracurricular or group work activities for the duration of the strike.
>
> The teachers were also asked to contribute to the strike relief fund, and to help maintain picket lines after hours.[9]

Teachers may also ponder the case of censorship imposed upon the Cleveland *Plain Dealer* by the Teamsters Union in August 1962. A rival union, competing with the Teamsters Union for membership, inserted a full-page ad in that paper which contained a paragraph objectionable to the teamsters. By threatening not to deliver the paper, the teamsters forced the editor to stop the presses and remove the offending paragraph. Is it too far-fetched to speculate that such censorship could be extended to textbooks or to the utterances of a teacher in the classroom if teachers were tied in with organized labor? Perhaps not. But it is an interesting question. (Subsequent to the writing of this statement, a ban on textbooks from the Kingsport Press did occur. See Chapter 13.) To recount the many attempts of other groups, especially business groups, to influence the curriculum and to intimidate teachers is no justification for similar efforts by organized labor. Both are immoral. The obvious conclusion is that teachers must forego affiliation with any special-interest group, must resist censorship, dictation, and intimidation from any and all organized segments of our society. (The foregoing was written in 1963. See Chapter 14, "The Price Is not Right," written in 1966), for subsequent events.

The long and drawn-out New York City newspaper strike was one in which the Newspaper Guild was not directly concerned. It had already concluded a satisfactory contract agreement. But the Guild was drawn into the strike to support the printers and lithographers, and while these groups readily found jobs in printing shops during the strike, many members of the guild were forced to subsist by driving taxis or doing other menial jobs they could find. Likewise, the long four-and-a-half-month newspaper strike in Detroit, beginning in July 1964, was one fomented by the pressmen. But guild members were pulled in, too.

The AFT's affiliation with organized labor means that its educational policies will likely be determined by AFL-CIO. There is no evidence that AFT has affected at all the educational policies of AFL-CIO. It has been pointed out elsewhere in this volume that AFT is inevitably caught in the web of AFL-CIO's school-tax policies, which are against the sales tax and other excise taxes, solid portions of school support in many states. This is AFL-CIO policy, not AFT policy, but AFT has conformed.

Another example: In the press on November 9, 1964, Charles Cogen, President of AFT, announced that the AFT Executive Council had endorsed The Proposed Elementary and Secondary Education Act, ostensibly to bring AFT policy more in line with AFL-CIO.

Al Shanker, president of UFT, immediately protested that this action had been taken without the sanction of any of the AFT locals or a vote of the AFT delegate body. Shanker said (in the *United Teacher,* September 23, 1964): "This stand by the Executive Council went contrary to a resolution approved by the AFT Convention in Philadelphia in 1961. That (resolution) stated, 'unalterable opposition to federal aid to private and parochial schools'. . . . [This] was the last general membership sentiment on the subject. . . ."

The point here is not to argue the question of private-school aid but to show the scramble of AFT (without prior authorization of its membership) to align itself with AFT-CIO policy.

This is for teachers to ponder.

In his Denver speech, James Carey referred also to engineers' professional unions. Doubtless some engineers in some industries are compelled to affiliate with the unions. But here is what their professional society thinks about union affiliation.

> The issue of professionalism or unionism in the engineering profession is today's challenge to the professional engineers of America. It is a challenge which must be quickly and decisively resolved. . . .
>
> What is the nature of this problem? It is simply whether the engineer will remain a professional man and advance as such, or whether he is going to allow the unionism philosophy to represent him in all his affairs as the device for resolving his economic problems. All side issues such as the theory of the "professional union," are mere side-stepping arguments which beg the main question.
>
> NSPE's position is clear and unequivocal. As a Society we have stated that "it is definitely unprofessional for a professional engineer, professionally employed, voluntarily to join a heterogeneous labor union, dominated by, or obligated to, non-professional groups." As long ago as 1948, our Society declared that "the individual responsibility and independent judgment required of a professional engineer are incompatible with the regimentation fundamentally inherent in unionization." Our statement clearly indicates that labor union affiliation necessarily means the sacrifice of professional status. And I would take it that our position includes the so-called "professional" unions as well as the trade unions. . . .
>
> The naked issue then is whether the temporary economic benefits the unions claim they can obtain for professional engineers are worth the long range loss of professional status. NSPE believes that we cannot have our cake and eat it too; we must make our choice. Some members of the profession are committed

> to the union philosophy, a greater number have clearly indicated their preference for development through professional societies, and the largest group stands in the middle, uncommitted to either position as evidenced by their failure to join either a union or a professional society.[10]

Also, the American Association of University Professors, toward which the AFT has directed overtures for merger, stated in the summer of 1966 ". . . our Association is not a trade union, it is not part of the trade union movement, and it does not seek identification with organized labor which trade union status would imply."

The drive of the teachers' unions is for members—any members—not just teachers. The drive is for school janitors, custodians, cafeteria workers, bus drivers—any school workers. Certainly these are honorable people who are entitled to economic justice. The point is that in attempting to serve all these interests, teachers will inevitably be called upon to fight the fight of these workers, to join picket lines, and to join in support of their strikes. Thus teachers are compelled to make a choice when choosing organization affiliation whether they want to be members of a craft or members of a profession.

9

The Teacher Unions: Philosophy and Practice

> The question of why the AFT insists on affiliation with the AFL-CIO does deserve an answer, however. The first and most obvious reason, of course, is that of practicality. In any dispute with city and school officials, or with state officials, teachers rarely have the force to go it alone against the power structure. In every major city, and in many state legislatures, the labor movement is a potent power bloc, and it is virtually the only friendly force available to teachers. You may not like everything that these "labor blocs" do, but they are there and they must be dealt with.
>
> When teachers are a part of organized labor they have an influence on its policy and action, reducing the possibility of adverse action as well as providing an opportunity to induce favorable action and support. This cannot be done when teachers are on the outside looking in, reacting to decisions after they have been made.
>
> —David Selden, "Why the AFT Maintains Its AFL-CIO Affiliation," *Phi Delta Kappan* February 1966

Obviously, AFT decided after New York to thrust itself into a full-scale alliance with organized labor. Whereas, prior to 1960, the alliance was somewhat tenuous and token, thereafter it was to be vigorous, aggressive, and vocal. Whereas, prior to 1960, there were muted, intermittent, and casual references to the ties to the labor affiliation, thereafter the strategy became one of proud assertion of the alliance. The peripheral connection gave way to a comprehensive adoption of labor philosophy and procedures. Two things had happened.

In the first place, labor, which had endured the long-time and ineffective alliance with AFT with an amused tolerance, now found that it needed to raid teachers' organizations to spearhead its life-saving campaign to organize public employees to get at the burgeoning and unorganized white-collar groups.

Secondly, AFT, getting nowhere in attracting the rapidly increasing numbers of public-school teachers to its ranks, was desperate for financial help and a respectable power structure. It was simply a case of all-out alliance with labor or perish. The coffers of AFL-CIO now opened invitingly. Ample organizing funds could be had for the asking. The political power of AFL-CIO in Congress, in the state legislatures, and especially in the cities was essential if AFT was to make more than a dent in the encrusted shell of professional loyalties of teachers.

Thus, after 1960 (the date is an approximation since this shift was developmental and did not happen all at once) AFT began to take on the full coloring of a trade union, embracing fully the philosophy, the tactics, and the strategy of the labor movement.

This was a bold gamble that paid off. It was a well-timed switch. Teachers in considerable numbers were ready for the harsh plunge into militancy.

Union Plans

The New York City situation was made to order, as has been pointed out elsewhere, for the launching of labor's drive to organize America's public-school teachers.

This decision by labor to capture the nation's teachers, as the most effective possible invasion of the white-collar field, was not a new one. Labor had known for several years that it must make the assault on teachers' professional organizations. Labor simply bided its time for the right situation. New York City was it. And the leadership of the AFT was made to order. Whatever may be the judgment on their tactics, Charles Cogen and David Selden proved to be vigorous, dynamic, and radical leaders of UFT, the AFT local in New York City, even to the point of shocking labor leaders. But they got away with unprecedented acts against the authorities and the law. Obviously they sensed the vacillation of the politicians and the wobbly position of the New York City Board of Education more perceptibly than had the labor leaders.

Teachers were the ideal group for the break-through for many reasons. For instance: (1) Teaching was a sellers' market, where there were more jobs than workers and where demand was likely to outrun supply for years to come. (2) Teaching presented a labor market in which economic rewards had lagged by comparison to other fields requiring comparable preparation and skills. (3) Teaching represented a field of eminent respectability. Only after New York City was the hush-hush Industrial Union Department (IUD) drive on teachers pushed out into the open. The facts were then too obvious to be longer obscured. At the time of the New York City campaign, AFT membership was only about 60,000, which could not possibly produce the money spent in that campaign. Estimates on the amount spent ranged from $250,000 to $500,000 in money and manpower. Knowledgeable observers surmised that this money had to come from the IUD, and this was later confirmed. Since the New York City campaign, the IUD has, through its literature and speeches by its officers, made it clear that it is managing and financing the campaign to organize the teachers of the United States. It is well known that the much-heralded UFT contract with the New York Board of Education was negotiated not by UFT teachers but by Jack Conway, then Director of the IUD, and Harry Van Arsdale, Head of the New York Central Labor Council.

The campaign in Milwaukee (which the AFT lost) was managed by Nick Zonarich, IUD Organizational Director, and Franz Daniel, one of his top assistants, with direct help from Walter Reuther, Vice-President of the AFL-CIO.

In his address to the annual convention of the AFT in August 1963, Carl Megel confirmed the out-and-out participation of labor as follows:

> We cannot boast of membership records without acknowledging the debt of gratitude we owe to Walter Reuther, Nicholas Zonarich, and all of the other IUD representatives who have given us so much help and assistance during the past two years. Their help in men and money was invaluable to the New York collective bargaining campaign which gave the impetus to New York for its spectacular rise in membership. Their direct organizational assistance to locals in Boston, Philadelphia, Newark, Chicago, West Suburban Milwaukee, St. Paul, Minneapolis, and Los Angeles contributed to the all-time gains in these areas.

It is well known, too, that as of March 1967 the IUD had raised a $4 million "war chest," in cash and contributed manpower, to organize white-collar workers, with first emphasis upon public-school teachers. The major contributors are the United Automobile Workers, the United Steel Workers, the International Union of Electrical Workers, the Textile Workers Union of America, and the International Association of Machinists. A direct appropriation of $362,000 was made in 1965 to AFT by IUD. The IUD has available over 200 union organizers on its own staff and on loan from other union staffs. The precise number of these assigned to organize teachers is not known, but it is believed to be significant.

Strategy of the Industrial Union Department

Labor's over-all strategy in the drive to organize teachers was indicated in the New York City elections.

The IUD program, obviously, was to concentrate initial efforts in school districts where conditions were like those existing in New York City. The psychology was to capitalize upon the success there, to be sure of initial success, and to generate the concept that a great tide was under way. Based on this psychology, it makes sense that the big push should be concentrated in Chicago, Detroit, Cleveland, Milwaukee, Minneapolis, Boston, Philadelphia, and Los Angeles. Thus there has been since New York continual agitation in most of these cities for collective-bargaining elections, circulating of petitions for elections, picketing, and repeated threats of strikes if school boards did not yield to demands for an election.

A second tactic of the IUD was to conduct holding actions in cities not yet deemed ripe for teacher unionization, until greater status could be attained for the teachers' unions, through victories in the favorable cities.

A third tactic was to attempt to downgrade the professional aspects of teaching by emphasizing that teachers, unlike members of private professions, are primarily workers. This tactic has usually taken the form of downgrading the notion that teachers should give priority to their obligation to children and to standards of practice. The blunt appeal is to self-interest, the "bread-and-butter" appeal. A corollary of this appeal has been to emphasize reduction of class size—to make the teacher's job easier and to improve working conditions—not in order to improve education. This gimmick—the effort to set a maximum class size—is found in the New York City contract without reference to the subject or caliber of students involved.

A fourth IUD method was to divide and conquer. The goal was to isolate the local professional association by separating it from its affiliated state association and from the NEA. The strategy was to attack both as rurally oriented unions and as company unions. Walter Reuther used the divide-and-conquer technique in his Milwaukee speech. He said: "For a group of classroom teachers to select as their bargaining representative an affiliate of NEA is like putting the fox in charge of the chicken house." Likewise, the NEA was to be pictured as a national colossus seeking to destroy the traditional local autonomy in the operation of schools. This gimmick has been so successful that many innocent school-board members began mouthing that propaganda.

The unions seek to sell the concept that teachers welfare is best advanced by an organized *local* work force hammering out a deal with the *local* school board. Of course, this concept is embellished with the promise of raw power to drive a favorable collective-bargaining agreement, backed up by threats of picket lines and strikes and the political muscle of organized labor. There are intimations that the teachers' brothers and sisters in the labor unions will back their demands for better working conditions. This did not happen in Newark or in the St. John's University strike in late 1965. Organized Labor refused to support these strikes.

This tactic, of course, avoids facing the fact that improved teacher welfare is dependent upon improved school financing. It also avoids the fact that, because trade unions are political organisms highly sensitive to and responsive to the economic interests of their members, these interests are often going to be in conflict with teachers' efforts to broaden the tax base for school revenues through sales taxes and other excise taxes. Thus school financing is treated in general terms so that the strengths of the professional association in this sensitive area will not be highlighted and the weakness of trade unionism will not be exposed.

This IUD tactic aims at isolating the local association from its state and national affiliate for the purpose, essentially, of setting up an uneven contest. If this isolation can be effected, the competition is then between a well-financed, tightly knit, seasoned national labor organization and an underfinanced underexperienced local association. In effect, it is then a contest between full-time professionals and rank amateurs. This is a neat trick if labor can pull it off, and it has in several situations.

And labor has been rather successful, because some local and state associations have not yet realized that these local elections are being run from the Washington, D.C. office of IUD. The local associations are not competing with amateurs in the local AFT, but with seasoned labor organizers. If this point needs substantiation, we can point to the fact that the secretary of the St. Louis AFT local resigned because an IUD organizer was sent to St. Louis and promptly took over the program of the local. In Philadelphia, the organizer for the brewers' union directed the election campaign of the teachers' union.

Finally, the IUD is gearing for a long war of attrition in the hope that the professional associations will exhaust their resources and grow weary of the fight.

There are some signs that the IUD may be altering some of its tactics. The Milwaukee election exposed the nature of the onslaught of organized labor against the professional associations. The Milwaukee election brought into focus the importance of an independent teaching profession as opposed to a teachers' organization financed and controlled by persons whose basic loyalties are elsewhere and who would use teachers as a stepping stone to bigger aspirations.

The Milwaukee election also revealed that professional associations are involved in a national conflict. It brought to light the fact that an attack on one professional association is actually an attack on all professional associations. The Milwaukee election forced the IUD to re-examine its concentration on welfare issues and to reappraise its soft-pedaling of professionalism.

Teachers' Union Tactics

The foregoing has dealt largely with the over-all strategy of IUD. There are a series of specific tactics which AFT locals use so repeatedly as to suggest a common, handed-down pattern or propaganda line. In sequence, here are the assertions and claims used by AFT locals to win converts and to influence elections.

1. Collective bargaining is a magic weapon, an inherent right of all workers. Teachers don't have it because administrators and school boards do not want them to. This picture is a good rabble-rousing stereotype. It is especially appealing when buttressed by stress upon its democratic-American way-of-life nature. This argument is based upon the assumption that teachers are workers and that there is no argument about whether they should be involved in the labor movement and in the processes established by law to serve employees in private industry.

2. The strength of unions, by which is meant the economic and political power of unions, is a great bulwark of protective power for the teachers. Unions are pictured as being able to protect teachers against the administraion, the school board, and the indifferent public. Again there is the image of the the enemy, a ploy designed to give teachers a bad guy to hate. Again, this is the image of organized labor as Big Brother, with power, money, and know-how to get for teachers their heart's desires.

3. An interesting switch of this power image is subtly used to the advantage of AFT. This is the David-Goliath analogy, in which the comparatively small AFT is pictured as a little David battling against tremendous odds with the giant NEA as the Goliath. Education writers like this analogy and propagate it with great vigor. But it conveniently overlooks the facts. The battle is really between AFL-CIO and NEA; and here the David is NEA and organized labor is Goliath. Big labor has 15 times the membership of NEA and hundreds of times the resources. But these facts are rarely alluded to in news stories.

This is a powerful propaganda gimmick making use of the American's traditional sympathy for the underdog.

4. Teachers are professionals and want to be respected. Teachers must have higher salaries to be respected because ours is a mercenary society where respect follows the dollar. This is a comparatively recent departure from the union designation of teachers as workers, not professionals. In the past the unions have sought (1) to impel teachers to give up their professional posture by belittling their aspirations in this direction, and (2) to intimidate teachers by calling them snobs who resist classification as workers.

The new line is that unions have as their goal the building of a profession based on adequate economic rewards and on the removal of barriers to the achievement of quality education; in removing these barriers the unions will work for reduction in class size, leaves of absence, and the right to bargain with administrators and boards about salaries and conditions of work.

5. The alleged ineffectiveness of the NEA is, of course, at the heart of the union tactics. The attack is seldom upon state associations or the local association. The attack is focused upon the NEA. The NEA is pictured as a group ineffective in securing teacher welfare, an organization that deals in

"abstract professionalism," publishes pamphlets, conducts research, and creates committees, but, so the propaganda goes, never really does anything to improve the lot of teachers.

Walter Reuther embellished this line in his Milwaukee speech with the statement, "You could put all that NEA has done for the welfare of teachers in one corner of your eye and not obscure your vision."

The teachers' union also has a well-mapped set of procedural steps for intimidating school boards.

Here are the steps in organizing techniques as outlined by Albert Shanker, 1967 President of the United Federation of Teachers, New York City, in a panel discussion on "Concepts of Techniques To Be Used Relative to Collective Bargaining," at the AFT convention in New York City, August 1963. (At the time of this statement Shanker was secretary and assistant to the president of UFT.)

1. [Have a] union officer tell a member of the board of education privately that a certain procedure is not good.
2. Send a letter criticizing the action and threatening, in a postscript, to use publicity.
3. Use publicity through a resolution by the union's executive board.
4. Call a larger meeting such as [a meeting of] the union's delegate assembly.
5. Circulate petitions.
6. Hold a protest demonstration such as a rally at a meeting of the board of education.
7. Have the teachers picket their own schools as the children arrive in the morning at the opening of school.
8. Strike.

Local AFT Tactics

The tactics of AFT locals follow a fairly common pattern to gain recognition and force an election to select an exclusive bargaining agent for the teachers. When an election is set IUD takes over.

Instructions for local AFT strategy would be about as follows: (1) Contact the superintendent and softly imply that if he keeps silent he will be given preferred treatment, thus robbing the school system of a protesting voice. Once the union is in, the superintendent becomes the target of vituperation. (2) Get a local, even if it has only 10 members. Refuse to divulge the names of members or the number of members, on the grounds of fear of reprisal or dismissal. This ploy is calculated to attract sympathy for the abused underdog. So deep is the devotion of Americans to the doctrine of fair play that this is a powerful posture. (3) Start shouting about the horrible conditions

AFT Will Back Kenosha Teachers if They Strike

Teacher Unionist Says Strikes Legal

Teachers Stage March on School Board

Angry Parents Force Talks In Teachers' Strike

Teachers Union Calls Off Strike In Louisville

1,000 Cheering Teachers Attend Class on Picketing

Teachers Give Strike Ultimatum on Bargaining

Teacher Strike Threat Revived

Teachers to Strike If Bargaining Bill Fails?

Teachers Drive For Collective Bargaining

Teachers put off strike threat

TEACHERS ON STRIKE-

Teachers Union Is Talking Tough

Turmoil, Turmoil

teachers are subjected to. The noise must be loud enough to convey the idea that the union membership, if not including a majority of the teachers, is several times what it actually is.

This loud breastbeating about teacher mistreatment is a sure-fire gimmick calculated to drive a wedge between the teachers and their professional association. This tactic is predicated upon the very human failing of learning to hate something before loving the alternative. It also capitalizes upon the willingness of human beings to accept the notion that they are not getting what they justly deserve. This is easy for teachers because, generally, they are not.

The gimmick is, first, to get teachers to hating their superintendents and school boards as the cause of their mistreatment. Second, it is aimed at getting the teachers to believe that their professional association is either a party to their troubles or is unable to do anything about correcting them.

Once the hate mechanisms are implanted, the notion that everything is wrong with the school system is easily sold.

The next step in the thought process is a natural: only the union is equipped to get the job done, and it promises in glowing language to do just that.

After gaining a foothold, the teachers' union begins purring softly, suggesting to the local association which still has a majority of teachers in its membership, that it wants to live and let live, to coexist peacefully, to work together toward mutual goals. At this point, the emphasis is heavy upon respecting the rights of the underdog (the union). If resistance develops, the union doesn't hesitate to remind members of the professional association of its code of ethics and admonishes them to be nice, to act like professionals.

Finally, if all goes well—if a sufficient number of teachers are attracted—the local union demands a bargaining election, whether legal or not, picketing and threatening a strike to intimidate the school board into acquiescence. When the election is won the sweetness and light go out of the window. The union no longer wants or will tolerate an equal role with the professional association. Suddenly all the horrendous problems the unions convinced teachers existed disappear. Everything is now all right by the single act of placing faith in the union.

A New Format

A new formula has come into being, judging from the utterances of teacher union leaders. Project an unfailing success story, talk big, act big, claim big, and never admit a mistake or a failure. The teachers' union leaders, faithful to the formula, emulate the language, the tactics, and the stereotyping of the big brother (AFL-CIO). Patented phrases are lavishly directed at the opposition—such phrases as *sweetheart contract; collective begging; bargain, don't beg; unfair labor practice; slave labor injunction; callous school boards;*

company union; and *tyrannical management* (used against school superintendents and boards).

An example of image-projecting is the sustained propaganda campaign to demonstrate that the professional associations have really made no significant contributions to the improvement of education and teacher welfare—propaganda that is something of an affront to credulity and a gross distortion of the facts.

This propaganda brushes aside the record of NEA, which has served both education and teacher welfare with some distinction for more than a century. It ignores the great contributions of the state education associations, ten of which antedated the NEA. These associations have been involved in virtually every gain for education, in virtually every advance in the welfare and status of teachers. Of course, no single organization or influence can claim exclusive credit for such gains. But to deny the key roles of these professional associations in bringing these to pass is to rewrite history, to say the least.

Consider the long, slow evolution of public education in the United States beginning with the magnificent innovations and influences of Horace Mann and his New England contemporaries. The professional associations assumed the obligation of implementing the dreams of these pioneers. The associations carried forward the crusade for universal free public education until free schooling was within the reach of virtually every American child, a complete system available to most. They fought to establish normal schools and fought for programs to prepare enough teachers for the ever burgeoning schools for the masses. They led the fight for raising standards of preparation and admission to teaching, for in-service growth programs for teachers, for broadened curricula in the schools, for the legal establishment of high schools and our public system of colleges and universities, for free textbooks, equalization of educational opportunity, the extended school term, increased school financial support, and nursery schools and kindergartens.

Concurrently, the professional associations kept up constant pressures to elevate the character of teaching and the status of teachers. Tenure laws, single-salary schedules, retirement systems, fringe benefits, academic authority and freedom—all these the professional associations labored over the years to bring to fruition.

Yet the AFT litany, as reflected in its publications and public statements, is that the record of the professional associations is one of vast and unvarying failure! This is parochialism run riot.

The West Allis Case

In the fall of 1963, AFT Local 1067 in West Allis, Wisconsin protested recognition by the school board of the West Allis-Milwaukee Teachers

Association as representing the majority of teachers. The protest was made to the Wisconsin Employment Relations Board on the grounds that (1) the West Allis Association was a company union because it included supervisors, and (2) no election on recognition had been held.

Incensed by these tactics, the California Teachers Association newspaper, *CTA Action,* on February 21, 1964, editorialized as follows:

Unpleasant Duty

"Why should the CTA and NEA oppose the AFT?" is occasionally asked by well-meaning members. "Aren't all these organizations interested in the advancement of the profession and the improvement of the teacher's lot?"

Unfortunately no. And when AFT's vaunted boasts of helping teachers turn out to actually be harming them, then it's the unpleasant task of CTA and NEA officials to oppose them and to set the record straight.

Recent action in Wisconsin is a good example of what we're talking about.

It involves a decision handed down by the Wisconsin Employment Relations Board on an effort made by AFT Local 1067 to disqualify the West Allis-West Milwaukee Teachers Association and the Wisconsin Education Association from representing teacher groups before their boards of education.

The AFT has been trumpeting that the decision marked a great victory for it. But the trumpeting masks a hat full of sour notes and several alarming facts.

The truth of the matter is that the decision is a significant victory for the professional organizations. It upholds the right of supervisors to be active members of the WEA and WA-WMTA as well as refuting charges that either group is "company dominated."

The decision also makes it clear that with the 415 WA-WMTA members out of a total of 514 classroom teachers in the district, there is no question . . . that the association is the valid spokesman for teachers in the area.

Since union policy favors the secretive approach, Local 1067's membership total is not known, but it's apparent that only a minority of those eligible belong.

Despite this clear-cut verdict on behalf of the associations, the board said there should be an election to determine the representative agency because when WA-WMTA was given recognition, union leaders should have been called in, asked to prove that they had majority support and then given advice on how to produce this proof.

Now, after raising the question in the first place, AFT leaders don't want the election. They're determined to stall it off because they lack the votes to win.

WA-WMTA and the WEA feel the election unnecessary but are eager to have it held—to clear the issue once and for all.

This may all sound like organizational maneuvering and not too important to the teachers.

But the legal uncertainty caused by AFT's challenge could force the school trustees to rescind a 4 per cent salary boost just negotiated by WA-WMTA. This is on top of a 3 per cent increase won a year ago and further indication of WA-WMTA's position as an able representative of the teachers.

With no doubt as to the result of an election and the possibility of losing a salary increase, why does AFT then stall and attempt to hold off the inevitable outcome?

The simple truth is that the AFT is not being run by teachers for the benefit

> of teachers. It is now a captive of the Industrial Union Department of the AFL-CIO, financed, dominated and controlled by non-teachers in IUD's Washington, D.C. headquarters. These professional organizers see teachers as a stepping-stone toward attracting white collar workers to union ranks. They see the Wisconsin situation as an opportunity to make some propaganda hay—particularly if the facts are ignored.
>
> IUD is concerned that another loss in Wisconsin would stall their propaganda drive in the big cities.
>
> Rejection of their bid to gain control in Milwaukee has only made them more desperate.
>
> They couldn't care less about the teacher who stands to lose a hard-earned pay raise because of its activity.

The West Allis-Milwaukee Teachers Association won the election on April 14, 1964 by a vote of 320 to 189, out of a possible 532 votes. This means that approximately 97 per cent of the eligible voters were voting. There were two votes for no agent and four votes contested.

The Butte Case

The AFT has vigorously and repeatedly charged that NEA membership is forced, that superintendents pressure their teachers to enroll.

The teachers' unions rarely discuss their own tactics for securing a closed shop, assuring, as organized labor phrases it, "union security."

The case of the Butte, Montana School District and the unions attempt to coerce nonunion teachers is a good example.

As is well known, Butte is a copper-mining area, the scene of bitter battles between labor and the powerful Anaconda Copper Company. As a result of this sustained bitter fight for the rights of the miners, Butte quite naturally became a town of intense loyalty to organized labor.

It was also quite natural that a teachers' union would have here a favorable climate and soil in which to grow. Thus it is no surprise that in 1956 the Butte School Board extended exclusive bargaining rights to the local AFT-affiliated teachers' union. The contract resulting from this recognition of the teachers' union contained a union security provision. The contract states:

> Union Security—As a condition of employment all teachers employed by the Board shall become members and maintain membership in the union as follows:
>
> All new teachers or former teachers employed by the Board shall become members of the union within 30 days after date of their employment and shall maintain their membership in good standing. . . .
>
> Any teacher who fails to sign a contract which includes the provision of this Union security clause shall be discharged on the written request of the Union, except that any such teachers who now have tenure under the laws of the state of Montana shall not be discharged but *shall receive none of the benefits nor salary increase negotiated by the Union, and shall be employed without contract,*

> *from year to year on the same terms and conditions as such teacher was employed at during the year 1955–56.*

The contract, for some reason not known, contained a discriminatory provision against married women:

> No married woman who is now economically self-dependent shall be hired unless a standing committee from the Butte Teachers Union agrees that all applicants from colleges and state teacher placement agencies have been contacted and none is available. If it becomes necessary to employ a married woman as a teacher, she shall be rotated on the job so that her work will not be continuous enough to give her tenure.[1]

Eight tenure teachers in the Butte system returned their contracts with the union-security clause deleted. The board ruled that these teachers would not receive the increment of about $300 and other benefits accorded the union teachers, but would serve under the terms of their contract in the previous year without contract. In other words, preparation and years of experience were ruled out as measures of competence. Only one measure was to be used in awarding salary raises: union membership. State tenure and continuing contract laws, which has been sponsored by the professional associations, protected these eight teachers from outright dismissal.

The teachers appealed to the Montana Education Association and the National Education Association for assistance in taking the matter to the courts. These two associations did come to the assistance of the eight teachers as joint petitioners in a court case; the AFT and the Montana AFL-CIO joined on the side of the school board. The teachers asked for voiding the union-security clause in the teachers' contracts and for judgment awarding them back pay.

The Montana District Court found in favor of the teachers and ordered the board to enter into contracts with the eight teachers, providing them the same pay as the schedule called for for union teachers and awarding them back pay due for the year.

The union appealed the case to the Montana Supreme Court. Appellants intervening for the teachers were the NEA and MEA, and for the Butte union the appellants were the AFT and the Montana AFL-CIO.

The Montana Supreme Court sustained the lower court's decision in the following language:

> Under our system, the Government is established by, and run for all the people, not for the benefit of any person or group. The profit motive, inherent in the principle of free enterprise is absent (from government employment). For the purposes of this case, it is for us to say that the school authorities have no power or authority to discriminate between teachers as to the amount of salary paid to each because of their membership or lack of membership in a labor union.

The Supreme Court of Montana has denied a petition for a rehearing of the

Butte case, having decided that a school board could not discriminate against nonunion teachers by denying them salary increases. The AFT had thrown its legal support behind its Butte local, which had a closed-shop type of contract with the local school board, while the NEA and the MEA fought for the rights of the nonunion members in the Butte schools. A news account of the results:

> $21,780 in back pay will go this month to 10 nonunion teachers in Butte, Montana. The Butte board voted to pay the teachers after all appeals had been exhausted in its fight, backed by AFT, to withhold salary increases from nonunion teachers.
>
> Suit on behalf of 8 of the 10 teachers had been brought by the Montana Education Association and NEA. The eight teachers were members of MEA and NEA.[2]

Picayune Potpourri

In 1957, the Contra Costa, California Local 866, AFT, asked the musicians' union to expel from membership William Bouton, a music teacher in the Richmond schools, on the grounds that (1) he served as president of the "local company union"—the Richmond Education Association, an affiliate of the California Teachers Association, (2) he was not a member of, nor did he lend support to, the teachers' union, and (3) on two occasions he had crossed picket lines of the teachers' union when the teachers union was trying to prevent the district governing board from holding regular meetings.

The musicians' union expelled Bouton, thus depriving him of supplemental income earned as a part-time musician. Bouton brought suit on December 19, 1957 to get reinstatement in the musicians' union. This suit was financed jointly by the NEA and the California Teachers Association. In his complaint, Bouton stated that he considered the objectives of the union shop and closed shop inappropriate to public-school employment and the use of threat of picketing, boycotting, and striking as detrimental to the teaching profession.

He stated that he considered the threatened use by the musicians' union of its economic power to compel him to join and support Teachers Local 866 against his will an abuse of rights and privileges which have been given to the musicians union for the protection of musicians, and for no other reason.

When the unions realized they could not win the suit, it was settled out of court in Mr. Bouton's favor under the following terms:

1. Locals number 6 and number 424 of the American Federation of Musicians of the United States and Canada will immediately reinstate Mr. Bouton to membership in good standing in each of the unions, restore to him all rights and privileges of said memberships . . . without prejudice or discrimination in any way due to any of the acts, positions or views of Mr. Bouton referred

to in the complaint in such action or due to the continued refusal of Mr. Bouton to join the defendent teachers' union.

2. The defendent musicians' union will pay to Mr. Bouton the sum of $1,000 as reimbursement for the expense of litigation.[3]

Thus ended an effort of an AFT local to enforce membership through use of the power of another union, a case which affected thousands of music teachers who also served as part-time musicians.

In San Diego, California, the following statement was given wide circulation among teachers:

Extra

Punish Teachers

Last month assemblyman Charles Chapel introduced AB 95, a bill which would have made it a misdemeanor for teachers to advocate the election of a candidate for public office.

Last week the CTA [California Teachers Association] appeared at a committee hearing in favor of the measure. The AFT was successful in having the bill killed in committee over the objections of the CTA and "scairt-agin" Sheridan Hegland, Assemblyman from La Mesa.

The facts:

A member of the [California] Assembly wrote to the President of the San Diego Teachers Association stating that the statement was "false and misleading in almost every detail." He labeled it as a "malicious attempt to assail the record of leadership of the California Teachers Association in protecting the rights of teachers."

[The bill] was designed to prohibit *any* public employee from engaging in *improper* political activity during the hours of his employment. . . .

In its original form, the bill did single out teachers and was broadened in scope *because of the strong objection of the California Teachers Association. . . .*[4]

The teachers' union did not have the bill killed; at no time did any representative of the AFT appear to offer any suggestions or comments or to raise any objection to the bill.

Oakland, 771, Blocks "Illegal" Practice

Oakland, California—The doubtful and allegedly illegal practice by principals here of releasing teachers from school to serve as "official representatives" of the non-union Oakland Teachers Association has been corrected at the request of the Oakland Federation of Teachers, Local 771.

George D. Stokes, Local 771 President, protested the release from duties required of other faculty members, to school Supt. Selmer H. Berg, and cited an opinion of its illegality from the attorney for the California State Federation of Teachers.[5]

Credit for salary increases in Hawaii has been claimed by the two island locals of AFT in a report to the *American Teacher*.

The territorial legislature, after hearing testimony by Robert McLain, NEA salary consultant, and the Hawaii Education Association, enacted a $900 salary increase for Hawaii's teachers. Mr. McLain spent two weeks in the islands working with the HEA, whose program was largely adopted by the legislature. Hawaii union membership reported to the AFT is 98. NEA and HEA membership is 4,758. There are 5,007 teachers in the islands.[6]

Credit for salary increases in Houston has been claimed by the new AFT local there, according to Mrs. Mary Heickman, President.

According to official AFT reports, the Houston local has 85 members. There are 7,326 teachers in Houston.[7]

AFT has notified the World Confederation of Organizations of the Teaching Profession (WCOTP) that it will withdraw from membership, thus leaving NEA as the sole national representative of the United States in this important world organization.

At the WCOTP convention, held at the NEA center in August [1959], AFT had only one delegate, based on a membership reported to WCOTP as only 6,440 members.[8]

Protests against closing of schools for an annual professional association meeting have been made by the Toledo (Ohio) Federation of Teachers.

The union charges that members are "coerced into buying tickets" for Northwestern Ohio Education Association meetings, that the meetings are not educationally valuable, and that the TFT could not get permission to have a program on the same day.

"The basic objection is that it's a company union," said the TFT president. NWOEA is a district of the Ohio Education Association.[9]

Credit for fighting residence rules in Newark, New Jersey, is claimed by AFT. . . . No mention is made . . . of the vigorous work of the Newark Teachers Association, majority organization in Newark, or that the New Jersey Education Association and NEA, which have provided free legal counsel and have pledged all-out support.[10]

I submit we are professional only in the same sense that a skilled bricklayer or carpenter [is] professional—a highly skilled laborer hired to do a job to the best of his ability.[11]

Teachers have the same problem as the fellow who carries the hod or fixes plumbing fixtures.[12]

"Teachers want to do things for themselves. They want the freedom and the power to control their own professional destiny. The AFT provides the means for achieving these objectives."[13]

The American Federation of Teachers condemns as obviously unfair any request of teachers to abandon the right to strike—the American labor movement has long maintained that the strike is an inherent right of all *workers*.[14]

The AFT does not believe in strikes.[15]

Strikes or threat of strikes by public employees as a device for negotiation have been rendered ineffective by no-strike legislation or injunctions—the AFT urges the repeal of no-strike legislation—and resolves that legislation be enacted or existing anti-injunction legislation be amended to guarantee public employees protection against injunctions in labor disputes.[16]

Students will learn to emulate us and to realize there are certain laws that should not be obeyed. This may sound like anarchy, but I hope it does not. We believe in the right to disobey an unjust law.[17]

SAUCE FOR THE GOOSE. An interesting reaction of a segment of organized labor to the doctors' strike in Saskatchewan in 1962 is contained in the editorial reproduced below. The statement seems ironic in view of the claims of the AFT president that the strike is an inherent human right.

The editorial is by William L. Dodge, Executive Vice-President of the Canadian Labor Congress, published in the July 12, 1962 issue of *The Machinist.*

Mutiny

The withdrawal of service by Saskatchewan doctors on the orders of the provincial College of Physicians and Surgeons can in no sense be considered a strike. It is a clear act of defiance of the government.

Trade union organizations, on occasion, take strike action. They do so according to rules clearly laid down in law and subject to further stringent requirements of the organizations themselves, and violations are subject to full legal recourse. Tens of thousands of Canadian trade unionists respected the Maintenance of Railway Operations Act when it was approved by Parliament. Trade union members respect other legislation approved by democratically elected governments, even when they strongly disapprove of it.

The type of political strike, which the College has now enforced, has been condemned frequently by the labor movement. The open and brazen defiance of constituted authority by Saskatchewan doctors is in no sense a strike. It could be more properly described as a mutiny and deserves the strongest condemnation by all groups which place any value on democratic government and its procedures.

Leaders of the Saskatchewan College of Physicians and Surgeons have assumed a heavy responsibility in advising medical practitioners to flout the terms of their Hippocratic Oath and to defy the laws of the Province. For purely political reasons these men have told the legally constituted government of Saskatchewan: "Do things our way, or not at all." [Italics supplied by author.]

There are legal as well as moral obligations being swept aside by those doctors who refuse to treat patients. A legal advisor to the medical profession has pointed out the legal obligation of doctors to their patients which cannot, at will, be severed. The medical politicians have stressed the importance of the so-called "doctor-patient relationships." In deserting their patients, the doctors of Saskatchewan have shown a callous disregard not only for the law but for the health and safety of the people of the Province.

The Integration Issue

The AFT regularly engages in loud self-applause for its stand against school segregation, and regularly denounces the NEA as being in favour of segregation. Virtually in every election the AFT local affiliate has injected the race issue.

The president of AFT in his annual (1963) convention address said:

> The American Federation of Teachers in 1956, by Convention action following the Supreme Court integration decision, required all segregated locals to be integrated. This was an historic act. . . . By this action, the American Federation of Teachers lost 7,000 members. But unlike NEA we have had no segregated locals for more than six years.[18]

This loss of 7,000 members is difficult to reconcile with AFT membership figures. It could be that reference was made to loss of members in places other than the South over this decision, but this is doubtful. Judging from membership figures in the South, there has apparently been no such loss. Table 9–1 indicates that during 1956 AFT in the South had only 24 locals with a total membership of 3,616, almost precisely one half of which (1,763) was in Atlanta. By 1963, the number of AFT locals had declined to 11, and the total membership to 776. The Atlanta group did withdraw in 1958, and AFT membership in the South showed a steady yearly decline from 1956 on, but not by any such number as 7,000. AFT never had any such membership in the South.

TABLE 9-1

Membership of AFT in Seven Southern States in 1956 and 1963*

State	May 30, 1956		June 30, 1963	
	Number of Locals	Total Membership	Number of Locals	Total Membership
Alabama	3	91	3	63
Florida	3	141	1	8
Georgia	4	2,124	1	122
Louisiana	5	668	2	321
North Carolina	2	14	1	10
Tennessee	7	578	2	227
Texas	0	0	1	25
Totals	24	3,616	11	776

* Arkansas, Mississippi, South Carolina, Virginia, and Texas had no AFT membership in 1956; the District of Columbia, Maryland, and Kentucky had a total membership of 757 in 1956 and a total of 795 in 1963.

Source: AFT annual releases of membership and estimates according to related factors.

And it can be assumed that in 1963 this AFT membership was segregated in the sense that virtually all members were Negroes.

The AFT's prideful claims conveniently ignore the record of its parent labor organizations. During the upsurge of the Civil Rights Movement in 1963 and 1964, the AFL-CIO was denounced time and again by Negro leaders for discrimination policies, particularly in the building trades in the large industrial cities of the East. In Philadelphia and New York, at construction site, picketing and riots by Negroes protesting the non employment of Negroes led to violence. Union plumbers walked off a public construction job in New York City in the spring of 1964 because Negroes showed up on the job.

That these building trades have maintained and perpetuated an apprentice system, tightly controlled, which gave priority to the sons of union members and effectively closed the door to Negro apprentices is widely known. The discrimination has continued despite pious platitudes in resolutions or social issues in recent annual conventions of the AFL-CIO. Only the rioting in 1963 and 1964 seems to have lessened the *de facto* discrimination to any great extent. Even while UFT and AFT were loudly denouncing NEA, during the New York City election, for its segregation policies two court suits were pending to force AFL-CIO unions to integrate.

What about labor affiliates in the South?

One commentator has written:

> Sharing enthusiastically in the mores of their region, Southern Unionists often turn out to be members of the White Citizens' Councils or at the very least advocates of Jim Crow locals. . . . Failure of the various Operations Dixie can be attributed to several factors, but not least to this one. It accounts, too, for the hollowness of labor-convention resolutions on segregation and the eloquent scorn with which they are regularly denounced by President A. Philip Randolph of the Brotherhood of Sleeping Car Porters.[19]

Paul Jacobs describes the problems AFL-CIO has had and is having with integration of membership in the union locals, as well as with job discrimination against Negroes.[20]

These problems are far from solved, and the repeated boasts of nondiscrimination both by big labor and the AFT, upon close examination of the facts, seem to contain as much bombast as reality. By subtle and covert tactics both integration of membership and equality of job opportunities continue to be as yet largely unsolved problems.

Elizabeth Koontz, a Negro teacher of Salisbury, North Carolina, and 1965–66 President of the NEA Department of Classroom Teachers (and President-elect of NEA in 1967) was challenged after a speech in Milwaukee in 1964 on the segregated professional associations in her state. Her heckler asked: "Why don't you bring in [to North Carolina] teachers unions; they are integrated?" Mrs. Koontz replied: "Heavens, we don't want any more double organizations. I have a brother who wanted to be an electrician. He knew he couldn't get work in North Carolina because the Union wont accept him as a member. I have another relative who is a plumber who gave up for the same reason."

The NEA continues to be a hot target for big labor and its teachers' union affiliates, AFT, on the integration matter. Certainly, there are some reasonable and valid grounds for such attacks on NEA. The plain truth is that both clusters of organizations have pursued a course of gradualism. In such a bitter issue it is, of course, arguable whether this is the better part of wisdom; that is, in terms of human justice, which is the better course?

NEA policies are made by its representative assembly—some 7,000 delegates from every state in the union. Obviously, the non-Southern States could at any annual meeting outvote the Southern States and impose integration as a prerequisite to affiliation of a local association. In 1964 the non-Southern States did so vote, the new ruling becoming effective in 1966. The only conclusion that can be drawn from their failure to so vote earlier is the conviction of the delegates of the non-Southern States that constant pressure toward integration was more effective than an overt edict. Obviously those delegates took the view that if the Federal Government with its vast powers could not bring about full school integration overnight, it was hardly feasible to expect a professional association of fewer than a million members to do so.

The NEA has never had membership requirements barring Negroes. To put the matter in reverse: the NEA always has had integrated membership (at least after 1877 when for the time women were admitted to membership). The point of attack, however, is that the NEA still permits segregated state and local associations to affiliate with it. Long before the school integration decision at the Indianapolis Convention in 1943, the NEA barred meetings of the association or any of its units in cities or in hotels practicing segregation. The resolution reads as follows:

> Be it resolved, that in choosing the city for its convention, the National Education Association shall see to it that only those cities shall be selected where it is possible to make provisions, without discrimination, for the housing, feeding, seating at the convention, and general welfare of all delegates and teachers regardless of race, color, or creed.

And it has quietly kept up constant pressure to bring about integration of its state and local affiliates.

Steady progress has been made under this policy of gradualism. Locals in Arlington, Alexandria, and Fairfax, Virginia; in Davidson County (Nashville), Tennessee; Dade County (Miami) and Duvall County (Jacksonville) Florida; and in the state associations in Kentucky, Maryland, Oklahoma, Florida, and Texas have been integrated and several more integrations are in process. By 1967 only six state associations are not integrated.

To put the matter bluntly, it appears that the NEA has felt that it could best serve its membership, and particularly its Negro membership, by keeping the channels of communication open rather than issuing an edict which would effectively close those channels by forcing the withdrawal of thousands of whites in the Southern States.

This viewpoint is, of course, denounced by many sincere people. Perhaps it would be well, then, to look at what happened to the "integrated" locals of the AFT. The teachers' union has made great propaganda gains with its 1956 edict to ban segregated locals from affiliation with the AFT. At that time, it had only a handful of locals in the Southern States. The immediate effect of its edict was the disbanding of these locals. In the years since, a few more have been formed, but, as the president of AFT has admitted, they are all still segregated; that is, their membership consists entirely of Negroes. True, whites are not barred—they just don't join.

This was admitted in an exchange between Dr. Ruth Stout, former NEA President, and Carl Megel, president of the American Federation of Teachers, in a debate in Topeka, Kansas.

> *Mr. Megel:* I was interested that Miss Stout even brought that [integration] up, because the American Federation has been so far in advance on this matter of integration that the National Education Association usually doesn't bring this up. . . . After the Supreme Court decision in 1954, we passed a resolution (actually in 1956) demanding that these locals (in the South) be integrated. We now have locals in the South; it is true that most of the white teachers have withdrawn from these locals, and we do have the Negro teachers in the Negro locals in the South.
>
> *Dr. Stout:* On the matter of integration, I asked this question particularly. There are a number of magazine articles lately that have referred to this and the attitude of the Negro toward labor, and the fact they are unhappy about it. But I asked for another reason—that I understood the [teachers'] union had claimed it had done a great deal in the South. We have at the present time NEA affiliates that are integrated in greater numbers in the eleven Southern states than the American Federation of Teachers has in the entire United States.
>
> The second point I would like to make is the point that Mr. Megel just made in connection with the matter of integrated locals; that they are disaffiliating any that are not integrated. Mr. Megel, I happened to be in the South when that edict came. I was meeting with both Negro and white teachers. I was told by the Negro teachers that you disaffiliated the units in the South, then you came back the next day and said to the Negro teachers, "We will re-affiliate this now and we will call it an integrated local, even though the whites don't join." This I got from the Negro teachers. Do you deny that this is what happened?
>
> *Mr. Megel:* Miss Stout, you are right. That is exactly what we did in the South. We said we were going to have integrated locals. Here is a Negro local and white local. They are going to be integrated. Now those of you that want to join, and those of you that don't want to join don't have to. The white teachers withdrew and we organized the local. Now it is true that most of them are Negro locals but we are making progress down there.[21]

PROGRESS IN DESEGREGATION OF NEA AFFILIATES. Separate professional associations for white and Negro teachers existed in 17 states and the District of

Columbia prior to the Supreme Court decision on school desegregation in May 1954. The states were Alabama, Arkansas, Delaware, Florida, Georgia, Kentucky, Louisiana, Maryland, Mississippi, Missouri, North Carolina, Oklahoma, South Carolina, Tennessee, Texas, Virginia, and West Virginia.

The difficulty in patiently working out the problem of integration of professional associations is set forth in the following editorial:

> Yet, somehow through an overriding moral urgency, person-to-person persuasion, and—most of all—a spirit of professional unity, NEA Convention resolutions have led the nation's teachers—Southern, Northern, white, and Negro—to a common endorsement of that Supreme Court principle. Only after you have been to such national meetings and personally faced Southern white resistance and Negro acquiescence can you appreciate what an achievement this NEA stand represents. In the latest step, NEA representatives last year endorsed the complete Kennedy civil rights proposals which are now before the Senate. . . .
>
> There will be those, however, who will again call for "immediate merger or out." If the NEA didn't have many members in the South, forgetting about them would obviously be the simplest way to handle the problem. . . .
>
> Then, who would send commission members in to assist with desegregation? Then, who would provide assistance and large-scale interest-free loans to enable Southern teachers to hold out against the threat of public school closings (as happened in New Orleans and Little Rock)? . . .
>
> If the teaching profession really means to encourage school integration in the Southern states, it must keep white and Negro teachers there united within the national organizations. The call for expulsion does not threaten the cause of segregation nearly as much as it does the cause of integration.[22]

The NEA Seattle Convention in July 1964 took a more aggressive posture toward stimulating the merger of segregated local and state associations in the South, as set forth in the following excerpt from a resolution:

> In the light of these principles, the Representative Assembly instructs the officers and directors of the National Education Association—
>
> To direct all local, district, and state associations affiliated with the National Education Association to take immediate steps to remove all restrictive membership requirements dealing with race, creed, or ethnic groups.
>
> To take immediate action to develop plans to effect the complete integration of all local and state affiliates whose memberships are now limited to educators of specifically designated racial, religious, or ethnic groups.
>
> Affiliates whose membership reflect the above-mentioned restrictions shall be given until July 1, 1966, to revise their constitutions and bylaws, where necessary, to take whatever steps are required to expedite the complete removal of all restrictive labels, and to present a plan to effect the complete integration of their associations.
>
> Should an affiliated association fail to comply with these requirements by July 1, 1966, the Executive Committee shall have the discretionary powers to take necessary action.

This resolution may or may not speed up the process. Doubtless, there will be some loss of membership, and even some state associations may withdraw from NEA. But the intent of the representative assembly is to remove as speedily as possible the racial bar to membership in professional-association affiliates.

The NEA Executive Committee, in a postconvention meeting at Miami Beach on July 2, 1966, in accordance with the Seattle Resolution, voted to suspend the Louisiana Teachers Association (the white association) because it had not removed the racial qualification for membership from its constitution nor proposed a plan for merger with the Louisiana Education Association (the Negro affiliate).

The Louisiana Teachers Association was directed to submit a plan for merger by October 1, 1966, or be expelled from NEA.

Also, at the NEA Miami Beach Convention in 1966, the NEA and the American Teachers Association (the national association of Negro teachers, with 40,000 members) voted to merge.

The passage of Resolution 12 at the NEA Seattle Convention in 1964 did indeed speed up the merger of affiliate associations. At the NEA Miami Beach Convention in 1966 it was announced that Arkansas, Alabama, Georgia, Mississippi, North Carolina, South Carolina, Tennessee, Texas and Virginia had no racial barriers in their constitutions.

The two Florida state associations merged July 1, 1966. The two Texas associations voted to merge in the summer of 1966. Although Louisiana presented no plans for merging, other plans for developing mergers were submitted at the Miami Beach Convention. In addition, hundreds of local associations reported mergers. This grave and troublesome problem of integrated affiliates appears to be on the way to complete solution. AFT propaganda against NEA has been extremely effective. This propaganda obscured the delicate and sensitive nature of the problems involved. The program of gradualism plus reasonable pressures had at long last borne fruit.

By the 1967 NEA Convention all Southern States had presented acceptable plans for integrating the associations as well as local affiliates.

The Sky Is the Limit

At the AFT 1964 National Convention, Nicholas Zonarich, IUD Director of Organization, urged the teachers' union to launch an all-out drive for the 1.5 million teachers who were not organized (that is, not organized by labor). The AFT president, in a previous address to the convention, had advocated a comparatively modest goal of 250,000 members. Also, Zonarich urged AFT members to contribute $1.00 each per month to the drive, and pledged that IUD would match such contributions, which would produce a total potential yield of $2 million a year.

In another power play for recognition, UFT in New York City pulled off a strike (by means of mass resignations, since the strike was illegal) of recreation workers in August 1964. This action closed 508 vacation camps serving about 2,000,000 children throughout New York City. This work stoppage occurred during the tragic Harlem rioting. The executive deputy superintendent of schools said: "Such an unwarranted action deprives thousands of children of needed supervision at a time when this city is beset by social problems which also have a significant impact upon children."

No immediate pay raise was gained. In three years the $3.88 hourly rate of regular teachers, which was the goal of the strike, would have been achieved in any case.

But UFT got the right to represent the workers.

About half the 2,800 recreation workers are teachers in the city school system. The remainder are largely college students hired for the summer under special teaching licenses.

Self-Defeating Actions

Myron Lieberman, the chief intellectual rationalizer of teachers' union philosophy, ran for the AFT presidency in 1962 and was defeated. In September 1963, upon assumption of his new post as head of the Foundations of Education Department at Rhode Island College, he was refused membership in the AFT local in Providence on the grounds he had become an administrator. This raised the question in many minds whether he was rejected because he had become tainted with administrative bias, or whether he had incurred the displeasure of the AFT hierarchy.

As one unionist has said: "What I need is a union to represent me before my own union."

Another case of what's good for the goose being *not* good for the gander is the suit of the AFT local in Albuquerque seeking to enjoin the school board from withholding, at the request of the teachers involved, the membership dues in the local, state, and national professional associations. This is the story as it appeared in the *Albuquerque Journal* September 13, 1964.

Action to Halt Schools Paying Dues is Rejected

District Judge Edwin L. Swope Tuesday declined to issue a temporary or permanent injunction against the lump sum payment of dues to three professional education organizations by the Albuquerque Public Schools on behalf of teacher-members.

The injunction had been requested by individual members of the Albuquerque Teachers Federation and other taxpayers, who filed suit Sept. 4 against the board of education and School Supt. Charles R. Spain.

The suit alleged the board was using public funds illegally by advancing

> members' dues to the organizations at the beginning of the school year, while collecting from the teachers on a monthly basis.
>
> The three organizations are the National Education Assn. (NEA), the New Mexico Education Assn. (NMEA), and the Albuquerque Classroom Teachers Assn. (ACTA).
>
> As its chief defense, the board contended that the money advanced is not in fact public funds, but earned money held in reserve for the teachers.
>
> Its argument was that the money is earned on the basis of 183 teaching days, but is paid in 12 monthly instalments. Thus, the defense said, each teacher has legally earned more than paid until the 12th payment is completed—and funds "in reserve" are legally the teacher's, not the public's.
>
> At the conclusion of the four-hour hearing, Judge Swope remarked, "I see nothing illegal about this." He then announced he would not issue an injunction, leaving the case to be heard on its merits at another date.

The Pawtucket, Rhode Island strike in October 1964, called by the local teachers' union at the insistence of AFT, was something of a puzzle. This was a six-day strike the fourth, incidentally, in Pawtucket by the local AFT over the years (and another strike was staged in November 1964).

Because of a court decision in 1957 that a strike by teachers is illegal, the union in 1964 got teachers not to strike but to stay away from the schools on sick leave. A court order to the Pawtucket School Alliance to stop picketing the schools was circumvented by the AFT by having members of other unions replace teachers on the picket lines.

The excuse for the strike, which was invoked by the AFT, was "no contract, no work." Yet the Pawtucket teachers had been without a contract since August 1962.

The settlement granted each teacher a raise of $150. This amounts to .823 cents a day for the 182-day school year. The six-day loss in salary, calculated on the basis of an estimated average salary of $6,000 (or $33.00 per day for a 182-day term) amounts to $198 or about $50 more than the increased annual salary.

The *Providence Journal*, in commenting on the strike said:

> "If the teachers had substantial grievances, their staying away from school could be understood, if not condoned. But a review of events . . . facts to shed a scintilla of evidence as justification for their course of action are absent. . . . Has the union closed the schools in the teachers' interest, or in its own self-interest?"

10

The Professional Associations: Strengths and Weaknesses

> Our professional associations have often been criticized for not doing more, but our members often lack the courage to support us in what we already do.
>
> Several years ago one of our districts fired 21 teachers. Our association got 20 of those teachers re-employed. We were instrumental in the school board firing the superintendent, and the community was instrumental in getting the school board to resign and a new board appointed. The next year we had fewer members than before. In another case, involving the faculty of one of our colleges, nine staff members were fired. Our Association employed an attorney, got five reinstated and a $22,000 settlement made by the Board of Trustees. We lost members in that institution the next year. Recently we had a case in which several teachers were fired. We had an investigation and published a report. We got all but one of the teachers reinstated. The community in that district recalled the school board and the new school board demoted the superintendent who in turn sued the Association. Our membership in that unit is less than it was before we intervened on behalf of the teachers.
>
> If we are going to become more aggressive, militant, and responsive in protecting the needs of teachers, they have to have the courage to support our actions. Some people want the executive secretary to act like a Jimmy Hoffa in short pants, but they desert him when he does.
>
> —Joe Chandler, Executive Secretary,
> Washington Education Association

Perhaps the most effective single propaganda gimmick the teachers' unions have is the charge that NEA is a company union. Of course, this is private-industry and labor phraseology. The analogy is not only not perfect, it is a distorted analogy. But it is effective, nonetheless.

The AFL-CIO at its meeting in Atlantic City in December 1957 took action to officially dub the National Education Association a company union. The AFT, of course, had repeatedly used this designation in referring to the NEA.

This action came in a resolution pushed by the American Federation of Teachers. According to newspaper reports, the motion ran into strong opposition from certain AFL-CIO leaders, including George Meany, President; Peter Shoeman, Head of the United Association of Plumbers; and George Harrison, President of the Railway Clerks. The heart of the resolution was contained in this paragraph:

> Furthermore, in most American communities classroom teachers are still without a genuine union organization of their own through which they seek redress from exploitation. The National Education Association (NEA) dominated as it is by the school administrators, does not and cannot fulfill that need because it is, in effect, a company union. In fact, in many instances membership in the American Federation of Teachers—the only *bona fide* trade union organization of classroom teachers in the United States—is subtly and even openly discouraged by school administrators and by school boards.[1]

In response to this resolution, the NEA Executive Secretary, William Carr, issued a news release which said in part:

> The resolution adopted by the AFL-CIO Convention (on December 11, 1957) was engineered by some members of the American Federation of Teachers who deny the independent professional character of their own calling. . . . It is misleading to apply the term "company union" to the National Education Association. Our public schools are not a company; they are government services; they are not operated for profit. . . .
>
> Although the National Education Association includes all professional persons, most of its members are classroom teachers. Seventy per cent of the 6,000 delegates to its 1957 Representative Assembly were classroom teachers. Hundreds of classroom teachers serve on major policy-making and controlling committees, and as officers of NEA local and state affiliates. . . .
>
> The independent, professional status of teaching carries with it no implications of hostility toward any other group. The NEA and its strong state and local affiliates have proven that the teaching profession is big enough to stand on its own feet. Any arrangement whereby the teaching profession becomes dependent upon any single section of our society would profoundly affect the nature of American education.

At that time it was believed that certain AFL-CIO leaders were lukewarm toward the resolution, that they doubted the wisdom of such categorical denunciation of the NEA. It is not generally known, however, that pursuant to this resolution, George Meany, President of the AFL-CIO, issued a directive that labor organizations and leaders should refuse to meet with the NEA.

The teachers' union litany that the NEA is a company union and that the unions only are pure classroom teacher organizations would seem to be a bit of Tweedle Dee and Tweedle Dum, in the light of the following advertisement in a New York City newspaper.[2]

Vote "Yes" for Trade Unionism

Dear UFT colleagues:

The Executive Board of the UFT voted to recommend that the American Federation of Teachers grant an AFT charter to the Union of School Supervisors. We urge you to read with care the reasons for this recommendation, which came after five years of study by the UFT.

The Union of School Supervisors consists of many present and former members of the UFT. Most of these members have devoted many years of loyal service to our union. They want to continue to serve unionism.

The UFT is now a powerful organization of more than 25,000 members. It is time for union-minded supervisors to form their own local union within the American Federation of Teachers. We have to provide a union home for UFT members who have been, are, or may become supervisors so that they may be able to work effectively on matters of concern to supervisors: grievances against their superiors, working conditions, freedom from chores that prevent cooperative and democratic supervision, and organized support in the fight for effective schools.

The basic goals of teachers and supervisors are essentially the same. It is better to settle whatever differences may arise WITHIN rather than outside of the House of Labor.

VOTE "YES". A YES VOTE IS A TRADE UNION VOTE.

THE UFT SUPPORTERS OF A SUPERVISORS LOCAL

No NEA proponent could have written a better justification for the inclusive professional association.

Under certain circumstances, the AFT constitution permits all administrators except superintendents to become members of the local teachers' union. Administrators may be barred from voting in collective-bargaining elections but not from membership. Like NEA locals, AFT locals are empowered to determine the membership of their organizations.

Actually, the AFT Los Angeles Convention in August 1965 refused to adopt a resolution barring administrative and supervisory personnel from membership in AFT locals. Apparently this was too hot an issue for the delegates; they referred the resolution to the AFT Executive Council.

The 1966 annual meeting of AFT amended the constitution to exclude administrators from principal up and making any organization of non-teaching personnel ineligible for membership. The new provisions are not retroactive. The voted amendments came after two decades of efforts to bring about their passage.

The Case Against the NEA

Putting aside the far-fetched charge that the NEA is a union of whatever kind, let's take a look at the teachers' national professional organization—a look at its weaknesses as well as its strengths.

The NEA is not invulnerable to attacks in the internecine warfare among teachers over organizational loyalties. It has great strengths and some obvious and significant weaknesses.

It is not a perfect organization. In its record of 110 years of service to education and to the nation's teachers, it would be a near-miracle if NEA had not bogged down at points, become encrusted at others, and attracted bitter criticism on many occasions and by many groups. The fact is that it has had to undergo several internal revolutions to survive. But survive it has. Maybe NEA now is entering a new evolutionary period of refinement and renewal. Like big labor itself, it has failed to change rapidly enough to keep up with the changes in society. And like AFL-CIO it must renew itself, and rapidly, or lose its influence and authority.

Although the AFT has been NEA's most publicized critic, there are other powerful and influential groups antagonistic to certain NEA aims and procedures. Behind the scenes in the educational world there are some strong currents of opposition, even of bitterness, toward the NEA. These rarely break into the news, but they are there. One needs only to attend some of the multitude of conferences on education held each year and listen to private comments and well-turned phrases in speeches to sense the extent of the opposition.

The reasons for these attitudes are many and diverse. Devotion to a cherished pluralism in education is perhaps the most basic—the fear of one giant organization forcing, intentionally or unwittingly, a stultifying uniformity upon education. Many impartial people in education have this honest fear. However far-fetched some of their presumptions may be, their apprehension nevertheless is real and persisting. Of course, there are some power groups which want such power as NEA admittedly has, or some portions of it, for themselves.

A few of the many reasons why people bear, with great intensity and great fear, particular attitudes toward the NEA are these: the many specialities in teaching and the several levels of schools, with both the specialities and the levels having their particular status symbols; the seemingly inevitable conflicts between public and nonpublic-school concept and procedures; the schools' struggle for financial support; the competition for the educational dollar; and the suspicion of ensconsed power groups in education and their bitter reaction to any threat to their status.

THE DISADVANTAGE OF SIZE. The very size of the NEA, particularly when considered in combination with its affiliated state education associations, engenders apprehensions all through the educational world. There is great fear that the NEA may indeed become, as it has repeatedly stated that it wants to be, the one all-inclusive, general organization of teachers in the United States such as the American Medical Association for medical doctors, the American Bar Association for lawyers, the American Dental Association for dentists, or the American Society for Engineering Education for engineers. Relatively, it already is just that. Its percentage of membership among the nation's public-school teachers is probably as high (52 per cent) as most of the other national professional associations have of persons working within their professions. And when the membership of its affiliated state associations is added, the NEA really is in a position to speak for at least 90 per cent of all public-school teachers.

As long as the NEA was relatively small (as late as 1950 its membership was only 453,797), this goal bothered few people. But when by 1962 its membership of 815,000 included more than 50 per cent of all public-school teachers (and, as pointed out above, counting the membership of its affiliated state education associations, the enrollment of public-school teachers reached 90 per cent and above), some higher-education and nonpublic-school groups became alarmed. NEA membership has continued to include above 50 per cent of all public-school personnel, reaching almost 1 million in 1966 and more than a million in 1967.

As long as the NEA presumed to be the spokesman for only the public-school teachers, there was no great stirring among other groups. But when an NEA unit began to assert that there was, or should be, one profession of teaching, that all people in education were members of a common body with common objectives, this was considered to be going too far and was resented by many groups. There were repeated charges that the NEA was out to dominate all of American education. The published report of the New Horizons Task force of the NEA National Commission on Teacher Education and Professional Standards (NCTEPS) especially aroused the ire of many higher-education and non-public school personnel because it presumed (1) to suggest the essentiality of the concept of one profession of teaching (this had no reference to membership in any association), (2) to suggest that preparation for teaching, including college teaching, should be a planned, purposeful program with specific orientation to the teaching function (as contrasted to the notion that a general education with a high degree of specialization was adequate for teaching), and (3) to imply that there should be a badge of admission to the profession such as legal licensure.[3] Considering the history and traditions of college teaching, it is not strange that this report was the focus of considerable controversy. In any case, it unleashed a new wave of apprehension and criticism of the NEA.

It should be noted that this was a report of a special task force of 35 educators appointed by the NCTEPS. The task force was given free rein in developing its recommendations. The report has in no way been endorsed by the NEA. Its purpose was to guide the NCTEPS in its future work. Actually, the NCTEPS has not given official endorsement or approval to the report as a whole, only to some portions of it.

The critics are not stilled by the fact that the NEA itself is a highly pluralistic entity, with 30 of its 33 departments (out of a total of 76 units) being independent of direction by the NEA—each being self-financed by membership dues, electing its own executive bodies and officers, choosing its own staff, and fixing its own policies. All 33 departments select their own officers and are largely autonomous in policy determination. Two—the Association for Higher Education and the department of Classroom Teachers—are wholly financed by NEA funds. But these two are largely autonomous also. Five other departments receive some financial support from NEA.

To some critics, the image of the NEA as a monolithic giant is too appealing a stereotype to be let go of. However, perhaps NEA's greatest weakness is its lack of central direction. But the myth of monolithic controls and direction persists. A good example of this belief was the reaction to a suggestion made several years ago by the executive secretary of one of the independent NEA departments (the National Association of Secondary School Principals) that high schools consider banning use of *Life* magazine for what he considered an unfair attack. Immediately the NEA, not the independent department, was accused of attempted censorship of the press. The fact was, and is, that neither NEA officials nor any of its governing bodies had any connection whatever with the suggestion or any control over NASSP.

The image of the NEA as a giant and dangerous monolith persists with especial doggedness among private schools and among colleges and universities, both public and private. Theirs is certainly a natural and, to a degree, logical apprehension. The NEA membership admittedly is preponderantly made up of public-school personnel. No figures are available on membership of teachers in nonpublic elementary and secondary schools, but it is doubtless fairly small. Among the some 300,000 professionals in higher education, only about 20,000 belong directly to the NEA, and they are presumed to be mostly professors of education who have a primary interest in the public schools. Figures are not available either on the number of college teachers who belong to the 32 subject-matter departments of the NEA (the thirty-third NEA department being the Department of Classroom Teachers). But a casual sampling would seem to justify the estimate of about 50,000 college teachers among the aggregate membership of about 475,000 in those departments. Thus not more than 70,000, or from 20 to 25 per cent, of college personnel are affiliated directly or indirectly with the NEA. At this point, it should be borne in mind that membership in an independent NEA department does not carry with it automatic membership in the NEA itself. Actually, only members of the executive committees of the independent departments are, under current policies, required to hold NEA membership.

In fact, many teachers in nonpublic lower schools and in institutions of higher education of all types tend to view the NEA as antagonistic to their aspirations for adequate financial support. This concept doubtless arises from NEA's vigorous drive over the years for Federal legislation providing financial support for the public schools and the implied, if not explicit opposition to the use of public monies to support private schools.

Too, there has been apprehensions about the powers and influence of NEA expressed by prominent laymen and politicians. Typical of the conservatives' fears at the alleged design of the NEA to control education are the remarks inserted in the *Congressional Record* by Congressman Ashbrook of Ohio:

National Education Association versus the School Boards

Mr. Speaker, for over a year now the National Education Association—NEA—that powerfully persuasive teachers' lobby for Federal Aid—has been quietly preparing an all-out war against the Nation's school boards, last bulwarks of traditional American local self-government. The NEA is proposing that, by State statute and/or school board rule, the local boards share their decision making authority on all matters including curriculum with the NEA's local affiliates—or else.

This is not to be a war of words only, Mr. Speaker. The NEA is planning the use of labor union tactics, including adaptations of collective bargaining, the strike and political action to reach its goals.

[The allegation that NEA planned to use the strike was not true.]

I have here on my desk the documentary evidence to prove these allegations and I feel the Members of Congress should have the opportunity to study this evidence before considering additional Federal aid to the public schools.

First of all, Mr. Speaker, I should point out that the National Education Association spokesmen do not admit that they are advocating the use of labor union tactics. On the contrary, they say they want—

First. Recognition of their professional autonomy and professional status. They want no part of the craft status of the AFL-CIO, nor of the private employer-employee relationship, nor do they want even to be school board employees. They want teacher-association representatives to be recognized as coequals with school board members in running the public schools.

Second. They want the right of what they call professional negotiation—in effect professional collective bargaining.

Third. They want the right of what they call professional sanctions—in effect, in ultimate form, a teachers' strike.

Fourth. They want to drastically change and formalize the relationship of teachers associations, school administrators, and school boards, by State statute if possible, otherwise by school board ruling. They want professional negotiations written into law and/or administrative regulations.

Fifth. However, they want teachers to remain outside the restrictions of Federal or State Labor law.

Please note that the NEA frankly states they want teacher associations to be in on curriculum planning and teaching methods; and this is control of education by whatever name.[4]

Raymond Moley, in his column in the New York *Herald Tribune* of June 22, 1963 also seemed to be singing the song of "NEA, the Big Bad Wolf," out to control American education:

> For a long period of its life of more than 100 years the NEA was essentially a professional organization (innocuous, one supposes). It published information helpful in the work of a classroom teacher. It worked for the improvement of the teaching art. Its annual conventions and meetings of state and local units offered lectures, inspirational and informative. Its efforts were to improve the quality of teachers and teaching.
>
> But in recent years it has consolidated itself into a very powerful pressure group working in Washington and in States for legislation favorable to schools and teaching. It is now essentially as much a political organization as is the AFL-CIO. And since the war, its concentration has been on Federal aid for school construction and teachers' salaries.

Now that Congress has passed a $3.1 billion appropriation for building construction for higher education, one wonders if higher-education organizations now become "political" ones, since it would be naive to assume that this much-needed legislation just passed itself. In fact, a few days after this comment was written, an article appeared in *Reader's Digest*, implying just such a role for the American Council on Education.[5]

We have also the testimony of a former United States Commissioner of Education, Dr. Sterling McMurrin talking about the NEA before a meeting of the Council for Basic Education a private organization:

> But, while we guard against Federal control, we should not lose sight of the possibility of national control—control of education by the bureaucracies of large and powerful educational organizations. These bureaucracies are just as real, and exhibit all the vices of a government bureaucracy. Their control of the schools is not beyond possibility . . . and there is no reason for believing that such control would be any more desirable than Federal control.[6]

The anti-NEA feeling became bitterly evident as an aftermath of the defeat of the Federal College-aid bill in September 1962. The bill had passed both the House and Senate, in one case with direct grants to private colleges and in the other with provisions for loans to such colleges. In the Conference Committee, agreement was reached to include direct grants. The NEA, which had favored the loans but not the grants, sent telegrams to members of Congress opposing these grants and cited as its grounds for opposition the separation of church and state guaranteed by the Constitution. The bill was defeated, but whether as a direct result of these telegrams or because enough Congressmen used them as an excuse for voting against the measure probably never will be known. But the NEA was credited with killing the measure. The resultant bitterness of the Administration and of college presidents was pronounced. The president of the American Council on Education, an association representing about 1,100 college presidents, issued a scathing criticism of the NEA. At the succeeding NEA Convention at Detroit in the summer of 1963, at the request of the NEA Legislative Commission, the NEA resolution was amended to provide not for direct opposition to the passage of such legislation but for the insistence upon inclusion of a judicial-review provision in any Federal legislation appropriating funds to private schools. Subsequently the College Aid Bill of 1963 was passed and became law without the bitterness over NEA opposition.

The Establishment

In recent years, there have been concerted and vigorous attacks upon NEA as the focus of what the critics call the educational Establishment. These attacks have charged that there is a coalition of organizations affiliated with NEA whose aim is to control education. Identified as co-conspirators in this alleged plot are the National Commission on Teacher Education and Professional Standards (NCTEPS), a dependent unit of NEA, representing about 1.8 million public-school personnel; the American Association of Colleges for Teacher Education (AACTE), an independent NEA department with a membership of some 700 colleges and universities that prepare teachers, generally indicted as representing the professors of education; the Council of Chief State School Officers (CCSSO), which has office space in the NEA building but has no official connection whatever with NEA; and the National Association of State Directors of Teacher Education and Certification (NASDTEC), representing state teacher-licensing authorities, which has no office in the NEA building and no official ties to NEA whatever.

This galaxy is usually identified as the Establishment (although there are other large and influential associations identified with NEA), largely, one supposes, because it makes up the sponsoring or constituent organizations of the National Council for Accreditation of Teacher Education (NCATE).

Around this council and its influence on teacher education and teacher certification, swirl the charges that the establishment seeks to dominate American education. The critics miss the target at two points.

First, these organizations, as well as the other NEA affiliates, are seeking some reasonable controls of the teaching profession, not of education itself. Controls of public education are of course vested in the respective state legislatures. Controls of a profession—standards of preparation, licensure, ethical behavior, professional growth—are almost without exception vested in the members of the professions through their professional associations.

Second, there is, to be sure, an establishment, or establishments, in every profession. Indeed, the free society is dependent upon establishments or special-interest groups. The alternative is governmental regulation of every aspect of group and individual life or the emergence and acceptance of self-appointed and self-perpetuating oligarchies.

Establishments are evil only when they become monopolistic closed bodies without the safeguards of checks and balances. Thus, there will always be, and should be, vigorous dissent and power struggles, particularly in education.

These are essential ingredients in the free society and the free system of education. And NEA, as long as it remains in an influential position, can expect incessant attacks and criticism. Again, this is at it should be. Controversy is the lifeblood of a free society, and so it is of a free profession of teaching.

As a result of the vehement attacks upon the Establishment since 1960—attacks led by the *New York Times* and certain of the slick magazines in collaboration with the prestige Eastern universities, their satellites, and the rich foundations—a new establishment in education has come into being. At the moment at least, this is *the* Establishment. It has been brought into power by the flow of Federal money.

The take-over of the new establishment, labeled by some as the Eastern Establishment, by others as the Establishmentarians, was evident at the White House Conference on Education of 1965 where the dominant influences were the United States Office of Education, the president of the Carnegie Corporation, leaders of foundation-supported projects, and a few private universities. Public-school personnel and the professional associations were definitely and obviously shunted to the sidelines and given only token representation and participation in the program of the conference.

Whether there are adequate checks and balances in the new establishment to assure its fairness and survival remains to be seen.

Administrative Complexity of NEA

As has been said, the sheer size (over 1,000 employees) of the NEA invites suspicion and opposition. This is a price that any big organization, public or private, must expect to pay for bigness. Such giants of the business world as General Motors, American Telephone and Telegraph Conpany, and the DuPont Company are prime targets for members of the Congress and others. The charge of monopoly is a natural concomitant of the size of these companies. And that danger of monopoly is always inherent in a giant corporation and must be carefully guarded against in the public interest. Indeed, AFL–CIO has these same inherent dangers. And NEA should be, and rightly, subjected to the same scrutiny, criticism, and reasonable checks and balances as any other large organization.

There are 76 separate units in the NEA: 33 departments, 18 divisions, and 25 committees, commissions and councils. As has been pointed out, 30 of the 33 departments are independent or semi-independent, 25 of them wholly independent. Five of the 33 departments get varying degrees of financial support (usually very small) from the NEA. They are created (or admitted to affiliation) by the NEA Board of Directors; they are furnished free office space, furniture, custodial services, and certain other general services by the

NEA. But they fiercely protect their independence, being quick to resent any policy of the NEA or any memoranda from the NEA executive secretary which could be given the interpretation of a directive. Here is an example of how fiercely they guard their independent status. Until 1958, NEA bylaws provided that the members of these departments were required to be members of the NEA also. But this provision was so rarely enforced that a change was made in the bylaws in 1958 to change this requirement. The change simply specified that the members of the respective executive committees of these departments were required to be members of NEA. Despite the fact that this requirement was recommended by a staff committee on which the departments had representation, and despite the fact that the new requirement was vastly more generous than the previous one for the NEA-affiliated departments, rebellion ensued, with a few departments threatening to withdraw from the NEA.

Of the remaining 43 administrative units at NEA, 18 are divisions and 25 are committees, commissions or joint councils. Most of these are subject to general direction by the NEA executive secretary. But that is an oversimplification. Each of these units, with the exception of some of the committees, have full-time professional staffs and a director or executive secretary, and several of the committees and all of the commissions have policy-making and directing bodies made up of NEA members, some appointed by the current NEA president and some appointed by the NEA Executive Committee. While they are expected to operate within policy determined by the NEA representative Assembly, many of these units are relatively autonomous in developing their own programs. Other than the limitations of budget allotments and policy decisions by the NEA executive secretary, the restrictions upon their freedom of action are minor. For example, the Association for Higher Education, a department fully financed by the NEA, had a policy of supporting the college-aid bill which NEA opposed in 1962, yet no retaliation whatsoever, financial or otherwise, was directed at AHE by the NEA. Furthermore, several of the committees and all of the councils are joint organizations of NEA and outside agencies as well.

How does such a loose federation operate effectively? Well, sometimes it doesn't.

Of course there is lost motion. Of course the organization is cumbersome; and, in terms of split-second timing and machine like precision, it is inefficient. But it is not a monolithic, monopolistic, goose-stepping organization. Its units are inter-related and cooperative.

It is fair to say that there is some community of viewpoints among all these diverse groups; otherwise they would not be together under one umbrella. But this is quite different from saying that there is a common commitment or common direction.

It is also fair to say that the NEA reflects the great diversity of American education. There are units or departments serving virtually every specialized interest in education, from the nursery schools through the graduate schools of the universities. Most of them, it is true, do emphasize elementary and secondary-school education, but many serve the interests of higher education as well. Included in the 33 departments are services in the fields of administrative women, art, audiovisual instruction, business education, classroom teachers, teacher education, driver education, educational research, educational secretaries, elementary-kindergarten-nursery education, elementary-school principals, exceptional children, foreign languages, physical education, higher education, home economics, industrial arts, journalism directors, mathematics, music, public-school adult educators, retired teachers, rural education, school administrators, school librarians, school public relations, science, secondary-school principals, social studies, speech, supervision and curriculum development, vocational education, and women deans and counselors.

But the very bigness of the NEA, plus the slowness of its official bodies to change policy, make it difficult for the huge bureaucracy to keep abreast of current developments. This can best be illustrated with the big-city problem. Other than the work of the NEA Defense Commission and the Committee on Tenure and Academic Freedom, (consolidated into the national Commission on Professional Rights and Responsibilities in 1961) very few direct services in the area of teacher welfare in large cities were provided until the late 1950's. These matters were left largely to the state and local education associations. The NEA did contribute heavily by providing current research on teachers' salaries and on policies regarding fringe benefits and working conditions as well as by furnishing expert consultive services. In 1957, NEA salary consultant services were added, and in 1960 a group-insurance program was inaugurated although it was vigorously opposed by many of the state associations. In 1962, the NEA Urban Project was established to provide direct services to big-city groups. In 1964, an NEA Investment Fund (mutual fund) for teachers was added. In 1966, an annuity program and group accident insurance were added. In 1966 a Special Services Division was created to handle these added welfare services.

Tax Status of the NEA

Another factor, often overlooked or not generally recognized, which has tended to keep the NEA from vigorous all-out efforts to improve the welfare provisions for its members is its tax-free status and the fear of endangering that status through activities not clearly covered by the NEA charter. The NEA was chartered by an act of Congress in 1906, with two broad functions listed: (1) to elevate the character and advance the interest of the profession of teaching, and (2) to promote the cause of education in the United States.

The nontaxable status of the NEA does not arise from its charter but from a regulation of the Internal Revenue Service. Under the IRS regulations the NEA is classed under the 501*c*3 section which covers nonprofit religious, charitable, and educational organizations. Any activity which has connotations other than the improvement of education, such as lobbying for legislation in Congress (by spending an inordinate amount of money), giving direct services to improve the economic condition of NEA members, or taking part in an activity of profit-making nature, can be suspect from the standpoint of the IRS. Lobbying activities of the NEA have been maintained because "no substantial part of its resources" are spent for this purpose (less than 2 per cent of its income). The IRS carefully audits the expenditures of the NEA Legislative Commission and the division of Federal and State Relations each year to ascertain if these lobbying groups stay within the bounds of IRS interpretations.

But when the NEA group insurance program was inaugerated in 1960, a separate insurance trust had to be organized to administer the program as a nonprofit body to avoid the hazard of being declared in competition with commercial insurance companies and, therefore, of violating NEA's nonprofit classification. Subsequently, an NEA mutual fund, a group accident insurance program, and a tax-sheltered annuity program have been organized, all under separate corporate status. This tax-exempt status is of great importance to the NEA, as it is to any nonprofit organization, not only because the organization is relieved of paying the usual property taxes on its headquarters building and income taxes on its membership dues, but also because of the substantial sums of money which its various units and departments receive from the philanthropic foundations. (In 1964, these totaled some $3.5 million.) These foundations are also tax-free and would endanger their own status if grants were made to organizations not so classified by the IRS. In this respect, the NEA is no different from hundreds of other nonprofit educational, philanthropic, or religious organizations, but its size, its fight for Federal support of education, and its competition with other similar organizations and business organizations which may object to its activities make it a sensitive target for those who would like to see its tax-free status taken from it.

Generally, state education associations and labor organizations also have tax-free classification but under a different category—the 501(c)6 designation: the "business league." Thus the NEA has been sometimes handicapped in meeting the burgeoning demands of its members for more direct welfare services. Because of the ever present danger of some activity being adversely interpreted by the IRS, the NEA may be compelled to group together the units dealing with direct welfare services and request classification for them under the business-league category, organizing the remaining units and departments (by far the greater portion of the total structure) under 501(c)3.

Both organized labor and some professions (medicine, for example) have organized separate entities to enable them to participate fully in lobbying and partisan political activities. However, NEA to this point has rested its case on the thesis that everything it does or sponsors is basically aimed at the improvement of education. There is no question that this position puts NEA in a disadvantageous position at some points with the teachers' unions. But it has doggedly stuck to this position.

The Company-Union Charge

The most vehement, persistent, and perhaps the most damaging charge leveled at the NEA by the AFT and its sympathizers is that of being a company union. This is of course labor terminology which has found legal sanction in the Wagner Act wherein management and labor are prohibited from belonging to the same organizations. In this concept and terminology management is the superintendent of schools and the school boards and labor consists of the teachers. Supervisory principals are generally not defined as management. Since the NEA is an all-inclusive association in which membership is open to all professional people in education who meet specified preparation requirements, it is dubbed by labor and AFT as a company union. The implication is that the association is dominated by school administrators and that teachers cannot be aggressive regarding salary and working conditions because they will be prevented from doing so by their supervisors. The American Association of University Professors takes substantially the same view as AFT and excludes college presidents and certain other administrative officers from its membership.

The NEA view is that teachers and administrators are members of the same profession, with common objectives and interests; that the superintendent is both a member of the teaching staff and a professional advisor to the school board. The NEA view also is that a school is not an industrial plant run for profit, that it is not private but public, that the continual struggle between management and labor over division of profits does not apply to the schools. Whether this view can be maintained is discussed in Chapter 15.

Incidentally, in this connection, one of the fallacies of the teachers' union approach to salary matters—collective bargaining—is that the same tactics can be used in education as in an industry. This approach breaks down at the source of the money. An entrepreneur can pass on the cost of higher wages by charging the consumer higher prices for the product. The school board cannot. Generally, its funds come from levies voted by local citizens, from appropriations of state legislatures, and up, to 1965, from minor sums from Federal appropriations. (Federal sums now are larger.) Generally, the only way additional monies can be made available is through the slow-moving procedure of the ballot or legislative enactments. However strong the threat of the strike may be, a school board cannot be forced to spend more money than it has from these sources. Collective bargaining and the strike may, it is true, arouse the public to provide more funds, but the public cannot yield funds which do not exist. Collective bargaining and the strike may also spur politicians to seek adequate funds, but politicians cannot at any given time force from the school board monies which it does not have. So at this point the management-labor analogy breaks down. (See detailed discussion of this point in Chapter 14).

Domination by Administrators

How much truth is there in the charge that the NEA is dominated by administrators? There is some, to be sure—quite a bit in fact. Perhaps the domination came not by intent but by default. It is a mixed picture. There is certainly enough truth in the charge to justify its being made and scrutinized.

In the annual meeting of the NEA Representative Assembly, which is NEA's top policy-making body, it is rare for an action to succeed over the opposition of the NEA Department of Classroom Teachers. By the same token, it is rare for a proposal which has the backing of the department to fail. The record is full of policy actions sponsored by the department. And, strangely enough, the department has seldom sought to use its power in a parochial manner, although it is often accused of doing so. In fact, it may be said with some degree of fairness that the department has not been aggressive enough or militant enough. It could be charged that this cooperative attitude by the DCT arises from its reliance upon the NEA for financial support, that its lack of militancy is due to its subsidiary, dependent status. To be fair about it, there are bound to be some signs of dependence in the organizational classification of the department. Yet occasionally members of the DCT become so aroused over an issue or a budget matter that they use the departments' power (the power of superior numbers) to ride over all opposition. It does not follow that the lack of domination by the DCT arises from fear of inferior status; observation leads one to believe that it arises from a sense of fair play, a desire to live together in a complex organization with all segments of education. Whether independent status for the DCT would put it into a more strategic position is a debatable question.

If the charge of administrator domination is true, one may fairly ask why and how the professional-negotiation and sanctions resolutions ever got passed. It is well known that school boards and administrators were deeply unhappy over the passage of those two resolutions.

Where the charge of administrator domination finds its best support is in the membership of the NEA official bodies—the Representative Assembly, the Board of Directors, the Board of Trustees, and the Executive Committee —and in the constituency of many of the committees and commissions. An examination of the statistics is calculated to make the defenders of NEA squirm a bit. Bearing in mind that from 85 to 90 per cent of public-school personnel are classroom teachers and that, presumably, this proportion applies to NEA membership, the break-down shown in Table 10–1 is subject to attack by critics. (This does not mean necessarily that DCT represents 85 or 90 per cent of NEA membership.)

TABLE 10-1

Make-up of NEA Executive Committee, Board of Trustees, and Board of Directors for 1966–67

Executive Committee—11 members	
Teachers (college and public school)	7
Superintendents	2
Principals	2
Total	11
Board of Trustees—5 members	
Teachers	3
Superintendents	2
Total	5
Board of Directors—83 members	
Teachers (college and public school)	37
Superintendents and assistant superintendents	12
Principals and assistant principals	18
College administrators	7
Supervisors	3
State association staff members	6
Total	83

Classroom teachers make up about 45 per cent of the membership of the NEA board of Directors; superintendents, over 14 per cent; all other administrative and supervisory personnel make up about 34 per cent; other classifications about 7 per cent.

It would appear, therefore, that the Board of Directors is somewhat out of balance, weighted in favor of administrative personnel. As for committees and commissions, the NEA Executive Committee has been mandated to see that classroom teachers make up at least 50 per cent of the membership of each (by a resolution adopted in 1965).

The figures in the table indicate that 70 per cent of the 7,222 delegates to the New York NEA Convention in 1965 were classroom teachers and 22.5

TABLE 10-2

Composition of NEA Representative Assembly, New York City Convention, June 27–July 2, 1965

Position of Delegate	Number Registered	Per cent of Total Delegates
Classroom teachers	5,054	70.0
Superintendents, principals, and other supervisors	1,617	22.5
Retired teachers	28	0.4
Staff members of state education associations	215	3.0
Other delegates	308	4.0
Totals	7,222	99.9

Source: Department of Classroom Teachers *Bulletin*, November 1965, p. 8.

per cent were superintendents and other administrators. When the other identifiable groups (principals and supervisors) who have been generally eligible for AFT membership are added, they, along with teachers, constitute at least 88 per cent of the official delegates. These figures hardly support the charges that NEA conventions are dominated by superintendents.

At the New York NEA Convention in 1965, a resolution sponsored by the Department of Classroom Teachers was adopted requiring the Executive Committee to increase the number of classroom teachers on committees and commissions to at least 50 per cent.

Let's look now at the companion propaganda suggestion of AFT that it—AFT—is the only strictly classroom teacher organization at the national level.

A report[7] prepared (in 1965–66) for the AFT Executive Council revealed that in 262 of its locals enrolling about 87,000 members (about 85 per cent of AFT's total membership) 18 per cent of the locals enrolled principals as members; 20 per cent enrolled assistant principals; 58 per cent enrolled department heads; and 15 per cent enrolled other supervisors.

Policy differences between NEA and AFT regarding membership are more apparent than real. AFT propaganda seeks to persuade teachers that superintendents, principals, and supervisors are their natural enemies. NEA, on the other hand, has contended that superintendents, principals, and supervisors are natural allies of the teachers and that historically there is much evidence to substantiate this viewpoint. Some recent examples are the Utah, Oklahoma, and Kentucky sanctions cases. Generally, superintendents and principals led, or were involved alongside, teachers in those statewide uprisings.

There appears to be imminent a new look at AFT's position on the inclusive membership pronouncements. For example, the AFT research director has declared:

> There is absolutely nothing sacred about the private employment experience in this area, which is generally read to say that they [administrators] should be kept out.... The question must be viewed anew. Administrators do have talents, could be effectively used at the bargaining table.[8]

Is it, in view of the above statements, fair to inquire if AFT has decided that its propaganda about administrator domination has reached the points of diminishing returns, that every bit of mileage has been squeezed out of it?

Compulsory Membership

The NEA defines itself as an independent, voluntary association of teachers. How true is this claim?

The AFT hoots at this posture, claiming that superintendents of schools force teachers to join their state associations and the NEA by impelling them to sign authorizations for withholding dues from their salaries. Is there any truth in this assertion? Yes, quite frankly, there is. But not as stated above. If the assertion were that superintendents often influence teachers to join their professional associations, this would be unarguable. They do. But the cases of coercion or downright pressure are relatively few.

To be honest about it, superintendents are a major force in state association and NEA membership. Why deny this or seek to obscure it? The AFT would give its right arm, so to speak, to have such loyal support. It is not known how many superintendents actually pressure teachers to join their professional association. But many, if not most, one suspects, do try to influence them to do so. And why not? Is there anything untoward about a superintendent wanting curriculum people on his staff and supervisors to be affiliated with the association for Supervision and Curriculum Development, or the mathematics teachers to join the National Council of Teachers of Mathematics?

In reply to this, the teachers' unions say that it is wrong for an employer to influence employees to join any organization; yet, through its union-security agreements or agency shop arrangement, organized labor uses the contractual power of management to enforce union membership or contributions.

Even in the 19 states with right-to-work laws, labor often compels employers to enforce the agency shop by withholding from nonunion employees money equal to union dues. This is precisely the same principle as the employer influencing or compelling membership.

All this is not as authoritarian as it is pictured. The NEA itself does follow very closely the principle of voluntary membership. So do most superintendents of schools. They simply subscribe to what they believe is a sound belief, or they follow procedures advocated by the majority of their staffs. The principle they follow is that it is the obligation of teachers to affiliate with their colleagues in concerted efforts to improve education. The concept here is that a member of a profession (any profession) has a dual role: (1) as a practitioner (in the case of the teacher he practices in the classroom), and (2) as a member of his profession.

A few superintendents—again it is not known how many because no definitive study has ever been made of the matter—insert in contracts that the teacher agree to be a member of his local, state, and national professional associations. On the face of it, this can be condemned as an authoritarian practice. And on the face of it, this practice is certainly subject to serious question. Actually, these superintendents conceive the obligation to join professional organizations as a factor in qualification for the job. To those who protest that this allows no freedom of choice, that it is compulsory, their (the few superintendents enforcing such provisions) position is that freedom of choice was exercised when the teacher chose his profession. After that choice, after the choice to prepare for teaching, there followed the obligation to join with professional colleagues to improve education and the status of the profession in general. This writer knows of one superintendent of schools, now retired, closely identified with the NEA, who enforced this provision so religiously that his school district had 100 per cent membership in the local, state, and national education associations for 38 consecutive years. As far as is known this is an all-time record, but that it was made under some duress is obvious. But this is a rare example, not a general one. To those who revolt against this, it can be asked, How much does this practice differ from the commom practice among trade unions?

One's answer all depends upon the point of view. In the 10 provinces of Canada, for example, law mandates membership in the provincial teachers' association—and this is only one among other provisions which acknowledge the associations as the spokesmen for teachers in the public schools.

The president of AFT dealt with so-called compulsory NEA membership in an article in the *Teachers College Record*, October 1964.[9] There was an answering article in the December 1964 issue of the same journal by Marion Street: "Professional Associations—More than Unions." Both articles in large degree, begged the question; the articles were largely parochial propaganda.

The extravagant nature of charges of the AFT president about "enforced" NEA membership led Clyde Russell, long-time Executive Secretary of the Maine Teachers Association, to write in protest to George Meany, President of AFT-CIO:

> One of my most treasured possessions is a parchment document which attests to the fact that I am an honorary member of the Maine CIO. It was given me almost twenty years ago in recognition, I suppose, of my efforts to combat

> (successfully) a right-to-work bill in a state-wide referendum. Since that time I have done whatever I could to oppose right-to-work legislation and so far we in Maine have been successful.
>
> Now, in the *Teachers College Record* for October there is an article written by Carl Megel which is the most plausible propaganda for the right to work that I have ever seen.
>
> This particular article may not be widely seen in Maine and it may not do us any harm, but Mr. Megel is playing with dynamite. If he continues this line, somebody, sooner or later, is going to notice that the President of an AFL-CIO union is saying—only more effectively—the same things that NAM does about right to work.
>
> I know that I don't have any influence with Mr. Megel, but I'm told tnat the financial support of AFL-CIO is all that keeps AFT alive. He must listen to you. Won't you tell him that the union attitude toward right-to-work or the right-to-ride-free or whatever you call it, is based on sound ethics and not on expediency and that organized labor does not have one set of principles for situations when a union is the minority and another for those occasions when it is the majority?
>
> Your organization and mine have many common interests. One of them is maintenance of the idea that the people who get the benefits of an organization should contribute to the support of that organization. I'll maintain that proposition against Goldwater or Megel. What do you say?

If, as AFT implies, all or most superintendents force teachers to join NEA, how is it that NEA has only 52 per cent of the nation's public-school teachers in its membership? How does it happen that at least 800,000 such teachers are not members?

A private survey among teachers made several years ago reported that 15 per cent of the respondents felt that they were pressured by superintendents to join NEA; 16 per cent reported that they joined because the mores or climate in their school districts made it "the thing to do."

THE MAGENHEIM CASE. The NEA has faced several cases in recent years that point up this problem. In Butte, Montana, where the labor-union movement is strong, the local AFT unit easily induced the school board to rule that unless teachers belonged to the teachers' union they were not eligible to receive the usual annual increments on the adopted salary schedule. (See Chapter 9). The NEA joined with its members in Butte to carry the question to the Montana Supreme Court, which held that the board's action was unconstitutional.

In California, a music teacher in a high school was compelled to join the local musicians' union in order to direct his high-school orchestra in a public appearance. Sponsored by the California Teachers Association and the NEA, a suit in the California courts led to upset of this decree. (Again, see Chapter 9).

But a case of some embarrassment to the NEA was the case of a dismissed tenure teacher in the Riverview Gardens (Missouri) School District—the Magenheim case. In this suit for reinstatement, this teacher based his plea on the nonspecification of reason by the school board for his dismissal. He inserted, also, the complaint that he has been compelled by board regulation to join his professional organizations.

Specifically, he cited the following rule in the board's salary schedule:

> Each person on this salary schedule shall join the professional organizations which include the Community Teachers Association, and the St. Louis Suburban Association.
>
> Failure to join such organizations precludes the benefits derived through the salary schedule and places such person outside the salary schedule.
>
> This provision is to be complied with on or before October 1 of each school year.

The teacher asked for declaratory judgment that this paragraph was unreasonable, void, and beyond the authority of the board to adopt. The teacher asked for an injuction against its enforcement, and for the award of a judgment of $32, the dues he claimed to have paid to two local associations involuntarily during his four years of employment. He stated that he had joined the NEA and the Missouri Teachers Association of his own accord. Incidentally, this teacher was a life member of NEA and a member of AFT.

The Missouri Apellate Court held on June 14, 1961 that the board had the legal right to adopt the rule regarding membership in the professional associations:

> In the teaching profession, as in all professions, membership in professional organizations tends to improve the interest, knowledge, experience and overall professional competence. Membership in professional organizations is no guaranty of professional excellence, but active participation in such organizations, attendance at meetings where leaders give the members the benefit of their experience and where mutual problems and experiences and practices are discussed, are reasonably related to the development of higher professional attainments and qualifications. Such membership affords an opportunity for self-improvement and self-development on the part of the individual member. It is the duty of every school board to obtain the services of the best qualified teachers, and it is not only within their power but it is their duty to adopt rules and regulations to elevate the standards of teachers and the educational standards within their school district.

On the face of it, this suit seemed to parallel closely the Butte case in which the court ruled out the resolve of the school board to include a union-security clause in the master agreement with the local teachers union. In fact, the teacher cited the Butte case in his plea before the Missouri court. The Missouri court justified its rejection of his plea as follows:

> Union membership *per se* has no connection with teaching competence. Plaintiff Magenheim was not *required* to meet the conditions stated in Paragraphs 15 and 18 of the Salary Schedules. Teachers employed by defendant District who do not choose to meet the conditions stated for compensation under the Salary Schedule will have an individually negotiated compensation.

The question may be logically raised, Why was not NEA a party to this teacher's suit as it had been in the Butte case?

The teacher did not request NEA to join in and aid in his suit. Instead, he sought assistance from the AFT local.

Had he requested assistance in the suit from NEA, he doubtless would have received it. Later, he did request NEA to enter the case to impel the board to give him a written statement of the causes for his dismissal.

The PR and R Commission subsequently did conduct a preliminary investigation into the Riverview Gardens School District and made certain recommendations. Among these were the following statements in a letter to the president of the board dated December 20, 1961:

> . . . We hope the Board will . . . re-examine its policy [on compulsory membership]. . . . Such a regulation is certainly beneficial to the organization we represent. But, in a larger sense, we believe the central purposes of NEA to elevate the character and advance the interests of the profession of teaching and to promote the cause of education will be advanced with more fervor and dedication in those schools where teachers voluntarily associate in professional organizations.

A letter from the president of the Riverview Gardens School Board to the PR and R Commission dated January 4, 1962 stated:

> The teachers voted twice to keep the provision in the salary schedule requiring membership in the professional organizations. The last action of the old Board was a 5–1 vote to eliminate that provision from the salary schedule despite the teachers' vote. . . . One of the first actions . . . of the new board was to put the professional membership provision back in the salary schedule.

This whole problem involves a bit of hypocracy on both sides. It is a well-established practice of labor organizations to prescribe the "check-off" system (withholding of union dues from workers pay checks) for their members in a given craft. This is understandable. It will doubtless apply to teachers if and when they affiliate with unions. The difference will be that they will have no choice whatever. They must join in a check-off system or be labeled as scabs. To remain aloof, to ride piggyback, will not suffice. Hence, the AFT charge that the NEA has a compulsory system at work for it is at least a little bit hypocritical. The fact is that, under either organizational membership plan, there will be pressures to join. The difference is that rarely, if ever, will teachers' jobs depend upon NEA membership.

The honest answer is that, whichever organization becomes predominant, the tendency will be to try to get, either by persuasion or sanctions, either directly or indirectly, universal requirements of membership. So the AFT has no grounds for a holier-than-thou posture. The best answer to the charge of compulsory membership by the NEA is the fact that only slightly more than half of its potential are NEA members. In spite of the fact that in some districts enforcement of NEA membership may be influenced by administrators, nevertheless one half of public-school teachers do not belong to the association. What would the AFT do in a similar situation?

Take the "hiring-hall provision," for example, in the contract of UFT with the Queens School (a private school in New York City) which provides that the union shall have the right to nominate candidates for vacancies. If the union cannot fill a given job in three days, then the school may employ a nonunion teacher. In essence this means the union not only is enforcing compulsory membership but has the right to say what teachers are employed.

In summary, the charge that the NEA advocates compulsory membership, condones it, or is a silent partner in some sort of *subrosa* pressure process to force membership is unsupported by facts. That there are pressures in some cases which arouse the resentment of some teachers cannot be denied. There is, however, no national pattern, no design for such pressures. Such cases as do exist arise from the concept that teachers willingness to join with their colleagues to improve education is a basic qualification for teaching; or else such cases arise from the subtle but effective pressures of a climate of opinion among the staff members of a given school system.

If the precise facts were known, the number of teachers who become members of the NEA through compulsory requirements of local school administrators probably would be comparatively small. Likewise, the number of cases of arbitrary withholding of membership dues from salary checks would be very small. Actually, the bulk of NEA membership, perhaps as much as 90 per cent, comes from membership campaigns of local and state education associations.

The professional associations certainly have many identifiable weaknesses. They also have many demonstrated strengths. For more than a century they have constantly advanced the cause of popular education as well as constantly advanced the status and prestige of teachers. The inclusive professional associations are under vigorous attack as being dominated by administrators. It seems reasonable to assume that the inclusive association will survive, but this will require some restructuring and a more definitive spelling out of appropriate representation and the respective roles of specialized segments.

Part Four

THE FLOW OF THE CONFLICT

11

From Omaha to Okinawa

> Looking at these schools on a national basis, the Overseas Dependents Schools are currently serving about one out of every two hundred youngsters enrolled in all American schools. As such, they are significant parts of education in the United States. Looking at these schools world-wide, they could offer a demonstration of the high value which Americans place on education, for here are schools serving our youngsters wherever these youngsters are to be found—in Europe, Asia, Africa, and the islands of the sea. The nation should meet its rightful obligation to these children who are wholly dependent upon the federal government for their education while overseas. . . . These schools need more money to erase a range of deficiency from the services of teachers to the adequacy of educational supplies. The present salary arrangements for teachers in these schools is indefensible.[1]

It is ironic (since the general assumption was that only individual school districts needed be involved) that the first two requests for the invoking of sanctions by the NEA, after the passage of the Denver resolution in 1962, involved the Federal Government and the state of Utah. Then, when the Utah case was settled, Oklahoma followed almost immediately, with Kentucky in the wings.

Almost before the newly adopted processes could be printed in the list of annual resolutions, the NEA found itself involved in a tussle with the United States Government over the conditions in the Overseas Dependents Schools, and, later in the school year 1962–63, with the state of Utah over inadequate educational facilities. This was starting off with a bang in the flexing-of-muscles business. Still later, after settlement of the Utah case in 1965, NEA invoked sanctions against Oklahoma.

Of course there were a few tentative inquiries about the possibility of declaring sanctions by local teachers' associations which had obviously misinterpreted the meaning of the new process, thinking it was to be invoked when even the slightest of disagreements arose in the school districts.

The AFT, some segments of the press, some news magazines, and many teachers had a field day scoffing at the NEA's ineptness and timidity in these two requests for the invoking of sanctions. The AFT referred to the overseas teachers as "innocents abroad." The implications were that sanctions were an insipid weapon as compared to the strike. As Goethe once said, "there are those who think that the answer to every problem is a punch in the nose."

But when the 300 days of the Utah case and the 133 days of the Oklahoma case yielded substantial victories, the snickering faded, with the scoffers asserting that "after all sanctions are really strikes."

Following is an account of the NEA's handling of the two situations (the Overseas Dependents Schools in this chapter and the Utah and Oklahoma Cases in Chapter 12).

The stories of these cases are included to present a balanced picture of events that have taken place in the struggle for teachers' rights and dignity since adoption of the sanctions resolution. Admittedly, NEA has not looked too good at many points as it sought to help these two clusters of teachers. In fact, in both cases, NEA appeared for a long time as a bungling, inept organization operating with inadequate know-how and ineffective weapons. It took time and a lot of muddling through to substantiate NEA's policies. But that is all the more reason why the stories should be told.

NEA was dealing with unprecedented situations—a state-wide situation and a Federally operated and controlled situation. NEA had never before dealt with such comprehensive and far-flung school operations, its previous experiences with sanctions having been in single school districts. That NEA floundered in many respects and muddled through these two cases no honest observer can possibly deny. NEA simply had no chart gained from experience and history to direct its course in these two cases.

Thus, the stories of the cases of the overseas schools and the Utah schools are largely sagas of bumbling and groping, frustration and failure, of muddling through to moderate success. Yet, when the whole stories are revealed, they indicate uncertainty with completely new problems and an exasperating slowness in finding solutions, rather than ultimate failure. Actually, success came in both efforts, but slowly.

The overseas school problems were largely resolved in 1965–66, but much remains to be done.

In the case of the Overseas Dependents Schools, there can be little doubt that the teachers had been flagrantly, even callously, mistreated in salary matters. Whether sanctions were justifiable on the general conditions of the schools can be debated. On the basis of the Department of Defense Survey Team Report in 1964, many weaknesses were discovered, also many strengths. Allowing for the obviously extraordinary circumstances under which these schools are operated as adjuncts of the military establishments in foreign countries and under somewhat temporary commitments, it could not be reasonably expected that they would or could have all the strengths of "state-side" schools in stable, long-existing communities.

But on the salary question alone, there were indisputable grounds for invoking sanctions. Having recognized that, however, one is immediately faced with the grave import of invoking so drastic a measure against the Government of the United States. Of course the blood-and-guts fighters can easily dispose of the matter by the easy answer of "So what?" But the measure of indignation against one's national government, especially in matters relating to education, are considerations not to be lightly brushed aside.

As for the Utah case in 1962–63, the NEA rendered every possible help short of actually declaring the sanction of withdrawal of services of its members outside Utah. In refusing to take this drastic step in the summer of 1963, the NEA official bodies at the Detroit Convention simply were adhering to the adopted procedures of taking such action only after impartial, objective, thorough study had revealed intolerable conditions in the schools. At the time, the uncompleted study of the NEA Commission on Professional Rights and Responsibilities had not uncovered such conditions. The NEA refusal at Detroit, therefore, simply sought to protect the integrity of the sanctions process. NEA did invoke sanctions in May 1964 after its study was completed.

The Case of the Overseas Dependents Schools

The case involving the Federal Government concerned the Overseas Dependents Schools for the children of military personnel stationed in foreign countries. The schools are administered by the Department of Defense.

Most Americans have only casual knowledge of the existence of these schools, which have been maintained since 1945 when the Government began sending abroad the families of men stationed in the armed services overseas posts. Actually, this is the nation's ninth largest school system, enrolling about 180,000 American children taught by approximately 8,000 American teachers recruited from state-side school systems. The system operates 327 separate schools in 28 countries at a cost of about $80 million per year. Actual operation of these schools began in October 1946, when 38 elementary and five high schools were opened in Germany with a total of 2,000 students and with 120 teachers.

The bulk of the enrollment of the overseas schools is in Europe, particularly Germany, but schools are maintained in such countries as Japan, Korea, Okinawa, Ethiopia, Taiwan, the Philippines, and Pakistan.

There has been an almost continuous hassle between the teachers and the Department of Defense ever since the founding of these schools. There are several reasons for this clash. In the first place, the schools are run by the military, with each of three branches of the armed services (Army, Navy, and Air Force) operating and directing their own schools under somewhat varying procedures and personnel policies. This command was ordered unified on July 1, 1964 presumably with all the schools in a given area being placed under the jurisdiction of one of the three services. But this arrangement has been effected only in part. Civilian personnel in the Department of Defense have key roles in the operation and administration of these schools.

Federally operated schools have rarely been shining examples of how schools ought to be run, especially from the standpoint of teachers with experience in good public-school systems. The schools of Washington, D.C., largely supported by and under the direction of Congress, have been notoriously underfinanced, underhoused, and understaffed. The ideological conflicts in Congress over school integration and even over how a school system should be run have had their adverse impact on the District of Columbia schools.

In the nation's capital, with a foreign embassy, so to speak, on almost every street, the school system should be a showplace, typifying the best in American public education. It is in some respects admittedly far short of this. There are, of course, many good schools in the district, but the system as a whole has glaring deficiencies. The basic cause of the neglect, even mistreatment, of the District of Columbia schools is not so much because of the pecadillos of members of Congress as the fact that it is a school system without a public. The parents are not able to vote or elect their local officials and school board, are without representation in Congress, and, therefore, are almost wholly without voice. This is also the basic cause of the trouble with the Overseas Dependents Schools. Critics of Federal support to public education frequently point to the District of Columbia schools as a horrible example of what Federal support would inevitably do to the public schools. But the crucial fact is often overlooked. It is not that the Federal money is so devastating, it is the act that the people in the district have no voice.

IN DEFENSE OF CONGRESS. To state the case fairly for Congress, it did enact in the summer of 1964 much more generous legislation for the District of Columbia schools, effective with the school year 1965–65. A significant increase in the teachers' salary schedules was enacted, averaging a 7 per cent raise. Before then, the scale for teachers holding bachelors' degrees ranged from $5,350 to $8,240, on an annual 13-step schedule, with three additional career increments above that, so that such teachers at the end of 19 years of service could attain a salary of $9,350. Teachers with masters' degrees and those with six years of college preparation had been accorded comparable increases. For the former, the new scale ranged from $5,830 to $8,740 in 13 steps, with the career maximum of $9,850 after 19 years of service. For the latter, the 13-step range was from $6,050 to $8,940, with the career maximum after 19 years of service reaching $10,050.

Congress also provided for new teachers and made substantial appropriations for new buildings. All these provisions still are not enough, but represent great gains. Finally, Congress made the district schools eligible for impacted aid amounting to about $4.5 million annually.

Under the impacted areas laws, Public Laws 874 and 815, Federal assistance is provided to small schools where at least 3 per cent, and to large districts where at least 6 per cent, of the total average daily attendance are pupils with a parent employed on Federal property.

The schools in the suburbs of Washington, D.C. received substantial Federal assistance under these laws because these suburbs are heavily populated by employees of the Federal Government. The schools of the District of Columbia, however, received (until the 1964–65 school year) none of these funds for two reasons: by the definition of a state in the law, the district is excluded; and the presumption is that Congress will make adequate direct appropriations for these schools.

Likewise, the schools of American Samoa were given only casual attention by the Congress of the United States from 1900, when the U.S. Navy assumed the jurisdiction of this possession, until 1961, when public outcries impelled Congress to attempt to atone for years of neglect of the Samoan schools. Unfavorable publicity directed at this neglect, coupled with the Conference of the South Pacific in Samoa in 1961, where existing conditions were again aired, resulted in prompt congressional action which quadrupled the appropriation for American Samoan schools to $9.6 million in 1961 rising to $13 million in 1962.[2]

For some reason, the Federal Government has been unusually generous in the operation of schools for children of the military and of U.S. civilian employees in the Canal Zone, where there are about 480 teachers for an enrollment of 12,500 children. Here teachers are paid salaries equivalent to those of teachers in the District of Columbia schools, plus a tropical-climate bonus of 25 per cent, plus post-exchange privileges and generous housing allowances.

The minimum starting salary for teachers holding bachelors' degrees in the Panama Canal Zone schools in 1964–65 was $6,250 (as contrasted with $4,535 in the Overseas Dependents Schools). If they have five years experience teachers with bachelors' degrees can begin in the Canal Zone schools at $7,706 and reach a maximum salary of $10,887. Teachers with masters' degrees can begin at $6,875; with five years of prior experience they can begin at $8,331 and reach a maximum of $11,512. In addition, Canal Zone teachers have all the fringe benefits that the teachers in the Overseas Dependents Schools have—fringe benefits which the Department of Defense has constantly used as an excuse for not giving salary increases to the latter. The only apparent explanation for this preferred treatment by Congress of the Canal Zone schools and teachers is that revenue from the Panama Canal accruing to the Federal Treasury is more than adequate to finance the Canal Zone Goverment and the Canal Zone Company.

The above comments are not intended to imply resentment toward the Canal Zone schools. They are simply intended to suggest that there is no good reason why comparatively low support should be given the Overseas Dependents Schools. The same Congress that appropriates about $650 per child for schooling the dependents of military personnel stationed in the Canal Zone, appropriates only $285 (actually only about $260) per child in the Overseas Dependents Schools. The latter sum was raised to $455 in the 1965–66 school year, but this increase was a rather meaningless lumping together of all school expenditures in the per-pupil limitation appropriation. Actually the increase per pupil was only $10 over that of the $285 limitation. This makes about as much sense as Congress providing over two times as much for the education of children with blue eyes as for those with brown eyes. But these are the facts.

It should be noted that the Department of Defense announced on July 28, 1964 a cutback from 25 to 15 per cent in the tropical pay that is, the bonus, allowed employees in the Canal Zone. The cut was not made retroactive but applied to new employees. The department stated that the basis for this bonus pay (hardship of the tropical climate) no longer existed, presumably because of air-conditioning. Also, Congress in 1967, liberalized controls of schools in the District of Columbia.

But back to the Overseas Dependents Schools. These schools are under the jurisdiction of the Department of Defense, the direct authority being centered in the Assistant Secretary of Defense for Manpower. Responsibility regarding educational policy and operation is delegated to the department of the Army, Air Force, and Navy. For the Army and Air Force, the commanders of the various theaters are in charge, and great authority is lodged in post commanders. In contrast, each Navy school is a separate entity, with a superintendent being responsible for the school at each naval station. This chain of command, with rather strict adherence to military red tape and protocol, is chafing to teachers, who find doing things through channels restrictive, cumbersome, and inhibiting. However, as previously mentioned, a unified school system was ordered to begin on July 1, 1964 with the Army in charge in Europe, the Navy in the Atlantic, and the Air Force in the Pacific. The school unification will be under the academic administration program developed by the Assistant Secretary of Defense for Manpower. This may bring some improvements.

Salary Discrimination Against Teachers Overseas

Prior to January 1960, teachers recruited from the states for the Overseas Dependents Schools were classified under civil service with the rating and salary of a GS–7, on a 10/12 basis, because of the length of the school term. These salaries, of course, moved upward as Congress adjusted the civil-service pay scale, but the salaries had only incidental reference to pay scales of teachers in the states.

In July 1959 Congress passed Public Law 86–91, "The Defense Department Overseas Teachers Pay and Personnel Practices Act" (effective in January of the 1959–60 school year). This law removed teachers from the civil-service pay scales and regulations and was passed because of difficulties in fitting teachers into the work year and other conditions of civil-service employees. Its intent was to establish personnel policies and pay policies in line with practices of school districts in the states. The act had the approval of the Department of Defense, the Overseas Education Association (an affiliate of the NEA), and the National Education Association. It specified that teachers' salary schedules be set in relation to those of teachers in similar positions in the United States, but were not to exceed the scales for teachers in the District of Columbia. Pursuant to the provisions of the law, the civilian wage board of the Department of Defense adopted regulations gearing the overseas teachers' schedules to salaries of teachers in state-side cities of 100,000 or more with periodic review, based upon data supplied by the NEA Research Division, of changes in state-side salaries.

However, only one real adjustment upward between passage of the law in 1959 and the school year 1965–66 has been provided for the overseas teachers.

This fact exists despite the clear intent of Public Law 86–91 and its implementing regulations adopted by the Pentagon wage board, despite the fact that teachers' salaries in the United States to which the overseas teachers' scales were to be adjusted have increased each year from 5 to 6 per cent, and despite four salary increases for civil-service employees aggregating 21 per cent on the scale from which the overseas teachers were removed. This one

TABLE 11-1

Original Teachers' Salary Scale Under Public Law 86–91 and the Adjustment of August 1960

Preparation Level	January 1960[1] Scale	August 1960[2] Scale
Bachelor's degree	$4,350–$5,550	$4,435[3]–$5,915
Master's degree	$4,550–$5,750	$4,635–$6,115
Master's degree plus 30 semester hours	$4,650–$5,850	$4,735–$6,215

[1] Eight annual increments of $150.
[2] Eight annual increments of $185.
[3] A $100 increase in the minimums was made for the 1963–64 school year.

adjustment, a modest one of 3.5 per cent, occurred in August 1960. The original scale adopted under the new law in January 1960 and the one increase adjustment in August of that year are shown in Table 11–1.

Immediately upon announcement of the scale (Column 1, Table 11–1) a sustained protest came from the teachers. The announced scale covered pay for 180 school days, annual leave, compensatory leave, holidays, and travel-duty pay. The teachers charged that this was discriminatory because all other Government employees were paid for these leaves and the travel time in addition to their regular pay. In other words, there was a charge that the Federal Government was treating these teachers as second-class citizens.

No further adjustment in the pay scale of teachers (until September 1965) was made after the modest one in August 1960 except for a $100 raise for the 1963–64 school year. It is estimated that the overseas teachers lost something like $8,704,000 (or an average of about $800 per teacher) from January 1960 to June 1964; in fact, with the fourth civil-service raise in the summer of 1964, the loss per teacher ran well over $1,000. This came about by the teachers consenting to being removed from the GS-7 civil-service scale and by the failure of Congress to implement fully the provisions of its own law and the rules of the Department of Defense wage board. But during this same period overseas school administrators were granted four pay raises by Congress. Moreover, the overseas teachers who were at the GS–7 salary level when Public Law 86–91 was passed, now—because of the callous disregard of the law's intent and the upgrading of pay in the civil-service classifications—found themselves at the GS–4 level of pay.

The reasons given by the Department of Defense and the House Subcommittee of the Defense Appropriations Committee for this cavalier treatment of these teachers were, first, that plenty of teachers can be recruited at the existing scale; and, second that teachers in the overseas schools get certain fringe benefits such as buying privileges at the military post exchanges and free housing or subsidies for housing. Neither of these excuses will bear up under critical scrutiny. These privileges are also accorded civil-service employees who have received four significant raises and are provided as well to Panama Canal Zone teachers, who receive 40 to 50 per cent higher salaries.

Whether the supply of overseas teachers is adequate is a serious question. Doubtless it is true that, quantitatively, enough teachers are available. But whether enough teachers with competence in the various specialized fields have been available is questionable. The records for the school year 1962–63 reflected that 6.3 per cent were "pick-ups" or "temporaries," wives and daughters of military men who happened to be on the spot but who only partially meet the requirements. Also, there is the suspicion, if not the demonstrated fact, of widespread misassignment of teachers. It is well known that high-school social-studies and modern-language teachers, because of the nature and content of their teaching fields, jump at the chance to teach abroad for a year or two where they can see, first hand history—past and present and in-the-making—and develop fluency in foreign languages. It is doubtless true that there is a glamour aspect to teaching in foreign countries that attracts many teachers who will even take these jobs at salaries below what they get state-side. The glamour aspect is a powerful magnet since life overseas appeals to teachers as an opportunity for cultural enrichment.

The Department of Defense survey team in 1962 hit this practice hard. It found that to a great extent the Overseas Dependents Schools were being staffed by transients. As evidence, the survey team found that, because of the department's failure to comply with the law and regulations on teachers' pay over 37 per cent of the teachers were in their first year of service in their particular schools; over 60 per cent were in their first or second year of service; and about 75 per cent were in their first, second, or third year of service.[3] In contrast, the annual turnover rate in state-side schools is less than 4 per cent.

Strangely enough, education officials of the Department of Defense have strongly supported the idea that teachers in the Overseas Dependents Schools can have a high rate of turnover. Stranger still is the support of this notion by some reputable state-side school leaders, including some superintendents, who take the position that it is good to use these schools for the cultural broadening of the roving teachers. Yet each of these would find such staff turnover in his own school system intolerable.

Assuming that these claims of an adequate supply are valid, does this absolve Congress and the Department of Defense from the cynical disregard for their own laws and regulations? Does it excuse the obvious deception of the teachers who agreed to being removed from the civil-service classification and pay scales on the explicit promise that they would be put on pay scales comparable to those in the United States? And how does one answer the question regarding civilian employees who have already been given four salary increases aggregating more than 20 per cent, while overseas teachers were held to a 3.5 per cent increase between 1960 and 1965 despite passage of Public Law 86–91? How does one justify the difference in pay for the Canal Zone teachers?

Overseas Education Association Sanctions

The Overseas Education Association, weary of getting the run-around three years in a row and despairing of getting a satisfactory adjustment by appeals to the House Subcommittee on Defense Appropriations and the Defense Department, declared sanctions at the October 1962 meeting of its executive committee. This was a unilateral action without prior consultation with NEA. A request was transmitted to the NEA that it invoke sanctions against the

Overseas Dependents Schools by requesting its members not to accept appointments to positions in these schools. This action came upon the heels of the adoption of the sanctions resolution by the Denver NEA Representative Assembly. This was an act of desperation, a natural reaction to continued mistreatment, but an unwise one, because a local association alone can rarely enforce sanctions effectively. Unless the total teaching profession supports sanctions, rarely will they work.

Also, the OEA had requested recognition by the Defense Department as the negotiating agency for the overseas teachers and for designation of the NEA as its Washington agent. This latter action was taken under terms of the President's Executive Order Number 10988, issued in January 1962, declaring the right of Federal employees to negotiate with their unit heads regarding working conditions, grievances, and salaries. The Defense Department rejected the request for recognition of the OEA on the grounds that its declarations of sanctions was tantamount to a strike, which is banned in the President's directive. This was strange reasoning, expressing more resentment than law. Even after the lifting of the sanctions by the OEA, the request was still denied because of an "Urgent Advisory" sent by the NEA to its members regarding conditions in the overseas schools, which are described in the next section of this chapter. This again was interpreted as a strike, or strike threat, by the Defense Department (by whatever tortured reasoning or lack of reasoning is not known). On February 7, 1964 the Overseas Education Association was finally granted formal recognition at the national level by the Department of Defense.

The request of the OEA to the NEA to invoke sanctions against the overseas schools was received at the time when the Cuban crisis was imminent. Obviously the NEA could not and would not take such a drastic action against the Government of the United States in a time of a threatened national crisis. The circumstances and the extent of the mistreatment of the overseas teachers was crystal-clear. There could not be at that time, nor now, any reasonable doubt that these teachers had been capriciously and unjustly treated. But the NEA refused to take this drastic step at that particular time.

When the Cuban crisis was over, another circumstance arose which held great promise for amicable and mutual agreement to rectify the long-standing mistreatment of the overseas teachers. This circumstance was a survey of the entire Overseas Dependents Schools system by an impartial, competent group of six outstanding educators selected by the Defense Department.[4]

Deficiencies in the Schools

This survey resulted from repeated requests of the OEA and NEA. Resolutions were adopted by the NEA Representative Assembly in 1960, 1961, and 1962 calling for such a study. The concern of the OEA and NEA in requesting such a survey was not primarily the teachers salary situation, although that was, of course, involved. The primary concern was to cure the administrative, building, equipment, and curriculum weaknesses in these schools.

As has been stated concerning the District of Columbia schools, the overseas schools, located in countries whose friendship and good opinions the United States intensely covets, should be impressive showplaces. They should reflect the best practices in American public education. The feeling of the OEA and NEA, especially of the NEA staff members who had visited these schools, was that the Federal Government could afford to divert a microscopic portion of the billions it was pouring out in foreign lands to make these schools models of a public-school system.

This criticism of the overseas schools is not intended as a blanket indictment. There are some fine school buildings and many excellent school programs. In many respects the system has worked much better than any thoughtful person could have predicted. Considering the schools' connection with the military and direction by the Department of Defense, practices which are certainly foreign to the American concept of operation and control of public schools, it is surprising that the schools have done as well as, in some respects, they have. The defense Department has on its staff of civilian personnel many capable and sympathetic educators who, under the handicaps of a slow-moving bureaucracy, inadequate financial support, and too much military domination, have earnestly sought to make these replicas of the best American schools.

But the handicaps are great. One example, which has now been corrected, was that under contract-awarding procedures of the Defense Department it sometimes took 18 months to receive delivery on a given order for textbooks. Too, there have been some attempts to interfere with the curriculum. One flagrant case was the military order to discontinue, for the sake of economy, the offering of classes in the language of the country where the schools were located. Only a vigorous and sustained protest from the teachers caused this order to be withdrawn.

Many observers feel that, considering logistics and many other problems, it would be extremely difficult to devise a better system of responsibility for these schools. Others feel that they should be transfered to the United States Office of Education. That office does, under public laws, operate some schools, and some competent authorites believe the dependents' schools should be among them.

There have been serious, observable weaknesses and serious interference in school-personnel matters because of the operation of these schools by the military. Military protocol, red tape, and the necessity of going through channels often fouled up both the educational processes and teacher morale. There have been cases of summary handling of teachers' personnel problems by the military who, quite naturally, often tended to deal with teachers on the basis of superiors delivering orders to subordinates. This, apparently, is not general, but it occurs often enough to be a serious irritant.

There are glaring neglects and deficiencies in these schools. The first schools built overseas were from funds specifically appropriated by Congress, and these are good school buildings. The Berlin American High School is in every sense adequate; in fact, it is the sort of desirable showplace previously referred to. To a somewhat lesser degree, so is the Paris American High School and the Frankfurt American High School. But after the first spurt of building schools overseas, Congress—one supposes because it visualized these schools and, perhaps, the whole American occupation, as temporary—began to rely upon post commanders' use of unappropriated military funds to provide new school buildings. This resulted in some shocking buildings for school children. Quonset huts used for schools are common; converted warehouses, abandoned company fire stations, and abandoned post community buildings have been pressed into school service.

A humorous incident was uncovered by the survey team: the story of the star-shaped school. A post commander had directed that a cluster of quonset huts, so grouped that children had to walk over cobblestones in freezing weather to reach the rest rooms, be renovated into a star shape, with all buildings being connected by enclosed, steam-heated passageways. When the renovation was completed, the post commander was so impressed with it that he decreed it too good for a school building and promptly ordered that, instead, it be made into the post's communication center.

In another dilapidated building, the survey team was observing recitation in a class of some 25 third-grade children. An enormous rat strolled in during the recitation. The team expected an uproar to ensue. Instead, nothing happened; the children paid no attention to it. After the period was over, the teacher said that this was a daily occurrence, that the rat's wanderings about the room had become so commonplace they no longer excited the children.

In brief, the survey team found shortages of supplies and up-to-date textbooks, a lack of specialized personnel, principals bogged down in military paperwork, an excessive teacher turnover rate, little provision for handicapped or superior children, inadequate and unsafe school facilities in many locations, unsuitable housing for teachers at some posts, and unprofessional salaries for teachers. All of these deficiences were confirmed by a subcommittee of the House Committee on Education and Labor, authorized by House Resolution 596 in the first session of the Eighty-ninth Congress in 1965.

The survey recommended that the administration of the schools be unified (this was ordered by the Defense Department, effective July 1, 1964) that the education program be strengthened, that school facilities be improved, that teachers be paid salaries provided by the law, that the per-pupil limitation be abolished ($285 per child in 1963–64), and that financial requirements of the schools be fully met by the Department of Defense and Congress. The per-pupil limitation, which the Department of Defense had been hiding behind as an excuse for inadequate financing was abandoned in the President's budget submitted to Congress in January 1966.

The situation in the overseas schools, as reported by the survey team, was confirmed by Major William J. Davis, President of the European Congress of Parents and Teachers, in an address before the annual convention of the National Congress of Parents and Teachers at Miami Beach in April 1963.

> I am president of the PTA in Europe, the Middle East, and North Africa, an area of American children overseas extending 4,000 miles south from Iceland to Ethiopia and 2,000 miles east from Spain to Turkey, a mere 2,500,000 square miles, or the size of the Roman Empire at its peak in 117 A.D.
>
> Here is our basic problem area: We are entirely dependent on Federal aid for the education of our children overseas. I represent the PTA; the Congress of the United States is our school board, located some 5,000 miles away. In effect, except for one or two trips a year like this, the National Congress of Parents and Teachers is our only means of contacting the Congress of the United States.
>
> Here are our six basic problems.
>
> 1. Do you have kindergartens in your school system? We don't.
> 2. Do you have an adequate number of classrooms for your children (which are not located, in some instances, in old quonset huts, office buildings, officers' clubs, etc.)? We don't.
> 3. Do you have teachers who consider their salaries to be adequate, and as stated in a Public Law (86–91) which keep them in consonance with those salaries earned in the previous year in certain portions of the United States? We don't.
> 4. Do you have adequate specialists, especially in the fields of guidance counseling and remedial reading (which is extremely important to children who average one move per year)? We don't.
> 5. Do you have adequate physical education facilities, where your children can attempt to carry out the dicta of the President's Council on Youth Fitness? We don't.
> 6. Do you have a continuing health program in school for your children? We don't.
>
> If your answer to any of these questions is yes, then you know the basic flaws in our system, which contains 160,000 children who are actually ambassadors to all of our United Nations today, not just a dream of tomorrow.
>
> Americans appeal to overseas countries for exchange students on the university level, yet our elementary and secondary school program overseas is so limited that, in addition to offering less than the best in education to our own children, we are obliged to turn away the English-speaking children of NATO officials who would welcome the opportunity to learn the doings of democracy and its educational system at this age. This is in sharp contrast to the local Communists who welcome every opportunity to teach them at this tender age, rather than when they have reached manhood or womanhood.

Aftermath of the Survey

The report of the Defense Department's survey team was submitted in early December 1962. It soundly denounced the government's treatment regarding salary of the overseas teachers, recommending either the significant raising of the per-pupil limitation from $275 to $310 or above, or the elimination of the per-pupil limitation as a means of financing the dependent schools. This limitation was raised in 1963–64 to $285. Incidentally, the per-pupil limitation is what we would call the per-capita (or per pupil) expenditure for current operating expenses (excluding capital outlay) in school districts of the United States. The $285 appropriation compares with the average per-pupil expenditure in the United States of about $450 for the school year 1964–65. Actually, only about $260 per child is available in the Overseas Dependent Schools because tuition payments for children of overseas civilian employees enrolled in other schools must be paid from this limitation. For example, $640 per child paid in tuition in the Canal Zone is taken from this limitation.

This per-pupil limitation does not represent by any means the total spending of the Federal Government on the overseas schools. A huge chunk comes from appropriations for the military. When the NEA protested from time to time about the low overseas per-pupil limitation rate as compared to stateside schools, the NEA officials were told that much additional money was spent on the overseas schools, that money could be found outside the per-pupil limitation for increased teachers' salaries. But when NEA officials pressed for an adjustment in these salaries, there always seemed to be some reason why this could not be done, although it was done for administrators' salaries.

With the submission of the survey team's report, the NEA, still debating the invoking of sanctions against the overseas schools, believed that surely now, with the report of its own survey committee before it pointing to horrendous mistreatment of teachers, the Defense Department would move immediately to cure the injustice. NEA officials especially felt that neither the Department nor the Congressional subcommittee could brazenly deny the simple human justice of the matter after the Department of Defense Advisory Committee on Education (a lay committee) had solidly supported the report and soundly denounced the unjust salary treatment of the teachers as a violation of the specifics and the intent of Public Law 86–91 and the Defense Department's own wage-board regulations. But the NEA was wrong. Scuttlebutt has it that the subcommittee told Secretary McNamara in blunt terms to give a hands-off treatment to requests for raises for the teachers.

But in the meantime, NEA officials were faced with the critical decision of whether to invoke sanctions against the Government of the United States. The survey team's report was placed under a secrecy ban by the Defense Department as confidential information. Finally in desperation, the NEA was able to pry the report loose by intervention of fair-minded congressmen and senators.

In back of NEA reluctance to get tough with the Federal Government on the OEA question is—let's face it—the whole history and tradition of the teaching profession in the United States; total reliance upon the impact of an aroused public sentiment to support adequate financing and decent treatment of teachers. This experience with our Government convinced some NEA officials (including this writer) that this is beautiful philosophy but that, in the dog-eat-dog kind of pressure-group society that has evolved in the United States, there are serious elements of weakness in such a posture.

Finally, in January 1963, after repeated delays, run-arounds, and backing and filling by the Defense Department, the word came through from Secretary McNamara's office that only a $5 raise in the per-pupil limitation for the Overseas Dependent Schools would be requested.

The $5 per-pupil limitation increase requested would make possible about a $100 increase in salaries for the overseas teachers for 1963–64. However, to provide a scale which would restore lost ground for the future and compensate for the losses in each of the last three years would have required a $25 to $35 raise in this limitation.

NEA Advisory

It was only then, after every avenue of appeal to reason and justice had been exhausted—and this includes efforts to get the story to the White House—the NEA decided to issue an "Urgent Advisory" to its members and affiliates. Some 40,000 letters were sent to state and local affiliates, superintendents of schools, boards of education, and college placement services. In addition, publicity was given to the advisory by national, state, and local association publications.

The advisory described the adverse conditions in the dependent schools and the salary mistreatment of teachers. It simply advised teachers who are considering appointments to these schools that they should know the facts. It did not request or suggest that they refuse service to these schools. The advisory also urged teachers who had accepted appointments to keep these agreements.

What was the impact of this advisory (aside from the wailing of some dissidents who professed to see in this mild action of the NEA a strike against the government of the United States)?

One can't be sure.

Some Defense Department officials boasted that its only effect was to advertise the overseas positions and to drum up more applicants. And this could be correct. There are too many variables to be able to pinpoint the effect precisely. However, Department of Defense officials admitted that the second advisory, sent out in the fall of 1963, did significantly cut the number of applicants. And, in the summer of 1965, officials admitted in testimony before a Congressional committee that a shortage of 200 teachers existed for the school year 1965–66.

The NEA had a few letters from teachers who were considering appointments saying, in effect, that they had confidence in their professional association and would decline. Also, a few letters were received denouncing the advisory as a communistic document. By and large, however, there was little reaction.

The Canadian Teachers Federation, which stands in the same relation to its affiliated provincial teachers' associations as does the NEA to its affiliated state education associations, had precisely the same problem with its government. Here is how the matter was handled.

> A number of teachers overseas complained to us through their provincial teachers organizations that when the salary limits were raised a year ago, equivalent adjustments were not made in the case of teachers then in service (i.e., beginning the second year of their two-year contract). We made a number of appeals to the Department of National Defense. . . . At each stage we received rather abrupt refusals and the Deputy Minister finally stated that he would do nothing at all about the matter, even though he granted that we had made "an interesting case" (to use his term). We suggested to him that his reluctance to take positive action was only because he felt that he had an adequate supply of teachers for his schools overseas and that his opinion might change if the supply dropped off. His reply was that they had thousands of applications on file.
>
> The rest of the story is quite brief. We simply contacted our provincial affiliates and suggested that they request their teachers to delay signing [Department of National Defense] contracts until further notice. We also got word to the Deputy Minister through a minor official that if we did not get settlement within two weeks, he would get no teachers. As the deadline approached, I heard that they had received four applications for the 175 vacancies which had to be filled during the present year. Before the deadline, I received a telephone call which assured me that the matter had been reconsidered and that there would be no difficulty in adjusting the salary limit for the teachers concerned. We notified our affiliates to this effect; the applications began to arrive in satisfactory numbers; and [the Department of National Defense] was as good as its word in making the adjustment.
>
> Our action was made possible by a number of factors. . . . One of these was our feature of automatic membership—compulsory membership required by law in the 10 provinces—(unkindly called "closed shop" by some of our colleagues in the United States). This makes it possible for us to reach virtually every teacher in Canada with a minimum of delay and to marshal support for any causes which can be justified on grounds of professional standards and ethics.

Explosion of Teachers' Anger

Finally, in November 1963, when a piddling raise of $100 came through (as a result of the Defense Department's request for the inadequate increase of $5 in the per-pupil limitation) for the overseas teachers for the school year 1963–64—their first raise in three years—the pent-up resentment of the overseas teachers began to explode. A group of twenty teachers in the American High School in Ankara wrote the Department of Defense, saying in part:

> In view of the too-little, too-late teachers' pay increase, we do hereby reject the $100 pay raise. . . . The amount of the raise offered is certainly an insult to the dedication, ability, and services of the teachers in the armed forces schools. We therefore ask that our salaries be returned to the level of the pre-raise era until a satisfactory pay increase is granted.

Other OEA teachers sent their checks for $100 to the NEA. Some were made out to the President, some to Defense Secretary McNamara, and some to the Secretary of the Treasury. Of course, the reaction of the Department of Defense was one of righteous indignation and refusal to accept the checks.

The Overseas Federation of Teachers (consisting at that time of two small AFT locals in Madrid and Weisbaden, organized in the fall of 1963) began circulating to all teachers in the dependents' schools a form letter to be signed and then mailed to congressmen, the Treasury Department, the President, or a member of the House Subcommittee on Defense Appropriations. An excerpt: "Enclosed find $2.08. This sum is the amount the Department of Defense raised my salary per month after four years. Figured on a per-hour basis, that raise amounts to two cents an hour."

CARDS STACKED AGAINST PROFESSIONAL ASSOCIATIONS. The tremendous odds that a professional association faces in seeking to represent its members before Federal agencies, under President Kennedy's Executive Order directing such representation and negotiation concerning working conditions, are indicated in an article from a Washington newspaper:

> An increasingly-pressing problem for Government agencies has to do with the role of professional associations under the Administration's labor-management program for Federal employees.
>
> The question is: Does the program offer professional groups the chance to represent their members before management in the same way as rank-and-file unions?
>
> The still-tentative answer seems to be that it does not.
>
> It seems to be that the associations must continue to fill the same role as in the past, that the labor-management program offers them nothing.
>
> It also seems to be that the program, while denying new opportunities to the professional groups, opens the door to increasing rank-and-file union raids on the membership of professional groups.[5]

Why is this? Frankly, organized labor is a superpower structure in the Federal Government. Those who administer the Presidential, or even Congressional, directives, tend to show every possible favor to labor. To put it bluntly, the cards seem to be stacked against the professional associations. Actually, the President's Executive Order was formulated, many believe, to help the unions reverse their sagging membership figures; it had been pursued to that end.

Fed up with getting polite run-arounds from the Department of Defense, the NEA sent out a second "Urgent Advisory" in November 1963 (well ahead, this time, of the Defense Department's recruiting teams) calling attention to the continued mistreatment of the overseas teachers and the unsatisfactory conditions and inadequate financing of the Overseas Dependents Schools. This advisory was effective, but still not enough.

Moreover, the NEA again (in February 1964) protested the nonrecognition of the Overseas Education Association as the representative of overseas teachers. (With a membership of about 4,000, the OEA is by far the largest organization of overseas teachers.) As a result, on February 7, 1964 the Defense Department extended national recognition to the OEA under the President's directive of January 1962.

In December 1963, the NEA learned that the Defense Department had retreated a little in the battle—to the extent of requesting in its budget a raise of $10 in the per-pupil limitation for the overseas schools. This would provide for the 1964–65 school year a raise of $200 per teacher, still far short of the mandate of Public Law 86–91 and the department's wage-board regulations, but some concession at least.

Unsatisfied with this still inadequate adjustment, the NEA directed its attorneys to file suit in the Federal courts of the District of Columbia, asking for a writ of mandamus against the Secretary of Defense and the secretaries of the three armed services, compelling them to take action to meet the requirements of the law and their own wage-board regulations in implementing salary policies for the overseas teachers.

From the outset, the outcome of this suit was questionable. Ambiguities in the wording of Public Law 86–91 and even of the Defense Department's wage-board regulations presented loopholes for the Government. However, the matter of equity could enter into court consideration of the matter. Should equity considerations result in a decision favorable to the overseas teachers, then the way would be cleared for action in the court of claims to recover past salaries back to the passage of Public Law 86–91 in 1959.

A Washington columnist pointed up the significance of the suit to compel the Department of Defense to meet the commitment of the law and its regulations:

> It's a long-shot possibility but the Federal courts could conceivably direct Uncle Sam to carry out his promise to Federal employees to pay them salaries which are comparable with rates in private industry.
>
> The Courts will have the opportunity in a pending case brought by Defense's overseas teachers. Rulings on it could have a profound effect on the classified

and postal pay systems which fix salaries of 1.7 million Federal employees. This is the background on it:

Salaries of the 7000 teachers in dependent schools are supposed to be comparable to salaries paid in this country in school districts of at least 100,000 population.

In fact, the 1959 law (PL 86–91) that laid down that principle was the first of its kind to embrace the comparability formula. It took the jobs of teachers out of the Classification Act and set up a new personnel system for them.

But Congress has refused to permit the teacher comparability pay law to be carried out as intended by the 1959 law just as it has failed to follow through on the 1962 law that bears the comparability principle for classified and postal employees.

The House Appropriations Committee wrote into Defense's appropriation act a per-pupil limitation on funds that could be used to pay teacher salaries and for other school operations. The limitation has effectively gutted the teacher pay comparability formula.

As a result, the Overseas Educational Association, the organization of teachers that has formal recognition from Defense, has asked the Federal court to direct Defense to pay the teachers comparable salaries as intended in the 1958 law. The Association is affiliated with the National Education Association here.

The case could have significance far beyond the salaries paid the 7000 overseas teachers. Classified and postal employees will watch closely the court's decision. There is talk of these employees appealing to the courts to force Congress to follow through on the comparability principle to their salaries.[6]

The United States District Court for the District of Columbia dismissed the suit in November 12, 1964 on the grounds that remedial action should be sought through Congress. The NEA filed notice of appeal to the higher court. District of Columbia Court of Appeals sustained the lower court's decision. In the meantime, the legal counsel of OEA entered a suit in the court of claims, in the name of 3,000 teachers and former teachers in the dependent schools, for back pay.

Following the court setbacks, there were threats of a one-day work stoppage by some 500 teachers in the dependent schools in 14 school centers in France, Spain, Germany, Italy, Japan, and the Netherlands, to protest their grievances.

This threatened step was a spontaneous reaction of teachers not sponsored by the Overseas Education Association or NEA. The genesis of the movement was in Paris, and the idea spread to the other centers.

The Department of Defense immediately advised military commanders to warn teachers that any work stoppage would be interpreted as a strike against the United States Government; that the offending teachers would be fired; and that they might be subject to charges by the Department of Justice of having committed a felony and, if prosecuted and convicted were subject to a fine not to exceed $1,000 or imprisonment for a term not to exceed one year.

The teachers, who called off their threatened protest actions, complained bitterly that the Defense Department was selective in its zeal to enforce the law; it seemed unconcerned about the law and regulations regarding the teachers' salaries, but invoked zealously the no-strike law. Of course this reaction was one of anger and frustration. But it illustrates the dangers of failure to redress long-standing grievances and, in effect, denying the aggrieved any effective means of redress.

And what if the NEA should invoke the sanction of asking its members to withdraw services to the Overseas Dependents Schools? The Department of Defense had already ruled that such an act would constitute the advocacy of a strike against the United States Government, if the action were taken by the Overseas Education Association as representative of the overseas teachers. What would be the legal implications should NEA take such a step?

The answer is not clear; and it is doubtful that the interpretation of sanctions as a strike would be sustained by the courts.

The threatened "protest day" of the overseas teachers, initiated by a group of teachers in Paris, brought to light some plans of the Department of Defense for improvement of the general school situation.

The Director of Education for the Army in Europe, Dr. Walter O'Kane, met with this group of teachers and apprised them of the developing Defense Department plans. Doubtless this information had much to do with the calling off of the protest. It had been the Defense Department's blank stone wall of indifference, the contemptuous ignoring of the teacher's repeated pleas over several years, that had produced a dangerous near rebellion on the part of the overseas teachers.

Pentagon officials, too, gave assurance that serious consideration was under way to remedy the situation.

From the teachers' viewpoint, the Defense Department has been the major bottleneck to correcting unsatisfactory conditions in the schools. Rightly or wrongly, the teachers have felt that the department officials responsible for the operation of the dependents' schools have persistently assured Congress that everything was all right in these schools and that only minor added appropriations were necessary.

At the end of 1964, there seemed to be some hope, in several areas, that the problems might be solved.

The President's budget for the fiscal year 1966, submitted to Congress on January 20, 1965 provided for a raise in the per-pupil limitation for the Overseas Dependent Schools from $285 to $455. At a glance, this seemed to be a shift in policy—an apparent raising of the limitation by $170. But it was done with mirrors. All expenditures for these schools were simply grouped into the per-pupil limitation, whereas previously much of the schools' cost had been in the "appropriated funds" of the Department of Defense. Only $11 of this increased limitation was to be applied to teachers' salaries, making a possible raise of $300 for the teachers. This raise, combined with the $100 raise in 1963–64, meant a total raise of $400 since 1960. This left the overseas teachers still $400–$600 short of the intent of Public Law 86–91 and the Defense Department's wage-board scales of 1959.

So, some progress had been made but far from enough.

Meanwhile, Dr. Walter O'Kane, who had met with the Paris teachers and was viewed by the teachers as a highly competent, sincere professional who consistently fought for better school conditions to the extent of bucking the military hierarchy, finally quit in disgust in the summer of 1965.

It seems incongruous, to say the least, for the Federal Government, with its war on poverty and its aid-to-education program emphasizing adequate educational opportunities for all children, to perpetuate inequities in the schools for the children of men in the military service.

The American Legion became concerned about this neglect, as reflected in its resolution demanding that the Overseas Dependents Schools be maintained at a level equal to those of the better schools in the United States. This resolution was adopted at the Legion's National Convention in September 1964 and was subsequently endorsed by the Jewish War Veterans.

Victory at Long Last

In the summer of 1965, the story of the continued mistreatment of the overseas teachers and the extent of the neglect of the dependents' schools got through to Congress. Led by Congressman Morris Udall of Arizona, the House of Representatives passed a bill to implement the intent of Public Law 86–91 and subsequent wage-board regulations to gear the salaries of the overseas teachers to those in cities with populations of 100,000 or more. This bill would increase teachers' salaries by $800. In the course of debate on the bill many Congressmen expressed indignation over the manner in which these teachers had been treated. There was also widespread indignation over neglect of the Department of Defense schools which began a movement to transfer control of these schools to the United States Office of Education. In addition, a subcommittee of the House Labor and Education Committee was appointed to survey the Overseas Dependents Schools after the first session of the Eighty-ninth Congress in 1965.

The Udall bill went to the Senate for consideration in August 1965 only to get caught in the filibuster over the proposal to repeal section 14 *b* of the Taft-Hartley Act. Thus action was deferred until the second session, beginning in January 1966. The Senate committee voted out the bill in the first few days of the session. Passage again was delayed by continuation of the filibuster. But senators Vance Hartke, Mike Monroney, and Frank Carlson

TABLE 11-2

Changes Effected in Pay Scales of Teachers in the Overseas Dependents Schools by Passage of Public Law 89–391 in April 1966

Steps	Teachers with Bachelors' Degrees			Teachers with Masters' Degrees		
	Scale as of September 1965	Scale after Passage of New Law	Scale Effective September 1966	Scale as of September 1965	Scale after Passage of New Law	Scale Effective September 1966
1	$4,835	$5,265	$5,505	$5,035	$5,680	$5,970
2	5,020	5,475	5,720	5,220	5,905	6,210
3	5,205	5,685	5,935	5,405	6,130	6,450
4	5,390	5,895	6,150	5,590	6,355	6,690
5	5,575	6,105	6,365	5,775	6,580	6,930
6	5,760	6,315	6,580	5,960	6,805	7,170
7	5,945	6,525	6,795	6,145	7,030	7,410
8	6,130	6,735	7,010	6,330	7,255	7,650
9	6,315	6,945	7,225	6,515	7,980	7,890
10	—	7,155	7,440	—	7,705	8,130
11	—	7,365	7,655	—	7,930	8,370
12	—	—	—	—	8,155	8,610

fought for justice for the overseas teachers, and on February 10, 1966 the Senate, by a voice vote, passed the bill.

Following the deliberations of a joint conference committee of the Senate and the House to reconcile certain differences in the versions passed by each, the bill was approved by both houses, and was signed by President Johnson on April 24, to become effective with the succeeding pay period of the teachers.

The new law (Public Law 89–391) amended the Defense Department Overseas Teacher Pay and Personnel Practices Act of 1959, directing the Defense Department to pay teachers in the Overseas Dependents Schools at the average range of rates existing in the 181 urban school districts with populations of 100,000 or more.

The new salary scale of the overseas teachers ranged from $5,265 for teachers with bachelors' degrees to $8,825 for teachers with doctors' degrees. The bill provided an average increase per teacher of $800. The range of increases was from $430 to $2,210.

The new scale provided by the bill added a fourth preparation level, provided greater preparation differentials, and increased the number of annual increments.

Table 11-2 indicates the extent of the adjustment upward of salaries of the overseas teachers from the September 1965 scale (including a raise of $300

Teachers with Six Years' Preparation			Teachers with Doctors' Degrees		
Scale as of September 1965	Scale after Passage of New Law	Scale Effective September 1966	Scale as of September 1965	Scale after Passage of New Law	Scale Effective September 1966
		$6,195			$6,460
$5,135	$5,890	6,435	No Scale prior to Public Law 89-391	$6,125	6,700
5,320	6,115	6,675		6,350	6,940
5,505	6,340	6,915		6,575	7,180
5,690	6,565	7,155		6,800	7,420
5,875	6,790	7,395		7,025	7,660
6,060	7,015	7,635		7,250	7,900
6,245	7,240	7,875		7,475	8,140
6,430	7,465	8,115		7,700	8,380
6,615	7,690	8,355		7,925	8,620
—	7,915	8,595		8,150	8,860
—	8,140	8,835		8,375	9,100
—	8,365	9,075		8,600	9,340

at that time) to the scale that was immediately implemented in May 1966 by passage of the new law, to the scale in effect for the school year 1966–67.

Not only was there, finally, satisfactory adjudication of the teachers' salary problem in the Overseas Dependents Schools, but there were also plans for rapid eradication of the educational deficiencies in these schools promised by the Department of Defense officials.

Dr. Lynn M. Bartlett, Deputy Assistant Secretary of Defense for Education, in testimony before the House Subcommittee on Appropriations on April 27, 1966 suggested a total appropriation of $182,869,000, for the overseas schools for fiscal year 1967, an increase of about $9 million over the fiscal year 1966. This represented an increase in per-pupil cost from $455 to $492, an increase of $37. Also, the per-pupil limitation which the NEA and OEA had protested for several years as a serious handicap to proper financing of the schools was eliminated from the 1967 fiscal budget.

Items marked for improvement in the testimony before the House Subcommittee on Appropriations included teachers' salaries, provision for kindergartens in the regular school program, provision for host-nation language and cultural programs for all students from grades 1–12, a world-wide survey of school facilities to enable the Department of Defense to keep abreast of school building needs, a remedy for the textbook deficiencies, and stabilization of administrative personnel by an improved salary and promotional system.

Thus, with the salary controversy settled, with some provisions already made, and with commitment by responsible officials for rapid improvement of existing deficiencies in the overseas educational program, NEA lifted on October 14, 1966 its advisory which had been in effect since February 1, 1963.

Senator Vance Hartke of Indiana, commenting on the inadequacies in these schools in hearings on Public Law 89–391, took the Defense Department officials to task for repeated mention of the travel advantages and the fringe benefits for overseas teachers (post-exchange privileges and housing) and said in effect; "Let's bury these arguments. They should never have been used in the first place. We are not running a tourist agency, but education for children."[7]

An exchange between Senator Hartke and Dr. Lynn Bartlett, Assistant Secretary of Defense for Education, in these hearings sums up the sustained position of NEA and OEA:[8]

> Senator Hartke:
>
> Now, gentlemen, you are going to have to make up your minds which side you are on in this thing. I am not asking you at this time to forfeit your position in the Department of Defense, but you are trying to educate children and this is a responsibility. We have a great struggle in this Nation educating our young people to keep up not alone with ourselves but with the competition in the world. If you are going to shortchange these children, then I would feel you would have a difficult time living with your conscience. I know you are dedicated people and I know you are operating under the hazard of budget restrictions and things of that sort, but you are in the field of educating children. If you want to do away with their educational system, why don't you advocate in addition certain sacrifices in the interest of country and love of man; that is fine.
>
> Dr. Bartlett. Senator Hartke, I couldn't agree with you more than in this statement. I think our primary function is to provide and secure the very best teaching possible.
>
> Let me make a statement that we made in the report in which I participated. I stated and I was responsible for this statement in that report and we have another member of the committee here whom I am sure will concur in it—I said and I still feel that this school system can and should be the most outstanding educational system in the world. I think together we can make it the most outstanding school system in the world.
>
> I think Congress and the Department of Defense must work together in seeing that this is accomplished. It was interesting to me to see the contrast in the equipment used for briefings in the military headquarters and that which was available in the schools on the bases. The contrast was very great and I don't think this should be the case.
>
> So, I greatly admire your stand, Senator Hartke, in trying to see to it that these schools are improved. Let me assure you that our office is in complete concurrence in doing everything we can to see the same thing accomplished.

Thus after seven solid years of effort and frustration, NEA and OEA were able to bring about a satisfactory correction of the deficiencies in the Overseas

Dependents Schools situation, with regard both to teachers' salaries and to subminimal conditions in the educational program.

While the victory demonstrated that, in time, the steady pressure of the facts and the appeals for justice are powerful forces, it cannot be denied that NEA did not look too good or appear to be able to get decisive action during this long drawn-out fight. It is astounding that so many of the overseas teachers stuck loyally to NEA through these years and that so few defected to the teachers' unions.

Whatever the reasons may be for the teachers' loyalty, the NEA certainly has to find quicker acting measures in the future.

12

After 300 Days

> You must stand up for what you stand for. You know what you are trying to do. Others have various vague notions of social growth. You know that there is only one true science of building a stable and broad-based democratic social structure. You know what you need for your work. Demand it as a right in the name of the children of the Commonwealth. In other words, never for a moment be afraid of that dying body of opinion which looks on the public school as a sort of educational orphan asylum. Stand to it, that it is the nursery of the leaders of the world, as by the high virtue of our invincible democracy it is!
>
> —Walter Hines Page[1]

The second request (after the Denver resolution on the summer of 1962) for the voting of sanctions by the NEA came from Utah. The total teaching force in the public schools of Utah requested that NEA invoke sanctions against that state in the spring of 1963. Happily, this turned out to be a success story for the Utah Education Association and NEA, although it was also long and drawn out.

After 300 days (sanctions were invoked May 19, 1964 and lifted March 13, 1965) NEA demonstrated in the Utah case that its sanctions weapon would work and work effectively. This was a landmark victory, a turning point in the battle with the teachers' union. This victory was quickly followed by another in Oklahoma, which required less than half as much time to win. Later came a victory in Kentucky, although sanctions were not involved.

The first intimation that something unusual was coming up in Utah came in early March 1963. This was a request from John Evans, Executive Secretary of the Utah Education Association (UEA), to the National Commission on Professional Rights and Responsibilities (PR and R Commission) to send an observer to a meeting of the UEA House of Delegates on March 15 and to a mass meeting of Utah teachers on March 16, both meetings to be held in Salt Lake City.

The observer was present and witnessed extraordinary solidarity in the vote of the special session of the teachers on a motion to withhold contract negotiations for the school year 1963–64, giving the right of attorney to local association officials. Despite the heaviest snowstorm of the year, some

8,000 teachers, 83 per cent of the state's total were in attendance. Only 189 voted against withholding negotiations, and it is believed that most of the "no" votes arose over dissatisfaction with the mildness of the action. Too, the NEA, was requested to inform its members of the action and urge them to refrain from seeking or accepting jobs in Utah until the controversy was settled.

Background of the Revolt

What was in back of this action of the teachers of Utah? There was a historical background of discontent among the teachers, and there was a current irritant.

Contrary to some press reports, the current unrest in the spring of 1963 stemmed not from salary demands alone, but from failure of the legislature to provide funds for upgrading the total school program in that state. The legislature had provided and increased appropriation ($11.6 million) which, if applied to teachers' salaries, could have underwritten an average raise of about $700 per teacher, or from $400 to $1,000 per teacher according to the wealth of the school district in which he was employed.

The revolt grew out of what the teachers considered a lack of any serious consideration by the Utah governor or legislature of a cooperatively developed proposal for school improvement. This proposal was called the CAPS Program (Cooperating Agencies of the Public Schools) and was developed by an informal coalition of organizations consisting of the Utah Education Association, the Utah School boards, the Utah Society of School Superintendents, the Utah State Board of Education, and the Utah Congress of Parents and Teachers.

The program, developed after long and careful study by these groups, called for an increased biennial state appropriation of $24.5 million. The increased funds were to be alloted as follows: 40 per cent for increased teachers' salaries; 20 per cent for employment of necessary new school personnel including teachers and special service personnel such as counselors; and 40 per cent for necessary new buildings, equipment, and instructional materials. In Utah, buildings are constructed on a pay-as-you-go basis from current appropriations as well as by bond issues. But most bond issues are paid off in short-time schedules, unlike the general practice in other states. Few of the bond issues in Utah extend over a longer period than 15 years. Thus about 35 per cent of current school money was going for buildings. The 1963 legislature actually appropriated only $11.6 million, about $2 million more than was needed to provide the requested increases in teachers' salaries. The original CAPS plan never got out of the sifting committee of the legislature (a committee roughly analogous to the Rules Committee of the United States House of Representatives) for debate.

The teachers felt that this was an arbitrary manner of dealing with what they considered a fair, carefully developed plan for bringing Utah's schools up to the desired standards. They felt that certain interests in the state vetoed the plan behind the scenes and were not willing to have the people's representatives even debate its merits.

A DECADE AND A HALF OF STRUGGLE. The historical aspect of the Utah teachers' revolt has two facets. First, the teachers fought bitterly against the ultraconservative J. Bracken Lee during his two gubernatorial terms in the early 1950's in efforts to secure adequate support for the schools. In order to gain any consideration at all, the teachers were compelled in 1953 to "stack their contracts" until some assurance was given that there would be a special session of the legislature. Public-spirited citizens of the state, together with the press, radio, and TV stations, pledged that if the teachers would return to the schools an all-out effort would be made to bring about a special session. The teachers agreed, and the session was held in late 1953. Only patchwork legislation was passed. The teachers signed their contracts, but they were far from satisfied with the funds provided.

This conflict with Governor Lee and his supporters (and one would presume that some of the same forces were involved in support of Governor Clyde in the 1963 battle) left some rankling scars among many of the teachers. They felt that they had been treated with contempt then and again in another controversy in 1960.

The second facet of the historical cause for bitterness among the teachers was their belief that Utah had not supported its public schools as generously as the people of the state had been led to believe. In 1947, there was a massive infusion of new funds, perhaps the greatest stride forward by the state in modern times. But since, steady deterioration in the state's educational situation had taken place.

The teachers felt that adequate state appropriations had been held down by statistics such as: "Utah ranks fourth among the states in per-capita support of the schools." The teachers contended that these statements were misleading because of the high number of children per family, resulting in more children to educate in proportion to the total population than in most other states. In 1963 Utah led the nation in its percentage of school-age population (ages 5–17): 29.5 per cent.

For example, Utah's per-pupil expenditure for education was equal to the national average in 1947–48. But in the succeeding 15 years, that expenditure declined significantly. Utah was able to make progress in education in this period largely because of the sacrifice of its teachers and administrators, who imposed higher and still higher standards of preparation and performance upon themselves.

In the meantime, the population explosion hit Utah with great force, requiring the construction of an extraordinary number of new school buildings and requiring some districts to borrow to the legal limits and, in addition, to supplement the bonding with high tax rates for capital outlay. The reluctance of the legislature to provide realistic state aid for capital outlay caused some school systems to restrict operating programs in order to provide taxing power for building needs.

During the administration of Governor J. Bracken Lee, taxes were actually reduced at a time when plans should have been made for financing schools for future increased enrollments that would result from the postwar baby boom. As a result, Utah was not adequately prepared when the children of the baby boom began to enter the first grade. The insistent warnings of the UEA in this connection were ignored by Governor Lee. And, thus, by 1963 the state had not yet been able to recover from this shortsightedness.

Table 12–1 indicates the deteriorating financial situation.

TABLE 12-1

Utah's Relative Position Among the States on Current Expenditures per Pupil 1947–48 to 1962–63[2]

Current Expenditures Per Pupil in ADA			Percentage United States Average Was Above Utah
School Year	**Utah**	**United States Average**	
1947–48	$179	$179	0.0%
1949–50	179	209	16.8
1951–52	196	244	24.5
1953–54	208	265	27.4
1955–56	240	294	22.5
1957–58	291	341	17.2
1959–60	322	376	16.8
1961–62*	349	415	18.9
1962–63*	354	432	22.0
Per cent of increase 1947–48 to 1962–63	97.8%	141.3%	

**Estimates of School Statistics 1962–63,* Washington, D.C.: National Education Association, p. 31.
Source: United States Office of Education, *Biennial Survey of Education in the United States.*

Thus by 1962–63, Utah instead of matching the United States average expenditure per pupil, was spending 22 per cent below that average, dropping in rank among the state from twenty-eighth to thirty-sixth.

To present a fair picture, it should be mentioned that Table 12–1 does not reflect capital-outlay expenditures, that is, expenditures for buildings. If these expenditures were added, of course, the total spent per capita would be sigificantly higher. But the table reflects the pinch on teachers and on children because of the diversion of normal current expenditure funds to capital outlay.

Moreover, the record showed that Utah had fallen behind the average current expenditure per pupil in the surrounding seven Mountain States (Arizona, Idaho, Colorado, Nevada, New Mexico, Montana, and Wyoming) by $100. Utah's per-pupil expenditure exceeded only that of Idaho. Besides, Utah had slipped to forty-ninth place among the states in improvement of teachers' salaries. The local boards of education were virtually powerless to rectify the situation since increased funds had to come from the state.

The situation was made to order for an explosion. The shape of things to come was indicated by the invoking of sanctions in the summer of 1962 by the local associations in the Jordan and Alpine school districts, in joint action with the Utah Education Association. The situations in these two districts were settled before the opening of schools in the fall, but these actions were a harbinger of deep teacher unrest. In fact, there were plenty of signs of rebellion to alert responsible authorities to the necessity of taking action in a deteriorating situation. But apparently the state's power structure assumed that only a slight effort was necessary.

Precisely what did the CAPS program propose? It proposed an increase of $100 per pupil, or a total increase in school funds of $24.5 million, to accomplish its goals:

1. A per-pupil investment in education equal to the Mountain States average.
2. Conditions of work, including salary, that would insure an adequate supply of well-qualified teachers.
3. Provision of adequate additional services to children, e.g., library, counseling and guidance, special education, and vocational education. (This would involve provisions for a greater percentage of non-teaching personnel.)
4. Greater utilization of present staff through an extended school year.
5. Provision of full-time kindergartens.
6. Elimination of half-day or double sessions.
7. State responsibility for school buildings on a continuing as well as an emergency basis.
8. Return to the former method of electing school board members.
9. Elimination of the costs to school districts of collecting taxes.
10. Earlier remittance of school funds from the state to the local districts.

Teachers' Appeal to NEA

Following the action of UEA members on March 16, 1963 to withhold the signing of contracts, officials of the Utah Education Association went to

Washington on April 17–18 to present a request that the NEA invoke sanctions and provide other assistance. The meeting was with the Interim Committee of the NEA, PR and R Commission, a committee empowered to make decisions, between regular meetings of the full commission, regarding investigations into troubled school situations. The interim committee explained that the procedures for invoking sanctions, as spelled out by the NEA Board of Directors, required that sanctions could be invoked only after a thorough, impartial, objective study had been made of a given situation by the PR and R Commission. The Interim Committee voted to make such a study of the Utah situation, and a committee was subsequently appointed to conduct the investigation. The study committee conducted its first inquiry June 2–5, 1963.[3]

In the meantime, the NEA agreed to assist the UEA in every possible way including two especially important items:

1. An immediate grant of $30,000 to help the UEA in publicizing its side of the controversy to the people of the state.
2. An immediate effort to publicize among NEA members in other states the fight of the Utah teachers for better school conditions, their unity of action in withholding contract negotiations, and their resolve to return to their positions upon reconcilement of the impasse; and to request that teachers employed in other states be mindful of their professional obligations to their colleagues in Utah.

During the period following this meeting and the visit of the PR and R study committee to Utah on June 2, negotiations were going on behind the scenes to bring about a resolution of the impasse between the governor of Utah and the UEA. Governor Clyde had become incensed at the action of the UEA, claiming that the only knowledge he had about the proposed action and the voted action was from the press. He claimed he had not been consulted. On the other side, UEA officials and members were incensed at what they described as the governor's contemptuous ignoring and bypassing of the teachers.

At Detroit, during the annual NEA convention, June 30–July 5, 1963, where the matter of the NEA's invoking sanctions became a red-hot issue before the Representative Assembly, it was obvious that Utah teachers were bitter most of all at the governor's ignoring them and his insistence upon dealing with them through intermediaries. The teachers charged, for example, at least in private conversations, that the only contact their executive secretary had with the governor was through telephone conversations with an intermediary in San Francisco, who attempted to mediate the controversy via telephone.

The NEA worked in every possible way to heal the estrangement between the governor and the teachers. It was a difficult and delicate job. But opportunities were opened by reasonable, wise, and public-spirited Utah citizens, some of whom had been influential in mediating the 1953 stalemate between the teachers and the former governor, J. Bracken Lee.

For example, Dr. O. Preston Robinson, general manager and editor of the *Deseret News*, the Mormon newspaper, took the initiative in arranging a meeting between William G. Carr, NEA Executive secretary, and Governor Clyde. In this meeting on May 5, the executive secretary urged the governor to place the school-appropriation proposal on the agenda of the upcoming special session of the legislature. The governor again refused.

The entire controversy had now developed into a situation of exploding tempers. Many observers felt that much of the teachers' resentment would have disappeared and their belligerent stand ended had the governor consented to full consideration by the legislature of the CAPS program (which it had not considered in regular session) even though it might refuse to act upon it.

The governor had publicly proposed to appoint a study committee on the school controversy but refused to let the UEA have any say in the make-up of the committee. This was the last straw for the teachers. They had had enough of studies, the purpose of which seemed to them to be to delay, to stall for time, to prevent the state's meeting its full obligation to its children.

However, the PR and R study committee, in the short time it had to investigate conditions in the Utah schools before the NEA Detroit Convention, was unable to find sufficient grounds for declaring conditions in the Utah schools intolerable and for recommending to the NEA Executive Committee that the facts justified the voting of sanctions against the state of Utah.

Controversy at Detroit

This set the stage for the NEA Detroit Convention (June 30–July 5, 1963) at which the Utah delegation made an all-out fight to influence the NEA Representative Assembly to override the NEA Executive Committee and Board of Directors, whose actions were based upon the recommendations of the PR and R Commission.

Some newspapers as well as the AFT strained to reflect the NEA in the worst possible light during its deliberations and actions on the Utah situation at Detroit. Such phrases as "NEA Backs Down on Utah," "NEA Runs Out on Utah," "NEA Rejects Utah Sanctions," and "NEA—A Paper Tiger?" appeared in the news media during the convention.

What actually happened at Detroit? Did the NEA run out on Utah?

The story begins prior to the opening of the Detroit Convention, when the NEA Executive Committee and Board of Directors, in customary pre-convention meetings, accepted the recommendations of the PR and R Commission that the decision to invoke sanctions in the Utah situation not be made "at this time." Both the NEA Executive Committee and the Board of Directors pledged themselves to offer every other possible assistance to the Utah teachers.

There was no decision, as some papers reported and as many of the Utah delegates believed, to deny the request for sanctions. There was only the decision "to withhold judgment at this time." The reason for this action was twofold.

First, as has been said, the PR and R Commission had not had time to complete its investigation; therefore, it did not have at that time such facts as would warrant its recommendation for the invoking of sanctions. The commission did not say that such facts did not exist. It simply said that, as yet, it had not been able to uncover, assemble, and interpret such facts. Some of the Utah delegates took the recommendation of the PR and R Commission to imply that such facts did not exist—and were incensed by this implication. Second, there was some evidence that Governor Clyde was ready to abandon his adamant attitude and to sit down with the UEA leaders and discuss a solution. That is precisely what did happen after the convention. In late July, the governor appointed a 12-member School Study Committee and receded from his previous stand that the UEA would not be consulted. The make up of the committee was jointly agreed upon. Channels had been opened for a settling of the impasse.

These behind-the-scenes developments—the progress in negotiations with the governor—were not known to the Utah delegates at the Detroit Convention or to the delegates from the other states, hence their anxiety that the NEA official bodies were not militant enough. The Utah delegates may have known something of the negotiations, but they did not know all the developments; and since much of these had to be confidential, NEA officials were not in a position to publicize the real situation. Thus they had to suffer in silence in the firm belief that their course was wise.

The President and the Executive Secretary of the UEA, Moroni Jensen and John C. Evans, did know every facet of the developments and of the continuing discussion with the governor. They too had to maintain a discreet silence. Thus we find Evans stating on June 26, in his summary of the Utah story:

> We (the NEA executive secretary and president) are agreed that present negotiations will be jeopardized if ultimate NEA sanctions are imposed against the state of Utah *at this time*. It is, therefore, our intention to ask that such NEA action be invoked after all possibilities for settlement of the controversy at the state level have been exhausted by the UEA.[4]

But a considerable portion of the Utah delegation obviously decided to go over the heads of their leadership and of the official bodies of the NEA, which of course they had every right to do. One might question the wisdom of their action but not their right to take it.

Meanwhile, the Representative Assembly of the Department of Classroom Teachers, which meets annually on the Monday of NEA convention week, adopted on July 1 a resolution calling upon members of the local associations not to accept positions in Utah, pending settlement of the crisis. This assembly also adopted a resolution to raise a subsistence loan fund for Utah teachers and for other teachers who might subsequently find themselves in a similar situation. To the Utah delegation this action by the Department of Classroom Teachers was clear evidence of the overwhelming sentiment of the majority of convention delegates in favor of invoking sanctions in their behalf, since presumably some 80 to 90 per cent of NEA membership is made up of classroom teachers and a majority of delegates are classroom teachers.

Therefore the Utah delegates launched an intensive campaign to impel the NEA Representative Assembly to vote sanctions against the state of Utah, thus overriding the decision of the UEA leaders and that of the NEA Executive Committee and Board of Directors, where authority for the invoking of sanctions had been lodged.

Throughout the week, members of the Utah delegation appeared before each of the other state delegations to plead their cause. On Tuesday and Wednesday they seemed to have the issue sewed up. But as the week wore on, and as more of the facts and the reasons for the decision of the NEA official bodies became known, sentiment began to change.

There have been insinuations that the hierarchy of the NEA official bodies and staff, along with the school administrators, gave out orders to the teachers to retreat from the resolution of the Department of Classroom Teachers. *Newsweek* published a letter from an alleged delegate to the NEA convention which read as follows:

> You mention the politicking which took place during the NEA Convention which led to the watered down version of a resolution to support the Utah teachers. . . . The main political activity consisted of administrators, especially superintendents, calling caucuses of the teachers who work under them and, in no uncertain terms, telling them to vote against support of the resolution. I, as a delegate, can hardly believe this was a convention in our democracy. How can teachers vote with their superintendents monitoring the voting?

This letter was signed by a teacher from Albuquerque, New Mexico. There was no delegate by that name at the convention, no one by that name is certified as a teacher in the state of New Mexico, no one by that name is employed by the Albuquerque School system, and no one by that name is listed in the Albuquerque telephone book.

But it was a good story anyhow and provided the opportunity for a burst of eloquence by the president of the AFT, who said: "The classroom teacher has once again been sacrificed on the cross of compromise."

Preliminary decisions on resolutions, on matters to come before the business sessions of the NEA Representative Assembly, and on other items of importance are made by the state delegations. Each morning of the convention the state delegations caucus and hear discussions of matters to come up that day in the business session. Each delegation then is polled, and the majority vote pledges the delegation to support or oppose the items under consideration. This vote empowers the chairman of the state delegation (who is elected by a majority vote of the delegation) to advise the NEA Representative Assembly of the position of his delegation. This, however, does not prevent an individual delegate from dissenting on the floor of the Representative Assembly or of voting his dissent.

Here in the state delegations caucuses is where most of the politicking at the NEA conventions really goes on; there is relatively little of it on the floor of the convention. The vast majority of the state delegations consists of classroom teachers. It is quite possible that some state delegations are dominated by administrators, but not numerically and certainly not because the superintendents of the teachers are present. Most likely, the superintendents of not more than 10 per cent of the classroom-teacher delegates attend the annual convention of the NEA. It is absurd, then, to claim that superintendents browbeat their teachers into voting "right."

It would be equally a distortion to claim that the NEA Executive Committee and Board of Directors did not seek support of their decision not to invoke sanctions against Utah "at this time." These bodies are charged with decision-making in such cases by the Representative Assembly. Thus when the threat arose to appeal the decision to that body, the Executive Committee and Board of Directors moved for a vigorous defense of their position. They developed a step-by-step description of the Utah situation and a step-by-step analysis of the decision they had made and the help they had given to the Utah Education Association. This was presented to the Representative Assembly and before state delegations.

The hassle over the Utah situation on the floor of the NEA Representative Assembly revolved around two issues. The first was whether the decision of the NEA Executive Committee was to be overriden and sanctions voted against Utah. The second was whether the Representative Assembly should adopt the practice of bypassing its official executive bodies and undertake the application of sanctions by so large a body as 7,000 delegates.

The matter came before the Representative Assembly in the form of a resolution proposed by the Resolution Committee, leaving that committee so late that it could not be printed with the others for distribution to the delegates.

The wording of the resolution was as follows:

> Resolution No. 3: Support of Educational Needs. The National Education Association commends and supports the stand taken by the Utah Education Association in its struggle to provide quality education for the children of Utah, and will do everything possible to assist the educators of Utah in meeting the

educational needs of the children of the state. *The Association recommends that all local affiliates urge their members not to apply for teaching positions in Utah until such time as this problem is resolved.*[5]

The last sentence was the key one. Its adoption would have meant a vote to invoke sanctions by the Representative Assembly. This was the final step that the NEA Executive Committee and Board of Directors had refused to take *at that time.*

Cecil J. Hannan, delegate from the state of Washington, moved to delete the last sentence of the resolution and to substitute the following paragraph in its place:

> The Representative Assembly commends the Executive Committee for its record of action in the Utah Crisis and directs the Executive Committee to remain ready at all times to continue such action and to take promptly such further action as the Committee deems the situation requires, including the use of sanctions and other necessary measures.[6]

Speaking in support of his amendment, Hannan brought clearly into the open the real issue. He said:

> My amendment to this resolution is designed essentially to do three things. It is designed, first of all, to help not only the teachers of Utah but the teachers of any other locality in this Union as they strive to work toward the improvement of education in their area. One of the things that seems to be clear about the subject of sanctions is that the procedure we follow must be very carefully considered. We cannot in these cases afford to wait for a meeting of this Delegate Assembly for action to occur. We must then say to the Executive Committee when these cases arise that it is sometimes necessary, in order to be helpful, to have swift action. . . . My second point is that of procedure to be followed. It is difficult for each of us here to be informed about the many details of the crisis in Utah or about crises which may in the future occur in any other state. Therefore, we must use the procedure that allows those who make the decisions to take the action after they have made the study. . . . Third, I think one of the greatest responsibilities we have as a Delegate Assembly is to express not only to the people of the United States, but more especially to the teachers of the United States, that we have confidence in the officers we have chosen to serve us. . . .[7]

After heated discussion, this proposed amendment was adopted by a decided majority of the delegates.

At stake here, basically, was preservation of the integrity of the procedure which had been carefully worked out by the NEA staff, carefully refined and approved by the NEA Board of Directors. This procedure provided that sanctions (withdrawal of services) would be invoked against a school district only after a careful, thorough, and impatrial study had been made by the Commission on Professional Rights and Responsibilities and conditions found which would make impossible quality services to children.

The NEA was on record before its members, before school boards, before state legislatures, in fact before the American people, pledging honorable, fair, responsible, and justifiable use of this powerful weapon of sanctions. Were it now, on the very first emotion-charged case to come before it, to abandon all these principles and swing over to a tide of blind partisanship, it could not expect respect and confidence of the American people nor even of its own membership.

Thus the NEA Representative Assembly at Detroit voted to uphold its official bodies.

The decision of the NEA Representative Assembly not to override the action of the Executive Committee in withholding judgment on the invoking of sanctions against Utah had immediate and favorable repercussions in that state. Together with negotiations which had continued throughout the convention, the NEA's leaning over backwards to be fair to all concerned at Detroit obviously had its effect upon Governor Clyde. He had privately told intermediaries that he was ready to move on steps to try to resolve the impasse but would do nothing until the UEA leaders returned from Detroit for fear that any actions by him would be considered unilateral and arbitrary. This was the first indication of a considerate and conciliatory posture by the governor toward the UEA.

On July 12 the UEA Board of Trustees issued a statement commending the idea of a school study committee but calling for a meeting between UEA leaders and the governor to resolve differences. The next day, July 13, Governor Clyde told the press he was ready to discuss any pertinent matter with UEA officers to help end the impasse. Then, on July 15, the president and the secretary of UEA met with the Governor, and the three agreed on direct consultation thereafter instead of the use of intermediaries and agreed also that the UEA would participate in selection of the remaining members of the School Study Committee, to be announced by August 1 with a timetable for a report on the committee's findings.

As a result of this fruitful meeting with the governor, the president and executive secretary of the UEA decided to issue a statement indicating that they would recommend to the UEA Board of Trustees that the present financial impasse be regarded as satisfactorily resolved and that Utah teachers proceed with the negotiation contracts for the 1963–64 school year. These recommendations, of course, had yet to be approved by the UEA Board of Trustees, House of Delegates, and, finally, by the full UEA membership.

At a meeting on July 19 the UEA Board of Trustees decided, subject to ratification by the UEA House of Delegates and the membership, that the School Study Committee to be appointed by Governor Clyde, its method of appointment, its timetable for reporting, and its functions offered hope of prompt and objective action to meet the needs of Utah schools. The board voted to recommend to the UEA House of Delegates that the impasse be regarded as satisfactorily resolved and that teachers proceed with contract negotiations for the 1963–64 school year.

On August 1 the governor and the UEA officials agreed on the members of the twelve-member study committee.

The UEA House of Delegates on August 2 adopted a resolution calling for resumption of contract negotiations but insisting upon a review of progress in the spring of 1964. The next day, August 3, 5,734 members of UEA met to pass upon the recommendations of the Board of Trustees and House of Delegates. After discussion and debate, the assembly voted by secret ballot for acceptance of the recommendation, 4,586 to 1,148. The vote, however, shows the doubts of one fourth of those voting that the impasse would be solved. In addition, the recommendations were amended to imply a clear threat of a walk-out in the spring of 1964 if the process then in motion did not secure needed improvements for the 1964–65 school year. This threat was in the form of a request to the Utah School Boards Association for setting aside two days in the spring of 1964, to be made up later in the year, for teachers' meetings. This request has been almost completely ignored, in the later general condemnation of Utah teachers for their declared recess of two days on May 18 and 19, 1964. The intent then and the intent in May 1964 was not a strike in the usual sense of the word, but a recess.

One other footnote should be added. In a postconvention meeting, the NEA Board of Directors authorized an interest-free loan of $500,000 to the Utah Education Association, to be made if requested by the UEA to carry on its campaign for adequate school support. (The money was never requested, and the loan was not made.) In addition the board authorized the raising of a special fund of $2 million or more for interest-free loans to Utah teachers or other teachers in similar situations, to provide a measure of subsistence in cases of mass unemployment. This was, of course, immediately labeled as a strike fund by some. A subsequent action of the NEA Board decreed that the special fund was to be built up to $2 million by transferring unexpended balances of budgeted funds at the end of each year to the emergency fund (which already had $1.2 million in it).

The NEA Executive Committee agreed to be ready for an emergency meeting at any time during the summer to take whatever action appeared necessary and justified. The PR and R Commission was directed to continue its study of conditions in the Utah schools.

Clearly, many of the Utah teachers felt let down and were disgruntled at the NEA. It was to be expected that perhaps thousands of teachers across the country, teachers who were not at Detroit and who got only the press accounts of the NEA's "backing off" from overt action in Utah, would visualize the NEA as inept and timid.

That additional thousands would have thrilled at a showdown of raw power also was to be expected.

And in the short view, it was certainly to be expected that the NEA might lose some members as a result of the Utah crisis. (This did not happen, however. As of May 31, 1964, the membership was higher than in 1962–63.)

Final Round-up

Following the Detroit Convention, the NEA Commission on Professional Rights and Responsibilities resumed its study of school conditions in Utah. In the meantime, the governor's School Study Committee got under way with the selection of a full-time director of its study.

The special committee appointed by the PR and R Commission finished its study and issued its published report on April 4, 1964.[8] The study, which required almost a full year to complete and publish, found serious weaknesses in the Utah schools and urged immediate remedial action by the state.

The special committee's task was to answer these two questions: Do conditions exist in the Utah school system which make it impossible, or at least unlikely and extremely difficult, for the educators in the public schools to conduct an effective program of education? If such conditions exist, are they so widespread and severe that they justify the imposition of professional sanctions at the national level? In essence, the committee's answer was yes on both questions.

Then, on May 13, the governor's School Study Committee made its long-awaited interim report. In effect, it corroborated the NEA report. Its recommendation to the governor stated:

> After much thought and consideration the Committee has reached the decision that some action should be taken at this time. If, as we believe, increases in the financial support for the elementary and secondary schools are inevitable, a beginning should be made now. Furthermore, we think that delay can serve no useful purpose. On the other hand, delay could cause serious harm to the program of education by perpetuating deficiencies which have existed for a long time in spite of commendable efforts made to eliminate them in the past.[9]

The governor's committee recommended specifically that a special session be called and that $6 million be appropriated and made available for the 1964–65 school year. The new funds were to be earmarked as follows:

> $700,000 for improvement of library facilities; $2,000 for additional certificated personnel, non-teaching personnel, books, supplies, and needed equipment in local school districts, and additional money for the State Department of Public Instruction; and $3,300,000 for salary increases to teachers on a selective basis (instead of across-the-board, blanket increases), with special emphasis to low salary areas and regards for advanced degrees.[10]

The reports of the NEA special committee and the governor's School Study Committee both substantially vindicated the claims of the Utah teachers. Hopes were high that at long last the current controversy, which began with the failure of the 1963 Utah Legislature to provide the needed funds for the schools, would be resolved amicably. Actually, the controversy had been in ferment for more than a decade, a long-sustained, bitter hassle between the teachers and the power structure of the state whose conservatism, of course, was reflected by the administration of the state.

But Governor Clyde dashed these rosy hopes within a few hours of his receipt of his committee's report. He flatly rejected the School Study Committee recommendation that a special session of the legislature be called because (1) the committee had not answered his question about the effect on the state's economy of the requested appropriation and (2) the committee had not specified where the new money was to come from.

Again the Utah teachers were in an uproar.

The UEA immediately called its Board of Directors into session and recommended to the House of Delegates meeting on Saturday, May 16, that a special assembly of all Utah teachers be scheduled for Tuesday, May 19, to vote on the withholding of contracts for 1964–65, and that the NEA be asked to invoke national sanctions against the schools of the state.

The House of Delegates adopted these two recommendations and added one of its own: that the teachers of Utah declare a two-day recess on Monday and Tuesday, May 18 and 19, for the purpose of staging a dramatic protest to the people of Utah over Governor Clyde's action in rejecting the recommendations of his School Study Committee. The UEA House of Delegates requested school boards to permit all teachers to attend the mass meeting on Tuesday. As previously pointed out, permission for this possible recess had been requested in August 1963.

Of course, this recess was generally viewed as a strike. The UEA contended that it was not a strike, that the teachers had committed themselves to make up the two days, that authorization for the recess was requested at a called meeting of the school boards and superintendents in Utah on Sunday, May 17.

Some reports charged that the school boards would have granted the request for the recess. But at this point T. H. Bell, the State Superintendent of Public Instruction, advised the school boards that they were without legal authority to extend the school term and that the two days, therefore, could not be made up. This official also sought a restraining order against the teachers from the courts. Whether justified or not, there was strong feeling among many Utah teachers that the state superintendent had acted under pressure from the governor to put the teachers in the posture of having violated their contracts and thus of having engaged in a strike.

At the May 19 meeting, with 7,500 of the state's 10,000 teachers present, only 355 voted against the action to withhold the signing of contracts for the 1964–65 school year.

The request to the NEA Executive Committee to invoke national sanctions was presented by telephone just a few hours before the teachers were to assemble at the fair grounds in Salt Lake City on Tuesday, May 19.

The members of the NEA Executive Committee were unhappy over the recess but agreed that all conditions for voting sanctions had been met. Thus on Tuesday, May 19, sanctions were voted and a telegram announcing the action was sent to John C. Evans, Jr., Executive Secretary of the Utah Education Association. Incidentally, the telegram did not reach Salt Lake City until near the time for adjournment of the mass teachers' meeting. But it did reach there in time and was read to the assemblage.

Having exhausted other professional means for assisting the Utah Education Association and the teachers of Utah to correct unsatisfactory education conditions in that state, the Executive Committee of the National Education Association hereby:

1. Invokes national sanctions by requesting members of the teaching profession to refrain from seeking employment or entering into employment agreements with Utah boards of education until the controversy has been satisfactorily resolved.
2. *Urges the teachers of Utah to observe their contracts with boards of education.* (This was to reaffirm NEA's position against strikes.)

This action, exercising the authority vested in it by the Representative Assembly in Detroit in July 1963, has been taken only after most careful study of the implications of the following events:

1. A carefully developed proposal which was prepared by representatives of the Cooperating Agencies for Public Schools (CAPS), consisting of Utah State School Boards Association, Utah Congress of Parents and Teachers, Utah State Department of Public Instruction, State Society of Superintendents, and the Utah Education Association, received scant attention from the State Legislature or the Governor, although it pointed out the need for immediate improvement of school financing for the state. Less than half of the requested increase in school support was granted by the Legislature.
2. The Utah Education Association suspended its action of urging its members to withhold services at the outset of the 1963–64 school year when the Governor appointed an eminently qualified committee to study the school needs. There were clear assurances that the recommendations of this committee would be given careful consideration.
3. NEA declined to apply sanctions at its July 1963 convention because its clearly defined procedures for invoking sanctions required that this grave step be taken only after a careful, objective study revealed conditions of such importance as to seriously jeopardize the possibility of rendering adequate educational services to the children of the state. There were indications that solutions might be worked out in cooperation with the Governor. An NEA investigation report in March 1964 indicated the need for emergency action, presenting evidence to show that:
   a. There are inadequate and dangerous school facilities which need to be replaced and improved.

b. There are overcrowded classrooms and conditions of work discouraging to students and to teachers.
c. The curriculum offered is narrow, and special programs and facilities normally available are lacking in most areas of Utah.
d. The salary schedules generally in force in Utah are inadequate to attract and hold competent teachers and school administrators.
e. Programs, personnel, and facilities for continuing education for school dropouts and for adults are generally lacking.

Other than from the Utah Education Association, the report and recommendations were not officially acknowledged by any agency in the state.

4. An interim report of the Governor's Committee reinforced the findings of the CAPS group and of the Special Committee of the National Education Association and urged that a Special Session of the Legislature be called to appropriate $6,000,000 immediately with more to be requested later. The committee recommended that "the Legislature be called into special session to consider the problems of critical need and appropriate funds required to meet these needs. This money should be made available at the beginning of the 1964–65 school year."

Failing to keep faith with the teachers and many other citizens of Utah, the Governor rejected the report of his own committee immediately after it had been presented. This last of a series of rejections of earnest efforts to improve conditions in Utah schools has aroused the teachers of the state. They are determined to bring about higher standards of education in Utah and their objectives deserve the support of their colleagues throughout the nation.

Robert H. Wyatt, President
National Education Association

This, then, covers the details of events leading to the first application of professional sanctions by the NEA after this procedure was approved by the NEA Representative Assembly at Denver in July 1962. Nobody, it seems fair to say, envisioned that sanctions would ever be invoked against the school system of an entire state.

There are many interesting and provocative question involved in this sudden denouement of both the UEA and NEA efforts to bring about a reconcilement of the struggle in Utah.

Did the NEA's action in invoking sanctions imply that it condoned the recess, or, in the popular mind, the strike? This question disturbed the NEA Execuive Committee as they discussed via telephone the motion to invoke sanctions. They did not want the NEA to be put in the position, even by implication, of supporting the violation of teachers' contracts or the interruption of service. That is why the sanctions action included the statement: "Urges the teachers of Utah to observe their contracts with boards of education." Since the UEA action, however, there have been several professional holidays, walk-outs, and clear strikes by NEA affiliates, without remonstrance from NEA.

There were other disturbing implications of the happenings in Utah.

Did the teachers alienate the support of many Utah citizens by their recess? Many people think so. There was general agreement that the teachers had the sympathy of the general public but hurt their cause greatly by the recess action. *Time* quoted a Utah citizen: "It isn't easy to be stupider than Clyde, but the teachers managed it."[11]

Governor Clyde's refusal to call a special session of the legislature was interpreted to mean that he did not intend to do anything to resolve the dispute. His position tended to confirm what the Utah teachers had said at Detroit—that the study was just another in a long series of delaying dodges.

Results of the Utah Case

On June 25, 1964, on the eve of the NEA Convention in Seattle, the Board of Governors of the Salt Lake City Chamber of Commerce sent to the NEA a letter of formal protest of its sanctions.

> This unfortunate and ill-conceived action by the NEA is a severe and ironic extra burden in our great efforts in Utah to improve the status of your profession here and to gain for our citizens the best possible education for their children. The NEA's gratuitous and unfair action has damaged the reputation of our state, hampered our efforts to expand our economy, provide more jobs, broaden the tax base and thus provide even more money for public education.[12]

Of course, there is much to be said on this side of the question. To invoke sanctions against an entire state is a tricky matter. While the over-all educational picture in Utah was not good, as reflected by both the PR and R Commission report and the report of the governor's own committee, doubtless there were, among 42 school districts in the state, some with wholly satisfactory programs. The question, then, "Why punish these districts?" is a valid one, and one that is difficult to answer. The only reasonable reply is that Utah districts are peculiarly dependent upon the state. Only action by the legislature can alleviate in large measure the plight of all Utah schools.

There is, too, the very disturbing problem of acting against a whole state. Without question, the public-school program in Utah is much better than the programs of several other states. What is the criterion for drawing the line between the acceptable and the unacceptable? Strictly on the basis of cold, comparative facts, there is no fool-proof answer to singling out Utah. The action can be justified only by the sequence of events in that state over the last decade and a half. The events include a steadily deteriorating situation, repeated slapping down of the teachers, and declining morale among the teachers as a result of continuous indifference, if not contemptuous treatment, to their pleas for remedial action. Admittedly, there are reasonable grounds for questioning the sanctions action and for commending it.

The Utah situation did not come before the Seattle Convention, which was held June 28–July 3, 1964. The solution, if any, was now within the state.

Obviously, the UEA made the decision to rest its case with the next governor, to be elected in November 1964, and with the next session of the legislature in January, 1965.

In late July, the UEA House of Delegates voted to resume contract negotiations for the school year 1964-65. Utah teachers in regional meetings afterwards ratified this action. NEA was asked to retain the sanction action for out-of-state teachers.

There were strong intimations that Utah would seek a restraining order from the courts, enjoining the NEA from the use of sanctions against the state. This effort was made against the California Teachers Association in the Little Lake case. The court in that case in an informal comment from the bench, implied that it would refuse to issue such an order on the grounds that the right to criticize and censure a public agency is inherent in the right of free speech. What the outcome might have been in the Utah case is a matter of conjecture. In another case, the governor of Oklahoma was angered at the refusal of the Oklahoma Education Association and NEA to lift sanctions after an unprecedented appropriation by the legislature. In advance of a vote on a constitutional amendment to permit local school districts to vote more taxes for schools, the Oklahoma governor ordered the state's attorney general to initiate a suit against the two associations. However, the suit did not eventuate.

The democratic processes do move slowly. The teachers of Utah, blocked by the power structure of the state and having lost valuable public support by the two-day recess, generally interpreted as a strike, resumed contract negotiations in July 1964.

The NEA sanctions against the state remained. The UEA organized a political arm called the Utah Council for the Improvement of Education (UCIE), the openly declared purpose of which was to seek justice at the polls by an organized campaign to elect officials sympathetic to the teachers' cause.

The teachers interviewed candidates for public office and distributed the results to teachers and other citizens, and on the basis of these interviews endorsed candidates for office.

In the general election in November 1964, a friendly governor was elected. The candidate for the United States Senate, who had fought the teachers at every turn, was defeated. Eleven teachers or former teachers were elected to the legislature, and some 30 legislators known to be committed to the teachers' cause were elected. A past president of the Utah Congress of Parents and Teachers who had demonstrated her concern for improvement of the schools was elected chairman of the Utah Board of Education

The incoming governor had pledged before the election to provide an additional $3 million for teachers' salaries for the remainder of the school year 1964–65. He had pledged to seek added appropriations from the legislature of $7.5 million for each of the ensuing two years for improvement of the schools.

In the meantime, national sanctions had had considerable effect. The Utah Chamber of Commerce complained bitterly that industries were refusing to locate in Utah until the sanctions were removed.

With the election and an apparent victory for the teachers, NEA was importuned by some Utah citizens to show statesmanship and lift the sanctions. Some of these pleas were made by undoubted friends of the teachers and of NEA. But NEA officials refused. They had shown two patient years of statesmanship only to be callously rejected by governor Clyde and treated contemptuously by the state's power structure. In effect, NEA said: "Let Utah now exhibit statesmanship by following through on the promised legislative program; when this is done the sanctions will be lifted immediately."

The newly elected governor recommended to the Utah legislature, in January 1965, that state funds for schools be increased by $8.3 million for each of the ensuing two years. This increase, with provision for school districts to increase local funds by $6.6 million, provided a total of nearly $15 million in new money for the schools each year of the biennium 1965–67. Average increase in teachers' salaries for the biennium was $874; for the 1963–65 biennium the average was $770. Thus, since the start of the controversy in the spring of 1965, teachers' average salaries were increased by $1,644 for the ensuing biennium, or $822 per year, and funds were made available for improving the total school program.

Thus on March 13, 1965, with Governor Rampton's signing of the new legislation substantially meeting the demands of the state's teachers, the NEA, upon request of UEA, lifted the sanctions against the state. How effective were the sanctions? Did they win the battle? Or was it a combination of factors that won? Probably the latter. The political action of the teachers certainly was a powerful factor. There is no question that national sanctions hurt in deterring new industries from locating in the state. Governor Rampton evaluated the effect of sanctions thus in a public statement:

> If I were asked if sanctions impelled the legislature and me to provide the new money, I should have to say "No"! If I were asked if sanctions influenced the people of the state to favor better support for the schools, I should have to say "Yes"!

It is clear that the teachers of Utah were vindicated in their fight for better education.

After 300 days, NEA proved that it had a potent weapon in sanctions.

Oklahoma, OK!

NEA's second venture into state-wide sanctions was the Oklahoma case.

The NEA Executive Committee announced the invoking of sanctions against that state on May 11, 1965. Only 59 days after lifting sanctions in Utah, NEA was called upon to invoke them against Oklahoma.

The sanctions applied involved three major phases: (1) calling upon all members outside the state not to seek or accept teaching positions within the state, (2) declaring that members who ignored this injunction might be judged in violation of the code of ethics of the education profession and subject to censure, suspension, or expulsion from membership and (3) establishing five relocation centers throughout the state to aid teachers who desired to leave Oklahoma to find positions in other states.

The language of the Executive Committee in imposing the sanctions was as follows:

> The National Education Association, in response to a request from the Oklahoma Education Association's Board of Directors, has authorized the imposition of professional sanctions on the state of Oklahoma, to include:
>
> 1. Censure through public notice and reports to the mass media. The National Education Association will at once advise business and industrial organizations and their leaders, agencies of government, and the general public that Oklahoma, despite ample resources, maintains a subminimal public education program.
> 2. Notification to professional agencies such as state departments of education, certification and placement services, and members of the teaching profession generally of the unsatisfactory conditions in Oklahoma schools. This notification will caution graduates of schools of education against acceptance of educational employment in Oklahoma.
> 3. Warning to active and student members of the National Education Association not currently employed in Oklahoma that acceptance of employment as a new teacher in any Oklahoma school district may be considered unethical conduct, and that such conduct, on recommendation of the Oklahoma Education Association, will be treated in accordance with established procedures of the National Education Association.
> 4. Assistance to OEA-NEA members presently employed in Oklahoma who desire to leave the state for educational employment under more favorable circumstances. In implementation of this program, NEA will establish relocation centers through which information about employment opportunities outside the state will be made available.
>
> By this action the National Education Association serves notice of its complete commitment to joining the Oklahoma Education Association in a combined effort to advance education and the welfare of students and teachers in Oklahoma. This step is taken only after serious consideration of:
>
> 1. The repeated massive efforts of the Oklahoma Education Association to secure public support for upgrading public education and eliminating the unsatisfactory conditions which exist.

2. The continued failure of the Governor of Oklahoma to act on the findings and recommendations for educational improvement contained in the Report on Common School Education prepared by a citizens committee selected by the Governor.
3. The general failure of the state legislature and of local and state officials responsible for the welfare of the schools to recognize the significance of the findings and recommendations set forth in the report of the investigation developed by the NEA Commission on Professional Rights and Responsibilities.
4. The need to impress upon the citizens of Oklahoma and their elected public officials that the level of public education in the state is far below any acceptable standard.

The National Education Association will consider the removal of these sanctions when governmental programs are implemented which assure significant elevation in the state's commitment to public education.

Recognizing the imperative need for total professional association involvement in seeking the resolution of Oklahoma's education programs the NEA will, on request of the Oklahoma Education Association and its local affiliates, assist in organizing:

(a) Clinics and workshops designed to increase the political effectiveness of the OEA membership at the local level.

(b) Committees to prepare lists of extra-curricular activities which may be eliminated or curtailed at the school district level during the 1965–66 school year pending satisfactory solution of the controversy.

The Oklahoma case involved several new steps by NEA, two being of major importance: threat of expulsion to out-of-state members and relocation assistance for in-state teachers.

The Oklahoma case was in many respects similar to that of Utah. Like Utah, state support of the school system had been allowed to fall behind the burgeoning needs since the late 1940's. Moreover, Oklahoma was falling farther behind the national average and the efforts of neighboring states. There had been no state-wide general tax increase since 1937. And year after year the schools were provided with inadequate portions of available state funds.

Events Leading to Sanctions

By the spring of 1963, Oklahoma teachers were determined to secure improvement in the rapidly deteriorating financial situation of the schools. At that time the minimum beginning salary was $3,800. The average salary was $5,257, more than $700 below the national average. A modest improvement in the salary situation was provided in a bill passed by the legislature. This bill carried an appropriation of $10.4 million, providing a salary increase of

$1,000 per teacher over a six-year period. The governor promptly vetoed the bill and the legislature was unable to override the veto.

In desperation, the teachers decided to take the skidding school-support issue to the people. In a series of teachers' meetings throughout the state during the remainder of 1963, proposals were formulated and submitted to the OEA Legislative Committee (including representatives of the State Congress of Parents and Teachers and the State School Boards Associations). In addition, a state-wide salary school, with representatives from each OEA local, made recommendations to the OEA Legislative Committee. In March 1964 the OEA Board of Directors approved proposals for submitting four referenda to the voters of the state through the initiative procedure. The OEA immediately began a campagin to secure the required number of voters' signatures to the petitions for the referenda, completing this task and filing the petitions with the secretary of state on April 24.

The four petitions (state questions 421, 422, 423, and 424) and their provisions were: (1) to amend the state constitution by repealing the existing 5-mill emergency levy and authorizing a 15-mill local levy instead, (2) to alter the school code by increasing state aid for other than capital outlay purposes, the effects of which would be to increase teachers' salaries, reduce class size, and stimulate other improvements, (3) to eliminate school districts providing less than a 12-year school program, and (4) to encourage county high-school districts to participate in a program of special services conducted by the county superintendents, and to increase the salaries of county superintendents.

After the filing of the petitions, the OEA requested the governor to call a special election before the November general election. Under Oklahoma law if the governor does not call a special election, proposed initiated acts go on the ballot in the next general election. Referenda votes in a special election require for adoption only a majority of the votes cast on a given petition. If a petition is voted on in the general election, it requires for adoption a majority of all votes cast in the election. Thus in a general election a given petition may receive a majority of "yes" votes out of all votes cast on the petition and still fail to be adopted, by the simple fact of voters in the general election failing to vote at all on the petition. For example, if 500,000 cast votes in the general election, the adoption of a petition would require more than 250,000 votes. If 100,000 voters failed to vote for or against the petition, it still must receive more than 250,000 votes to be adopted. In a special election, if 400,000 voted on the petition, only 200,000 or more affirmative votes would be needed for adoption.

The governor refused OEA's request for a special election on the grounds that state funds were not available to pay the election cost of $165,000. However, the governor subsequently did call a special election in September 1964 to vote on the reapportionment of the legislature, but the school petitions were not included in the election. Thus, the four initiative proposals of OEA were voted on in the November general election and defeated by the "silent vote"—by voters failing to vote either way on the proposals. Of the 946,000 votes cast in the general election, more than 300,000 voters failed to vote on the petitions on the ballot. All of the OEA-sponsored petitions failed to be passed although one did receive a majoriy of the votes cast on it, but none received a majority of the 946,000 votes cast in the election.

This clever ploy of counting upon the silent vote to defeat the petitions angered the teachers to the point of open revolt. A special meeting of the OEA Board of Directors requested the governor to call a special session of the legislature to consider school problems. The governor declined.

In Tulsa and Midwest City (a suburb of Oklahoma City) teachers were granted a "professional day" to protest defeat of the petitions. Observers believe that this day off prevented a probable walk-out, so angry were the teachers.

Some 1,200 teachers from 75 school systems met at Midwest City and unanimously proposed ten items for the attention of the legislature when it convened in regular session. One of the proposals was that teachers' salaries be raised by $1,000 per teacher by March 1, 1965, salaries thereafter to be kept at 100 per cent of the national salary average. Oklahoma City Teachers subsequently held a professional day and made the same demand, adding that they would seek sanctions if these demands were not met by March 1, 1965.

On November 14 the OEA Board of Directors requested the Governor to call a special session of the legislature and requested an investigation of the school situation in the state by the NEA Commission on Professional Rights and Responsibilities.

The governor again declined to call the legislature into a special session. But, obviously concerned over the near-revolt of the teachers, he invited the state's teachers to meet with him in two meetings, one in Tulsa, one in Oklahoma City in December to discuss proposals to improve the school situation. The governor proposed at these meetings his "operation Giant Stride." The heart of his proposal was a $500 million highway bond issue which would free for school use general funds allotted to highways and free other monies as well. He proposed also school-district reorganization, abolition of the office of county superintendent of schools, and a referendum to increase local levies to 15 mills. The OEA Board of Directors declined to support the governor's proposal. Again the school situation was at an impasse.

The NEA's PR and R Commission quickly began its investigation of Oklahoma school problems following the protest meeting of teachers after the general election of November 3, 1964. A preliminary inquiry was conducted as a forerunner of the full-scale investigation requested by OEA. The preliminary report issued on December 15, 1964 stated:

> On the basis of its investigation the Committee finds subminimal conditions in the public school system of Oklahoma in almost every area of the school program. The state salary schedule is a non-competitive minimum. There are also gross deficiencies in physical conditions of buildings, maintenance, health and safety standards, textbooks, teaching aids, libraries, special education, counseling, teacher load, and other provisions basic to an effective educational program. These subminimal conditions are by no means uniform in all schools in all localities, but they are prevalent to a degree which, in the Committee's judgment, demands widespread public knowledge in order that a well-formed citizenry can support basic reform in Oklahoma public school finance.

The full report of the PR and R Commission's Special Committee was issued in February 1965. The major recommendations in the report were:

> Provision for major reorganization of school districts.
>
> Equal tax assessments at 35 per cent of market value or a change in the system.
>
> Removal of local millage limitation on school districts and authorization for local school boards to levy taxes needed.
>
> Immediate increase in state taxes for school support.
>
> Provision for job security for teachers by amendment of continuing contract law.
>
> A change in the status of state superintendent to appointive instead of elective.

Even in the face of near-rebellion by the state's teachers and the findings and recommendations of the NEA's investigating committee, the state's power structure continued its dilatory tactics. The legislature passed a bill appropriating money for increased teachers' salaries to be derived from an increase in the sales tax. But the legislature used the well-worn gimmick of ducking responsibility by referring the act to a vote of the people. The proposal was defeated at the polls in April, 1965.

Following this debacle, the Oklahoma Education Association declared sanctions against the state and called upon NEA to do likewise.

The NEA action elicited a storm of protest and denunciation from state officials and other citizens.

The Outcome

Out of the turmoil of political in-fighting, the impact of sanctions, and the adverse publicity received by the state, several developments occured. In June 1965, the Oklahoma Legislature passed a school appropriation bill providing $28.6 million of new money for the schools. The bill was signed by the governor. This added money was sufficient to provide an average raise in teachers' salaries of about $550 throughout the state. The range of salary increases made possible was from $400 to $1,000, with the teachers in the cities getting about $800 on the average.

This appropriation also provided additional money for general school purposes. In addition, the legislature enacted legislation making social security available to the state's teachers and providing improved sick leave and retirement benefits. A professional-practices act was passed conferring certain rights and responsibilities on the teaching profession.

The legislature also authorized a state-wide referendum which, if adopted, would enable local school boards to raise millage levies by 10 mills.

On the heels of these favorable actions by the legislature came insistent demands from the governor and other influential citizens that OEA and NEA sanctions be lifted. Both OEA and NEA refused, pending the outcome of the referendum. These refusals were based upon the fact that unless the people voted to authorize the millage increase, the school program of the state could not be lifted to the needed level of quality.

However, the voters of Oklahoma did vote overwhelming endorsement of the increased millage levy on September 14, 1965.

NEA and OEA almost immediately thereafter lifted sanctions against the state.

THE EFFECTS OF SANCTIONS. As in Utah, the precise impact of sanctions in Oklahoma may never be known. It is reasonably clear that state officials, business groups, and citizens in general were greatly concerned about the effect of the sanctions upon the industrial development of the state. It is reasonably clear that the unfavorable publicity hurt the pride of Oklahoma citizens and caused deep-seated resentment. It is also reasonably clear that in their anger and resentment, the people of the state were prodded into a realization of the critical extent that school support had been allowed to lag.

One thing the sanctions did prove beyond question. If the teaching profession ever seriously undertakes the responsibility of inducing presently employed teachers to leave a sanctioned state or school district, it will have great effect. Within a few weeks after the teachers' relocation centers were established, NEA had requests from superintendents throughout the United States for about 10,000 teachers. Available evidence indicates that only a small number of Oklahoma teachers sought relocation. An OEA survey in September 1965 found that about 580 teachers had left the state to take new positions. But jobs were available had 20 times this number elected to leave.

As for the ban on teachers coming into the state, there is little evidence on this point. What will happen if and when the profession seriously seeks to enforce such a ban remains to be seen. This problem must be faced realistically (now that the feasibility of migration out has been established). This will involve at least three crucial factors: (1) the willingness of the profession to enforce its code of ethics on violators of the ban by censure, suspension, or expulsion from membership, (2) the willingness of placement services to refuse to refer candidates for employment in a sanctioned district, and (3) the willingness of superintendents of sanctioned school districts to refuse to recruit teachers from outside the district.

At the NEA New York Convention in July 1965, the sanctions resolution was tied to the code of ethics and implied that either the offering or accepting of a position in a sanctioned district might be construed as a violation of the code. While the only discussion of the amendment before the convention referred to the code being equally incumbent upon teachers and administrators, obviously it was aimed more at the offering of jobs by superintendents. This amendment may have been inspired by rumored indignation of Oklahoma teachers at reports in the state's papers saying that some superintendents were having no difficulty in filling vacancies by employing teachers from outside the state.

A blistering editorial appeared (see *Nation's Schools*, September 1965) on this amendment, charging that it was imposing impossible and intolerable conditions on superintendents and suggesting that American Association of School Administrators (AASA) must withdraw from affiliation with NEA.

While notable success was achieved in Utah and Oklahoma, as has been pointed out many times, the impact of sanctions, albeit powerful, was relatively slow in producing results.

However the debate may be decided about the impact of professional sanctions, it may be said that in conjunction with an aroused teaching staff the momentum is well-nigh irresistible. There appears to be considerable evidence that few if any states in the future are going to let conditions come to the point of inviting sanctions by a united profession. Florida did in June 1967.

The case of Idaho has been described. This might well have been a sanctions case, but with the Utah situation clearly visible next door, the authorities in Idaho acted on the facts dug out by the NEA investigation and significantly raised school support. In Kentucky, the teachers were so aroused that they staged a one-day professional day, which was exactly what it was. Teachers met in groups all over the state with lay people—in spite of 18 inches of snow—and discussed the problems of improving education with no hell-raising or loud threats. The laymen were impressed with the fairness of the teachers cause, and public sentiment backed them. The Kentucky Legislature, led by the governor, appropriated money to assure significant raises in teachers' salaries. Also, the legislature enacted legislation to give the professional day a place in the school year. But the KEA advised its membership to insist on making up the day.

Sanctions coolly applied, backed by facts, teacher anger, and teacher integrity, are forces of grave power.

13

Box Score and Evaluation

> For all its talk of action, the [AFT] convention last week spent a lot of time drafting resolutions. Delegates dutifully wrangled in fourteenth-floor committee rooms over the wording of 60-odd pronouncements on everything from world disarmament to the working conditions of school librarians. When the time came to vote on a president for the next two years, Megel's opposition split into two factions, and an all-night caucus finally nominated Myron Lieberman of Shaker Heights, Ohio, to run against him. Lieberman campaigned on a platform calling for still greater militancy in negotiations and more push in organizing AFT locals. (Only 4 per cent of the nation's teachers are now AFT members, he pointed out.) The insurgent had the backing of the union's 20,000-member New York local, but most delegates decided on reflection that there was such a thing as too much militancy. In the New York delegation's "hospitality suite," films of students jeering teachers during last April's strike inadvertently convinced viewers that professional dignity had its points. Megel won a sixth term by a 2-to-1 margin.
>
> —*Newsweek*, September 3, 1962

By the end of the 1965–66 school year, the professional associations were slugging it out in a vigorous, all-out dog fight with the teachers' unions. Buttressed by state professional-negotiation laws in California, Connecticut, Washington, and Oregon as well as by a superficial law in Florida, the associations were winning the great majority of elections. They were also winning almost all of the stipulations wherever the boards under existing laws could recognize the majority membership organization upon verified membership figures, or where there was no contesting organization. And the associations were also winning by big margins in the three states (Massachusetts, Michigan, and Wisconsin) with labor-sponsored legislation for public employees including teachers. (Rhode Island now also has a labor-sponsored law that was passed in June 1966.)

But the teachers' unions continued to win overwhelmingly in the big industrial cities. During the school year 1965–66 AFT won elections in Hartford, Boston, New Rochelle (where the NEA affiliate had won in 1965), and Chicago (the educational association did not contest this one). (See Table 13–1.)

NEA affiliates had won in Portland (Oregon), Seattle, Flint, Newark (second election), Toledo, and Fort Worth.

During the 1965–66 school year, according to Table 13–1, of 225 elections or stipulations, NEA affiliates won 196, or 87 per cent, while AFT affiliates won 26, or 11 per cent, with no choice in 3 districts. Of the 592 stipulations, NEA won 588 and AFT only 1, with no choice in 3. Combining the totals of these two procedures, (election and stipulation) NEA affiliates won 784 or 96 per cent, and AFT affiliates won 27 or 3 per cent. (See partial itemization of these in Table 13–2.)

TABLE 13-1

Partial Box Score of Elections and Stipulations in Five States*
During 1965–66 (as of May 1, 1966)

Number of Elections or Stipulations Held	Number Won by NEA Affiliates	Number Won by AFT Affiliates	Number of Cases of no choice of Affiliation	Per cent of Elections won by NEA Affiliates	Per cent of Elections won by AFT Affiliates
225 (Elections)	196	26	3	87+	11
592 (Stipulations)	588	1	3	99.3	—
Totals					
817	784	27	6	96	3

* The five states are Connecticut, Massachusetts, Michigan, Washington, and Wisconsin—Connecticut and Washington with progessional negotiation laws, and the other three with AFL-CIO sponsored laws.

Source: Urban Reporter (Newsletter of NEA Division of Urban Services) March–April, 1966.

In Connecticut NEA-CEA affiliates have won exclusive negotiation rights in 104 out of 108 elections or stipulations (winning 30 of 32 elections while AFT won 1, and in 1 there was joint representation). In designations, the NEA-CEA affiliates were designated in 14 districts, the teachers' union in 0, and in 2 districts teachers chose either joint or nonaffiliated organizations.

The remainder of the districts in Connecticut continue to negotiate with school boards under CEA-sponsored provisions.

In Massachusetts, only 2 elections were held by June 1, 1966 under the new AFL-CIO-sponsored law, of which the NEA-MTA affiliates won 1 (Lowell) and the AFT affiliate won 1 (Boston). NEA-MTA affiliates won 20 official recognitions through stipulation, as provided by the new law, so 21 of 22 exclusive representation rights have been won by professional associations. (In June 1966, the MTA affiliates won elections in Springfield and Pittsfield.)

In Michigan, NEA-MEA affiliates as of June 1, 1966 held 442 of 464 exclusive representation rights determined to date. NEA-MEA affiliates have won 48 of 68 elections held; the teachers' union won in 19 districts, including Detroit (in 1964) and the unaffiliated was chosen in 1 district. In addition, NEA-MEA affiliates have won 394 of the 396 representation rights through stipulation, and the union won no such stipulation. The associations in Michigan with these victories now represent 51,900 teachers; the teachers' union represents 15,770 teachers (including 10,500 in Detroit).

In the State of Washington, NEA-WEA affiliates have won 99 of 100 elections under the new professional negotiation law; the teacher unions, 0; 1 junior college chose an unaffiliated group.

In Wisconsin, NEA-WEA affiliates have won exclusive representation rights, through elections and stipulations, in 118 districts; of 23 elections the associations have won 18 and the unions 5.

Thus it is evident that the professional associations can meet the teachers' union challenge—in collective-bargaining elections under labor laws, or in elections or stipulations under professional negotiation laws. To date, the AFT affiliate has won 1 undoubted, clear-cut and significant victory—New York City—and has won several other elections the significance of which is unclear. For example, in Chicago, Cleveland, Detroit, and Philadelphia bargaining is superficial or nonexistant. No break-through such as occurred in New York City has yet developed. There has been much shouting and bombast, but the predicted sweep of the teachers' unions has not materialized. The AFT president in his address before the annual convention of that organization in 1966 claimed representation rights in only 58 school districts.

Thus by mid-June 1966 AFT had won bargaining rights in the following six large cities: New York, Detroit, Cleveland, Philadelphia, Boston, and Chicago. The teachers' unions had failed in strikes in New Orleans, Perth Amboy, and Newark. They failed to force representative elections for exclusive rights in St. Louis, Los Angeles, Baltimore, and the District of Columbia. They did force elections in the districts of Columbia and Baltimore in the Spring of 1967.

NEA affiliates had won exclusive negotiation rights by election or stipulation in Seattle, Portland, Toledo, Milwaukee, Rochester, Newark, Flint, Miami (Dade County), Tampa (Hillsboro County), Fort Worth, and Tulsa. In Los Angeles and San Francisco, NEA affiliates were in control of the joint negotiation councils established under the new state law.

Combining the box scores in elections discussed in Chapter 4 (Table 4-1: January 1, 1963 to June 1, 1965) and that of elections and stipulations discussed in this chapter (Table 13-2: September 1, 1965 to June 1, 1966), the total score for the period since January 1, 1963 (or since the New York City election) to May 1, 1966 reflects the following:

	Won by Affiliates		No Choice of Affiliates
Total Elections: 262	NEA: 219 (84%)	AFT: 39 (15%)	4 (1%)
Total Stipulations: 592 (in five states)	NEA: 588 (99.3%)	AFT: 1 (—%)	3 (—%)
Totals: 854	NEA: 807 (94.5%)	AFT: 40 (4.7%)	7 (—%)

It should be pointed out that the above figures are not complete reports. For example, there are many recognitions not yet reported to NEA of NEA affiliates through professional-negotiation agreements where there is no contesting organization.

In summary, by mid-June 1966, AFT affiliates had exclusive bargaining rights in less than 60 districts. NEA affiliates had exclusive rights in at least 1,000 districts.

Table 13-2 shows the actual score on these elections.

TABLE 13-2

Box Score Teacher Representation Elections September 1, 1965–June 1, 1966. Data by School Districts*

Date of Election	School District	Number of Teachers Eligible to Vote	Affiliated Organization Votes Received	
			NEA	AFT
September 8, 1965	Hartford, Conn.	1120	503	535
September 22, 1965	Stratford, Conn.	490	356	117
September 27, 1965	Berlin, Conn.	133	81	51
September 29, 1965	Highland Park, Mich.	458	188	247
October 4, 1965	Meriden, Conn.	448	343	105
October 4, 1965	Grandview, Wash.	100	88	—
October 4, 1965	Monroe, Wash.	60	38	—
October 7, 1965	Manchester, Conn.	486	366	110
October 7, 1965	Arlington, Wash.	94	82	—
October 11, 1965	Aberdeen, Wash.	244	227	—
October 11, 1965	Bellingham, Wash.	360	253	—
October 11, 1965	Ellensburg, Wash.	129	84	—
October 11, 1965	Enumclaw, Wash.	120	89	—
October 11, 1965	La Center, Wash.	22	20	—

Date of Election	School District	Number of Teachers Eligible to Vote	Affiliated Organization Votes Received	
			NEA	AFT
October 11, 1965	Grays Harbor College, Wash.	52	51	—
October 11, 1965	Mount Vernon–La Conner–Conway, Wash.	152	99	—
October 11, 1965	Northshore, Wash.	344	311	—
October 11, 1965	Othello, Wash.	85	79	—
October 11, 1965	Peninsula, Wash.	100	70	—
October 11, 1965	Peninsula College, Wash.	28	24	—
October 11, 1965	Selah, Wash.	91	75	—
October 11, 1965	Sunnyside, Wash.	166	151	—
October 11, 1965	West Valley, Wash.	167	110	—
October 11, 1965	West Valley of Yakima, Wash.	114	108	—
October 11, 1965	Winlock (Western Lewis County), Wash.	25	25	—
October 12, 1965	Edmonds, Wash.	1024	959	—
October 12, 1965	Kelso, Wash.	207	194	—
October 12, 1965	Pullman, Wash.	120	104	—
October 12, 1965	Shoreline, Wash.	700	625	—
October 12, 1965	Shoreline College, Wash.	82	44	—
October 12, 1965	Skagit Valley College, Wash.	75	69	—
October 12, 1965	South Central, Wash.	99	83	—
October 13, 1965	Kitsap, Wash.	132	103	—
October 13, 1965	Richland, Wash.	368	282	—
October 13, 1965	Walla Walla, Wash.	140	124	—
October 13, 1965	Wenatchee, Wash.	266	243	—
October 14, 1965	Wayne, Mich.	783	467	265
October 14, 1965	Franklin Pierce, Wash.	329	257	—
October 14, 1965	University Place, Wash.	132	100	—
October 14, 1965	Upper Snoqualmie Valley, Wash.	90	71	—
October 18, 1965	Crestwood, Mich.	175	125	34
October 18, 1965	Puyallup, Wash.	343	322	—
October 19, 1965	Bridgeport, Conn.	1040	908	not on ballot
October 19, 1965	Bethel, Wash.	145	57	—
October 19, 1965	Moses Lake, Wash.	300	251	—

Date of Election	School District	Number of Teachers Eligible to Vote	Affiliated Organization Votes Recieved	
			NEA	AFT
October 20, 1965	Longview, Wash.	360	308	—
October 20, 1965	Sumner, Wash.	122	107	—
October 20, 1965	Washougal, Wash.	71	59	—
October 21, 1965	Lake Stevens, Wash.	82	64	—
October 22, 1965	Evergreen, Wash.	147	119	—
October 25, 1965	East Hartford, Conn.	538	417	not on ballot
October 25, 1965	Ridgefield, Conn.	184	159	not on ballot
October 25, 1965	Highline, Wash.	1165	1,069	—
October 25, 1965	Warden, Wash.	33	31	—
October 26, 1965	Highline College, Wash.	66	36	—
October 27, 1965	Rham Conn.	44	27	16
October 27, 1965	Auburn, Wash.	295	256	—
October 27, 1965	Northwest Peninsula, Wash.	52	40	—
October 28, 1965	Bristol, Conn.	477	360	94
October 28, 1965	Spokane, Wash.	1,606	1,409	—
October ?, 1965	Omak, Wash.	69	57	—
November 2, 1965	Mead, Wash.	129	115	—
November 2, 1965	Sedro Wooley, Wash.	132	114	—
November 2, 1965	Stanwood, Wash.	54	34	—
November 3, 1965	Wethersfield, Conn.	268	191	79
November 3, 1965	Southgate, Mich.	183	102	73
November 4, 1965	New Milford, Conn.	118	88	28
November 7, 1965	East Valley, Wash.	86	75	—
November 9, 1965	Boston, Mass. (not affiliated)	4,000	1,116	1,602
November 9, 1965	Oakville (Grays Harbor County), Wash.	16	15	—
November 9, 1965	Okanogan County, Wash.	44	34	—
November 10, 1965	Groton, Conn.	444	391	18
November 10, 1965	West Hartford, Conn.	717	539	not on ballot
November 10, 1965	West Haven, Conn.	405	224	146
November 10, 1965	Birmingham, Mich.	720	545	not on ballot
November 10, 1965	Wenatchee Valley College, Wash.	65	32	—
November 11, 1965	Van Buren, Mich.	275	173	64
November 12, 1965	Stamford, Conn.	869	428	351

Date of Election	School District	Number of Teachers Eligible to Vote	Affiliated Organization Votes Received	
			NEA	AFT
November 12, 1965	Windham, Conn.	164	141	19
November 12, 1965	Clover Park, Wash.	650	574	—
November 12, 1965	Ephrata, Wash.	91	70	—
November 15, 1965	Simsbury, Conn.	178	147	23
November 15, 1965	Riverview, Mich.	148	120	not on ballot
November 15, 1965	Nooksack Valley, Wash.	45	44	—
November 18, 1965	Grosse Pointe, Mich.	527	318	195
November 18, 1965	Moxee (Yakima County), Wash.	55	49	—
November 23, 1965	Bainbridge Island, Wash.	82	65	—
November 24, 1965	Redford Union, Mich.	405	277	103
November 24, 1965	Oak Harbor, Wash.	185	150	—
November 30, 1965	Breitung Township, Mich.	74	68	not on ballot
November 30, 1965	Royal Oak, Mich.	793	434	297
November 30, 1965	Bellevue, Wash.	922	835	—
December 1, 1965	Trumbull, Conn.	273	241	—
December 1, 1965	Dearborn, Mich.	1,050	353	665
December 2, 1965	Chaplin, Conn.	11	6	4
December 2, 1965	Saginaw, Mich.	828	647	not on ballot
December 6, 1965	Melvindale, Mich.	219	97	105
December 7, 1965	Oak Park, Mich.	382	143	178
December 8, 1965	Reeths-Puffer, Mich.	159	122	not on ballot
December 9, 1965	Rapid River, Mich.	20	17	not on ballot
December 9, 1965	Wyandotte, Mich.	353	240	49
December 14, 1965	Ecorse, Mich.	194	69	120
December 15, 1965	Clarenceville, Mich.	124	94	not on ballot
December 15, 1965	Frankenmuth, Mich.	37	not on ballot	26
December 16, 1965	Lamphere, Mich.	214	116	74
December 20, 1965	Milford, Conn.	548	380	109
December 21, 1965	Middletown, Conn.	298	217	55
December 23, 1965	Cadillac, Mich.	120	108	not on ballot
January 6, 1966	Lakeview, Mich.	263	203	not on ballot

Date of Election	School District	Number of Teachers Eligible to Vote	Affiliated Organization Votes Received	
			NEA	AFT
January 11, 1966	Avondale, Mich.	131	66	64
January 11, 1966	Chelsea, Mich.	86	47	36
January 11, 1966	Midland, Mich.	489	420	not on ballot
January 12, 1966	West Ottawa, Mich.	136	105	not on ballot
January 13, 1966	Frazer, Mich.	189	151	8
January 13, 1966	Hamtramck, Mich.	149	9	130
January 14, 1966	South Lake, Mich.	207	172	not on ballot
January 17, 1966	Ansonia, Conn.	154	79	71
January 17, 1966	Farmington, Mich.	464	447	not on ballot
January 18, 1966	South Redford, Mich.	343	339	14
January 20, 1966	Manton, Mich.	25	11	not on ballot
January 25, 1966	Van Dyke, Mich.	270	133	153
January 25, 1966	Portland, Ore.	3,600	(association candidates won all positions on a 9-member negotiating council)	
January 28, 1966	Harper Woods, Mich.	95	43	49
February 2, 1966	Walled Lake, Mich.	333	259	not on ballot
February 2, 1966	Eatonville, Wash.	43	43	
February 3, 1966	Flint, Mich.	2,200	1,035	701
February 8, 1966	Garden City, Mich.		265	153
February 8, 1966	Whitehall, Mich.	78	72	not on ballot
February 10, 1966	Southfield, Mich.	646	465	not on ballot
February 10, 1966	New Rochelle, New York	662	278	342
February 15, 1966	East Detroit, Mich.	474	150	299
February 17, 1966	Roseville, Mich.	515	131	341
February 18, 1966	L'Anse Creuse, Mich.	204	160	not on ballot
February 22, 1966	Allen Park, Mich.	259	100	156
February 23, 1966	Willow Run, Mich.	186	134	not on ballot
February 24, 1966	Waterbury, Conn.	830	519	33
February 24, 1966	Lawrence, L.I., N.Y.	404	216	170

Date of Election	School District	Number of Teachers Eligible to Vote	Affiliated Organization Votes Received	
			NEA	AFT
February 28, 1966	Huron Valley, Mich.	192	171	not on ballot
February 28, 1966	Ypsilanti, Mich.	326	196	98
February ?, 1966	Fort Lewis, Wash.	119	84	—
March 3, 1966	Patchogue, L.I., New York	391	259	116
March 16, 1966	Olympic College, Wash.	—	87	not on ballot

* This is a partial listing. Listings are for elections where full data were available. This does not include any election with only the winner reported.
Source: Tabulations of NEA Division of Urban Services.

BOX SCORE THROUGH 1966-67. The Negotiation Research Digest of the NEA Research Division, for May 1967, summarized the competitive fight between the professional associations and the teachers' unions as follows: out of 7,157 school systems surveyed, with 5,549 or 77.5 per cent responding. These 7,157 school systems employed 1,428,836 members of the instructional staffs and 1,299,104 classroom teachers. A total of 1,353 systems (24.3 per cent), employing 574,621 members of the instructional staffs, had written negotiation procedures; 4,196 systems (75.6 per cent) did not have written negotiation procedures. There were no agreements in seven states (Alabama, District of Columbia, Georgia, Hawaii, Louisiana, Mississippi, and Tennessee). The range in number of school district agreements by states was from one in seven states (Arkansas, Kentucky, Nevada, North Carolina, North Dakota, South Carolina, and Virginia) to 215 in Michigan and 256 in California. Among the 1,353 school systems with agreements, 1,262 organizations held representation rights. Among these 1,262, NEA affiliates were the representing organizations in 1,179 districts; AFT affiliates were the representing organizations in 35 districts; in three districts the representing organizations were independent of affiliation; and in 45 districts there were two or more representing organizations. Thus NEA affiliates had by June 1, 1967 won representation rights in 93.4 per cent of the districts with agreement; the AFT affiliates had won in only 2.8 per cent of the districts. NEA affiliates represented 395,918 teachers or 78.9 per cent of professional personnel under agreements; the AFT affiliates represented 103,095 teachers, or 20.5 per cent of professional personnel under agreements.

Chicago was not included because although the AFT won the election there, no written agreement had been signed by June 1, 1967. Chicago would be one more district in which AFT has representation rights and 20,000 more teachers represented.

TABLE 13-3

Teacher Representation Elections
September 1, 1966 to June 16, 1967, by States

State	Date	School District	NEA Affiliate Vote	AFT Affiliate Vote
Colorado	March 1967	Denver	2,361	1,355
Connecticut	Oct. 1966	Hartford	638	758
	Nov. 1966	Wethersfield	163	100
	Dec. 1966	Middletown	195	72
	Dec. 1966	Groton	275	136
	Feb. 1967	Ansonia	78	80
District of Columbia	Apr. 1967		2,119	3,540
Illinois	Oct. 1966	Joliet	not on ballot	252
	Nov. 1966	Dolton	86	48
	Nov. 1966	Roxanna	113	not on ballot
	Jan. 1967	Cahokia	149	164
	Jan. 1967	Miles Township	89	312
	Apr. 1967	Springfield	548	370
	May 1967	Rockford	934	496
Indiana	Feb. 1967	South Bend	737	765
	March 1967	Gary	267	1,529
Maryland	June 1967	Baltimore	3,358	3,678
Massachusetts	Oct. 1966	Salem	96	168
	Nov. 1966	Lynn	228	339
	Nov. 1966	Peabody	71	226
	Dec. 1966	Gloucester	173	72
	Dec. 1966	Chelsea	107	131
	Dec. 1966	Lowell	361	148
	Dec. 1966	Malden	290	130
	Jan. 1967	Billercia	150	100
Michigan	Oct. 1966	Hazel Park	236	66
	Oct. 1966	Dearborn #8	135	93
	Oct. 1966	Lincoln Ark	260	240
	Oct. 1966	Gibraltar	44	51
	Nov. 1966	Grand Rapids	1,151	172
	Dec. 1966	River Rouge	95	86
	March 1967	Harper Woods	44	53
	March 1967	Oak Park	163	170
	Apr. 1967	Frazer	111	84
	Apr. 1967	Melvindale	106	121
	Apr. 1967	Willow Run	101	77

State	Date	School District	NEA Affiliate Vote	AFT Affiliate Vote
	Apr. 1967	Imlay City	34	38
	Apr. 1967	Van Dyke	121	159
	Apr. 1967	Detroit	3,709	6,410
New Jersey	May 1967	Jersey City	800	745
New York	May 1967	Schenectady	425	351
Ohio	Apr. 1967	Struthers	53	63
Rhode Island	Sept. 1966	Cranston	249	not on ballot
	Sept. 1966	Woonsocket	not on ballot	100
	Sept. 1966	Portsmouth	88	not on ballot
	Sept. 1966	Barrington	172	not on ballot
	Sept. 1966	Tiverton	71	not on ballot
	Sept. 1966	Jamestown	20	not on ballot
Rhode Island	Oct. 1966	Warwick	412	252
	Oct. 1966	Newport	266	withdrew
	Oct. 1966	Scituate	60	not on ballot
	Oct. 1966	Burrillville	65	not on ballot
	Nov. 1966	North Kingston	123	not on ballot
	Nov. 1966	East Providence	188	not on ballot
	Nov. 1966	Lincoln	71	not on ballot
	Nov. 1966	Chariho	42	not on ballot
	Nov. 1966	South Kingston	105	not on ballot
	Nov. 1966	Coventry	109	82
	Nov. 1966	Warren	53	not on ballot
	Nov. 1966	West Warwick	not on ballot	98
	Nov. 1966	Johnston	not on ballot	111
Wisconsin	Jan. 1967	Fond Du Lac	201	127
Totals	Elections: 62	Won by NEA: 39		Won by AFT: 23

Source: Division of Urban Services, National Education Association (mimeographed).

The Growing Turmoil

The school year 1965–66 reflected growing turmoil in the schools resulting in part from the bitter organizational rivalry. Obviously, AFT propaganda was paying off as indicated in the escalation of strike threats and actual strikes.

The constant appeal for teacher militancy as well as the constant urging of the strike upon affiliates, sometimes with the flimsiest of excuses, were having their impact upon the teachers' union affiliates and upon NEA affiliates as well.

In Michigan, for example, in the last month of the school year 1965–66, there was a rash of teachers' strikes. Strikes by AFT affiliates occurred in

Ecorse, Melvondale, Taylor Township, and North Dearborn Heights. The school board in Ecorse, despairing of a settlement after 14 days of the strike, summarily fired about 200 teachers on its staff on June 16, 1966. Later, the teachers were reinstated.

Five affiliates of the Michigan Education Association (and thus of NEA) staged strikes. The five districts were Flint, Gibraltar, Warren, Crestwood, and Wayne. These strikes were actions of the local associations protesting at what they felt were arbitrary positions of the school boards. Although they had won by election under Michigan law exclusive rights of negotiation, these associations were confronted with unilateral action of the boards in refusing to engage in any real negotiation. The associations called their walk-outs professional days but there can be little doubt that these were full-fledged strikes.

In addition there were strike threats or strike votes in several other AFT locals including Detroit where the federation was demanding $15 million in additional salary money.

What was the attitude of MEA and NEA toward these walk-outs? Neither counseled the associations to strike. MEA attempted to head off the strikes by declaring sanctions against the school districts, but to no avail. Neither MEA nor NEA denounced the strikes or criticized them. Both did what they could to assist the teachers in all possible ways.

The flurry of strikes in Michigan may be related to a court interpretation of the labor-sponsored amendments to the Public Employment Relations Act passed by the 1965 Michigan Legislature.

Although the law forbade strikes by public employees, a four-judge panel court refused to enjoin the Flint teachers from striking. The Flint School Board had requested an injunction. The judges refused, in effect, on the grounds that collective bargaining, by the passage of the labor-sponsored law, had become official policy of the state and its inevitable companion was the strike. The panel held that they could only enjoin the strike of the Flint teachers if it could be shown that life or property were threatened by the strike. This was an unexpected and sweeping decision, the import of which was to give legal sanction to strikes by teachers. Whether this view will be sustained by higher courts is a moot question. But there are grounds for believing that it encouraged teachers' strikes in Michigan both by NEA and AFT affiliates.

While it is simply speculation that this decision influenced the rash of strikes at the school year's end. There were at least two other significant factors. First is the fact that Michigan is heavily oriented to the philosophy and practices of organized labor. This is especially true in metropolitan Detroit, although it is generally true over most of the state. In such a climate, the strike is simply a companion piece to collective bargaining. Second, there appears to be considerable evidence that the school boards involved were not prepared to accept in good faith the provisions of the new law. Although they authorized the negotiation elections, it appears that they bitterly opposed negotiating with the winning organizations.

The Michigan Association of School Boards adopted a resolution on May 30, 1966 calling upon local boards to observe faithfully the amended Hutchinson Act. This amended act erased the automatic-dismissal penalty for a strike by public employees and required public employers to bargain with their workers. Under the act, when an impasse occurs provision is made for appeal to the State Labor Mediation Board. But the association went further and urged boards to take action, including dismissal or demotion, to discipline striking employees. The resolution also urged boards to seek court injunctions to bar teacher's strikes, and urged that whenever a teachers' strike or its equivalent occurs negotiations with teachers' organizations be discontinued and not resumed until such strike is ended.

Many observers judged that this get-tough resolution increased teacher unrest and encouraged strikes.

At the tail end of the 1965-66 school year there was a flurry of sanctions applications and several requests for investigations by NEA. As previously mentioned, the Michigan Education Association invoked sanctions against several districts, but strikes occurred in several of these districts anyway.

The Maine Teachers Association voted sanctions on the Portland and Hermon school districts, where the teachers won their demands in both cases, and the sanctions were lifted. The Baltimore Public School Teachers' Association voted sanctions against the Baltimore School Board and called upon NEA for a thorough investigation of the total school situation in that city. Likewise, the Minnesota Education Association requested in mid-June 1966 a thorough investigation by NEA of the Minneapolis School Board. The Detroit Federation of Teachers on June 18 voted to strike in September if the board failed to provide substantial salary increases.

All in all, the school year 1965–66 was a turbulent one. The problems that brought about the Oklahoma sanctions were settled in September. The Kentucky uprising of teachers was met by the statesmanlike action of the governor and solved to the satisfaction of the teachers. The Knoxville teachers called for an NEA investigation and invoked sanctions against the district. Walk-outs, strikes, or professional days occurred among NEA affiliates in Kentucky, Newark, and the five Michigan districts enumerated above. These situations will be discussed later in this chapter.

Red Faces on Both Sides

Several work stoppages occurred during the 1965–66 school year that caused the public and the teaching profession to wonder about the policy differences between NEA and AFT.

Children Will Respect Teachers Who Have the Courage to Violate the Law

Stanley Elam, in an editorial in the *Phi Delta Kappan* (May, 1966) advocating a merger of AFT and NEA, stated in effect that there were no philosophical, ideological, or procedural differences between the two organizations that constituted insurmountable obstacles to merger. This statement irritated many NEA staff members who assumed that Elam was equating the programs and philosophies of the two. But a fair assessment of the behaviour of AFT locals in general and of many NEA local affiliates would puzzle the most partisan NEA protagonists. In the closing weeks of the 1965–66 school year, especially in Michigan, some NEA-MEA affiliates appeared to embrace the strike with an enthusiasm and aggressiveness that often matched or exceeded that of the AFT locals. And there was no remonstrance from either

NEA or MEA. Thus the impartial observer and the general public were compelled to the view that the differences, if any, between NEA and AFT were rapidly disappearing, at least in some sections of the country. However superficial this conclusion may be, there are admittedly some grounds for it.

In Perth Amboy, New Jersey the AFT local staged an abortive strike on November 1 to force the school board to hold a collective-bargaining election. The board contended that state law forbids collective bargaining and strikes for public employees. This was a standard AFT gimmick to force on school boards an extra legal step.

About half of the district's 281 teachers went out on strike and picketed the school. The board immediately secured a court order enjoining the union from striking or picketing. Reports were that AFT forced the strike upon its local to compel an election. The strike continued for two weeks, ending on November 13 with the board's agreement to call a collective-bargaining election. The members of the Perth Amboy Teachers' Association, which was offered a similar agreement, rejected it as meaningless and also denounced the proposed election, refusing to take part in it. The Association contended that the union got only rights which the state constitution guaranteed to all teachers.

This opinion was confirmed by State Commissioner of Education Fred Raubinger on December 5 when he ruled that both the strike and settlement agreement were illegal. He ruled that the intervention of the state's board of mediation was not authorized by law. Thus the collective-bargaining election —for which the union strike was called to force board action—was not held.

THE NEWARK FIASCOS. Fresh from another "overwhelming victory" in Perth Amboy by operating beyond, to use a union phrase, "the horizon of the law" (which was negated by the action of the state commissioner as described), AFT attempted another coup in Newark in late November 1965 by pressuring its local to demand a new collective-bargaining election before the contract of the winner (the Newark Teachers Association) of the first election had expired.

The NTA contract was to end on July 27, 1966, but negotiation on a new salary scale had been postponed by the school board pending definite budget information for the 1966–67 school year. Sensing that the NTA would be able to secure significant gains in the upcoming negotiations, the AFT urged its local to demand an immediate election and to threaten a strike if the board refused to call the election. This was simply a union ploy to prevent NTA from getting credit for the new salary schedules. This was bad unionism, and many trade unions refused to back the position of the teachers' union. The UFT in New York City, however, gave all-out backing to the strike despite warnings from the school board that the strike was illegal, that the agreement with the NTA could not be abrogated during its term, and that the board would seek a restraining order from the courts. The Newark Teachers Union voted to go out on strike on December 2. Speakers from the AFT and UFT urged in impassioned language that the strike vote be *yes*. The Newark local was told that a vote in favor of the strike would bring the board to its knees, implying that the strike itself would not be necessary, that only the threat of a strike was needed.

Only about one fourth of Newark's 3,200 teachers went on strike on December 2. No schools were closed. The workers of the custodial and cafeteria union crossed the picket lines.

The board sought and secured a court injunction against the union, but the walk-out of about 800 union teachers continued for two days. The court cited ten union officers for contempt. The ten leaders appeared in court and pleaded guilty.

The Newark Teachers Union was fined $1,000. The president and executive vice-president of NTA were fined $350 each and the remaining eight officers, $250 each. Thus total fines of $3,700 were imposed by the court upon the union and its officers.

Here was another fiasco resulting from AFT's stated policy of operating beyond the horizon of the law through intimidation of the school board. This time, as in New Orleans and Perth Amboy, the tactic failed.

Impressions by a Non-Union Observer of a Strike Meeting of the Teachers Union in Newark, December 1965. Recorded in the Form of a Lesson Plan

LESSON PLAN: HOW TO RUN A UNION MEETING

Primary Objective:
To get your members to vote a strike.

Secondary Objective:
To torpedo any other organization working to help teachers.

Resources:
1. Representatives of other unions.
2. Stooges planted in audience.
3. "Cheerleaders" in aisles.
4. Loud emotional appeals.
5. A big gavel for pounding dissenters "out of order."

Definitions [*of Union Phraseology*]:
1. Union organizer—*a man who gets paid while others are out on strike.*
2. Condition of a local which has not struck: *on its knees.*
3. Group which has a contract—*company union.*
4. Any day you negotiate—a *reopener.*
5. Everyone else: *the enemy.*

Procedures:
1. Have representatives of other unions tell Newark teachers it's their duty to strike. *"You can't be a union without going through this action."*

2. Limit the debate to 30 minutes if possible. "*The Executive Board says the vote must come at 5:15.*"
3. Let members speak only once, for no more than three minutes, and prevent members from yielding the floor to other union members. *"I rule you out of order."*
4. Have the "cheerleader" run up and down the aisle proclaiming, "I'm going to strike Monday if I have to go out alone" and, during one of the disorders, "Mr. Chairman, do you need a sergeant-at-arms? *We may need one yet.*"
5. Duck questions like "The Perth Amboy union struck for 11 days, and the teachers got nothing. Couldn't the same thing happen in Newark?" and *"Is there any legal basis for a strike?"*
6. Pull favored nonmembers out of the audience, yield the dias to them, and let them have liberal portions of the limited discussion time.
7. Shout down dissenters. Interrupt them with "point of order." Tell them: "Go home."
8. [Allow members], when they don't want to strike, . . . to delay the date two weeks.
9. Use any means to get as large a vote as possible. *"Hold your hands up for the photographer."*
10. Get your "plant" in the audience to stand up after the strike vote and cry: "I move that we make it unanimous." *A simple majority then makes it so.*

Under provisions of the New Jersey Constitution strikes by public employees are forbidden. Collective bargaining for public employees also is not provided in the constitution. The New Jersey Constitution reads:

> Persons in *private* employment shall have the right to organize and bargain collectively. Persons in *public* employment shall have the right to organize (and) present to and make known to the state or any of its political subdivisions or agencies, their grievances through representatives of their own choosing.

It was under these provisions that the Perth Amboy board was over-ruled by the state commissioner of education in its agreement to hold a collective bargaining election. The Newark board contended it was without authority to conduct a collective-bargaining election. Consequently, it agreed only to selection of the representative of the teachers in an election in 1964 conducted, by agreement between the teacher's association and the teachers' union, by the American Arbitration Association. This is the reason for the issuance of an order by the New Jersey State Board of Education requiring local school boards to establish grievance and negotiation procedures to be mediated by that board in cases of impasse.

The teachers' union claimed to have been vindicated in the fiasco. But this was refuted by the president of the school board. Likewise, a fact-finding panel appointed by the mayor rejected both the legality and the validity of the strike. The union came out with nothing that it did not already have—the right to a new election within from 30 to 60 days before the termination of the NTA contract on July 27, 1966. The teachers' union lost this second election in May 1966, by a slim margin.

SECOND NEWARK STRIKE. Following the failure of the Newark Teachers Union in its strike (on December 2 and 3, 1965) to force a premature election, leaving the Newark Teachers Association as the negotiating agent for the teachers, the association itself got into a hassle with the school board. The board obviously was determined, in view of state constitutional provisions, to avoid full-scale negotiation or collective-bargaining procedures. The efforts of the NTA to negotiate a new salary schedule for the school year 1966–67 quickly reached an impasse. The NTA voted a strike against the board which took place on February 10 and 11. The strike was ended by a court injunction and court fines were levied against the association and its officers. The association was fined $1,000 and 30 individuals were fined a total of $16,500 on contempt charges. The three top officers were fined $1,000 and given suspended sentences of 90 days. Fines of $500 were assessed against four members of the strike committee, together with suspended sentences of 60 days. Twenty-three other teachers were fined $500 and given suspended sentences of 30 days for striking and picketing.

Here was another impasse resulting in dual control of the schools. The school had to depend upon the mayor and his appointed finance committee for approval of its budget. There was evidence that the mayor was jockeying for a favorable position in his coming campaign for re-election by forestalling efforts to increase school expenditures significantly. The NTA quickly found itself in a game of "pass the buck" between the school board and the mayor. Failing to get satisfactory action, the NTA voted sanctions against the Newark School District on January 31, 1966. There were reports that the mayor feared the invoking of sanctions because large billboards advertising the sanctions were placed throughout the city, which was not good publicity in the mayoralty election. There were also reports that the mayor hoped NTA would be drawn into an illegal strike, with the law and action of the courts already made clear in NTU strike. With the strike on February 10 and 11, both sides agreed to the appointment of a well-known university professor as arbitrator. He recommended a settlement on more liberal terms than the NTA had proposed. The bachelor's degree schedule was stepped up to a $6,300– $10,700 range) the master's degree schedule to $6,700–$11,100) and the master's degree plus 30 hours schedule from $7,100–$11,500. Teachers not at the maximum level received raises of $1,000–$1,100. Raises were secured also for permanent substitutes, summer-school teachers, and auxiliary personnel, and provisions were made for the employment of 300 teachers' aides.

A picture was published in some newspapers showing members of the Newark Teachers Association picketing and stamping the restraining court order underfoot, which on the face of it was as drastic as anything the AFT affiliates had ever engaged in. The *NEA Reporter*, which had hooted at the AFT strike in December and its fiasco, was relatively silent on the NTA strike and the flouting of the court injunction. Whose face is red?

As one NEA observer said: "It is simply impossible for a teacher in Nebraska, or any other rural area, to conceive of the ugly manipulation by politicians, of the partisan politics, the run-around, buck-passing, cynical ducking and dodging, anything to delay and dodge meeting the issue, in the hope that low school costs attract the attention of taxpayers." But NEA silence on the incident—without explanation—automatically put it alongside the teachers' unions in tactics in the eyes of many.

The reply of the executive secretary of a state education association to a question raised by the governor of that state perhaps best states the position of NEA and its state affiliates.

"Is your association advocating these strikes?" asked the governor.

"No," replied the executive secretary.

"What are you doing about the striking teachers?"

"We are doing everything we can to help them," replied the state association official. "We are in the position of a parent whose son has got into trouble. That parent grieves over the situation. He doesn't advocate or condone what has been done. But he must help his boy."

The Strike Dilemma

The walk-out, professional days, and outright strikes among NEA affiliates during 1965–66 have been recounted at some length to emphasize the dilemma in which NEA found itself at the close of the school year.

Its historic policy has been against the use of the strike by teachers. While, as has been pointed out several times, NEA has had no categorical no-strike policy, its tacit policy has been against the strike, and its adopted policy advocates the use of professional sanctions to remedy unsatisfactory conditions.

The two-day professional holiday in Utah and the one-day professional day in Oklahoma and Kentucky did not pose a problem requiring NEA action, inasmuch as there were extenuating circumstances in all three cases, since teachers had made firm or token efforts to avoid the appearance of engaging in concerted strike action. But the Newark strike and the Flint strike (and strikes in two or three other Michigan districts) were clear-cut cases of deliberate use of the strike by NEA affiliates.

What was to be NEA's reaction? Should it now denounce the striking affiliates and reassert its traditional opposition to the strike as a weapon?

These questions imposed an agonizing dilemma both for the NEA and the state affiliates involved. Would not failure to react adversely serve to demonstrate that the professional associations were beginning to embrace the AFT philosophy and procedures? Would not some slapping of the wrists be necessary to avoid the growing concept that AFT propaganda, the organized labor concept of industrial warfare, was winning broad acceptance by teachers? Had not the time come for NEA to clear up its ambivalent position on the strike? Or at least to declare flatly a *yes* or *no* position on the strike?

To be frank, after the Newark and Flint strikes a lot of soul-searching took place among the NEA staff on these points. Few favored an outright recommendation of a flat no-strike statement. However, the general consensus of the members of the staff who participated in the discussion was that NEA should retain its flexible position. It was suggested that this be done by two means: (1) by seeking state legislation similar to that prepared in New York in the spring of 1966 (as recommended by the governor's committee on public employee relations), to provide reasonable and fair means of solving impasses between boards and teachers, or (2) by a careful spelling out of ground rules and procedures when impasses arise so that overt and illegal action of teachers in very frustrating circumstances could probably be avoided.

The NEA Executive Secretary William Carr, in his 1966 convention speech said:

> *As future legislation is developed, let us seek procedures that will in the words of the NEA Charter advance the interests of the profession of teaching* and *promote the cause of popular education.* These ends are not attainable by merely copying procedures designed to regulate traditional labor-management controversy. . . . If the newly achieved power of the organized profession of education is not to corrupt, it must be exercised with responsibility within the framework of a code of ethics and with due regard to the public interest. Strikes and threats of strikes should not be a requirement for successful agreement between responsible boards of education and responsible education associations. There is an urgent need to explore complex ethical, political, economic, and legal problems relating to concerted work stoppage. . . . Under what conditions, if any, could a strike be considered necessary? Under what conditions is a strike specifically unprofessional and unethical? Should professional discipline be applied in the event of an improper work stoppage?

Carr then advised the Representative Assembly that he had recommended to the NEA Board of Directors that a blue-ribbon panel be appointed to prepare a comprehensive position paper on the resolution of impasses for the guidance of NEA and its members.

There is one significant difference between the use of the strike by AFT and NEA affiliates that ought not to be obscured in this discussion.

The AFT has consistently (at least since 1962) urged the use of the strike upon its locals to press beyond what it has termed "the horizon of the law," to force the calling of collective-bargaining elections, to intimidate school boards, and to deliberately create an image of aggressive conflict with school superintendents and boards. The use of vituperation and vilification has been grist to its mill, always with the potent power of AFL-CIO as a convenient reinforcement.

Moreover, in the last year or two, the strike apparently has been used as a gimmick for getting more union members. The relatively few NEA affiliates that have used the strike were forced to this extreme as they sought to negotiate with boards. No NEA strike occurred as a means of forcing elections or as a prime means of attracting members.

The Moving Tide

Whatever the casual factors may be, and they are clearly complex and often obscure, the *status quo* of teachers and their professional associations is in the process of drastic change. Perhaps the very swift and powerful flow of the times is the overriding cause. However, no fair evaluation could possibly obscure the impact of the propaganda and aggressive action of AFT and its affiliates. The successes of AFT in forcing elections and bargaining by strikes in several instances have without question impressed many thousands of teachers. There is no question, either, that the professional associations have been dragged along, albeit often reluctantly, to more aggressive, militant action.

Union propaganda suggesting administrator domination in NEA affiliates —that is, the accusation of NEA being a company union—has, it appears, about run its course largely through the revelation that there has been little difference in this regard between NEA and AFT—that the constant harping on these by the teachers' unions has been overdone is becoming evident.

What does remain is the increasing militancy on the part of teachers, an increasing demand that their associations find ways and procedures to improve teachers' negotiation rights.

Finally, the NEA 1966 Miami Beach Convention (June 26–July 1) clearly reflected, for those willing to see the fact, that the younger new breed of teachers was taking over from the old guard and the middle-aged members. In at least a half-dozen cases, the convention overrode the established leaders to vote liberal provisions and procedures.

Thus it seems evident the future will witness a drastic overhaul of NEA and its allied professional associations, their philosophic positions, their policies, and their procedures. In time, therefore, there will be a radically different view of the meaning of the professional concept and of the rights and responsibilities of members of the profession. Teachers' unions may continue to contribute to this change, but it may be that their major contributions have been made. In the future, they will have a struggle to keep abreast of the militancy of the once self-satisfied professional associations.

Part Five

PROJECTION OF THE STRUGGLE

14

The Price Is Not Right

Chicago, August 22, 1966: In this city where "White Power" and "Black Power" have been clashing on the streets, members of the American Federation of Teachers, AFL-CIO, yesterday were given a lesson in "teacher power."

Teachers arriving here for the AFT's 50th annual convention all received booklets outlining the strategy and rationale of teacher strikes. . . .

Chief conclusion of the 24 page booklet, written by Pete Schnauffer, is that crisis bargaining and shock tactics, including *illegal* strikes, are the best way to impose contracts. To gain the creative tension necessary to make deadline negotiations meaningful, Schnauffer writes, "You need an impending social crisis (such as a strike threat)." He concludes that, "Strikes will tend to be more affective when they violate laws prohibiting public employees to strike, since they will be more startling."

Since schools are more custodial and less educational than even the most cynical social critic probably realizes, a strike has the effect of dumping children back on their parents for day-long and week-long care.

The booklet adds that those who state that "schools exist for children," or "the children must come first" are simple-headed.

—Richard H. DeLone
Philadelphia Bulletin, August 22, 1966

Presently both NEA and AFT are woefully irrelevant to the pressing needs of teachers. But the NEA moves into the self-renewal period with overpowering advantages. It already has a vast program of professional services which would require years for AFT to match, even if it had the will and the resources to do so. NEA, on the other hand, given the will, which is steadily evolving, can rapidly change the nature of staff relationships *vis à vis* the school board and administration. This is the primary problem; welfare matters are, of course, important, but they are only a part of the problem. First of all, the prediction that public-school teachers will not defect to the teachers' unions in a giant migration is based upon the clear evidence that the price of such affiliation is too high.

The teachers will conclude, as have the provincial associations in Canada and the National Union of Teachers (NUT) in England, that, despite certain advantages of affiliation with trade unions, the price is too costly. For example, the AFT has scored heavy successes in New York City because of the political power of labor in that city, specifically the New York City Central Labor Council. But the teachers' union is now having to pay a heavy price for that support, as will soon be pointed out.

The price of labor affiliation for teachers is too high in terms of loss of academic freedom and loss of academic authority, in terms of labor's use of teachers to fight labor's battles on the picket lines, in terms of the threat of regimentation, in terms of labor's opposition to excise taxes for schools, in terms of labor's expecting teachers to be advocates of labor's dogma in the classroom.

The idea that labor would exploit teachers if they affiliated through the teachers' unions has been repeatedly scoffed at by some writers. It is true that when the union movement was jumping ahead dramatically, big labor had little need of teachers' help. That is no longer true. There are specific examples now to demonstrate that AFL-CIO will use teachers to further labor goals. In fact, such use in the future appears inevitable.

THE KINGSPORT PRESS STORY. The secondary boycott sponsored by AFL-CIO is a good example of labor policy engulfing the teachers' unions.

In March 1963 three graphic arts unions and their locals (International Printing Pressmen and Assistant's Union, International Stereotypers and Electrotypers Union, and the International Brotherhood of Book Binders) went out on strike against the Kingsport Press, in Kingsport, Tennessee. The International Union of Machinists and the International Typographical Union also represented a few workers at the outset of the strike, but since then NLRB has negated their bargaining rights because their members at Kingsport Press voted against the unions. The company and these unions could not reach agreement after several months of bargaining on a new three-year contract, and the company began hiring nonunion printers. The union, charging unfair labor practice, appeared before the National Labor Relations Board in September 1963. The National Labor Relations Board ruled against the union.

Again in March 1965, NLRB refused to act upon union charges of unfair labor practices against the Kingsport Press. The company has continued to operate with union and nonunion labor. Nearly one half of its total of 2,000 employees have returned to their jobs.

Of the original five striking unions, two early lost their bargaining rights at the plant by virtue of losing elections conducted by the NLRB. On April 27, 1967, the other three unions lost the right to represent workers in the plant being rejected in elections by vote of the workers. In effect, NLRB held that the company was within its legal rights. The union, having exhausted their resort to legal adjudication of the dispute, called upon other unions to boycott the products of the Kingsport Press. Many acts of violence were reported.

Those Are Simple-Minded Who Say that Children Come First

The products of the Kingsport Press included educational books and encyclopedias for 170 leading publishers of materials for schools. Kingsport Press is not a publisher; it is a printing plant which prints books on contract for reputable publishers.

Pressures were brought upon the New York City Board of Education by the New York City Central Labor Council to ban from the schools all books printed at the Kingsport Press.[1] This effort succeeded in March 1966, by a vote of five to four. The UFT in New York was asked to pressure the board of education to ban the books. The UFT, in formal negotiations, asked the board to agree not to purchase textbooks and other teaching materials manufactured, transported, or handled by firms which have discriminatory hiring practices or are antilabor. A teacher in the city, a member of the UFT, expressed in a letter to the president of UFT her dismay that labor would seek to use its teacher members to censor teaching materials in the school. The president replied that "it seems strange that teachers would expect help from other unions [in money, picketing, support of their strikes] and not expect to help these unions when they needed help."[2]

The Cleveland Board of Education, under pressure from union members in December 1965, ordered the superintendent to withhold new purchases of books printed by Kingsport Press and to order replacements only.

A New Jersey school board voted to ban Kingsport Press books but rescinded the action at its next meeting.

The annual convention of the AFT in Los Angeles in August 1965 adopted a resolution calling upon its locals throughout the country to pressure their school boards to boycott all books printed by the Kingsport Press.

The resolution reads:

Resolution # 103 American Federation of Teachers
Textbooks Produced By Strikebreakers

Submitted by Los Angeles Teachers Union, Local 1021

WHEREAS: the free public schools of this nation came into being as a result of tremendous efforts on the part of labor unions, and

WHEREAS: these free public schools derive their major support from laboring people, and

WHEREAS: this continued support is only possible in a society where good wages and fair working conditions are the rule, and

WHEREAS: one of the major suppliers of textbooks is Kingsport Press of Kingsport, Tennessee, and

WHEREAS: management of this company has refused to maintain wages and working conditions standard in the textbooks industry and did, on March 11, 1963, by its refusal to bargain, force its employees to go on strike in an attempt to gain good wages and fair working conditions, and

WHEREAS: the company continues to maintain a partial production by the use of imported strikebreakers, and

WHEREAS: history demonstrates that strikebreakers contribute nothing to the economy and only bring to the community disunity and distrust, be it therefore

RESOLVED: that this 49th Convention of the American Federation of Teachers does hereby go on record deploring the use of strikebreakers and the maintenance of poor working conditions and unfair wages in the production of textbooks for use in our public schools, and be it further

RESOLVED: that the AFT strongly urges member locals to call on their local boards of education to refrain from purchasing books printed by the Kingsport Press, and be it further

RESOLVED: that copies of this resolution be forwarded to George Meany of the AFL-CIO; United States Department of Health, Education and Welfare; United States Department of Labor, and to R. W. Ayers, Secretary, Allied Kingsport Press Unions.

In a lengthy resolution, the sixth AFL-CIO constitutional convention in San Francisco in January 1965 supported a boycott of all books being produced by "scabs and strike breakers" at the Kingsport Press and denounced the use of public funds to purchase books printed in the plant.

Charles Cogen, President of AFT, defended the resolution of that AFL-CIO affiliate and its pressures on school boards to ban Kingsport books as follows:

> I think it is quite obvious that we, as *the* organized teachers in this country, are very much involved in this struggle, because we have to teach with these instrumentalities, the textbooks, and encyclopedias that are being put out by scab labor. So we, through our Executive Council, have taken a very direct and unequivocal stand on this issue. We have stated that we support the workers in this long, drawn-out strike, and we urge boards of education and teachers everywhere to boycott the products put out by the Kingsport Press.
>
> As a result of the position that we have taken, the National Education Association, the NEA, *the company union*, the organization that has been officially declared *a company union* by the AFL-CIO, has taken this occasion to attack the American Federation of Teachers as violating academic freedom.
>
> I want to make it perfectly clear as we have tried to do in our answer to their statement, that our position on this issue has nothing whatsoever to do with the issue of academic freedom. We are not making any efforts whatsoever to censure the contents of the textbooks and encyclopedias involved. What we are trying to do is to see to it that the books and encyclopedias sold to the public schools and private schools of this country are books that are published under decent conditions, decent working conditions. We think that this is in consonance with the free rights and privileges of the American teachers to see to it that this is done. We are urging the American teachers throughout the country, to see to it that the books and encyclopedias put out by the Kingsport Press are not purchased for use in the schools in this country.
>
> We urge all teachers to stand with us on this score.[3] [Italics supplied by author.]

Cogen's reference to the NEA referred to a statement of Richard Batchelder, 1965–66 NEA President, in a public address:

> It should be noted that the decision of the American Federation of Teachers and its affiliates to force the disuse of the textbooks on this blacklist [books

printed at Kingsport Press] was completely unrelated to the educational value of the books or to whether acceptable alternative books were available. The decision was made solely on who published them.

Although the National Education Association can well appreciate the feelings of these members of the union in Kingsport, in the interest of academic freedom and the good of American education, the NEA must and does stand firm in its insistence that the only criteria for the use or disuse of books or other instructional materials in public schools is in their educational value and appropriateness. The teaching profession must not become embroiled in secondary boycotts growing out of labor disputes.

When we are faced with choosing between secondary involvement in a labor dispute and the welfare of millions of children, we will stand with the children every time. Here, perhaps, we have one of the main differences between the National Education Association and the American Federation of Teachers. Here, we have one of the main issues of independence. The National Education Association puts the children and teachers first. The American Federation of Teachers must put its union obligations first, because it is dependent on union support for its very existence.

An editorial in the January 1966 issue of *The American Teacher* (AFT publication) set forth the AFT position. Below are exerpts from that editorial.

For almost three years, the printing craftsmen in the Tennessee town of Kingsport have attempted to meet with their employer to collectively bargain in the democratic tradition that is their right, both legally and morally.

For three years, management has ignored them. Instead, *scabs and strikebreakers have been hired*, the regular skilled workers have been walking the picket line since 1963, and the makings of another Kohler strike are apparent.

Classroom teachers who talk about the virtues of democracy and a respect for one another's rights to their students are hypocritical if they do not, at the same time, point out the flaunting of law and morality by the Kingsport employer to their boards of education.

It is not "bookburning" or a "secondary boycott"—as some politically motivated detractors have charged—to urge publishers to choose another printer for their books. Neither is it "blacklisting" to ask boards of education to spend taxpayers' money with firms that practice democracy, not strikebreaking. Many school boards were instrumental in getting publishers to integrate school texts; they can be as effective in urging publishers to stop dealing with strikebreakers. [Italics supplied by author.]

A report issued by the Kingsport Press refutes the editorial assertion that it has refused to bargain and that it has flouted law and morality, citing two decisions of the NLRB dismissing charges of "unfair labor practices."[4] The editorial charges concerning morality and disregarding of the rights of others ignores some 800 cases of reported violence.[5]

The National School Boards Association, concerned by the pressures upon local boards to ban the textbooks printed in the Kingsport plant, called upon the general counsel of the association for a legal opinion in the matter. Exerpts from the opinion stated:

It would appear that school boards exceed their authority and violate both the constitution and the laws of their states by adopting such a boycott resolution as proposed by the unions. . . .

Several state courts have held that the refusal of a public agency, such as a school board, to purchase goods merely because they are not made by members of a union is an abuse of discretion wholly outside the power of such a public agency and a violation of the well established rule governing the spending of public funds. . . .

It is not the function of a school board to take sides in a labor dispute. Both the federal government and state agencies amply cover this area and provide adequate remedies for the parties to a labor dispute should one of them violate the law.

For a school board to adopt such a resolution would be discriminatory in nature and rank favoritism in preferring union shops over non-union shops. This would be particularly onerous in the printing industry where more than 60% of the employees are not organized by labor unions.[6]

The New York City Board of Education adopted, on March 16, 1966, by a vote of five to four, a resolution banning the use of the books printed at the Kingsport Press. This action was taken contrary to the opinion of the New York City Corporation Counsel, the legal representative of all the city departments.

The counsel refused to represent the board of education in any litigation arising from its boycott.

The Kingsport Press secured a temporary stay of the boycott until a hearing could be held.

A New York State Supreme Court justice, on October 13, 1966, voided the action of the New York City Board of Education in boycotting books printed by the Kingsport Press.

The *New York Times* commented editorially on March 19, 1966, on the boycott as follows:

The position taken by the Board throws doubt on its judgment and independence. The proposal had been introduced by Morris Iushewitz, secretary of the Central Labor Council, and was approved by a 5–4 vote of the Board. That action was bad enough; but in taking it the Board also brushed aside an opinion by the city's Corporation Counsel on the legality of the move, and it ignored the views of the three lawyers among its own members, including Lloyd K. Garrison, its president.

In pleading against an action that has the earmarks of a secondary boycott, Mr. Garrison warned that the move *will lead to intolerable pressures on principals to select textbooks "against their better judgment" and for other than educational reasons.* Moreover, the potential elimination of a substantial roster of books, many of them published by a wide variety of the most reputable firms, *raises questions of censorship which far transcends the labor issue involved.*

The ruling, which may jeopardize the quality of instructional materials, was clearly taken for one reason only—*to pander to union demands.* The Board thus has invited the conclusion that it has permitted pressure backed by political power to outweigh the proper considerations of educational trusteeship.

Labor's explanation of the boycott was quite different.

The *AFL-CIO News* of March 26, 1966 said: "The action of the New York City Board of Education . . . is a milestone in the historic relationship between the labor movement and education."

This statement, along with the AFT resolution on the Kingsport Press dispute, contains (or implies) a rationalization which has become a refrain in AFL-CIO and AFT literature in recent years, a rationalization for unionizing teachers and for using union tactics to force union dogma into the public schools. That refrain is that organized labor was responsible for the origin and spread of the free public schools in the United States. This is a bit of historical fiction. Union labor had virtually nothing to do with the founding and early development of the American public-school system, for the obvious reason that there was virtually no organized labor in this country prior to the middle of the nineteenth century. True, there was a sprinkling of unions of a sort beginning about 1800. But these were weak, small in number, and largely benevolent in nature, with little or no power to influence social or economic trends.

The historical fact is that from the time of the Massachusetts laws of 1642 and 1646, generally considered to be the forerunners of the American public-school system, to well into the twentieth century, the impetus for the development of the public schools came from many segments of society. But the major element appears to have been the settlers, the homesteaders, and the farmers. As soon as a new settlement was established, a common school and one or more churches came into existence. This devotion to the common school arose, of course, from the same ideal that has motivated organized labor to support the schools vigorously in later years. That ideal was for a better chance for the children to move up the economic and social ladder.

Of course, it is true that organized labor has, throughout its existence in the United States, fought for free schools. And from the early years of this century the labor movement has been aggressive and influential in its espousal of free schools. But this is a different thing from labor's asserting that it was the driving force in the origin and early development of the public-school system in the United States. If the assertion is that the masses of laboring people of all kinds, farmers as well as workers, formed the backbone of support for free schools, there is much evidence to sustain that assertion. But this is far different from the claim that labor unions were the motivating force in the first 250 years of the history of public schools in the United States.

Obviously, the price of unionism for teachers is too high in the case of the strike against the Kingsport Press, the price being loss of academic freedom and loss of the right of selection and use of textbooks solely on the basis of the quality of their contents. This is a case of a secondary boycott in which teachers affiliated with labor were asked to take on the unions' battle to win a strike through an economic boycott. Obviously the unions decided they could not win on the picket line or in negotiations with the company under existing law, but only with a nation-wide boycott. At this point it must be borne in mind that the complaining Kingsport unions had exercised their legal rights under Federal labor law and their appeals for interference by the National Labor Relations Board were rejected by that board on the grounds that the company was not guilty of unfair labor practice but was within its legal rights. It must also be borne in mind that, nation-wide, some 60 per cent of the workers in the printing industry are unorganized, unaffiliated with organized labor. In fact, the issue here is the international union's attempt to enforce the pay scales of some New York City unions upon unions in other parts of the country.

Naturally, the unions resorted to the usual propaganda weapons of referring to what happened at Kingsport as strike-breaking and strike-busting, and to the replacements as scabs and scum. Yet the Federal law was not violated and the NLRB said as much. It will be noted that the proposal of UFT to the New York City Board of Education was worded in such a way as to leave the unions to define unfair labor practice. That definition, however, is the role of NLRB and the courts. To transfer this authority to the unions themselves is to invite tyranny.

But the unions did not stop with the pressures of UFT and AFT. The unions related to the typographers' union—notably the bookbinders' and the local typographers' unions—conducted a national campaign to get local school superintendents and boards to ban the books printed at the Kingsport Press. The Cleveland School Board gave way, in part, to the pressures. And the Seacaucus, New Jersey Board succumbed and notified Kingsport Press in a letter on December 8, 1965, but rescinded its action on December 14, presumably after learning the full facts.

Seniority and Standardization

Two other good reasons why the price of affiliation with trade unions is too high for teachers are the entrenched policies of the unions regarding seniority and standardization. Neither of these policies are appropriate or feasible in the public schools.

The policy of seniority (that is job preference or priority on the basis of years of service in a given industry) simply will not work in a school, or perhaps in any professional endeavor, because the principle assumes a mass approach to an industry and ignores areas of specialization. This was illustrated in the costly, long-drawn-out 40-day union strike against the five

Author's note. The reader who desires a comprehensive description of the Kingsport Press Case should read *The Kingsport Strike*, by Sylvester Petro, New Rochelle, New York: Arlington House, 1967.

newspapers in New York City in April, May, and June 1966. The American Newspaper Guild insisted that all writers, regardless of specialization, be ranked according to seniority on the five papers, as if they all had been members of one staff, and that those with the longest tenure receive priority in employment on the papers remaining after the merger. This created an impossible situation for the three remaining papers (the *Herald Tribune* having gone out of business during the strike). For example, a given paper might find itself saddled with too many sports writers, fashion writers, or whatever, and too few or none for other specialities. This impasse was finally resolved by about half of the ANG members agreeing to resign.

The operation of the seniority principle in a given high school, for example, would inevitably end up with teachers in assignments for which they had little or no preparation. There has already been too much of this, largely as a result of the shortage of qualified teachers in certain fields. The application of the seniority principle to teaching would, in the long run, make a shambles of a school system, with, conceivably, kindergarten teachers assigned to teaching physics in the high school or vice versa.

The principle simply will not work in the schools.

Equally unworkable in the public schools is the standardization of work rules. The basic obligations of a profession cannot be reduced to a hard and fast formula of hours and duties. The eight-hour day (or less) certainly is feasible and acceptable in industry. But the full responsibility of teaching children cannot be confined to an 8:00-to-5:00 schedule or any other fixed set of hours. The period of classroom performances can, of course, be prescribed in hours, and is. But much of the essential part of teaching is elsewhere; preparation for classes, grading of papers, individual pupil guidance, study, reading—all of these cannot be encompassed within a standardized format.

Refusal of UFT in New York to permit teachers to remain after school for 30 minutes for a closed-circuit TV presentation by the school administration is an illustration of the point.

Here is a bit of relevant satire from the pen of columnist Art Buchwald in a syndicated column:

"Win One For Hoffa!"

Mr. James R. Hoffa of the Teamsters' Union has offered to organize all the professional athletes in the United States into his union. The sport that needs it the most, they say, is pro football. While there may be many advantages to having the pro footballer players in the Teamsters' Union, there could be some disadvantages, as you will see if you come into the locker room of the Washington Toughskins. It is half time and the Toughskins are behind 34 to 0.

The coach is standing in front of his blackboard.

"You're playing like a bunch of bums. Higgledorf, why didn't you take out the left end on play number 31?"

"I'm not supposed to take out ends. The union contract says I only have to take out tackles. If I took out the end, I'd be taking a job away from a blocking back."

The coach, trying to keep his temper: "All right, let's forget that. Mickazinski, why did you drop that pass that was right in your arms?"

"I caught my quota for the half. If I caught another one, the guys would have thought I was trying to speed up the game."

"Well, if you drop another pass, I'm pulling you out of the game and putting Wallnicki in."

"You can't do it. I've got three years seniority over Wallnicki. If you pull me out, the entire team walks off the field."

The coach clenches his teeth. "Harrison, you're the foreman as well as the quarterback. Can't you get any more work out of the men?"

Harrison says, "You're lucky we're here at all. We're not supposed to play on Sunday."

The coach says, "But you're getting time-and-a-half."

"We want double pay, and we also want to be paid for the time we spend going to and from the locker room."

"All right, bring it up at contract time. But right now I'm concerned with winning the game. The defense has been lousy. What happened to you, Brantowski, when they made that hole through off center?"

"I was resting. It says here. 'The linebackers are entitled to take a rest after every three plays.' If I didn't take that rest, I would have been fined by the union."

The coach wheels on his defensive back.

"And where were you, Eberhardt, when they threw the screen pass?"

"Screen passes aren't in my jurisdiction. My job is to cover the flanker. If you want me to cover screen passes, you're going to have to get authorization from the local."

"Okay, okay," the coach says. "Now I wasn't going to tell you this, but it looks like I've got to. Just before Jimmy Hoffa went to the Supreme Court to appeal his jail sentence, he said to me, 'Coach, if ever things get rough, and the team is down, and they're getting the hell beat out of them—tell them to win one for The Hoffa.' "

Tears start welling in the players' eyes.

"Gee, coach," the halfback sobs, "You wouldn't be kidding us?"

The coach looks at them. "Those were the last words Jimmy Hoffa said to me. Well, what do you say, team?"

The foreman jams on his helmet and shouts, "Let's go out there, guys, and murder the bums."

Union Dogma in the Classroom

Labor's drive to raid teachers' professional organizations goes far beyond the concern for teacher welfare. Apparently labor expects in return to be presented in a favorable light in classroom discussions of unions and their virtues.

Here are pronouncements of a vice-president of the AFL-CIO.

> A fiery plea to educate the nation on the labor movement by capturing the classroom was made today to the 10th annual convention of the New Mexico State AFL-CIO at the Alvarado.
>
> Herrick Roth, president of the Colorado State Labor Council, told delegates the labor movement will not reach its ultimate in America until "union shop signs are hanging in every classroom."
>
> He said the teachers of America have not yet realized the value of the labor movement to them. "Teachers need to know," he said, "that they must get more deeply involved in the labor movement."
>
> "The trade of teachers must have union shops," Mr. Roth said. The labor movement needs to be taught not from a book, he added, but by teachers who understand its value to the nation. And he emphasized that they do not now understand.
>
> Roth stressed his belief that the labor movement "is the only hope of this country and the world."
>
> And he added that if labor is able to get its perspective into the homes and schools, no legislator will ever again raise the issue of right-to-work in this state.[7]

Of course big labor has every right to expect of teachers a fair assessment of its aims and its goals, what it has done for the working man, and what it may reasonably be expected to do in the future. There is no justification for bias in a teacher's discussion of these matters, just as there is no justification of teacher bias in discussion of the position of businessmen, lawyers, farmers, or doctors.

But big labor has no right, legal or moral, to expect preferred treatment in such discussions. The price of teachers' affiliation with trade unions is too high if teachers are expected to present such preferred treatment. Such treatment would violate both academic freedom and academic authority.

Use of Teachers in Labor's Battles

Many of the proponents of teacher affiliation with the labor movement have jeered at the notion that labor would use teachers to fight its battles.

This is, in large measure, refuted by the preamble of the UFT Constitution in New York which reads:

> The objective of the United Federation of Teachers shall be to cooperate to the fullest extent with the labor movement and to work for a progressive labor philosophy, to awaken in all teachers a labor consciousness and a sense of solidarity with labor.

Certainly Charles Cogen, President of AFT, has been categorical in his advocacy of thrusting the teacher unions into full-scale involvement with the trade unions.

For example, in his address before the Forty-ninth Annual Convention of AFT, in Los Angeles in August 1965 he said:

> Closely intertwined with our need for greater influence over state legislation is the need for greater integration of our union into the labor union movement. It is a simple, incontrovertible fact that where we have been successful we have been closely allied with the rest of organized labor. I can say unequivocably that in New York City, we could not have succeeded without the support of our brothers and sisters in the other AFL-CIO unions, and I dare say that the same is true in Chicago, Detroit, Cleveland, Philadelphia and many a smaller school district. I wish to state in no uncertain terms that any AFT local which is not affiliated with its appropriate AFL-CIO city central body and state federation—and we have all too many such dangling locals, unfortunately—is not a union in the complete sense.
>
> Every AFT member knows the practical need for making sure that our brothers and sisters in other unions are there when we need them. They will be ready to help us if we are "there" when they need *our* support. Such solidarity is imperative, even though we know that the labor movement, including ourselves, has some shortcomings.

There have been cases where the teachers' unions have gone on picket lines and even on strike to aid other unions. In Granite City, Illinois, as has been mentioned, the AFT local supported a strike by janitors and cafeteria workers and closed the schools on April 6, 1964. In New York the teachers' union locals were asked to picket a department store in sympathy with the members of another union. In New York City, as previously stated, in the summer of 1964 the United Federation of Teachers called out the city's recreation workers. This occurred during the Harlem riots, but it proved an effective organizing ploy for UFT.

LABOR'S TAX POLICIES. Time and again—for examples, in Indiana, Philadelphia, Oklahoma, Louisville, Toledo, Kentucky, St. Louis, New Orleans, and Jefferson Parish, Louisiana—big labor has turned its back on teachers when tax proposals to increase teachers' salaries came up against the tax biases of workers. The philosophy has been that labor will help teachers if somebody else can be made to pay the bill. This position is no different than that of chambers of commerce, the Farm Bureau, the National Association of Manufacturers, or any other vested-interest group. Where, therefore, is the deep attachment of labor to teachers' economic problems?

This tax problem to support schools and the persistent opposition of AFL-CIO to excise taxes is one of the biggest, if indeed not the biggest, millstone around the neck of AFT in its drive to affiliate teachers with labor. Time after time, AFT and its locals have been compelled to support AFL-CIO policy and oppose sales taxes. In many cases, the sales tax has been the only source for improved school support and teachers' salaries. As long as AFT is bound to labor policy, it will be compelled to continue to oppose the sales tax.

The Indiana Story

The Indiana story of 1963 is a case in point. It illustrates rather clearly that big-labor support of teachers' salaries is a sometime thing.

Robert H. Wyatt, Executive Secretary of the Indiana State Teachers Association and NEA President in 1963–64, in his more than a quarter of a century of service to the ISTA, has earned a solid reputation as an effective

What's Bob Wyatt Got That We Haven't Got?

battler for the schools and teachers. His achievements, however, have made him the target of certain newspapers and business interests who resent his effectiveness with the legislature.

Wyatt's long patience and his silence in the face of the extravagant claims of the unions exploded in 1963 in an editorial in the *Indiana Teacher*:

Acres of Diamonds in His Own Backyard

The Indiana Supreme Court has rejected by a unanimous vote the efforts of the AFL-CIO Union to block the collection of the Sales Tax which was passed for school purposes.

The AFL-CIO suit blocked the collection of the tax from July 1 to October 24 and in so doing cost the public schools $22 million in state funds.

What does this mean to you? It is the equivalent on a state-wide basis of approximately $650 per instructional unit in the local school systems of this state. It cost thousands of teachers badly needed increases in salaries. It forced local school tax rates to unprecedented heights.

The Indiana State Teachers Association fought this case through the Indiana Supreme Court in support of the State of Indiana and the Governor and the Lieutenant Governor. We did so because in the final analysis it proved to be the only means by which the schools of Indiana could be saved from shortened school terms in at least one-fourth of the communities, and from disastrous financing and tax rates in all.

It is a little ridiculous that letters have been received in this office from teachers

> *in certain communities stating that the Union is now seeking to get the money from the Supreme Court victory for the teachers.*
>
> The program of the Indiana State Teachers Association in the 1963 Legislature, with the aid of other individuals and groups, produced increases in state funds equivalent to approximately $1,460 per instructional unit. This amount is now reduced by approximately $650 due to the AFL-CIO suit, but the schools may look forward to a net gain of approximately $810.
>
> The teachers of Indiana should read the facts of current history. In the past 10 years, annual state funds appropriated for schools have risen from $64,300,000 to $155,200,000. In the same decade, the average salary paid instructional personnel has risen from $4,047 to an estimated $6,460.
>
> From these facts, it is not difficult to compute that state funds have risen from $2,663 per instructional unit in 1953–54 to an appropriated amount of $5,223 for 1963–64, which is now reduced by the AFL-CIO suit to $4,574. . . .
>
> *Everybody in this state—politicians, press, public, taxpayers, opponents of adequate schools—everybody except school teachers seem to know the driving force [ISTA] behind this progress in education—seems to understand the broad, comprehensive, all-round program that has enhanced the image of the organized teaching profession to the place where its position and point of view are held in respect.* [Italics supplied by author.][8]

The background of this editorial presents an interesting example of how easily some teachers can be confused about issues and facts. During the 1963 session of the Indiana Legislature, the ISTA was successful in securing an increased appropriation of some $100 million a year for the ensuing biennium for the schools. This increase approximated $1,500 for each teacher unit in the state, from which teachers had reason to expect substantial increases in salaries.

A case was filed in an Indiana circuit court in July 1963 questioning the constitutionality of the 2 per cent sales tax, the major source of revenue for the increased appropriation. The suit was supported by the Indiana State AFL-CIO, the Indiana Farm Bureau, and the Indiana State Chamber of Commerce. The court ruled out the sales-tax collection. The ISTA appealed to the state supreme court, and in October the lower court was reversed and the tax upheld. But in the meantime, the schools had lost $22 million in expected revenue and teachers had their anticipated raises cut proportionately.

Of course the state AFL-CIO had every right to institute such a suit, even if successful court action would cripple the schools, because this was a matter of basic tax philosophy. But apparently what roused Wyatt's ire was that some members of the teachers' union were now claiming credit for the legislation and for the court victory; and some teachers naively accepted this assertion.

AFL-CIO TAX POSITION. The Indiana story points up an opinion of organized labor on what kinds of taxation are appropriate for the support of the schools

—an opinion which is bound to cause negative reactions among most teachers.

As it has every right to do, labor has consistently opposed many of the flat-rate taxes such as sales and cigarette taxes. Labor opposes these taxes on the grounds that they fall mainly and unequally on the working man. Labor has also opposed increases in property taxes, taxes on beer, and other taxes which its organizations consider regressive. As a general rule, labor cannot seem to bring itself to accept wholeheartedly anything but graduated income taxes on individual and corporate incomes. Yet it is debatable whether the regressive taxes hit the worker harder than the income tax.

Teachers' professional organizations have generally supported all these types of taxes for support of the public schools. Labor seems to pass over the fact that the cost of public-school support cannot be met solely by state and local income taxes.

Currently, more than 40 per cent of school funds provided by the states comes from sales taxes, less than 20 per cent from income taxes.

THE PHILADELPHIA STORY. The Indiana story has been told. The Philadelphia story is another indication of labor's secondary interest in teachers' salaries.

The Philadelphia Board of Education, in 1965, backed by the Philadelphia Teachers Association (an affiliate of NEA and Pennsylvania State Education Association), and, originally, by the Philadelphia Teachers Union, proposed to the Pennsylvania Legislature certain sales, liquor, and hotel taxes to provide badly needed funds for the Philadelphia schools.

Angered at the slow action and accusing the board of education of bad faith in not pushing for passage of the legislation, the Philadelphia Teachers Union picketed the board offices at the time when the board had organized a motor cavalcade to the state capitol at Harrisburg to lobby for the legislation.

Suddenly, the members of the PTU had the rug pulled out from under them by the parent body, the AFL-CIO—at least by those AFL-CIO unions that had a vested interest in defeating the proposed taxes. Almost at the time the PTU was picketing the board because of alleged nonaction, the labor unions affiliated with PTU deserted it, leaving the members of the teachers' union to withdraw with red faces.

The Philadelphia *Evening Bulletin* said editorially:

> The outright opposition of the Pennsylvania AFL-CIO to parts of the Philadelphia school tax program, coupled with the fact that the Philadelphia AFL-CIO Council has now reversed its executive Board and withdrawn its support for the package, reduces the chances for enactment of the taxes.
>
> This is unfortunate because the schools need money and the hour is late.
>
> The state labor body specifically opposes the proposed taxes on tobacco and alcoholic beverages, and has already notified legislators to that effect. The action

of the Philadelphia Council presumably leaves the decision on whether to fight parts or all of the package up to its component unions. And Philadelphia locals representing hotel, restaurant and brewery workers and musicians have indicated that they will fight the taxes which would affect their particular industries.

The fact that the state labor body got into the act at all points to one of the great weaknesses in the need to have Philadelphia school taxes authorized by the Legislature, and it offers a strong argument for home rule. Why should out-of-city organizations have a strong voice in determining the level and type of support which Philadelphians can give to their public schools?[9]

What about the alleged miracles performed by collective bargaining and strikes in getting salary gains for teachers? How much of this is a mere selling pitch?

In the spring of 1966 AFT issued a report on teachers' salaries in school systems enrolling 6,000 or more pupils,[10] claiming a salary advantage of $831 in districts where AFT locals had bargaining rights. *The American Teacher*, February 1966, gave the following explanation for this claim:

1. That the union teacher, by his very presence, prods the school board into giving teachers a raise.
2. That the competition of a teachers' union has beneficial effects on teacher militancy.
3. That the union teachers win the bargaining elections and negotiate aggressively for all teachers.

The NEA Research Division issued a dissenting memo[11] with the following foreword:

> The members of the NEA Research Division staff who prepared this memorandum undertook the task reluctantly. The role of the Research Division is to produce factual research data on problems confronting American education. To divert attention from this positive role in order to analyze a piece of misleading propaganda has been done with some distaste.

This memo points out that (1) teachers' salaries depend largely upon the economic strength of the school system, (2) AFT locals are organized chiefly in high-income states, (3) highest local-salary schedules are predominantly in nonunion systems, and (4) professional associations are in overwhelming majority in winning sole negotiation rights.

On the salary issue, the memo pointed out that in its annual study of schedules in districts enrolling 6,000 or more pupils, the 1965–66 study found that of the 101 highest schedules (of 1,071 reporting districts) 66 were from school systems having no AFT locals at all, and in only one of these 101 districts did an AFT local have exclusive rights in negotiating the salary schedule.

With reference to the AFT claim that "union teachers are winning the bargaining elections," the memo suggests that this is a bit of fiction. Citing

Connecticut, Michigan, and Wisconsin, the memo points out that union teachers have not mustered enough following to permit them to enter election contests in 566 districts in the three states. Under the laws in these states, teachers' organizations may be accorded sole negotiation tights by stipulation where no contest exists and where local teachers approve. Professional associations were thus recognized in 562 districts, while the union was recognized in one district. Moreover, where the unions did enter contests the professional association received the majority vote in 30 out of 31 elections in Connecticut, 45 of 63 in Michigan, and 18 of 23 in Wisconsin. Of these 117 elections, the professional association won 93, or 78 per cent, of the elections. Combining stipulations and elections, teachers have chosen the professional associations in 655 out of 685 school systems, or 96 per cent, in the states of Connecticut, Michigan, and Wisconsin.

The so-called magic formulas for bludgeoning out of school boards ever-increasing economic gains for teachers apparently are grossly over-rated. In the first place, local boards do not have a cornucopia of economic resources to be bludgeoned out of. Unlike private industry they cannot pass on added wages forced by a strike, to the consumer, in the form of higher prices of products, the school boards are limited by existing legal provisions. Currently some 40 to 50 per cent of school revenues come from the state governments.

The percentages are much higher in some states. The property tax is the heart of local support, and in many cases that source has reached its potential. If this be true, how can any bargaining weapon, either collective bargaining or professional negotiation, force more economic rewards for teachers from local school boards? In isolated cases, it might be possible to force substantial gains at the local level, but such cases will be few.

It follows, therefore, that additional money is increasingly coming from state appropriations, and in the future the really significant increases must come from state and, perhaps, Federal sources. And what influence is almost exclusively responsible for added state money for the schools?

The answer to that question is so obvious as to defy argument. The influence for added state money is the state education associations. So, in most places, whatever fulminations, hurrahs, and bombast may be broadcast about miracle weapons, any increases in teachers' salaries that may be forthcoming will not often arise from local revenues but from state sources, at least until there is substantial general federal support. All the miracle weapons can do is to fight for the added funds the state education associations can secure through state legislation.

A good example of the difference between the positions of the unions and the professional associations occurred in Oklahoma. After repeated rebuffs by the governor, the legislature, and the people through defeat of referenda proposals to enforce financial support of the schools, the Oklahoma Education

Association vigorously supported legislation proposing a sales tax for the schools. The legislation was referred to the people for approval and was soundly rejected. The state AFL-CIO and the AFT locals had vigorously opposed the tax. After defeat of the proposal at the polls, the few AFT locals called upon the OEA to join with them in "solving" the school financial problems. The OEA and NEA proceeded to impose sanctions on the state—and got remedial action.

St. Louis Blues

The *St. Louis Globe Democrat*, incensed by the tactics of the local teachers' union, blasted the local editorially:

> The St. Louis Teachers Union, Local 420, which claims membership of about a third of the city's public school instructors, has flatly refused to support the proposed 29-cent school tax increase, in an attempt to bludgeon the Board of Education into meeting its terms over issues of policy and administration.
>
> This is an overt case of trying to intimidate the St. Louis school system at a time when the schools are critically in need of funds to maintain and improve the education of our children.
>
> In its arbitrary purpose, the union is clobbering its own self interest, all too often the case with union leadership. Twenty-three cents of the rate rise has been earmarked for boosting teachers' salaries and hiring more teachers. . . . There was never any justified reason for a teachers union in the first place. Teaching is a highly reputed profession. It is a tax-supported public function, a part of government.
>
> The Teachers Union in the St. Louis schools should be disbanded! It has jeopardized interests of the schools at a crucial time, when teachers above all should be helping with the new tax rate. . . . The Teachers Union has discredited itself. There was never any justification for its existence, as far as we can determine. It has now effectively proved a hindrance and obstructionist influence in St. Louis schools. It ought to be read out of existence by its own members.[12]

The New Orleans Fiasco

In an effort to force collective bargaining upon the New Orleans School Board, AFT's local there staged a three-day strike beginning on March 11, 1966. All schools operated and the strike failed. An interesting sidelight on this abortive strike is that many observers felt that it was timed to conflict with the opening of the campaign to induce voters to pass a 1 per cent sales tax for the schools, which were in deplorable condition financially. The proposed tax was backed by the school board and the professional associations. While the AFT local made no statements for or against the tax, the state AFL-CIO opposed it, as it did in similar elections in two other Louisiana cities. Press accounts that the AFT local actually was against the levy were not denied. This seems strange because without the sales tax there would have been nothing to bargain about. The tax was passed by the voters on May 3, the first local tax rise for schools in over a century. Nearly $8 million of the levy was allotted by the board to raise teachers' salaries.

Apparently, here was another case of a strike dictated by AFT to force a collective-bargaining election at the same time as the AFL-CIO policy against the sales tax was being imposed upon the teachers' union.

Question of Who Sets Educational Policy

The matter of determination of educational policy is where, above all, teachers' affiliation with labor will mean paying too high a price. Policy determination of educational matters by AFL-CIO will continue to happen to AFT. There is virtually no evidence that AFT has influenced the educational policies of AFL-CIO. The one outstanding example in which AFT did influence AFL-CIO policy was the resolution declaring NEA a company union. But this could hardly be termed educational policy. Rather, it was political in nature.

Charles Cogen, President of AFT, in late 1964 announced the decision of the AFT Executive Council to support the proposed Elementary and Secondary Education Act of 1965 (Public Law 89–10) and said that this action was taken "to bring AFT policy more in line with that of AFL-CIO." This decision was made without consultation with AFT membership, and the president of its largest local, the UFT in New York City, immediately protested (on the aid proposed in the program for private and parochial schools). As a result of the protest a mail vote of the membership was instituted by AFT. This poll was still in progress 60 days after the bill had been passed in Congress and been signed into law by the President. (NEA, incidentally, vigorously supported the measure.)

On the matter of freedom to formulate educational policy turns the crucial issue of teachers' affiliation with organized labor. This freedom is the point that many observers feel will, in the long run, be neither to the advantage of AFT or of AFL-CIO.

It is at this point that many observers feel that it is inappropriate for teachers to be affiliated with—to the point of becoming in effect a subsidiary —any other segment of our society, be it business, agriculture, labor, or whatever. AFT's classic response to this viewpoint is to accuse those who espouse it of being antilabor. This is of course nonsense. Any of these powerful groups could be as destructive of the independence of teachers as labor. All should be allies of teachers in the pursuit of the best possible education for children. But none should be in a policy-making role for teachers. Teachers must be in a position to present all viewpoints in the classroom with balance and fairness.

Wherever and whenever teachers have been tied to a vested interest, and their policies dictated or influenced heavily by outside groups, virtually without exception teachers have been demeaned, their profession has been debased, and the public good has suffered.

It is easy for teachers to fall into the trap of affiliation with outside power groups because of the appealing sophistry that a certain amount of political and economic power is indispensible to the welfare of teachers and the interests of the schools. This reasoning, however, is illusory. The cost of such help is more than the profession should be willing to pay and more than the public interest can tolerate. Again, wherever and whenever affiliation of teachers with outside power structures has occurred, teachers have been used and education has tended to become doctrinaire and ideological. Always, of course, this has occurred under the aegis of cleverly phrased high-sounding rationales. Teachers will never achieve the status of a true profession by borrowing some other group's prefabricated image. Teachers will create their own professional image or they will have an inferior one.

This danger of exploitation of teachers by big labor has been stated by Donald Wollett, an industrial-relations attorney who has served as NEA consultant in some of the big-city elections:

> The only place in the United States where unionism has produced dividends for teachers is New York City. . . . The United Federation of Teachers owes its success in large measure to the support of Mr. Harry Van Arsdale and his confreres, who represent every important AFL-CIO union in the metropolitan area. And so the United Federation of Teachers is heavily indebted to its fellow trade unions. Creditors expect debts to be paid. . . . Thus the price of effective teacher unionism in New York City is the loss of the teachers' freedom to select textbooks [which], in the exercise of their professional judgment, will afford the maximum learning opportunities for their students.
>
> The Alberta Teachers' Association has demonstrated that the job can be done without sacrificing the freedom of teachers to teach. The National Education Association and its state and local affiliates have proved the same thing in this country. I invite a comparison of the group contracts negotiated by professional associations in Milwaukee, Wisconsin; Newark, New Jersey; Rochester, New York; and Denver, Colorado, with anything that has been accomplished by the Teachers' Union in the cities where it is the negotiating representative. These documents are tangible proof that the job can be done without forging chains on the freedom of teachers.
>
> Lest I be misunderstood, let me make it clear that I am not critical of trade unions for behaving like trade unions. I do not fault Albert Shanker, president of the United Federation of Teachers, for stating publicly that unionized teachers must help other unions achieve their objectives so that they can get the support which teachers need when they are in trouble.
>
> I believe in trade unions and I believe in collective bargaining, and I expect

unions to behave like unions. I think it was Arthur Goldberg who once said that it is not the job of a union to protect the public interest or to produce a better product; it is the job of the union "to protect the fellows."

But I do say that trade unionism is wrong for public education and wrong for public school teachers because it "protects the fellows" at the expense of their freedom to teach and at great cost to the quality of the education program.[13]

Big Business and Teachers

Obviously it would be unfair to inveigh against teacher's affiliation with organized labor without applying this same principle to other powerful segments of society. Through the years, although there has been no organizational affiliation nor has there been informal connection with big business, the close ties of schools (especially boards and administrators) to the business community is subject to several questions, if not criticism. The ties have been informal and incidental, largely through businessmen serving on school boards, through education committees of local and national chambers of commerce, and through participation of administrators in local civic clubs heavily oriented to business interests.

That these close relationships with the economic and civic power structures of the communities have yielded some significant fruits for the schools, there can be little question. But schools and teachers must be as wary of undue influence of business (or any other power structure) as they must be of big labor.

Just now, with the flow of Federal money into education, big business has suddenly discovered the schools as a source of inviting sales and profits. Several hundred giant corporations have, through mergers or establishment of subsidiaries, gone into the educational textbook and hardware business. Of course this is entirely legitimate and understandable.

Here, too, schools and teachers must be extremely cautious in protecting their independence. While no efforts such as labor has attempted have been made or probably will be made to entice teachers into formal affiliation with big business, nevertheless there are subtle dangers of undue influence upon the curriculum, teaching methodology, and educational materials. There are proposals that the most efficient way to high-quality education is for school boards to contract with business concerns to operate the schools.

Schools and teachers are as obligated to reject the bid of business to take over the schools as they are to reject the danger of labor doing so.

The price is not right—either for teachers or society—in either instance.

15

What of the Future?

> It would be hard to over-emphasize the importance of pluralism in helping a society to escape the cycle of growth and decay. The ever renewing organization is not one which is convinced that it enjoys eternal youth. It knows that it is forever growing old and must do something about it. It knows that it is always producing deadwood and must, for that reason, attend to its seedbeds. The seedlings are new ideas, new ways of doing things, new approaches.
>
> —John W. Gardner[1]

A strong case can be made for the proposition that the major problem of education, if not the major need, is to achieve a viable, effective, and unified organization of teachers.

Thus any unbiased observer must decry the organizational fight between the AFT and the NEA. It is, from one angle, a tragedy for teachers and for the future of education. The divisiveness engendered, the dissipation of energies that should be devoted to securing the needed resources for education the diversion of organization funds—all these are regrettable.

Certainly any thoughtful person wishes for some magic formula to heal the widening schism. But on the assumption that such a formula is not likely to arise quickly, if at all, what then of the future?

First, despite James Carey's polemic, it is clear that teachers can afford integrity and they can afford it without unionism.

Second, it is now reasonably clear that the price of affiliation with teachers' unions may be too high and that the price of affiliation with professional organizations may be too low.

These theses raise some fundamental questions.

What is to be the outcome of the current all-out drive of organized labor to seize control of the nation's public-school teachers?

Who will win the juridictional fight? More important, who will win the ideological fight?

What kind of organization will teachers predominantly choose: the labor-oriented organization or the professional association? Is teaching to become a craft or will it continue to drive for recognized professional status?

Can the NEA withstand the concerted assaults of labor and other groups jealous of its power and influence on education?

Above all, can the NEA renew itself in time? Can it refine its structure to meet new demands?

These are the crucial questions.

Probably neither organization will continue in its present form. The needs of teachers appear to call for an organization with much of the militancy of the unions and most of the professional aspirations of the NEA.

Prophecy is a risky sort of business. Life is flowing too fast, too tempestuously for any fallible human being to be cocksure about what will happen tomorrow even, let alone in the indefinite future.

Sir Richard Livingston once wrote:

> A river is always flowing; over most of its reaches the flow is so slow and peaceful that the direction of the current can hardly be discerned and may even be mistaken, but at times the stream bed falls rapidly and it hurries in a turmoil of broken water. As with rivers so with the individual; change is always taking place, but only at certain periods of life can it be clearly perceived. . . . So too with the State. It is always changing, for the most part imperceptibly. . . . But there come times when the nature of the pace or change is such that no one can mistake it. . . .[2]

Such a time is now. There is no difficulty in discerning the pace or change. The problem is assessing the true nature of it and what it portends. The hopeful prophet cannot be too hopeful.

Enthusiasm and partisan devotion may be fine ingredients for a rooting section but, as the saying goes, the outcome depends more on who has the horses.

The shrill boasting of organized labor at each new contract may be the cover up of a deep-seated frustration over the unprecedented problems it is facing. Likewise, the blatant trumpeting by the AFT of every miniscule happening as an "overwhelming victory" is simply the outward expression of a deep inner sense of insecurity. And NEA's continuing talk about the "sweet virtue of professionalism" (whatever that may mean) is losing some of its power. Such bombast ought to be readily discernible to thoughtful people. But so inured have we become to the brash, loudmouthed, extravagant "messages" of our commercial advertising that many soak it all up as the truth. The chips are down. What does the future hold?

This observer seeks to avoid the cheering-section approach.

But, despite the dangers of prophecy, the author feels that in the long look it seems that the winner of the struggle for the allegiance of America's teachers has to be the free, independent, voluntary, unaffiliated professional association—whether it be NEA or some other such organization—but with vastly changed procedures and objectives.

With all their weaknesses—and the professional associations have plenty which only time, new perspectives, and a new sense of responsibility of their members will cure—this observer believes that the professional associations will eventually win the fight. At least they will win the struggle against becoming adjuncts of organized labor. That the professional associations may themselves be drastically changed in this struggle seems too obvious to debate.

But repulsing the labor drive is only a part of the task ahead. A much more difficult part is the professional associations' remaking themselves into organizations that can unify teachers' objectives and cure the distressing fragmentation of teachers' organizational loyalties.

Of course it would be naive to predict the quick folding of the teachers' unions as such. They will hang on, prosper a bit, and starve a bit, with bursts of growth, plateaus, and declines fluctuating with conditions in society generally. (They will certainly win in some more of the larger cities.) And their winning is, momentarily at least, probably good to act as a needle and ever-present stimulant to the existing and servicing professional associations.

Admittedly, the prediction that the professional associations will endure is based upon certain assumptions. If these assumptions are not implemented, then the prediction may not hold.

The Giant Ifs

It is easy to identify and evaluate the opinions, the dedications, the preferences of public-school teachers. But any predictions about the future of professional associations will depend basically upon whether teachers are enabled to achieve the self-realization, the joy of creativeness, the dignity of identification and recognition which inevitably nurture the soul of every human being. This is where the assumption, the giants *ifs* come in.

NEW PERSONNEL RELATIONSHIPS. First, there must be a new era of personnel relationships in school systems. And professional associations must drive vigorously to this end. The present vertical and unilateral bureaucracy must give way to horizontal, co-equal, collegeal roles.

This is the key not only to teacher satisfactions but to ever-improving school programs. Enlightened administrators and enlighted school boards are beginning to sense this, and both are moving now to bring such relationships into reality. The big question is whether they will move fast enough. Unfortunately, at the moment there are not enough administrators and school boards who are acting in this direction. Unfortunately also, there are still too many of both who cling to the archaic notion that their positions and their legal power set them apart, endowing them to speak unilaterally and arbitrarily. Thus both administrators and school boards instinctively brace themselves against giving to the teachers freely and willingly a place of real dignity and respect in the policy-making structure, in a venture to which the teachers are devoting their lives.

In the resistance to the coming of a new day, there is always the anguished cry: "Teachers are trying to take over and run the school system." There is always the breast-beating defense: "We represent the people; we have the legal authority." The chief threat to local autonomy in the management of schools is neither the NEA nor the teachers, as some boards charge; it is the unwillingness of some boards to adapt to changing conditions.

Both of these reactions by school boards are largely rationalizations of the *status quo*. Any knowledgeable administrator in the New York City schools, if he is in a confidential mood, will admit without reservation that an encrusted board and administrative bureaucracy literally drove New York City teachers into the union. Moreover, he will say that progressive administrative regulations had been on the books for thirty years before unionization —and ignored' The teachers thought they had no place to go for redress. It could happen here—anywhere.

Except in rare instances, teachers don't want to take over control of the schools. They don't want to usurp the legal authority of the board. They don't want to bypass the superintendent or infringe upon his very important role. They want to be listened to, talked to, and given honest consideration before decisions of importance to them are made. They want recognition and participation and voice in policy determination. They want to be a real part in the creative task of shaping the best possible educational program.

They are fed up with role of the timid hired-hands, with being told when to come and go. They know that they are professionally competent to contribute significantly to constant improvements in the school system. And they yearn to be treated as competent professionals. In fact, they are going to demand it in the future. They know that their own indifferent standards of preparation and licensure in the past marked them as only playing at being professionals and justified such inferior status. But they know that this period is past—or rapidly passing.

Lieberman, in a comprehensive analysis of the problem of teachers' strikes, points out that society must find ways to provide teachers, as well as other employees, with reasonable bargaining power.[3] Especially is this true if teachers are to be enjoined by law from striking or if they voluntarily renounce the right to strike.

The principle of simple justice would seem to demand such provisions. It is very easy for honest people to use unwittingly the majesty of the law to deny teachers their fundamental human rights, to deny them any measure of voice in determining their conditions of work or employment. This can be done in good conscience, under the sacrosanct name of the sovereignty of the state. One assumes that there never was a reactionary school board or an arbitrary superintendent who did not believe he was acting under God's will because the law was on his side. The law must be changed.

The old, old privileged sovereignty of the state, the concept, "the king can do no wrong," the injunction that a plain citizen cannot sue the state or any subdivision thereof—all these are falling by the wayside because of decisions of the courts. Schools and teachers are being sued, by decisions of state courts, on almost every conceivable ground. The same is happening to whoever governs the schools.

The civil-rights issue is a case in point. Always the states standing on state rights invoked the majesty of the law. But whose law? A prejudiced majority in the enactment and enforcement of law can no longer be used to deny human rights either to Negroes or to teachers, or to any other demeaned group.

There have been teacher strikes; there will predictably be others. There will be others whether or not the NEA or AFT will them, condone them, condemn them, or reject them, because conditions sometimes go beyong the point of human endurance. By the nature of their work, their preparation, and occupational viewpoints, teachers as a group are a dedicated lot. There will, of course, be individuals among them who do not care about these attitudes very deeply, who are constantly looking for rebellious causes. However, there are relatively few of these in the total teaching personnel.

But the number could grow if the state cannot or will not seek a better balance in the teacher's negotating position. What needs to be done, probably—although no one is wise enough at the moment to prescribe precisely how to do this—is to enact special state legislation spelling out the right of teachers to negotiate conditions of work and the right of appeal. The inevitable consequence of failure to cure this void will be enactments forcing teachers into labor procedures. A law spelling out teachers' negotiating rights was proposed to the New York Legislature in 1966. This law was passed and became effective September 1, 1967. This law holds great promise of a solution to teachers' problems. It is not far-fetched to assume that school boards in the future, as is now largely the case with regents of universities, will become to some extent legislative bodies enacting the policy recommendations of the staff. Of course, this will not be an exclusive function of boards, but will be an important one.

CHANGES IN THE PROFESSIONAL ASSOCIATIONS. The second big *if* is that the professional associations must seek to refine the quality and nature of their services to teachers.

The old, tired routines dressed up in neat, nice slogans and clichés, in which appeals to professionalism are supposed to uplift their members and still all dissent, are obsolete. In the future these professional associations must concern themselves with the bread-and-butter issues without diminishing their efforts to make teaching a profession in every real meaning of the word. After all, professionals are entitled to a decent pay scale and a decent standard of living; they can't and won't any more, subsist at low levels and receive in recompense the knowledge that they have been ever faithful to the task.

The school year 1966–67 opened with a shortage of teachers so vast as to shock even the experts. The shortage was largely a result of new Federal programs draining off almost 100,000 qualified teachers, but losses to industry because of higher salaries and drains of the war in Vietnam were sizeable factors. The nation must take a new, realistic look at the status of teaching.

One of the big drives has to be for fringe benefits. In this area have been the big gains of labor in recent years. Between 1933 and 1960 wages of workers in industry moved up 500 per cent, but fringe benefits increased 3,500 per cent.[4] Every teacher should have adequate insurance paid for in part by the school board: life insurance, accident insurance, liability insurance, automobile insurance (damage and liability), burial insurance, unemployment-compensation insurance, and major-medical and hospital insurance. Retirement benefits should be upped to at least one half of the average salary during the five most lucrative years of the teacher's career. Moreover, more effective reciprocity provisions in state retirement plans must be effected so that teachers are free to move across state lines and not remain indentured in a given state.

Recently there have been serious proposals that the Federal Government guarantee (because of automation, the increased productivity of our society, and the diminution of job opportunities in many occupations) an adequate annual wage to every American, whether he works or not. It would seem therefore not to be radical to make a proposal to provide teachers who have spent 30 to 40 years in dedicated service with a retirement benefit roughly equivalent to at least half their earnings in their best-paid years. Moreover, the Federal Government now provides most of these benefits for its employees.

And salary: there should be no dilly-dallying in the drive to achieve teachers' salaries of $10,000 to $20,000. In fact, Federal funds eventually must be the base for establishing such a scale nation-wide. To spend half as much on a child's education in Mississippi as in New York makes no more sense than tolerating similar differentials in teachers' pay in these two states, or anywhere else.

MORE PUBLIC INTEREST AND SPENDING. The public has to give up its traditional reliance upon lip service only to the importance of education and teachers.

This giving of lip service only is an historic posture. The public, however sincere, has simply assumed that all that was necessary to keep teachers in line, to keep them from pressing too much for adequate salaries and financial support of education, was to speak in extravagant terms of the essentiality of teachers and or education.

The time has come for such lip service to our public schools to end. The people of the United States are only now realizing that the truism about the importance of education and teachers is literally true. Sooner or later we shall have to match expenditures for defense with those for education. The education laws and appropriations passed by the Eighty-ninth Congress in 1965 constituted a significant step toward meeting the nation's commitment to education. But, as the President himself said this must be only a beginning.

OVERHAUL OF PROFESSIONAL ASSOCIATIONS. A fourth big if is whether the NEA and its affiliated state associations will move and move fast enough to bring about a greater democratization of their structures.

Whatever length one goes to, to disprove the litany of the teachers' unions that the NEA is a company union dominated by and run in the interests of administrators—and this writer has gone to some length to rebut this—one must not stop until he has destroyed whatever intimation of this that remains.

Like Caesar's wife, this is a matter in which not only must evil be avoided but the appearance of evil as well. No attempt has been made herein to make a definitive analysis of the respective state education associations on this charge. There is too little data that bears accurately on the point.

A survey of the practices of state education associations, made in October 1963 by the National Association of Secretaries of State Teachers Associations, revealed that the median percentage of classroom teachers in the delegate assemblies was 75; the median percentage in the governing boards was 50; and the median percentage on committees and commissions was 60.

The range in percentage of classroom teacher members of the state delegate assemblies was from 35 in Oklahoma to 95 in Alaska and Montana. Thirty-one of the states reported percentages of 70 and above. The range in percentage of classroom teacher members of the state association governing boards was from 8 in Oklahoma (this has now been changed—upward) to 83 in Arizona, and 27 states reported percentages of 50 or above.

The range in the percentage of teacher members on state association committees and commissions was from 20 in Iowa to 95 in Alaska; 24 states reported percentages above 60 and seven below 50.

But simple observation leads one to believe that some state associations tend to be dominated by administrators. At least there is heavy evidence of too many of the top offices consistently going to superintendents of schools. Obviously, it would be unfair to leave the observation at this point. It should be added that many of the state education associations are superbly balanced in regard to representation by people from various positions and specialties which make up their membership. This balance prevades the associations' structure, their elected offices, and their policy-making machinery.

Of course, the above observations are far from precise scientific accuracy. There are exceptions at many points and in many places. But they are a rough generalization of things as they appear to be or were in 1963.

To advocate precise proportional representation by position, group, or speciality in the membership of a professional association is of debatable wisdom.

The precise professional quota system is probably impossible and certainly undesirable. If this principle were applied to Congress, for example, the number of lawyers would be held to a handful, the number of college graduates would be insignificant, and the number of representatives with meager education would dominate Congress.

The problem is to select the best qualified people, whatever their positions or specialities. To argue that, since classroom teachers make up 90 per cent (let us say) of the membership of the NEA, therefore 90 per cent of NEA delegates and officers and members of committees and commissions should be classroom teachers, is sheer nonsense. This kind of fallacious reasoning would make of the professional associations the divisive, warring, bitter factions that impel most teachers to reject the teachers' union philosophy. The real key to democratization of the professional association is, as William Carr said at Denver: "Each member with one voice, one vote, no more and no less." It is assumed, of course, that this means one voice and one vote free and untrammeled and uninhibited. Such a vote and voice enable each member to exercise them in the interest of the group as a whole as well as furthering the parochial and essential interest of given segments within the whole.

The reform that has to come is a classroom-teacher unit at the local level. While the inclusive local associations work well in some places, in many places they do not. The fact, or the suspicion, of the inclusive association being a rubber stamp for the administration must be altered. Teachers are going to demand their own organization where problems and grievances can be discussed freely without fear of reprisal. Even if there is no intent by administrators to dominate the inclusive associations, there is always apprehension on the part of the teachers. Both administrators and classroom teachers will feel more secure with an untrammeled teacher unit. The plain fact is that administrator interference or domination is all too prevalent in many local associations. Some administrators automatically assume that any efforts to establish a free teacher association stem from trouble makers. There have been many cases where leaders in such movements have been fired or transferred. Such treatment has to end—and quickly—for the preservation of the professional associations.

In a recent study the NEA Research Division found in 1964–65 that, of all NEA local affiliates, 12 per cent were exclusively classroom-teacher organizations and 27 per cent of all urban affiliates were.

But professional associations clearly have yet a long way to go in updating structures and machinery to guarantee one vote and one voice, no more, no less, to every member.

Doubtless both the size and the delegate structure or the NEA Representative Assembly must be overhauled.

This proposed organizational housecleaning cannot be done by the NEA alone. It must be a joint effort of the national and state associations and the urban associations. For example, delegates to an NEA convention are selected by and within state associations. The NEA has no control over these elections. The NEA can and should accept leadership in stimulating needed revisions, but it cannot dictate them. The NEA itself recognizes this. Both the Department of Classroom Teachers and the NEA Representative Assembly adopted resolutions at the Seattle Convention, in 1964, requiring a study of restructuring the NEA. This two-year developmental study has been completed by an impartial team. Implementation of it must be made by the Representative Assembly.

New Directions for the NEA

That drastic reorganization of NEA structure is indicated is crystal clear. That new directions, services, and processes for the NEA are imperative is also crystal clear. One of the built-in weaknesses of any bureaucracy is that it tends to grow by accretion. Attrition rarely happens. Divisions or units hang on and often grow in size after the purposes for which they were created have been accomplished or become obsolete. This is true of the NEA.

The difficulty is in charting the needed new sweeps.

First, the NEA has to attack the problem of clarifying the processes of professional negotiation and sanctions. The situation is now confused, especially as to the real differences between professional negotiation and collective bargaining and between sanctions and strikes.

Many teachers, administrators, and school boards are honestly confused and can see no real differences between these two sets of processes. Obviously if professional people are confused, the public can be expected, almost universally to be so.

It is always easier to borrow from tradition and past practices than it is to create a new, unique set of procedures. What the NEA has to do is to derive truly professional approaches to these problems. Adopting the propaganda lines of the teachers' unions and emulating their tactics and strategy could be disastrous. If there are no real fundamental and abiding differences between the NEA approach and the unions' approach, teachers and public could more easily be persuaded that, if there is to be indeed a class war with a management pitted against labor or vice versa, then the teachers' unions have all the advantages. And under such conditions the unions could eventually supersede the professional associations.

The difficulty is that the only material available in these areas is labor legislation, court decisions regarding such legislation, and the experience of applying these to industrial employees.

However, some helpful new precedents are developing as a result of the President's executive order conferring the right of negotiations upon Federal employees and also as a result of similar provisions in certain cities, notably New York and Philadelphia, and in the laws of a few states, But it is apparent that organized labor instead of seeking to develop processes appropriate to public employees will seek gradually to impose collective bargaining and, eventually, the strike as used by nonpublic employees.

One reluctantly comes to the conclusion that the teaching profession must seek state legislation spelling out procedures for negotiations and for the settling of impasses through an appeals system—both within educational channels. This will be new and it will require the charting of hitherto uncharted procedures. (See Appendix B.)

This conclusion is arrived at because of two factors. First, teaching will eventually be forced into using labor processes and labor machinery because of the increasing pressures of the AFL-CIO to pass legislation conferring the right to collective bargaining for public employees, including teachers, in the respective states. This effort has been described elsewhere in this book. For the teaching profession to assume that, without positive action on its part, it will not be engulfed and swept into an alliance with organized labor whether it likes it or not, is simply naive to say the least.

What should be the ingredients of such legislation? This is a complex question. No complete answer is possible at the moment. It is an evolving, developmental process.

Some of the ingredients are readily apparent:

1. The declaration of teaching as a profession.
2. The declaration of the right to join or not to join an organization.
3. Spelling out the right to negotiate with school boards regarding conditions of work, personnel policies, grievance machinery, determination of salaries and other welfare provisions, and the right to participate in virtually all policy matters relating to the educational program.
4. Delineating machinery within education channels for settling impasses; in other words, guaranteeing the right of appeal.
5. Prohibiting the strike as a means of settling disputes but placing penalties such as fines and suspension of negotiation rights upon the association rather than upon its members.

THE 1967 NEW YORK LAW. The Public Employee Negotiation Statute was passed and signed into law on April 21, 1967, and became effective on September 1, 1967. This law resulted from the recommendations of the Governor's Committee on Public Employee Relations, called the Taylor Report.

The new law was developed after an intensive search for fair, workable legislation to supplant the old Condin-Wadlin Act, which had not served to prevent strikes of public employees, and in several instances proved to be virtually unenforceable.

Key provisions of the new law are:

1. Establishes for public employees the right to organization and representation for the purpose of collectively negotiating conditions of employment.
2. Repeal of the Condin-Wadlin Law.
3. Empowers public employers to establish procedures for determining the organization to represent the employees, to establish procedures to resolve impasses in the course of negotiations, and to enter into written agreements.
4. Establishes a public employment relations board, to assist local governments and school districts and employee organizations in resolving disputes, providing panels of qualified mediators or fact-finding boards.
5. Prohibits the strike by public employees.
6. Provides injunctive relief from strikes. Public employees who strike, and are found guilty of criminal contempt, are subject to fines not to exceed $250 or jail terms not to exceed 30 days.
7. Provides when an employee organization willfully disobeys a lawful mandate of a court of record may be fined for each day that such contempt exists, in amount equal to 1/52 of the total amount of membership dues of the organization, or $10,000, whichever is the lesser, in any event not less than $1,000 per day. In addition, representation rights of the employee organization may be forfeited for a period not to exceed 18 months including dues check off.

Emphases in this legislation are:

1. The rights of public employees are carefully spelled out, with every possible recourse for fair settlement of differences provided.
2. The setting up of a new, specialized mediation and fact-finding service—the Public Employment Relations Board—thus divorcing public employees from mediation by the state labor department (to which teachers generally object); and presumably, from the state education department, to which teacher union members generally object, both on the ground of partisan sympathies.

The penalties for violation of the strike prohibition, which under the old Condin-Wadlin Act were assessed against the individual striking teachers, are largely shifted in the new law to be assessed against the employee organization. All these provisions appear to be solid steps toward a fair and workable law.

One of the toughest problems is the determination of the role of the superintendent of schools in the future. The long ingrained belief of the professional association is that he is an equal member—equal in voice and vote with all other members of a school's professional staff—and that he is also the professional adviser of the board.

It is doubtful that boards of education are going to be willing to accept this concept. Increasingly, boards are insisting that the superintendent is exclusively their man; that he is their executive officer; that he represents them and only them. If the professional association's view of the superintendent breaks down, it probably will be at this point. This writer believes it will not come from pressures of teachers who reject the all-inclusive concept of the professional associations, although admittedly there are evidences of a growing trend of thought in this direction.

Such a development, should it eventuate, need not destroy the all-inclusive concept. After all, the unions attempt to serve both industrial workers and professional employees. The AASA could remain an integral part of the NEA structure pretty much as it is now. Of course, the teachers' unions, with some qualifications, embrace in their membership all administrative personnel except superintendents. Too, there are many all-inclusive unions in private industry. (The AFT Convention in the summer of 1966 for the first time adopted a resolution barring from membership nonteaching personnel from "principals on up" and barring unions of such members, but this was not made retroactive.)

The problem is to spell out the "inness" and the "outness" of administrative and supervisory personnel. In the negotiating unit the superintendent will be out. In all other matters of professional concern, both the superintendent and other administrative and supervisory personnel will be in. There is no good reason why all administrative and supervisory personnel (except the superintendent) cannot be included in the negotiating unit.

FUTURE STATUS OF NEA DEPARTMENTS. It has been pointed out that there are 33 departments affiliated with NEA, all but five of them wholly independent. But this plan of loose affiliation has built-in irrations for both NEA and the departments. It is obvious that this structure must be overhauled.

There appear to be two alternatives. (1) The departments could be made integral parts of the NEA, with membership in NEA being prerequisite to membership in a department. This was the original concept of departments. But over the years the departments steadily retreated from this concept. Presently, only members of a department's executive committee must hold NEA membership, except that if a new department is created, NEA membership is a prerequisite to department membership. It is extremely doubtful that many of the departments would now accept a return to the original concept. (2) The plan most likely to be acceptable both to the departments and the NEA would be to remove the NEA membership requirement completely, making such membership voluntary for any and all department members. A good guess is that this would stimulate NEA membership among members of departments. All departments would be expected to be wholly self-supporting, to pay rent on office space and furniture, and to finance fully custodial and utility services. Presently these expenses are paid by NEA from NEA membership funds. If the departments demand absolute independence, it would appear that this ought to apply to their financial support.

The Department of Classroom Teachers

Perhaps the knottiest problem facing the NEA is the future structure and status of the Department of Classroom Teachers. Presently, the DCT is an NEA unit dependent upon annual appropriations from the NEA. In almost every other aspect it is an autonomous unit, with its governing and directing bodies chosen by its members, and it is in large measure self-directing. However, as long as it is dependent financially upon the NEA, no fair appraisal could contend that it is wholly independent.

There are presently pressures that the DCT be made an independent NEA department subsisting on its own membership dues, electing its own official bodies (as it now does), and making its own policies (as is now largely the case.)

The key question here is what this change would portend for NEA income. It has been stated that at least 90 per cent of NEA membership consists of classroom teachers. It it is assumed that all classroom teachers would join the independent DCT and not the NEA, this would be disastrous for the latter. But this assumption does not necessarily, or even probably, follow.

ENLARGED SCOPE OF DEPARTMENT OF CLASSROOM TEACHERS. Whatever direction the restructuring of the NEA Department of Classroom Teachers takes, it seems obvious that the scope of its activities must be broadened.

William G. Carr, NEA Executive Secretary, saw this clearly at the outset of labor's drive to organize teachers. At a meeting of the NEA Executive Committee in Atlantic City in 1961, he recommended that the DCT become more visible in the teacher-welfare field. The DCT Executive Committee bluntly rejected this proposal on the grounds that the department would thereby project the image of teachers as pursuing only selfish goals.

The feeling of the DCT Executive Committee was that the best service it could perform for teachers, for NEA, and for the profession, was to continue its broad program of disseminating information on the total spectrum of the work of the NEA, with special emphasis upon the improvement of instruction.

Now it appears that the department might well be assigned responsibility for the salary and welfare consultant service, which includes the development and adoption of professional-negotiation procedures and agreements. Also, the newly created (in 1966) Division of Special Services might be assigned to DCT. (This would cover insurance, tax-sheltered annuities, mutual funds, and so on.) There are strong arguments that the newly created (in 1962) Urban Services Division should also function as an integral part of the Department of Classroom Teachers. Already there is a crucial struggle between the two for association funds, with the threat that the Urban Services Division will increasingly take over not only many of the functions of DCT but of other existing NEA units as well.

Adaptations in an Inclusive Association

Among the several major issues between the teachers' union and the professional associations—the NEA and its affiliated state and local associations—is the basic one of the exclusive classroom-teacher organization versus the inclusive membership organization. This is really overstating the issue since teachers' unions (prior to 1966) really exclude universally only superintendents of schools but accept other administrative personnel, although with some restrictions on voting and office-holding. Or they accept administrators' and supervisors' unions into affiliation much as the state and local affiliates of NEA, and NEA itself, accept affiliation of the specialized departments.

Perhaps the most difficult problem facing NEA and its affiliates is adaptations between total inclusion and total exclusion—adaptations both in structure and membership. That some adaptations must be made seems to be clear and inescapable.

Some accommodation to the inclusive membership must be developed which will at the same time protect the vital interests of teachers and allow the fullest possible participation of administrative and supervisory personnel. It is apparent that this can be done without wrecking the inclusive membership concept.

Obviously, AFT would dearly love to see NEA cut its own throat by embracing the union's persistent and loudly trumpeted concept of exclusive devotion to classroom-teacher interests. Its major propaganda efforts are toward driving NEA into this corner. NEA would achieve the ultimate in stupidity to accept any such unqualified philosophy. To do so would be a complete surrender to the alleged management-worker dichotomy in the schools. In the labor concept, the superintendent would be exiled to outer darkness. This is neither necessary nor justifiable, for reasons which have been stated repeatedly in these pages. It has been pointed out that AFT in

August 1966, after it had secured all the possible mileage out of the propaganda that it was the only true organization for classroom-teachers, when in fact there was little difference in its structure and NEA's, adopted a resolution excluding from future membership all administrators from principals and above. NEA has only to fall for this "sucker punch" to be pulled all the way into the labor posture.

It is not easy to chart a restructuring of the professional associations that will accomplish the ends of protecting teachers' interests and allowing participation of supervisors and administrators. Before we come to the NEA structure we must begin with the local affiliates. The situation currently with these local affiliates is somewhat chaotic, and under the stresses of new problems and issues, the structure is probably obsolete.

Section 4 of the NEA bylaws reads:

> Any local professional education association located within a city, county, or other local school administrative unit of any state, commonwealth, or the District of Columbia, shall be eligible for affiliation with the Association and shall be designated as a local affiliate. In addition, any association recognized as a local unit by a state affiliate shall be eligible for affiliation. A local professional education association shall be interpreted to mean any local organization of educators whether its membership is open to all professional educators, or all classroom teachers, or all administrators within the jurisdiction boundaries of the organization, or to all members of a university or college staff. Such affiliate shall be entitled to representation at meetings of the Representative Assembly as provided in Article VIII, Section 5 (one delegate and one alternate for each 100 active or life members, or major fraction thereof).

Obviously, under this provision a member holding membership in several local associations can be counted more than once—several times in fact—when the number of delegates to the NEA Representative Assembly is determined. The above bylaw should be amended to provide that there be a local association of classroom-teachers as an independent entity. The other possible affiliates could remain as an all-inclusive association or an administrators' association. It may be that a classroom-teachers' department of an all-inclusive local association would work universally and satisfactorily, but this is doubtful. It could in some situations. There is too much suspicion to be passed over lightly that the deliberations of all-inclusive associations tend to be inhibited by administrators' participation. Teachers contend that administrators' groups have their own separate organizations at state and national levels, and often at the local level in large school systems, to discuss their own peculiar problems. Why, these teachers ask, should not classroom teachers have this opportunity also? Why should classroom teachers be restricted exclusively to an all-inclusive organization? These contentions are not made in an antagonistic spirit, but in a spirit of fair play and reasonableness.

One other point: It appears that the superintendents would want to remove himself from any voting right or obligation, in the local association. And this voluntary removal is probably what will happen, rather than a mandate from the NEA.

One of the great strengths of the plan outlined above would be the mandate that there must be an exclusive classroom-teachers' association (or department) as a prerequisite to local affiliation with NEA by any organization. When this requisite is met, there would be no restriction on what other kinds of locals are to be organized and affiliated. The great strength here is that classroom teachers would be assured of an organization and could not then be accused of being trouble makers by organizing their own local, as has happened in many instances. It is true that the mandating of a classroom-teacher local would not, per se, guarantee the independence and effectiveness of such a local. Doubtless many would exist, for some time at least, as paper organizations. In some places there might not even be a need for such an organization. But the mandate would guarantee that teachers would have the untrammeled and uninhibited opportunity for their own organizations without having to be subject to the suspicion of divisiveness.

In connection with the reorganization of the local association there are two other indicated changes. First, the counting of members, for the purpose of determining representation in the NEA Representative Assembly, should be restricted to one local association and the state association. Under present rules, one member may be counted several times by separate NEA affiliates. This practive tends to give certain associations a weighted representation. Second, the present size of the NEA Representative Assembly is unwieldy and must be reduced. The size now runs from 7,000 to 8,000 delegates, and the potential under the present quota system could run to 10,000 or more. This is too many people to assure democratic representation, full discussion of issues, or efficient operation. If the Congress of the United States can be truly representative of nearly 200 million pepole with 535 members, it would appear reasonable to assume that a similar size for an association of about a million members would be fair and feasible. At least, the size should be reduced to some acceptable and efficient point.

THE ROLE OF DISSENT. Another essential provision in the restructuring of the NEA, especially with reference to the proposed reduction in size of the Representative Assembly, is a formal organization for the expression of dissent regarding existing policies and programs. In any such organization as large as the NEA, there must always be, whether evident or not, a sense of frustration on the part of many members who never have an opportunity to be heard at the national level. They tend to feel that their national organization is a huge bureaucracy operated by a few officials, a handful of key leaders in the Representative Assembly, and the official bodies. They tend also to feel that the NEA staff has too much power in determining association policy and procedures. And this, all too often, is true. Whether their opinions are well-founded or not, these individuals feel that they have virtually no influence on policy formation. This feeling can be relieved to some degree by providing a forum which could have an impact on the policy-makers. The Annual Representative Assembly of the Department of Classroom Teachers, which is now held on Monday of Convention Week, preceding the deliberations of the NEA Representative Assembly, could, with some modifications, serve this purpose. In fact, it does now serve this purpose to some extent. But, in some views, not enough. One can visualize an assembly meeting on the Saturday and Sunday preceding both the DCT and the NEA Representative Assembly meetings—an assembly where any NEA member who registers in advance might have the opportunity to express his views on existing policies and proposed new policies to come before the convention, or propose new policies himself. The views expressed and the actions taken by this assembly would not be binding, only advisory, on the Representative Assemblies. This would institutionalize dissent, which any democratic organization needs.

Political Action of Teachers

Traditionally, public-school teachers have shunned direct political action to improve their lot and that of the schools. They have done so, one surmises, because (1) such action, it has seemed to them, would be inappropriate regarding a public institution and public employees, and (2) because such action would suggest selfishness on their part. Passage of the Hatch Act symbolized the public's support of the concept that public employees should not participate in partisan affairs, especially those relating to their own tenuse and pay.

This ingrained position, however, is breaking down. Teachers have learned the hard way that unless they concern themselves with getting school needs before the public, those needs are not likely to be presented effectively. Either they will not be presented to the public at all, or the needs will be downgraded by some taxpayer groups.

The facts of life are that as long as teachers accept the role of political eunuchs they will be treated as such by the public and contemptuously ignored by the politicians.

Here are some examples of the worm's turning.

In Waterbury, Connecticut repeated vetoes of the school-board budget by the incumbent mayor forced the teachers to enter directly as a group in the campaign to defeat the mayor for re-election. Joined by civic groups, they were successful. The incumbent was defeated, and his opponent, who had pledged to support the teachers in their efforts at salary raises and other needed school improvements, was elected. The newly elected mayor delivered on his promises immediately. The recumbent mayor's defeat was the only solution to a steadily deteriorating school situation.

The Omaha Education Association has for many years participated vigorously in political campaigns affecting the schools—school-board elections, bond elections, and school-tax levies. The OEA has always worked through an over-all organization called Friends of the Schools, in which membership is open to all citizens.

The Utah Education Association, despairing of repeated appeals to the politicians and to the economic power structure of the state, in order to rectify intolerable conditions of school support, decided in the summer of 1964 to take the issue to the voters. The UEA organized a political arm called the Utah Council for the Improvement of Education (UCIE) which other groups sympathetic to the schools joined. The council interviewed and endorsed candidates, and conducted an all-out campaign to elect favorable candidates. The UEA's candidates made an almost clean sweep in the election. Thus, after 15 years of turmoil, after seeing every kind of appeal to reason and justice rejected by the politicians, the Utah teachers went to the people directly.

The Indiana State Teachers Association has organized a County Citizenship Committee in each of the 92 counties of the state. All told, about 6,000 ISTA members serve on these committees. All levels and segments of the profession are represented, including all superintendents, all principals, all local association presidents, all members of local legislative committees, all officers of ISTA and the Indiana Classroom Teachers Association, and others. Every school building in each county is represented.

Among the major functions and purposes of the committees are these: conducting a teacher-by-teacher campaign to have every teacher registered and eligible to vote; helping to develop from the grass-roots level the ISTA legislative proposals; becoming thoroughly acquainted with the educational legislative program and being fully prepared to explain it and interpret it; and organizing interview teams of three members each from the personnel of the county committees so that each candidate for the legislature is interviewed by one of these teams.

Nowhere in this program is there any reference to political parties. It is a nonpartisan approach. The emphasis is upon the improvement of education.

There are several ground rules that teachers must observe when they engage in group political activity. They should not exploit their privileged relationships with pupils for partisan purposes. They should not use the school time or school facilities for political purposes.

Above all, except in rare instances, they should not appear alone in the political arena. They should join with other citizens' groups in the community concerned with school improvement. There are always such groups whose membership represents all segments of the population and all political interests.

The Republican Policy Committee of the Senate, in 1964, ahead of the General election, issued a document titled "Where the Votes Are," in which teachers were identified as the largest single specialized occupational group in the country. Teachers are just beginning to realize their potential as a political action group.

UNIFIED MEMBERSHIP. One of the clear musts for the professional associations if they are to repel the raid of labor, is to adopt the unified membership plan. This plan requires that a teacher join all three types of general professional organization—local, state, and national—if he joins any. Presently, nine states (Washington, Arizona, Alaska, Oregon, Nevada, Montana, West Virginia, Hawaii, and Idaho) have put this plan into effect. There are several reasons why this is imperative. Without the unified membership (which AFT has except in the 25 states where there is no state AFT organization) NEA can be attacked by labor and pictured as a far-away organization that has little meaning for a local group of teachers. Seldom does AFT attack a local association or a state association. Almost invariably, NEA is the target. This ploy is, of course, to isolate NEA from its local and state affiliates—the divide and conquer technique.

From the NEA viewpoint, it is often shocking to analyze its membership in local associations where NEA services and money have been made available. Take Milwaukee, for example. The local association won a collective-bargaining election from AFT, with extensive aid from NEA. Out of 4,571 members of the local association, 3,156 belonged to the Wisconsin Education Association, but only 419 were NEA members.

In Rochester, where the local association won a recognition election over the AFT affiliates, with considerable NEA assistance, only about 30 per cent of the teachers were NEA members.

A local association recently requested a sizeable grant from the DuShane Defense Fund for legal fees to defend a past officer who was fired from his teaching position. A check of membership figures revealed that fewer than one fourth of the teachers in that local association were members of NEA. Despite the fact that such aid is not restricted to NEA members, there is persistent grumbling among NEA membership about free-loaders.

Still another argument for unified membership is that both state and local associations have generally raised dues in recent years to rather substantial levels.

While these dues are not excessive or unreasonable, they are much higher than teachers have been accustomed to paying. Without unification of membership, it is likely that NEA will be the one to suffer membership losses.

The ironic aspect of this situation is that NEA has backed a vigorous drive to induce urban associations to employ full-time executive secretaries and has subsidized this effort in many cases. As soon as the local association begins to develop a program of its own, with an employed staff to advance the program, it almost immediately discovers that the program is underfinanced. A raise in membership dues is then necessary. The NEA, which largely stimulated and partially financed this development, often finds itself forgotten in the membership scramble.

A major consideration, however, apart from the money to finance services, is the essential matter of a united front in seeking legislation, in negotiation of policies at the local level, and making effective professional sanctions wherever it becomes necessary to invoke them.

The Possibility of Merger

An intriguing proposal is that the NEA and AFT find common grounds for effecting a merger. The horrendous costs of the continuous struggle between competing national teachers' organizations is, of course, a compelling factor in the suggestions. There are other serious factors involved.

Lieberman has proposed such a merger and has suggested bases.[5]

> Essentially, there are two basic issues which divide the two organizations. One is the fact that the NEA has no restrictions upon administrator membership. The other is AFT's affiliation with the AFL-CIO. . . . On the side of AFT, it must be recognized that the policy of affiliation with labor has reached a dead end and must be abandoned. . . . On the other issue—administrator membership—one-fourth of the NEA affiliates already exclude administrators. Administrators need not give up their affiliation at the national level, but they should get out of local associations which represent the teacher employees.

Candor compels one to admit the perceptiveness of Lieberman's analysis of the situation at the time he wrote it (in 1960) and of his projection of future developments if the merger were not effected. However, much has changed since then. Now organized labor apparently is determined to use the AFT as the vehicle for its life-saving break-through to the white-collar groups. The AFT, in all probability has become an inescapable captive of labor. The time is past, it appears, for such a merger, because the AFT cannot now effect a divorce.

Carl J. Megel also has proposed a merger of NEA and AFT, but under the banner of the AFL-CIO. Of course, a merger would have many advantages to commend it. But under such a program this would be extinction insofar as NEA is concerned. It won't happen under these terms.

A meeting was held by a small invited group during the NEA Convention in New York City in July 1965 to explore the possibility of a merger. The impetus for the meeting was provided by outsiders, presumably impartial observers. There is no known evidence that either NEA or AFT leadership had any part in calling the meeting or in its discussions. There were no discernible results from this meeting.

What the proponents of a merger of NEA and AFT overlooked is that should the two conditions prescribed by Lieberman (abandonment of labor ties by AFT and restriction of administrator membership by NEA) be met, organized labor would in all probability immediately create another teachers' union. Thus the fight would start all over again.

There are grounds for the belief that much of the present discussion of merger of NEA and AFT is merely a propagandizing effort to convince NEA members that there is really little or no difference between the two organizations. Stanley Elam has stated that there are no philosophical, organizational, or programatic differences in the way of merger.[6] This is an amazing assertion in view of the fact that AFT has virtually no professional program, while NEA has 76 units covering every spectrum of professional effort and the improvement of education.

Richard Batchelder, 1965–66 NEA President, made a similar proposal to the 1966 Convention in Miami Beach.

> One way to strengthen and unify our profession would be to avoid the conflicts that we have within the profession. These teachers who have decided to join a federation under the AFL-CIO must now recognize that this decision has not solved teacher problems or satisfied education's needs.
>
> We have responded to these needs, not with a mere whisper of a stop-gap superficial program of "pamphleteering," but with an effective program of state and national action—a program which has focused on the urbanized problems of education—a program which has guaranteed by state statute for tens of thousands of American teachers the right to negotiate collectively with school boards—a program which has unified the organization of white and Negro teachers concomitant with their professional interests—a program which has negotiated through the nation's strongest "school board," the Congress of the United States, a five billion dollar package of benefits for children and teachers in the needy school districts of this country—a program of collective action which has pricked the educational conscience of some reluctant Americans from the little Island of Nantucket to the great plains of Oklahoma—and most important, a program of action for teachers which was organized by teachers, operated by teachers and paid for by teachers. We owe no debts.
>
> Indeed, my colleagues in the American Federation of Teachers, your notion that teachers can only be strong if they merge with one segment of American society has been answered far more militantly, far more effectively and far more responsibly by your fellow teachers in the National Education Association and its local and state affiliates.
>
> I, therefore, invite our colleagues in the AFT to sever ties with labor and to unite with the National Education Association so that we can present one common front for the improvement of the teaching profession and can assure that all teachers can serve the needs of all children.

Of course, Charles Cogen, AFT President, immediately rejected this bid.

There are pervasive reasons why all-out efforts should be made to achieve a single national general organization of public-school teachers. But it will require an ecumenical movement of revolutionary proportions to bring about a merging of the two existing ones. It is quite possible, perhaps probable, that the NEA and AFT will, in time, move so closely together in terms of programs and services as to invite amalgamation. Obviously such a development cannot be predicated upon a demand of unconditional surrender from either side. There are, however, some essential prerequisites. The AFT would have to withdraw from its affiliation with organized labor. This, probably, it will do in time in its own interest, when it has been demonstrated that such affiliation is disadvantageous. On the NEA side, there must be changes in structure, membership, representation, and voting rights, and greater emphasis must be place upon the role of classroom teachers. These too, it appears, are inevitable developments in the future.

But these projected changes may take years, even decades. What are possible ways of ameliorating the current costly and divisive conditions?

A Program for Coexistence

A feasible, workable plan to ameliorate the bitterness, to ease the great stress on the funds of both organizations used in competitive fights for local organizations, and to end the pulling and hauling over educational policies is possible.

As some observers visualize it, this plan could be applied by organized labor to all professional groups. This plan would enable AFL-CIO to bid for professional members solely for the purposes of representing them in certain situations where economic welfare matters only are involved. In other words, the argument goes, AFL-CIO should take the posture of urging members of all professions to join and support their professional associations, both general and specialized. This should be AFL-CIO's position for the following sound reasons. First, loyalty to professional associations is traditional with the members of all professions. Professionals have an irrevocable commitment to improvement in the quality of their services and advancement of their field or fields of knowledge.

Second, AFL-CIO has no possible contributions to make to these goals and should frankly acknowledge the obvious. Third, conceivably AFL-CIO can provide—in certain situations at least—quick, powerful, and great services for economic improvement for members of professions.

Thus, organized labor might attract thousands of members of professions to union membership and the professional associations might be strengthened at the same time. Whether such a program would or could work is anybody's guess.

The Indispensable Commitment of the Professional Association

There is still another consideration—one of supreme importance. This is that the basic purpose of a professional association to be the guardian and the stimulator of appropriate standards for its members. This means a constant appeal to the membership to impose still greater demands upon themselves to raise their professional standards, still greater effort to grow toward perfection in performance.

Teachers respond with great enthusiasm to such a challenge because it is a challenge to their altruism and their pride in their profession. Professional associations could easily, in this struggle, make the mistake of taking the seemingly easy road of appealing only to the selfish, financial instincts which exist to some degree in all of us.

Pressures from the teachers' union could conceivably influence professional associations to concentrate upon welfare services, to hold out the glittering promises of more and more economic rewards. That pressure could conceivably persuade the professional associations to lower their standards for membership and thus to try to become rag-bag catch-all organizations opening membership, for the sake of dues, to every school employee and to laymen as associate members. This is what AFT is now doing, and if the professional associations seek to compete on this basis, they are licked in advance. Morevoer, such competition will inevitably lead to the lowering of standards, to the reduction in certification requirements, to the abolition of national accrediting, and to nondescript, indifferent programs of teacher education. If these things should come to pass as a concomitant of the scramble for members then the professional associations would indeed offer little choice to teachers in choosing between them and the unions.

In September 1964 the NEA membership prerequisite of a bachelor's degree became effective—as was already the case in 28 state education associations. In the near-panic to compete with the unions, there were strong movements in NEA to rescind this requirement. This would have been, from any unbiased view, a catastrophic retreat.

All this can be summed up as follows: It is a mistake to assume that welfare services, geared solely to the utilitarian hungers of teachers, even if expanded to the sky, will alone attract members. Organized labor is now paying the price of workers' indifference by embracing this philosophy. In the professional association at least a large part of its attraction has been the drive for social horizons; for more humanistic causes than the payroll envelope.

Teachers are different. The appeal of associational services of a welfare nature alone will never secure their loyalties. They hunger, too, for appeals to self-sacrifice, to dedication, to motivations in the public interest. This, one surmises, is the greatest weapon—if one wants to term it that—the professional associations have. And these associations can forget this stricture only at the peril of their survival.

The Public Stake

However, the reaction will be decisive when the public finally becomes fully conscious of what really is at stake in the struggle between the teachers' unions and the professional associations for the organizational loyalties of teachers.

This requires elaboration. As a matter of realism the public doesn't care a hoot about who wins a jurisdictional fight for membership of teachers. In general, the public couldn't care less whether the NEA or the AFT survives or goes down.

What the public does care about—and will get excited about—is the control and direction of the public schools. There can be little doubt of the deep loyalty of the American people to their free mass system of education. People may not shout about it, but they know deep down what this system has meant to our egalitarian dream, what it has meant in terms of an equal chance for the common man and his children.

Let this system be obviously threatened—especially by domination, control, direction, or undue influence by any one segment of our society—and, once this trend becomes visible to the public, the public will react with anger. And this reaction, ultimately, will be vehement, whatever the group seeking such undemocratic powers—be it bankers, industrialists, lawyers, politicians, chambers of commerce, farmers, labor, or what not.

The public, to be sure, is a somewhat disparate entity, slow to grasp the impact of movements, slow to be stirred, and even slower to anger. But once aroused over a great international, national, social, or economic issue, its power is irresistible.

It is simple-mindedness raised to the *n*th power to assume that the public will not sooner or later grasp the full meaning of teachers' affiliation with and ultimate subservience to big labor.

First, the public will demand a disaffiliation by its teachers from this untoward combine. This demand will develop either in the form of pressure—the pressure of public opinion which, if intense enough, is as effective as law—or in the form of state legislation.

Second, assuming the unlikely failure of these demands the public will abandon support and patronage of the public schools in such numbers as to imperil their very existence. This will not come cataclysmically, but there will be a steady decline in financial support and a steady defection of children to private schools. Eventually, what will be left of the public schools will be only the legal substance of them. They will continue as mere shadows of their former robust splendour. They will eventually become the recourse only for the children of economically and culturally deprived families.

The children of the upper- and middle-class families will have departed for the superior teaching climate, the independent marketplace of ideas offered by the untrammeled private schools. Thus, the public schools will have become the havens of mediocrity and of pedestrian, routine, lock-step teaching, institutions to be shunned by the capable student and the sensitive parent.

In the long look, with or without the above suggested eventualities coming to pass, domination of public-school teachers and schools would be bad for labor. It would be bad in terms of creating an enmity toward labor that would be far more costly than any sporadic and ephemeral gains that might accrue to labor.

Sooner or later, even the most power-hungry labor leaders are bound to see this elemental fact.

Moreover, as has been stated, union members themselves will ultimately rebel at this unwarranted labor power grab which now is for members but will eventuate in untoward influence on the public schools. *Union members will rebel because the public school is their one great hope that their children may have access to that social and economic mobility which is fundamental to a free society. Class stratifications are the chief threat to the promise of such mobility. Class control of the public schools—by any class—or even undue influence, would inevitably defeat itself. The laboring man will not miss this point. And organized labor will feel his wrath.*

Yes. Teachers can afford integrity. If they can't the public schools are on the way to extinction, or, worse still, on the way to a mediocrity which will earn the contempt of all those who have high hopes for their children—and this ultimately means virtually every American parent.

James Reston wrote in the *New York Times* (December 20, 1964): "The Great Society is not an accumulation of things but of values, if it means anything at all—it is not easy to reconcile the truth the spirit knows, with the truth the mind knows. . . ."

It is precisely the task and the yearning of teachers to effect such reconciliation. In this reconciliation, they can afford integrity—and they will accept no lasting compromise, however bitter the struggle may become for their organization loyalties.

The turmoil in teaching will continue, but teachers' devotion to their professional obligations will also continue. The blandishments of labor will have their appeals, here and there, but they will not obscure the essential loyalties of teachers for the better way to educational quality for those they teach.

PROTECTION OF TEACHERS. One other essential forward sweep of the professional associations should be emphasized. This is the necessity that the association establish a unified, integrated, aggressive program for immediately coming to the assistance of a teacher dismissed under capricious or arbitrary circumstances, without the benefit of boards following due process. Every member of the profession should know with certainty that if such an improper dismissal happens to him, he shall have instant recourse to the resources of his professional organization. NEA is in the process of developing a million dollar fund (the DuShane Fund for Teachers Rights). This probably should be built up to a $10 million trust fund, from portions of members dues.

The glaring weakness in this program, presently, is the inaction or reluctance of some state and local associations to move immediately and vigorously to protect teachers from unfair treatment. This timidity most often arises from political considerations—the fear of offending school boards and administrators, and the fear of, thereby, jeopardizing success of state legislative programs.

ME-TOOISM. NEA and its affiliated professional associations must present a clear alternative to the union approach to school board-staff relations. They must do this for the welfare of the public schools and for their own welfare. Neither the little or big Sir Echo approach will suffice. Me-tooism will inevitably result in the total equating of the labor context in private industry with the professional context in public employment. There is a real question whether the associations can win if this eventuates.

16

Afterword

It seems necessary for me to add this afterword, in the light of the personal comments and viewpoints expressed in the foreword.

It must be obvious to the reader that as the successive chapters were written, the viewpoint of the writer tended to change from one of general hostility toward the teachers' unions to one of recognition—if somewhat reluctant—of their constructive contributions. These contributions are reflected in two clusters. First, the teachers' unions have contributed to a new and needed attitude of aggressiveness by teachers. Second, they have stimulated NEA and its affiliates to move positively to meet new needs of teachers in a new format and in a new context.

And just here arises the need for this afterword.

The grave danger inherent in the developing competition between NEA and AFT and their affiliates, between the teachers' professional associations and the teachers' unions, is that competition will get far out of bounds and become one vast bitter shouting contest, with each group trying to outdo the other in demands on school boards, each trying to outdo the other in a heady brinkmanship, until the very threshold of a constant destructive turmoil in the public schools is approached.

Already the situation has become one of bitter vituperation, invective, and name-calling between the two major competing teachers' organizations. On one side some members of the staffs of the professional associations are calling the teachers' union leaders vultures who constantly stir the froth of discontent, creating strife where none existed before. On the other side, some teachers' union leaders are calling the opposition finks and scabs and innocuous do-gooders, accusing them of selling out the teachers.

I have pointed out NEA's steadily increasing tendency to match or exceed AFT's activism. It may be that this is the only way that NEA can win the war. But, if this is so, the price of winning may be too high for the good of public education.

A contest that degenerates into a race to "outradical" each other has catastrophic implications. The Civil Rights Movement offers a reasonable analogy. Currently, the movement which began with appeals for justice for American Negro citizens shows signs of foundering on the rocks of defiance, violence, and parochialism. Martin Luther King, with his nonviolent program and his appeals to reason, to the good conscience and sense of fairness of the American people, attracted people of goodwill everywhere, in every section of the country. Of course, he exerted pressures—the pressures of facts: the facts of history, of public neglect, of indifference to the deplorable state of a great race. Now the movement is being fragmented by extremists.

But extremism feeds on extremism. It grows from an incident to a more violent incident to still greater violence until the lust for insurrection and chaos is limitless. Through the summer and on into the fall of 1965, and beyond, it became increasingly clear that Americans were turning away from the Civil Rights Movement in great numbers. They were asking themselves: "Where does it (or will it) all end?"

The responsibility for this turn of events can be placed almost equally on two groups. First are the leaders of some of the Negro organizations who, with their lust for power, seem willing to pull down upon themselves and their followers the whole temple of American society. Slogans such as "Black Power," "Get Whitey," and "Burn, Baby, Burn," reinforced by lawlessness, destructive demonstrations, blackmail by fear, and intimidation by violence have inevitably elicited revulsion from the public. Well-known and respected moderates, including candidates for governor in some states, were rejected in 1966 by the voters in favor of avowed and belligerent racists. The progressive city of Atlanta, for years a leader among Southern cities in earnestly seeking to solve the problem of inter-racial relations, was torn apart by strife. California was ripped by riots, looting, burning, until the reasonable and moderate office-holders were left with no moorings.

The other group contributing to this sad denouement in the Negro's upsurge for his just rights is what is called the new left, the far-out liberals who have seized the civil-rights issue in the name of liberalism to beat down authority and order and ostensibly to seek a state of anarchy. This movement, in some of its aspects, reflected a vengeful hate campaign against one section of the country.

The current turmoil in teaching could move toward the same kind of point of no return.

The surest way to damage the cause of teachers—and in some aspects that cause is as righteous as the Civil Rights Movement—is for the two general national teachers' organizations to engage in a contest of shouting more, promising more, inciting to illegal action more, denouncing school boards and administrators more, and boasting of radicalism more than the other.

This is the shortest and surest road to alienation of reasonable citizens from the cause of teachers.

It is a new experience in the United States to note that the headline-grabbers in 1966 were not the industrial unions but the striking professionals—those with no-strike policies or traditions: teachers, nurses, doctors, and others, all with little or no union backgrounds. Add to this the striking public employees—firemen, policemen, and other city workers—and there is a disturbing situation. The easy explanation is that this stems from young hotheads who are rebelling at tradition and the docile posture of these groups in the past, and there is some truth in this thesis. But there is another aspect. The public simply has to face the reality of the situation of these groups in comparison to the remuneration and rights of industrial employees. Appropriate legislation defining more realistically the rights of public employees is another part of the answer.

Such legislation certainly must face up to the growing gap in the equalization of power between workers and employers in the bargaining process. This equalization was the prime theory of the Wagner Act. The fact is that, with the unrestrained use of the strike, labor has become more equal than industry. The country has found itself increasingly beset with strife while large segments of the population are immobilized or grievously hurt economically. No man with a social conscience, with a decent urge for fairness and justice for every human being, could do less than hail this enlightened legislation of the Wagner Act as a landmark of social and economic justice in the history of the United States. But here again extremism feeds on extremism. Power begets power—and often corrupts. The ever widening gap between the power of labor and the power of employer led to corrective provisions embodied by the Taft-Hartley Act.

Since that "Slave-Labor Law" was passed, the cards are again becoming stacked, with a steady diminution of the rights of employers and a steady escalation in the collective rights of workers. Now that labor, with pious acceptance, has brought into existence the President's Executive Order Number 10988, with its specific declarations and restrictions, there has been a steady erosion in labor's acquiescence. Step by step, organized labor is impelling the Federal Government into an unequal negotiating situation by subtly moving toward the full collective-bargaining and strike provisions of the Wagner Act. And already labor is beginning to talk of the inherent right to strike. At first the talk was surreptitious, but now it is open and vigorous. Of course, these are trial balloons, but the future directions are clear. Unless checked, strikes against the Federal Government and other public units will become widespread either by sanction of amended law or by defiant flouting of existing law.

Here is where the analogy with teachers and teaching becomes disturbing. Like the teachers' unions up to 1962 with respect to collective bargaining, the NEA and its affiliated associations began advocating professional negotiation in muted tones and with promises of responsible and reasonable action by teachers. Gaining a foothold in some places now, teachers' associations and unions are exhibiting increasing truculency and growing demands. Turmoil and strife have grown alarmingly in frequency. Teachers could eventually negate this new-found power, a power long needed, by improper and arrogant uses. If the philosophy that power must be taken from society is to become generally accepted—as it now appears to be among public employees' groups—society will be forced eventually to consider this a two-way street and end up by taking some of the power back.

With one sixth of the nation's total work force now public employees (about 10.5 million) and steadily mounting, society may be forced to take some restrictive steps. Otherwise the alternative clearly is anarchy. The movement to take power from society is fast gaining momentum by unchecked successes. Society has to find some answer besides continued retreat and acquiescence in the erosion of the general welfare. It would seem that the general public's disinterest toward the asserted position of several groups that "If you don't like a law, violate it," must surely end this side of general civil obedience. No nation can survive with this philosophy running riot and uninhibited.

It is my conviction that the professional associations can secure the passage of enlightened legislation guaranteeing the long neglected rights of teachers, the rights of negotiation and appeals, without the use of tactics and weapons which, in the long view, could eventuate in what amounts to insurrection against society.

I know of course that in the conditions of modern life, with the swift flow of events and forces, the chaotic comingling of sky-high asperations and jumbled value judgements, this view is considered old-hat by the activists. But I know, too, that this nation must have some anchorages in responsibility, accountability. These anchorages constitute a complex of factors—teachers, ministers, home, church and synagogue, mass media, the enlightened community, and others. These anchorages must reflect and defend some reasonable norms of dissent and behavior.

The argument that a relatively small group such as teachers is lost in a vast morass of mass mores and is powerless to affect the national climate tends to deny the basic premise for the very existence of the public schools.

The evidence seems to indicate that the turmoil in teaching is just beginning. The number of work stoppages by teachers in the school year 1965–66 about equalled the number in the decade 1955–65. At the beginning of the school year 1967–68, there were work stoppages, strikes, or mass resignations in about 40 school districts in six states. There were withdrawals of teacher services in Florida, Illinois, Kentucky, Michigan, New York, and Ohio. These strikes, by whatever name, involved about 100,000 teachers and 1,500,000 children. In addition, there were threatened strikes in five other states (Connecticut, Maryland, Massachusetts, Rhode Island, and South

Dakota). The strikes delayed the opening of schools in Detroit and New York City for nearly three weeks. Another aspect of these work stoppages is that they are growing in length. The short one-day exciting adventure is receding. Also, the teacher strike is becoming a recurring phenomenon in many places. In New York, for example, there have been three strikes and three threatened strikes since 1960. Also, there were almost 150 strikes by public employees in 1966. In New York City and Florida, mass resignations obviously were used to avoid the legal penalties of the strike.

Prior to the New York City case in September, 1967, AFT locals had avoided penalties of anti-strike laws by securing, as a part of the settlement, assurances from the school board of no retaliation. This had become an integral part of the use of teacher strikes. The AFT recoiled with indignation when a judge in Chicago insisted upon enforcement of the law.

President Cogen, in his address to the AFT Fifty-first Annual Convention (August, 1967) said:

> Serious roadblocks are being placed in our way. More states are passing what they consider to be enforceable anti-strike laws. Judges are increasingly imposing fines and even jail sentences in injunction violations. This has happened even in an instance like the Cook County College local's situation, where a settlement had already been reached between the contesting parties. In this case, Judge Covelli stated: "Teachers have been coddled too long; it's about time they were paddled." What judicial arrogance this is.

This indignation stems from the free use by courts of the injunction (usually favoring management) prior to the Norris-LaGuardia Act, which put a stop to the loose use of such injunctions. Since then, court injunctions against strikes by public employees have continued because such strikes are illegal.

It remains to be seen whether New York state public officials will seek to enforce the new law. The enforcing board (PERB) has the authority, if the courts declare the mass resignation a strike, by enforcing the fines against the union, in voiding the recognition of the offending union for 18 months, and by eliminating the dues check off for the 50,000 UFT members for the same period. This could prove to be very costly to UFT. If public officials will not seek to enforce such penalties against the public employees' organizations, there remains only one logical answer—the repeal of legislation prohibiting strikes of public employees. In either instance, the road ahead is a dangerously growing turmoil in teaching and other public services, with the potential of chaos in the offing.

APPENDIXES

APPENDIX A

Notes to Chapters

Chapter 1. Big Labor Launches the Big Push

1. William G. Carr, "The Turning Point," *Addresses and Proceedings*, (One-hundredth Annual Meeting, Denver, July 1962), Washington, D.C.: National Education Association, 1962. p. 28.
2. James A. Carey, "Address," *Addresses and Proceedings*, *op. cit.*, pp. 48–49.
3. *Ibid.*, p. 52.
4. *Addresses and Proceedings*, *op. cit.*, p. 142.
5. William G. Carr, *op. cit.*, pp. 22–23.
6. James W. Goodsell, "Different Breed of Cats: Organization of 'White Collars' Calls for New Approaches," *AFL-CIO News*, vol. 3 (December 27, 1958).
7. James E. Allen, Jr., in an unpublished address to the Regent Institute for New School Board Members, Albany, August 15, 1964.

Chapter 2. Evolution of the Organizational Struggle

1. American Federation of Teachers, Commission on Educational Reconstruction, *Organizing the Teaching Profession* (*The Story of the American Federation of Teachers*), Glencoe, Ill.: Free Press of Glencoe, Inc., 1955. p. 21.
2. Frederick M. Hunter, from an unpublished address to the NEA Board of Directors, Detroit, July 6, 1963.
3. Howard Mumford Jones, Francis Keppel, and Robert Ulrich, "On the Conflict Between the Liberal Arts and Educationists," *Newsletter of the American Council of Learned Societies*, vol. 5 (No. 2, 1954).
4. Harold H. Martin, "Has Success Spoiled Big Labor?" Part I, *Saturday Evening Post*, vol. 235 (December 8, 1962), p. 77.
5. "Trends and Changes in Union Membership," *Monthly Labor Review* (May 1966), Vol. 89, No. 5. pp. 510–513.
6. H. James Neary, "American Trade Union Membership in 1962," *Monthly Labor Review*, vol. 87 (May 1964), pp. 501–507.

7. Arthur F. Corey, "Address," *Addresses and Proceedings*, (One-hundredth Annual Meeting, Denver, July 1962), Washington, D.C.: National Education Association, 1962. p. 143.
8. T. M. Stinnett and Albert J. Huggett, *Professional Problems of Teachers*, 2nd ed., New York: The Macmillan Company, 1963. pp. 420–26.
9. John H. Fischer, "Board-Staff Relations: Issues and Alternatives," address before the School Board Dinner of the Metropolitan School Study Council, November 28, 1962. 8 pp. (Mimeographed.)
10. National Education Association, American Association of School Administrators, *Roles, Responsibilities, Relationships of the School Board, Superintendent, and Staff*, Washington, D.C.: American Association of School Administrators, 1963. pp. 7–8.
11. As quoted in American Federation of Teachers, Commission on Educational Reconstruction, *op. cit.*, p. 10.

Chapter 3. Battleground: The Big Cities

1. "Indelible Blot on the UFT's Record" (editorial), *New York World-Telegram* (April, 1962).
2. *Business Week* (December 30, 1961).
3. Paul Woodring, "The New York Teachers' Strike," *Saturday Review*, vol. 45 (May 19, 1962), pp. 51–52.
4. Fred Hechinger, "The Story Behind the Strike," *Saturday Review*, vol. 45 (May 19, 1962), pp. 54–56.
5. Robert Kaye, as quoted in the *New York World-Telegram* (December 17, 1964).
6. David Selden, "Class Size and the New York Contract," *Phi Delta Kappan*, vol. 47 (March 1964), pp. 283–287.
7. "Above the Law," (editorial), *Washington Evening Star* (September 7, 1963).

Chapter 4. The Campaign Shapes Up

1. Stanley Elam, "Organizing the Teachers," *The Nation*, vol. 198 (June 29, 1964), p. 652.
2. John K. Norton, "Report of the NEA Project on Urban Services," Washington, D.C.: National Education Association, 1962. 49 pp. (Mimeographed.)

Chapter 5. Collective Bargaining and Strikes

1. Arthur F. Corey, "Address," *Addresses and Proceedings*, (One-hundredth Annual Meeting, Denver, July, 1962), Washington, D.C.: National Education Association, 1962. p. 143.
2. *Board of Education of City of Minneapolis vs Public School Employees Union*, 45 N. W. (2d) 797, Minnesota (1951).
3. National Education Association, Office of Professional Development and

Welfare, *Guidelines for Professional Negotiation*, Washington, D.C.: the Association, 1963. p. 7.

4. Irene Thorne, *Collective Negotiation: A Survey and Analysis of Teacher Group Collective Negotiation Contracts with School Boards* (unpublished doctoral dissertation), New York: Teachers College, Columbia University, 1961. p. 13.
5. "Keeping Abreast in Education," *Phi Delta Kappan*, vol. 44 (January 1963), p. 198.
6. American Federation of Teachers, Commission on Educational Reconstruction, *Organizing the Teaching Profession*, Glencoe, Ill.: Free Press of Glencoe, Inc., 1955. pp. 272–73.
7. Myron Lieberman, *Education as a Profession*, Englewood Cliffs, N.J.: Prentice-Hall, Inc., 1956. p. 30.
8. A. H. Raskin, "The Big Strike: A Thing of the Past?" *Saturday Review*, vol. 46 (November 16, 1963), pp. 20–22.
9. Max Lerner, "A Way Out of Our Strike Dilemma," *Look*, vol. 27 (April 23, 1963), p. 86.
10. Robert Bendiner, "What's Wrong in the House of Labor?" *The Reporter*, vol. 25 (October 12, 1961), p. 41.
11. A. H. Raskin, "Making Strikes Obsolete," *The Atlantic* (June 1966), vol. 217, No. 6, pp. 48–52.
12. Myron Lieberman, "Teachers Strikes: An Analysis of the Issues," *Harvard Education Review*, vol. 26 (Winter 1956), p. 41. This is perhaps the most comprehensive and thoughtful analysis in educational literature of the strike problem as related to teachers.
13. Myron Lieberman, "Teachers Strikes: Acceptable Strategy?" *Phi Delta Kappan*, vol. XLVI, No. 5 (January 1965), pp. 237–240.

Chapter 6. Professional Negotiation and Sanctions

1. "Sanctions Settle Problems" (editorial) *San Gabriel Valley Tribune*, Covina, Cal. (February 1, 1964).
2. Arthur F. Corey, "Address," *Addresses and Proceedings*, (One-hundredth Annual Meeting, Denver, July 1962) Washington, D.C.: National Education Association, 1962. p. 143.
3. *Ibid.*, p. 145.
4. It is significant that this negative paragraph was dropped from the resolution by the 1964 NEA Representative Assembly at Seattle.
5. National Education Association, American Association of School Administrators, *Your AASA in 1963–64*. Washington, D.C.: American Association of School Administrators, 1964. Resolution No. 21, p. 186.
6. National School Boards Association, *School Boards in a Changing Society, Proceedings of the 1963 Convention*. Evanston, Ill.: the Association, 1963. Resolution No. 4, p. 327.
7. The survey of state activities with reference to collective bargaining for public employees was abstracted from *From the State Capitals*, issues covering the period March 18 to September 1, 1963. Asbury Park, N.J.: Bethune Jones.

8. Frederick L. Redefer, "The Morale of Teachers," Research Memo 1963–18. Washington, D.C.: Research Division, National Education Association, August 1963. p. 20.
9. Donald H. Wollett, "The Public Employees at the Bargaining Table: Promise or Illusion," *Labor Law Journal*, vol. 15 (January 1964), pp. 8–14.
10. Margaret Lindsey, ed., *New Horizons for the Teaching Profession*, Washington, D.C.: National Education Association, National Commission on Teacher Education and Professional Standards, 1961.
11. This idea is vigorously opposed by some colleges and universities. For criticisms see James D. Koerner, *The Miseducation of American Teachers*, Boston: Houghton Mifflin Company, 1963, and James B. Conant, *The Education of American Teachers*, New York: McGraw-Hill, Inc., 1963. The fact is that the National Council for Accreditation of Teacher Education, which gives national professional accreditation for teacher education, is vigorously opposed by many colleges and universities, especially those which have not achieved accreditation by this agency.
12. For a detailed outline of this procedure see National Education Association, National Commission on Professional Rights and Responsibilities, *Guidelines for Professional Sanctions*, Washington, D.C.: the Association, 1963.
13. For a detailed description of the North College Hill case see National Education Association, National Commission for the Defense of Democracy through Education, *North College Hill, Ohio: An Example of Some Effects of Board of Education Interference with Sound Administration of Public Education*, Washington, D.C.: the Association.
14. Richard B. Kennan, "Professional Sanctions," in an unpublished address delivered to the NEA Department of Classroom Teachers Annual Study Conference, Washington, D.C., November 23, 1962.
15. National Education Association and Washington Education Association, *Report of the NEA-WEA Investigation Committee on Kelso, Washington,* Washington, D.C.: National Education Association, June, 1950.

Chapter 7. A Comparative Analysis

1. See Wesley A. Wildman and Charles R. Perry, "Group Conflict and School Organization," *Phi Delta Kappan*, vol. XLVII, No. 5 (January, 1966), pp. 244–251.
2. National Education Association, Office of Professional Development and Welfare, *Guidelines for Professional Negotiation*, Washington, D.C.: the Association, 1963. 45 pp.
3. *Ibid.*, rev. ed., 1965. 54 pp.
4. For a definitive analysis of state legislation on collective negotiation for teachers, see T. M. Stinnett, Jack H. Kleinmann, and Martha L. Ware, *Professional Negotiation in Public Education*, New York: The Macmillan Company, 1966. Chapters II and VIII.
5. "Work Stoppages Involving Teachers, 1940–1962," (summary release), United States Department of Labor, Bureau of Labor Statistics, November 1963. 8 pp.
6. *Ibid.*

7. Mary McGough *Addresses and Proceedings*, (Eighty-fifth Annual Meeting, Cincinnati, July 1947), Washington, D.C.: National Education Association, 1947. pp. 130–131.

Chapter 8. Conflicting Rationales

1. Samuel P. Capen, "The Teaching Profession and Labor Unions," *Journal of General Education*, vol. 1 (July 1947), p. 277.
2. James B. Conant, *The Education of American Teachers*, New York: McGraw-Hill Inc., 1963.
3. Alan A. Kloss, "What Is a Profession?" *The British Columbia Teacher* (January 1963), pp. 136–39. (Reprinted from *The Canadian Medical Association Journal.*)
4. Myron Lieberman, "Teachers Choose a Union," *The Nation*, vol. 193 (December 2, 1961), pp. 447, 460.
5. David Selden, "Class Size and the New York Contract," *Phi Delta Kappan* vol. 47 (March 1964), pp. 283–87.
6. National Education Association, Research Division, "Does Union Membership Mean Higher Salaries for Teachers?" (NEA's Urban Research Series), Washington, D.C.: the Association, April 1966. 15 pp. (Mimeographed.)
7. "The Press," *Time*, vol. 80 (August 10, 1962), p. 46.
8. *Illinois State Journal* (April 7, 1964).
9. *New York World Telegram and Sun* (March 9, 1964).
10. T. Carr Forrest, "Profession or Unionism—Facing the Issue," *American Engineer*, vol. 24 (March 1954), p. 23–25.

Chapter 9. The Teacher Unions: Philosophy and Practice

1. *The Montana Standard* (May 27, 1956).
2. NEA Union Release No. 16 (January 28, 1960).
3. Releases of California Teachers Association Field Service, January 2, 1958; news releases of California Teachers Association, April 4, 1958; *CTA Journal* (May 1958).
4. NEA Union Release No. 10 (July 11, 1958).
5. *The American Teacher*, vol. 5 (January 1959), p. 3.
6. NEA Union Release No. 14 (November 1, 1959).
7. *Ibid.*
8. *Ibid.*
9. NEA Union Release No. 15 (December 7, 1959).
10. NEA Union Release No. 16 (January 28, 1960).
11. Herbert Clark, Past President, Minnesota Federation of Teachers.
12. George Meany, AFL-CIO.

13. Charles Cogen. Address before AFT's 51st Annual Convention, August, 1967.
14. Carl Megel, AFT President, at the AFT Convention in 1962.
15. Harvey Otterson, Executive Secretary, Minnesota Federation of Teachers.
16. Official Policies of the AFT, adopted in 1958.
17. Charles Cogen, President of the New York Teachers Union.
18. Carl J. Megel in an address to the Forty-eighth Annual Convention of the American Federation of Teachers, AFL-CIO August 1964.
19. Robert Bendiner, "What's Wrong in the House of Labor?" *The Reporter*, vol. 25 (October 12, 1961), p. 42.
20. Paul Jacobs, "The Negro Asserts His Rights," *The State of the Unions*, New York: Atheneum Publishers, 1963. pp. 152–169.
21. "Debate on Teacher Unions and Professional Organizations," Topeka Teachers Association Spring Meeting, March 20, 1963, 19 pp. (Mimeographed.)
22. "Common Endorsement" (editorial), *NJEA Review* of the New Jersey Education Association, vol. 37 (April 1964), p. 486.

Chapter 10. The Professional Associations: Strengths and Weaknesses

1. NEA Union Release No. 1 (December 30, 1957).
2. UFT Advertisement, *New York World Telegram and Sun* (February 27, 1964).
3. Margaret Lindsey, ed., *New Horizons for the Teaching Profession*, Washington, D.C.: National Education Association, National Commission on Teacher Education and Professional Standards, 1961.
4. *Congressional Record* (Proceedings and Debates of the 88th Congress, First Session), vol. 109, (June 25, 1963), pp. 10,880–10,881.
5. Paul Friggens, "Federal Aid to Colleges: Boon or Bane," *Reader's Digest*, vol. 84 (January 1964), pp. 139–143.
6. Note: Former Commissioner McMurrin was referring to opposition to his concepts of Federal aid to education, specifically, to categorical aid, that is, appropriations for specific purposes such as science and mathematics and cooperative research. These are gimmicks which public and private colleges had found to be a bonanza and which the American Association of School Administrators and the Council of Chief State School Officers opposed as a means for the Federal Government to duck its responsibility for general support of the lower schools. The association and the council are independent organizations affiliated with the NEA.
7. T. Schnaufer, *Report on Supervisory Membership in AFT and in other International Unions*, prepared for the Executive Council of the American Federation of Teachers, December 3, 1965. 10 pp. (Mimeographed.)
8. *Ibid.*
9. Carl J. Megel, "Teacher Conscription—Basis of Association Membership," *Teachers College Record*, vol. 106 (October 1964). pp. 7–17.

Chapter 11. From Omaha to Okinawa

1. Overseas Dependent Schools: Recommendations for Improvement (Report of Survey Committee appointed by the Department of Defense) Washington, D.C.: December, 1962, pp. 60, 61.
2. For material on schools in American Samoa see Hubert V. Everly, "Education in American Samoa," *Report of Study Committee to the Committee on Interior and Insular Affairs*, United States Senate. Washington, D.C.: Government Printing Office, 1961. pp. 137–51; 1960 *Annual Report of the Governor of Samoa to the Secretary of the Interior*, Washington, D.C.: Government Printing Office, 1960 and 1961; and Ross R. Allen, "Forgotten Island—American Samoa," *Overseas*, the Magazine of Education Exchange, vol. 2 (February 1963), pp. 15–19.
3. Department of Defense, Overseas Dependent Schools: Recommendations for Improvement, Report of Survey Committee, Washington, D.C.: the Department, December 1962. Table 2, p. iii.
4. Members of the survey team were Dr. Lynn Bartlett, Michigan State Superintendent of Public Instruction; Miss Waurine Walker, Assistant Director of the Division of Teacher Education and Professional Standards, Texas Education Agency; Dr. Hazel Davis, Associate Director of the NEA Research Division; Dr. Alva J. Gibson, Director, Division of Instruction, West Virginia State Department of Education; James E. Gibbs, Jr., Chief of the State School Systems Section of the United States Office of Education, Washington, D.C.; and Edward J. Meade, Jr., Program Assistant for the Ford Foundation, New York.
5. John Cramer, "The Role of Associations Is a Problem," *Washington Daily News* (December 30, 1963).
6. Jerry Klutz, "The Federal Diary," *The Washington Post.*
7. "Overseas Teachers Pay." Hearings (on S.2228) before the Sub-committee on Civil Service of the Committee on Post Office and Civil Service, United States Senate, Eighty-ninth Congress (First Session), August 2 and 3, 1965. Washington, D.C.: Government Printing Office, 1965. p. 8.
8. *Ibid.*, p. 38.

Chapter 12. After 300 Days

1. Walter Hines Page, *The School That Built a Town*, New York: Harper & Row, Publishers, 1952. p. 64.
2. John C. Evans, *Utah School Crisis of 1963*, Salt Lake City: Utah Education Association, 1963. p. 6.
3. Members of the NEA Special Committee to investigate the Utah situation were (1) Chairman: Oscar E. Thompson, Professor, State College of Iowa, Cedar Falls; Chairman, NEA Commission on Professional Rights and Responsibilities, 1962–63. (2) Oby T. Brewer, Jr., member and past President, Board of Education, Atlanta, Georgia. (3) Mrs. Bertha P. Boyd, educational program specialist, State Department of Public Instruction, Harrisburg, Pennsylvania; Vice-Chairman, NEA Commission on Professional Rights and Responsibilities, 1963–64; Interim Committee member, 1962–63. (4) Roy Frantz, past President,

National School Boards Association and Colorado School Boards Association; President, Pueblo, Colorado, Board of Education. (5) William P. McLure, Professor and Director, Bureau of Education Research, University of Illinois, Urbana. (6) G. Warren Phillips, Superintendent of Schools, Valparaiso, Indiana; Executive Committee member, American Association of School Administrators. (7) Audra May Pence, classroom teacher, Elmhurst, Illinois; Chairman, NEA Commission on Professional Rights and Responsibilities, 1963–64, Vice-Chairman, 1962–63. (8) Mrs. Gladys Perry, classroom teacher, Seattle, Washington; President, Seattle Teachers Association. (9) Raleigh R. Steinbach, Professor, University of South Dakota, Vermillion; President, South Dakota Education Association.

4. John C. Evans, *op. cit.*, p. 51.
5. *Addresses and Proceedings* (One-hundred-and-first Annual Meeting, Detroit, June 30–July 5, 1963), Washington, D.C.: National Education Association, 1963. p. 192.
6. *Ibid.*, p. 207.
7. *Ibid.*, p. 207.
8. National Education Association, National Commission on Professional Rights and Responsibilities, *Utah: A State-wide Study of School Conditions*, Washington, D.C.: the Commission, March 1964.
9. *Interim Report of the Governor's School Study Committee*, May 13, 1964. 55 pp. (Mimeographed.)
10. *Ibid.*
11. *Time*, vol. 83 (May 29, 1964), p. 63.
12. *Deseret News*, Salt Lake City, Utah (May 23, 1964).

Chapter 14. The Price is Not Right

1. *New York World Telegram and Sun* (April 1, 1965).
2. *New York World Telegram and Sun*, Education Page (April 8, 1965).
3. *Proceedings* (Sixth AFL-CIO Constitutional Convention, San Francisco, January 1965). pp. 76–77.
4. "The Kingsport Strike," Kingsport Press, February 1, 1966. 12 pp. (Mimeographed.)
5. Michael C. Gardner, "The Kingsport Strike," *Wall Street Journal* (April 22, 1964).
6. "School Boards Beware of Book Boycotts" (opinion of general legal council) National School Boards Association, February 14, 1966. 3 pp. (Mimeographed.)
7. *Albuquerque Tribune* (October 16, 1965).
8. Robert H. Wyatt, "AFL-CIO Effort to Kill Sales Tax Caused Teachers Severe Loss," *Indiana Teacher*, vol. 108 (November 1963), p. 125.
9. *Philadelphia Evening Bulletin* (May 10, 1963).
10. *Less than an Egg a Day*, Chicago: American Federation of Teachers, 1966. (Mimeographed.) p. 8.

11. National Education Association, Research Division, "Does Union Membership Mean Higher Salaries for Teachers?" (NEA Urban Research Series), Washington, D.C.: the Association, April 1, 1966. 15 pp.
12. *St. Louis Globe Democrat* (February 12, 1963).
13. Donald H. Wollett, "The Price of Teacher Unionism," *Connecticut Teacher* (November 1965), p. 6 *et seq.*

Chapter 15. What of the Future?

1. John W. Gardner, *Self-Renewal: The Individual and the Innovative Society*, New York: Harper & Row, Publishers, 1963. p. 68.
2. Sir Richard Livingston, *Education for a World Adrift*, New York: The Macmillan Company, 1943. p. 1.
3. Myron Lieberman, "Teachers Strikes: An Analysis of the Issues," *Harvard Educational Review*, vol. 26 (Winter 1956), pp. 39–69.
4. Jack F. Kleinmann, *Fringe Benefits for Public School Personnel*, New York: Columbia University Press, 1962, 178 pp.
5. Myron Lieberman, *The Future of Public Education*, Chicago: University of Chicago Press, 1960. pp. 230–236.
6. Stanley Elam editorial in *Phi Delta Kappan.*

APPENDIX B

Supplementary Materials to Chapters

Chapter 2. Evolution of the Organizational Struggle

Membership of American Federation of Teachers and National Education Association in Selected Years, 1918–1966

Year	Number of Members (Nearest Thousand)	
	AFT	NEA
1918	1,500	10,000
1920	10,000	53,000
1930	7,000	172,000
1940	30,000	203,000
1950	41,000	454,000
1958	53,000	617,000
1959	55,000	667,000
1960	59,000	714,000
1961	61,000	766,000
1962	71,000	812,000
1963	82,000	860,000
1964	100,000	903,000
1965	110,000	943,000
1966	125,461	986,113
48-Year Growth	123,961	976,113

Source: NEA Handbook, published annually by the National Education Association; and Report of Annual AFT Convention.

NEA and AFT Memberships by States 1962–63

State	Total Number of Public-School Personnel	NEA Membership	Estimated AFT Membership
Alabama	28,669	19,307	63
Alaska	2,225	1,732	24
Arizona	14,925	12,741	66
Arkansas	16,431	9,747	None
California	143,700	72,863	4,915
Colorado	20,063	13,299	334
Connecticut	23,700	6,188	1,408
Delaware	4,299	1,920	176
District of Columbia	5,266	3,638	291
Florida	46,800	22,803	8
Georgia	36,771	25,293	122
Hawaii	5,730	4,695	804
Idaho	7,186	6,375	93
Illinois	86,708	37,438	16,579
Indiana	41,500	24,188	3,320
Iowa	31,275	22,242	787
Kansas	24,371	23,248	25
Kentucky	26,740	20,574	56
Louisiana	29,725	2,555	321
Maine	8,800	5,546	14
Maryland	28,354	17,770	448
Massachusetts	41,600	8,815	2,841
Michigan	75,980	26,295	8,649
Minnesota	33,050	14,318	5,837
Mississippi	20,475	3,826	10
Missouri	35,400	23,892	1,781
Montana	7,045	6,032	463
Nebraska	14,730	7,493	None
Nevada	3,584	2,887	72
New Hampshire	4,940	2,510	141
New Jersey	54,600	25,398	1,658
New Mexico	10,366	8,043	97
New York	94,100[1]	25,264[2]	19,372[3]
North Carolina	43,300	35,734	None
North Dakota	7,660	4,411	152
Ohio	84,800	47,913	4,170
Oklahoma	23,000	15,995	None
Oregon	19,160	17,929	245
Pennsylvania	85,439	56,958	1,307
Puerto Rico	17,309	3,918	None
Rhode Island	6,810	533	1,710
South Carolina	22,201	10,892	None
South Dakota	8,300	3,743	11

State	Total Number of Public School Personnel	NEA Membership	Estimated AFT Membership
Tennessee	31,273	24,736	227
Texas	96,000	32,791	25
Utah	10,404	8,880	None
Vermont	3,566	1,699	None
Virginia	37,500	21,394	None
Washington	30,380	26,013	519
West Virginia	17,275	16,497	None
Wisconsin	33,450	13,525	2,229
Wyoming	4,510	3,570	None
Canal Zone			262
Overseas Dependents Schools	7,262	2,374	39
Miscellaneous		1,065	9
TOTALS	1,665,065	859,505	81,680

Per cent NEA membership is of total public-school personnel: 52.0
Per cent AFT membership is of total public-school personnel: 4.9
Per cent state education association (affiliated with NEA) membership (1,481,002) is of total public-school personnel, excluding New York City: 91.0

[1] Plus 46,000 in New York City.
[2] Includes 1,470 members in New York City.
[3] Includes 17,200 members in New York City.

NEA and AFT Memberships by States 1965–1966

State	Total Number of Public-School Personnel	NEA Membership	Estimated AFT Membership
Alabama	31,200	21,273	137
Alaska	3,040	2,177	68
Arizona	17,110	13,924	361
Arkansas	17,649	10,352	—
California	172,300	81,790	8,648
Colorado	23,260	14,806	660
Connecticut	29,100	8,355	1,854
Delaware	5,320	2,482	232
District of Columbia	6,625	3,440	758
Florida	55,330	27,797	34

State	Total Number of Public-School Personnel	NEA Membership	Estimated AFT Membership
Georgia	41,537	25,059	76
Hawaii	6,722	5,236	1,036
Idaho	7,730	6,852	69
Illinois	93,460	40,650	17,913
Indiana	50,000	30,108	4,335
Iowa	30,000	25,551	577
Kansas	25,632	24,731	48
Kentucky	29,300	23,348	171
Louisiana	34,750	3,675	1,393
Maine	9,930	6,542	44
Maryland	34,870	22,261	1,022
Massachusetts	48,450	13,801	4,062
Michigan	80,440	33,099	11,999
Minnesota	38,050	19,756	6,831
Mississippi	21,950	4,669	—
Missouri	39,986	27,639	1,696
Montana	8,350	7,110	476
Nebraska	16,375	10,007	—
Nevada	5,000	4,153	171
New Hampshire	5,975	3,371	154
New Jersey	65,075	29,190	2,385
New Mexico	12,100	9,431	192
New York (State)	107,802	30,245	4,337
New York City	56,898	1,861	37,291
North Carolina	48,845	37,211	—
North Dakota	7,652	5,189	173
Ohio	95,000	50,295	5,314
Oklahoma	25,100	17,312	50
Oregon	21,770	19,871	489
Pennsylvania	97,634	61,566	4,181
Puerto Rico	19,300	3,448	—
Rhode Island	7,513	902	1,940
South Carolina	24,745	12,809	—
South Dakota	9,300	4,731	—
Tennessee	34,000	28,251	258
Texas	109,000	41,535	9
Utah	11,997	10,034	—
Vermont	3,944	2,046	—
Virginia	43,700	24,806	—
Washington	32,200	32,533	802
West Virginia	17,643	16,753	76
Wisconsin	40,230	15,116	2,325
Wyoming	4,684	3,656	
Canal Zone			290

State	Total Number of Public-School Personnel	NEA Membership	Estimated AFT Membership
Overseas Dependent Schools		2,308	484
Foreign and Others		1,000	
TOTALS	1,885,573	986,113*	125,421

Per cent NEA membership is of total public-school personnel: 52.0
Per cent of state association (affiliated with NEA) membership (1,639,083) is of total instructional staff: 90.0
Per cent AFT membership is of instructional staff: 6.6

* Does not include 124,257 student NEA members. If these associate members were counted, the total NEA membership would be 1,110,370.

Chapter 3. Battleground: The Big Cities

This Is the Law

. . . No person holding a position by appointment or employment in the government of the State of New York, or in the government of the several cities, counties, town or villages thereof . . . or in the public school service . . . shall strike.

. . . Any public employee who violates the provision of this section shall thereby abandon and terminate his appointment of employment. . . .

A person violating the provisions of this section may subsequent to such violation be appointed or reappointed, employed or re-employed, as a public employee, but only upon the following conditions:

(a) His compensation shall in no event exceed that received by him immediately prior to the time of such violation:

(b) The compensation of such person shall not be increased until after the expiration of three years from such appointment or reappointment, employment or re-employment; and

(c) Such person shall be on probation for a period of five years . . . during which period he shall serve without tenure and at the pleasure of the appointing officer or body.

(The final paragraph of the law gives persons presumed to be violators to establish, in writing, that they were not and to state the reasons for their absence.)

Is the law harsh? Yes, but so is a strike against the public school system of New York City.

School officials have pledged themselves to enforce the law. There is no turning back. To do so would be to invite every other public-employee union or group in town to use the same blackjack methods with impunity.

It is clearly true that only a fraction of the city's 40,000 teachers are members of the United Federation of Teachers. It is equally true that only a fraction of the

UFT's members voted on the strike question. Finally, it is true that the strike was voted by only a narrow margin.

The question arises: Is it fair to punish a majority of teachers for the irresponsibility of a minority?

The answer, as we see it, is this: Only those teachers who strike can be punished. Those who do not want to engage in this strike certainly owe no loyalty to a union that calls on them to violate the law!

—*New York World Telegram*
1962

Board President's Statement

Following is the text of a statement issued when it was announced that the New York Board of Education would seek a court order to end the strike.

The board expresses this statement with great sorrow. We have attempted to exhibit every ounce of patience throughout these trying days. We have negotiated with the collective bargaining agent of the teachers for many, many weeks. The board itself has been intensively involved in negotiations now for several days. We have negotiated in good faith, with complete sincerity, in an effort to reach an accord which would have eliminated that dreadful calamity which has occurred in our public school system.

We have negotiated even under the threat of a closing of the schools, if demands were not met. We did that and have continued to do that, because our transcendent duty is to a million children attending our schools—and out of respect for our teachers.

Violation of Law

Our position has been clear and explicit. We are unanimous in the view that a strike by teachers is illegal. It is a violation of law. It is the duty of this board to obey the law. Under the circumstances that prevail the strike is particularly immoral, for this board has done all that could be done within reason, to meet the legitimate demands of our teachers.

Those teachers who have abandoned their positions have betrayed their duty. They have been guilty of irresponsible behavior. The leadership of a union which encouraged and incited this strike has been guilty of recklessness and irresponsible leadership. We believe it is also a betrayal of responsible unionism.

In November, 1960, when there was a one-day stoppage by teachers, responsible union leaders in this city gave public assurance that there would never be a recurrence. The leadership of this union, which has ordered this strike, has betrayed that pledge.

There is no reason to misunderstand against whom this strike is directed. We know that the effort has been made to call this a strike against City Hall and a strike against Albany, but City Hall is open and functioning today and Albany is functioning today. It is the schools which are not functioning as they should be today.

It is the school children who are being deprived of their right to an education today, and there can be no escape from the fact that this is a strike against one million children attending our schools.

This board, in the exercise of every conceivable restraint, did not go to court heretofore. It felt that there was no need to do so in view of its clear position with respect to the law. It did not wish to create any chasm between the teachers and the board. It did not wish to take any step that some might construe as provocative and inflammatory. Despite this patience, despite this attitude, despite the willingness to work with the teachers, a dreadful strike took place this morning.

—Max J. Rubin
President of the New York City Board of Education

New York's Disgrace

In November, 1960, the United Federation of Teachers went on a one-day strike in New York City. This was settled when the Board of Education, after being told there would never be another strike by city teachers, gave collective bargaining rights to the federation.

This no-strike assurance didn't amount to much. For now New York has had another one-day teachers' strike—this time over pay demands which the city says it cannot afford to meet. This latest strike was accompanied by minor riots staged by some students. But why not? If the teachers set an example of contempt for law, why expect anything better of pupils? . . .

—*Washington Evening Star*

Behind the Strike

On the eve of the strike vote by the United Federation of Teachers in New York last week, a young woman who teaches elementary school in a slum neighborhood was close to tears. "I love those children," she said. "I won't discuss the strike with them. But I just wish you could understand how exciting it is to think that we have the courage to stand up and fight for our rights. I hope we'll go out on strike." She made it quite clear that the illegality of the strike was of no concern to her.

In this teacher's plea and mood, reflected in the words and actions of so many of her colleagues, was the clue to much of the confusion, courage, bitterness and absence of rational thinking which marked the New York story.

Teachers' grievances are real and of long standing. The huge educational bureaucracy has made them voiceless pawns in a machine. In New York City, they have even come to accept punching a time clock, hardly the sign of the professional. They are inevitably aware that many of those who boss them are superior merely in political know-how or in college credits in "educational administration" rather than in ability. . . .

The feeling of being pushed around is probably a more serious, nagging grievance than the salary issue. Without this background of low morale, that led to a belligerent demand for a strike against the last-minute plea for moderation by the U.F.T.'s president, it would be hard to explain the strike. Pay increases giving teachers an average of at least $700 more annually, plus improved fringe benefits, pensions and working conditions had already been offered. Even in any comparison with the suburbs, the dollar gains were impressive U.F.T. victories; but the comparison in a teacher's way of life and "professional status" makes the suburbs greatly preferable. . . .

The result has been something of a contradiction. The militant element in the U.F.T. was able to create the impression among many teachers that going on strike, even if it was unlikely to change the outcome of the negotiations, was a show of strength that would give the profession a new image. The problem, which this approach failed to resolve, was how to prevent the "professional" image from being blurred. Even devoted union members in other fields find it hard to picture striking physicians, the profession to which teachers like most to compare themselves.

Differences Confusing

If the disparity between the professional and the trade union image is confusing, the difference between collective bargaining conditions in industry and in education is even more marked. In industrial disputes labor confronts a management that knows what its assets are. Teachers bargain with a board of education, which lacks fiscal independence in the form of taxing powers. It is a kind of shadow boxing. At best, they can expect a promise that the board will recommend a certain amount to the city authorities. . . .

Final Paradox

The final paradox is that the leadership of organized labor looks on the teachers' action with lack of enthusiasm, if not downright disapproval. Perhaps partly as a result of inexperience at labor procedures, partly because of a power struggle among the teachers' own leaders, and partly as a result of the tendency toward teachers' individualistic obstinacy, the New York local was known to have acted without prior consultation with either its parent union, the American Federation of Teachers, or the AFL-CIO, of which it is an affiliate. The general labor leadership was known to have been opposed to the strike threat.

. . . It is only after all . . . answers are in that the majority of teachers in the big cities will be able to tell where to find their place, how they want to be represented, and what is to be their public image.

—Fred Hechinger
New York Times

Chapter 4. The Campaign Shapes Up

Urban Education Associations that Employed Full-Time Executive Secretaries in 1965-66

Albuquerque Classroom Teachers Association, Albuquerque, New Mexico
Anne Arundel County: Teachers Association of Anne Arundel County, Annapolis, Maryland
Arlington Education Association, Arlington, Virginia
Atlanta Public School Teachers Association, Atlanta, Georgia
Baltimore: Public School Teachers Association of Baltimore, Baltimore, Maryland
Baltimore County: Teachers Association of Baltimore County, Towson, Maryland
Brevard County Classroom Teachers Association, Cocoa, Florida
Broward County Classroom Teachers Association, Fort Lauderdale, Florida
Charlotte Classroom Teachers Association, Charlotte, North Carolina
Chicago Education Association, Chicago, Illinois
Cleveland Education Association, Cleveland, Ohio
Dade County Classroom Teachers Association, Miami, Florida
Davis County Education Association, Farmington, Utah
Dayton Classroom Teachers Association, Dayton, Ohio
DeKalb Education Association, Decatur, Georgia
Denver Classroom Teachers Association, Denver, Colorado
Des Moines Education Association, Des Moines, Iowa

Detroit Education Association, Detroit, Michigan
District of Columbia Education Association, Washington, D.C.
Duval Teachers Association, Jacksonville, Florida
Fairfax Education Association, Fairfax Virginia
Flint Education Association, Flint, Michigan
Fresno Teachers Association, Fresno, California
Garden Grove Education Association, Garden Grove, California
Glendale Teachers Association, Glendale, California
Grand Rapids Education Association, Grand Rapids, Michigan
Granite Education Association, Salt Lake City, Utah
Hayward Unified Teachers Association, Hayward, California
Hennepin Division, Minnesota Education Association, Minneapolis, Minnesota
Highline Education Association, Seattle, Washington
Hillsborough County Classroom Teachers Association, Tampa, Florida
Houston Teachers Association, Houston, Texas
Indianapolis Education Association, Indianapolis, Indiana
Kansas City Education Association, Kansas City, Missouri
Kenmore Teachers Association, Kenmore, New York
Lansing Schools Education Association, Lansing, Michigan
Lincoln Education Association, Lincoln, Nebraska
Livonia Education Association, Livonia, Michigan
Long Beach: Teachers Association of Long Beach, Long Beach, California
Los Angeles: Affiliated Teachers Organizations of Los Angeles, Los Angeles, California
Los Angeles Teachers Association, Los Angeles, California
Louisville Education Association, Louisville, Kentucky
Maricopa Urban Teachers Association, Mesa, Arizona
Milwaukee Teachers Education Association, Milwaukee, Wisconsin
Minneapolis: City of Minneapolis Education Association, Minneapolis, Minnesota
Montebello Teachers Association, Montebello, California
Montgomery County Education Association, Rockville, Maryland
Mt. Diablo Unified District Education Association, Concord, California
Nashville: Metropolitan Nashville Education Association, Inc., Nashville, Tennessee
Norwalk-La Mirada Teachers Association, California
Oakland Education Association, Oakland, California
Omaha Education Association, Omaha, Nebraska
Palm Beach County Classroom Teachers Association, West Palm Beach, Florida
Parma Education Association, Parma, Ohio
Pasadena Education Association, Pasadena, California
Philadelphia Teachers Association, Philadelphia, Pennsylvania
Pinellas Classroom Teachers Association, Clearwater, Florida
Portland Association of Teachers, Portland, Oregon
Prince Georges County Teachers Association, Bladensburg, Maryland
Racine Education Association, Racine, Wisconsin
Richmond: Association of Richmond Educators, Richmond, California
Riverside City Teachers Association, Riverside, California
Sacramento City Teachers Association, Sacramento, California
Saginaw Education Association, Saginaw, Michigan
St. Louis Suburban Teachers Association, St. Louis, Missouri
St. Louis Teachers Association, St. Louis, Missouri

Salt Lake City Teachers Association, Salt Lake City, Utah
San Bernardino Teachers Association, San Bernardino, California
San Diego Teachers Association, San Diego, California
San Francisco Classroom Teachers Association, San Francisco, California
San Jose Teachers Association, San Jose, California
San Juan Teachers Association, Sacramento, California
Seattle Teachers Association, Seattle, Washington
Sioux City Education Association, Sioux City, Iowa
Spokane Education Association, Spokane, Washington
Springfield Education Association, Springfield, Massachusetts
Stockton Teachers Association, Stockton, California
Tacoma Association of Classroom Teachers, Tacoma, Washington
Torrance Education Association, Torrance, California
Tucson Education Association, Tucson, Arizona
Warren Education Association, Warren, Michigan
Wichita City Teachers Association, Wichita, Kansas
Worcester, Educational Association of, Worcester, Massachusetts
Youngstown Education Association, Youngstown, Ohio
Overseas Education Association, APO New York, New York

Chapter 9. The Teacher Unions: Philosophy and Practice

NEA Convention, July 1964

Desegregation in the Public Schools

The National Education Association views with deep concern the problems which accompany the evolving process of desegregation in the public schools in response to the changed legal status of the public schools initiated by the Supreme Court decisions on desegregation.

The National Education Association pledges continued support of the United States Supreme Court decision on school desegregation. . . .

. . . the Representative Assembly instructs the officers and directors of the National Education Association—

a. To direct all local, district, and state associations affiliated with the National Education Association to take immediate steps to remove all restrictive membership requirements dealing with race, creed, or ethnic groups.

b. To take immediate action to develop plans to effect the complete integration of all local and state affiliates whose memberships are now limited to educators of specifically designated racial, religious, or ethnic groups.

Affiliates whose memberships reflect the above-mentioned restrictions shall be given until July 1, 1966, to revise their constitutions and bylaws, where necessary, to take whatever steps are required to expedite the complete removal of all restrictive labels, and to present a plan to effect the complete integration of their associations.

Should an affiliated association fail to comply with these requirements by July 1, 1966, the Executive Committee shall have the discretionary powers to take necessary action.

—Resolution adopted at NEA Convention, July 1964

Chapter 12. After 300 Days

Strikes by Teachers Violate Public Trust

Action of the Utah Education Association's House of Delegates calling a two-day "recess" in the public schools of the state can be regarded only with consternation and regret.

A "recess" called unilaterally by an employe group is really a strike. Thus the UEA leadership resorts to the prime weapon of trade unionism, a movement with which the National Education Association is locked in grim conflict.

STRIKES BY TEACHERS fall into the same category as strikes by doctors, hospital employees, police, firemen, sanitation workers and others engaged in necessary public service. Such walkouts make a mockery of the professional status which members claim.

The resolution calling for the strike over Monday and Tuesday ("to be made up") was taken to "protest the refusal" of Governor Clyde to act upon the recommendations of his school study committee, and "to give time for all teachers to meet in Salt Lake City on Tuesday, May 19, to determine, as a body, a further course of action."

The 600-odd member House of Delegates representing local teacher organizations also requested that the National Education Association "immediately impose national sanctions against the state of Utah. . . ."

If the NEA complies, teachers throughout the U.S. will be urged to follow customary union procedures and to refrain from accepting school positions in the state, thus aggravating an already complicated problem.

The group also urged the Governor's School Study Committee, which last week recommended a special legislative appropriation of six million dollars for Utah schools, to complete its final report.

WE CAN ONLY PRAY that cooler heads in the Utah Education Association membership will prevail and that the error in judgment of the House of Delegates will not be compounded. As the Tribune said in 1957 and again in 1963 when teacher strikes were threatened, the high calling of Utah's educators and their expressed concern for the children's welfare face an acid test.

Alternatives suggested by the UEA House of Delegates, to be placed before the 10,000 Utah educators, include "an indefinite extension of this recess," which would mean a strike to the finish; curtailment of summer programs; cutting the school year from 180 to 170 days, "thus concentrating available finances toward quality education during a lesser period," but without cutting pay of personnel.

Another alternative would be mass refusal to sign contracts until either the Legislature is called into special session to make the proposed emergency appropriation or the State Board of Education shortens the school year.

It is hard to see how compressing the school year would save funds of consequence or assure "quality education."

Since a large proportion of school operation budgets goes for salaries, the savings likely would be less than 1 per cent in most districts.

School funds are apportioned according to students in daily classroom attendance. With most Utah schools within a week or two of closing, it is hard to see how lost classroom time can be made up.

IT IS UNDERSTANDABLE that Utah teachers are angry and frustrated because the governor refused to follow the unanimous recommendations of his own study committee. A great deal of public sentiment doubtless swung to the teachers after this action. If the majority of Utah's 10,000 educators now go out on strike, however, it will only register callousness and result in erosion of their reputation.

The UEA membership is aware that Governor Clyde, wrong or right, is adamant. He will never call a special session during the remainder of his term. Even with initiative action, no relief is in sight until January, when a new governor, a completely new House of Representatives and half the Senate members take office. Instead of displaying anger and force with the strike weapon now, the Utah educators and their friends would be better advised to take their case to the people of Utah in the political arena this summer and fall.

During one New York school crisis, Max Lerner, himself a prominent teacher and articulate spokesman for education, wrote in his syndicated column:

"AMIDST THE CHARGES and countercharges, the pulling and pushing, it is the children who are in danger. . . . A bus strike is an inconvenience; a school strike is a disaster!

"The strike as a weapon just doesn't make sense here. There are plenty of opponents of public education across the nation. Any widespread and sustained use of the strike weapon will play directly into their hands.,'

A strike against the children and the public with attendant publicity and degeneration of Utah's reputation will not win friends and influence people either at the polls or in the next State Legislature. It could prove to be a disastrous boomerang.

—*Salt Lake Tribune*
May 17, 1964

They Fought on Other Side

The Look magazine article names leaders who fought on the other side in the battle for teachers rights in Oklahoma.

Dale Porter, a Kay county school board president, was named as one who headed up the campaign that resulted in the defeat of the four statewide teachers petitions.

Teachers recoiled, the article reported "as if they had been slapped in the face," and they rose up in mighty indignation.

"The uprising leapt from Midwest City to Tulsa, back to Oklahoma City. It erupted, it exploded, it raced like a prairie fire. Its spark crackled and sputtered among the new, younger teachers. New leadership burst out of their ranks," the magazine article declared.

"Once begun, the turmoil would not be contained. Teachers went to the legislature to lobby. Governor Bellmon proposed 'Operation Giant Stride'—a program of wildly imaginative promises to meet teacher demands. Teachers rejected it as impractical . . . [their wives] marched on the capitol, demanded—and got—an audience with the Governor."

Look tells us about the sanctions and Bellmon's calling them "unjustified . . . disgusting," admitting "they reminded him of 'The Grapes of Wrath.' "

But, says the magazine article, "sanctions were unquestionably the most telling blow dealt in this war. Without them, nothing unusual would have come out of the legislature."

In conclusion, the Look article says: "Oklahoma was not, after all, the 'Okie State' of an earlier day—it was a theater of war. And Oklahoma's education war was part of a grass-roots revolution of national scope. A new generation of teachers is putting down the old rural idea and speaking out for its role in the urban society.

They are revolting not AGAINST, but FOR—for recognition, for a new role, for a voice. In Oklahoma last year, they fought and won. Before they are through, their revolution may sweep the nation."

—Editorial
Oklahoma Journal
January 12, 1966

Chapter 13. Box Score and Evaluation

Arbitration Issue—Teachers Union Criticizes Rival

The Newark Teachers Union criticized last night the rival Newark Teachers Association for agreeing to compulsory arbitration to end the NTA's two-day strike.

A resolution embodying the censure was adopted by the union after conciliatory attempts from within the union itself and by NTA members were unavailing.

The union also characterized as "undemocratic" the method by which the NTA called off the strike and insisted there would have been greater gains for all teachers if the association had accepted the union's offer of united planning and execution.

On Teacher Unity—

The union also rejected a resolution that it "explore every possibility of organizational unity with the NTA" in favor of a less emphatic agreement to "keep open every means of communication with the NTA with a view to possible teacher unity."

The union aired its feelings in the wake of the strike settlement at a meeting at the Essex House, attended by upwards of 300 of its members.

The meeting emphasized the peculiar organizational dichotomy of Newark's teachers. NTA members were present and spoke their piece and even gained the support of some union members against the resolution of censure. Wistful talk of unity contrasted with a hardline approach to the NTA.

For its part, the union applauded the "united" action of teachers for gaining at least a $700-a-year increase and the action of the "vast majority of teachers who showed their determination to improve their salary schedule and working conditions."

Looks to Election—

The NTU, while barred from strike strategy planning by the NTA, had, however, urged its members not to cross the picket lines. As one NTU member shouted last night: "We made your damned strike and we'll beat you in the election."

If such a representation election is held, it will take place in the spring. The NTA nosed out the union in an election for bargaining agent in 1964.

The critical resolution, drawn up by the union's executive board, was proposed to the membership by Semour C. Heck, executive vice-president.

NTA member Sam Shapiro immediately stood up to insist that this was no time to be pointing out mistakes.

"This is the time to unite teachers," he said, "such a resolution won't help anybody and will do more damage than good. It's easy to find fault."

Sidney Rosenfeld, NTU president, replied that the NTA had, in effect, left itself open to criticism by rejecting the union's offer to participate in the strike strategy.

Stephen Adubato, a member of the NTU and legislative representative for the State Federation of Teachers, the parent organization, suggested a moderate resolution from which the "negative" references to the NTA would be deleted.

Rosenfeld ruled Adubato out of order, precipitating a parliamentary wrangle during which Adubato accused the present of "undemocratic" procedures. But Adubato lost out on an appeal to the membership as a whole, and the resolution was carried with only scattered "noes" in opposition.

'Brother Teachers'—

After the meeting, Adubato explained to a reporter that the NTA members are "our brother teachers and not people from Mars."

"We have the same objectives and when we work together we will benefit public education generally," he said.

Critical portions of the resolution read:

"We regret, however, the decision of the NTA leadership to abandon its responsibility to negotiate for teachers those matters which only teachers are best qualified to deal with. Compulsory arbitration as an alternative to the already united demonstrated strength of the classroom teacher is not the best way to handle the interests of teachers and education, and is indeed an abdication of responsibility to capitalize on the proven numerical strength of Newark teachers."

"We deplore the undemocratic method by which the NTA leadership suddenly called off its strike action without first consulting the teachers who should have been permitted to make such a decision. A fuller utilization of the united strength and wishes of all teachers would have undoubtedly resulted in greater gains."

"We regret also the decision to call off the strike before proper negotiations had been completed."

"We feel also that the acceptance of the NTU's offer of united planning and execution would have resulted in greater gains for all teachers."

—Thomas J. Hooper
Newark Evening News
February 14, 1966

APPENDIX C

Summary of Work Stoppages

The NEA Research Division tabulated in July 1966 the work stoppages by teachers from January 1940 to July 1966. These stoppages were for different periods and in a different format from the tables contained in Chapters 6 and 13. The tables follow.

TABLE 1

Summary of Withdrawals of Service by Teachers, January 1940 to July 1966, by Type of Organization Involved

Type of organization	Withdrawals of service		Personnel involved		Man-days idle	
	Number	Per cent of total	Number	Per cent of total	Number	Per cent of total
1	2	3	4	5	6	7
CIO Affiliate*	14	9.86%	865	1.16%	4,820	1.49%
AFL Affiliate*	59	41.55	51,413	69.05	238,768	73.99
Independent organization	9	6.34	925	1.24	4,140	1.28
No organization	27	19.01	1,290	1.73	18,520	5.74
Professional organization	33	23.24	19,968	26.82	56,466	17.50
Total	142	100.00%	74,461	100.00%	322,714	100.00%

* Beginning with 1956, withdrawals of service involving unions affiliated with the AFL-CIO are shown as AFL in this table.

TABLE 2

System-By-System Listing of Withdrawals of Service by Teachers, 1960–61 to 1965–66

Year	Beginning date	School system (board of education) involved	Type of organization involved	Approximate duration in days	Approximate number of personnel involved	Approximate number of man-days idle
1	2	3	4	5	6	7
1960	August 29	Macoupin County, Illinois	AFT	1	60	60
1960	November 7	New York, New York	AFT	1	5,000	5,000
1961	May 26	Portola Valley, California	Professional organization	1	20	20
1962	April 11	New York, New York	AFT	1	22,000	22,000
1963	May 2	Anderson, Indiana	AFT	5	200	1,000
1963	May 28	Gary, Indiana	AFT	1	2,000	2,000
1964	March 4	Jersey City, New Jersey	Professional organization	1	600	600
1964	May 18	East St. Louis, Illinois	AFT	5	510	2,550
1964	May 18	Utah (state-wide)	Professional organization	2	10,000	20,000
1964	June 2	Hoboken, New Jersey	Professional organization	1	170	170
1964	June 8	New York, New York	AFT	1	700	700
1964	September 8	East St. Louis, Illinois	AFT	5	400	2,000
1964	October 5	Pawtucket, Rhode Island	AFT	9	360	3,240
1964	November 2	Lakeview, Georgia	Professional organization	7	30	210
1964	November 4	Louisville, Kentucky	AFT	6	250	1,500
1965	March 19	Belleville, New Jersey	Professional organization	1	263	263
1965	March 25	Pawtucket, Rhode Island	AFT	13	380	4,980
1965	April 26	Hamtramck, Michigan	AFT	4	120	480
1965	May 11	South Bend, Indiana	AFT	6	300	1,800

TABLE 2

System-By-System Listing of Withdrawals of Service by Teachers, 1960–61 to 1965–66 (cont).

Year	Beginning date	School system (board of education) involved	Type of organization involved	Approximate duration in days	Approximate number of personnel involved	Approximate number of man-days idle
1	2	3	4	5	6	7
1965	November 1	Perth Amboy, New Jersey	AFT	12	130	1,560
1965	December 2	Newark, New Jersey	AFT	4	800	3,200
1966	February 10	Newark, New Jersey	Professional organization	2	1,500	3,000
1966	March 8	Plainview, New York	AFT	4	400	1,600
1966	March 11	New Orleans, Louisiana	AFT	3	507	1,521
1966	March 24	Thornton Fractional High School, Calumet City and Lansing Divisions, Illinois	AFT	2	120	240
1966	April 12	Tallmadge, Ohio	Professional organization	1	132	132
1966	April 12	Wallace Village for Children, Bromfield, Colorado	AFT	2	13	26
1966	April 28	Highland Park, Michigan	AFT	2	310	620
1966	June 2	Crestwood, Michigan	Professional organization	7	158	1,106
1966	June 2	Flint, Michigan	Professional organization	$2\frac{1}{2}$	1,550	3,875
1966	June 2	Melvindale, Michigan	AFT	2	130	260
1966	June 2	North Dearborn Heights, Michigan	AFT	3	117	351
1966	June 2	Taylor Township, Michigan	AFT	2	420	840
1966	June 3	Ecorse, Michigan	AFT	11*	185	2,035
1966	June 7	Wayne, Michigan	Professional organization	4	710	2,840
1966	June 14	Northville, Michigan	Professional organization	2	105	210

* Plus 16 days of summer school for personnel who would have been employed; withdrawal of service lasted until July 11.

TABLE 3

Summary of Withdrawals of Service by Teachers, 1960–61 to 1965–66, by Type of Organization Involved

Type of Organization	Withdrawals of service		Personnel involved		Man-days idle	
	Number	Per cent of total	Number	Per cent of total	Number	Per cent of total
1	2	3	4	5	6	7
American Federation of Teachers, AFL-CIO	24	66.66%	35,412	69.92%	59,563	64.75%
Professional organization	12	33.34	15,238	30.08	32,426	35.25
Total	36	100.00%	50,650	100.00%	91,989	100.00%

TABLE 4

Withdrawals of Service by Teachers, 1960–61 to 1965–66, Subsequently Made Up by Personnel Involved or not Counted as Days Lost by Boards of Education Involved (Not Included in Summary Tables 1 and 3) *

Year	Beginning date	School system (board of education) involved	Type of organization involved	Approximate duration in days	Approximate number of personnel involved	Comments
1	2	3	4	5	6	7
1964	November 9	Louisville, Kentucky	Professional organization	1	2,080	Days subsequently made up by personnel involved.
1964	November 9	Midwest City, Oklahoma	Professional organization	1	700	Counted by board of education as one of five planning days allowed by law.
1964	November 12	Oklahoma City, Oklahoma	Professional organization	1	2,200	Counted by board of education as one of five planning days allowed by law.
1965	May 11	Oklahoma (various school systems)	Professional organization	1	8,000	Counted by boards of education as one of five planning days allowed by law.
1966	February 3	Kentucky (state-wide)	Professional organization	1	26,600	Days subsequently made up by personnel involved.

* Prepared by Jack H. Kleinmann, Assistant Director, Research Division, National Education Association.

APPENDIX D

Bibliography

"Administrators Give Reluctant Approval to Sanctions: Condemn Strike Three to One" (opinion poll) *Nation's Schools*, vol. 70 (November 1962), p. 71.

American Federation of Teachers, Commission on Educational Reconstruction, *Organizing the Teaching Profession* (*The Story of the American Federation of Teachers*), Glencoe, Ill.: Free Press of Glencoe, Inc., 1955.

Barbash, Jack, "Bargaining for Professionals and Public Employees," *American Teacher Magazine*, vol. 43 (April 1959), pp. 7–8.

———, "Union Philosophy and the Professional," *American Teacher Magazine*, vol. 42 (December 1957), pp. 7–8, 18.

"Bargaining Has Not Failed," *Nation's Business*, vol. 47 (September 1959), p. 112.

Bendiner, Robert, "What's Wrong in the House of Labor?" *The Reporter*, vol. 25 (October 12, 1961), pp. 41–46.

Brameld, Theodore, "The Teacher and Organized Labor," *Educational Forum*, vol. 4 (March 1940), pp. 253–261.

Brickman, W. W., "Teachers' Organizations and Labor Unions," *School and Society*, vol. 89 (March 11, 1961), pp. 96.

Brooks, George, "A Case for Teachers' Unions," *Monthly Labor Review*, vol. 87 (March 1964), p. 292.

Buder, L., "Teachers Revolt," *Phi Delta Kappan*, vol. 43 (June 1962), pp. 370–76.

Bunzel, John H., "Pressure Groups in Politics and Education," *National Elementary Principal*, vol. 43 (January 1964), pp. 12–16.

Butler, Henry E., Jr., and Wyatt, Robert H., "Who Helps the Aggrieved Teacher?" *NEA Journal*, vol. 48 (February 1959), pp. 50, 72–73.

Caliguri, J., "Do Associations and Unions Have the Same Goals?" *American School Board Journal*, vol. 147 (December 1963), pp. 9–10.

Capen, Samuel P., "The Teaching Profession and Labor Unions," *Journal of General Education*, vol. 1 (July 1947), pp. 275–278.

Carr, William G., "The Assault on Professional Independence," *Phi Delta Kappan*, vol. 46 (September 1964), pp. 17–18.

Carroll, Mollie R., *What is Collective Bargaining?* New York: Longmans, Green and Co., 1949.

Cherry, Howard L., "Negotiations Between Boards and Teacher Organizations," *American School Board Journal*, vol. 146 (March 1963), pp. 7–9.

Cogen, Charles, "Departure From the Old Ways: The First Year of New York City Bargaining," *American Teacher Magazine*, vol. 48 (October 1963), pp. 5–6.

"Collective Bargaining vs. Collective Begging." *American Teacher Magazine*, vol. 41 (October 1956), pp. 11–12.

Conant, James B., *The Education of American Teachers*, New York: McGraw-Hill, Inc., 1963.

Corey, Arthur F., "Why Teacher Strikes Must Be Rejected by the Profession and Why Sanctions Should Be Considered," *Nation's Schools*, vol. 70 (September 1962), pp. 69–72.

Davies, Daniel R., "Norwalk Sets a Precedent," *Teachers College Record*, vol. 48 (December 1946), pp. 148–154.

Dawson, G. G., "Doctoral Studies on the Relationship Between the Labor Movement and Public Education," *Journal of Educational Sociology*, vol. 34 (February 1961), pp. 260–269.

Denemark, George W., "Schools Are Not Factories," *NEA Journal*, vol. 53 (March 1964), pp. 25–27.

"Denver Sweetheart Contract," *American Teacher Magazine*, vol. 47 (April 1963), pp. 16–17.

Eby, K., "Labor's Program for Teachers in the Postwar World," *Teachers College Record*, vol. 47 (October 1945), pp. 38–42.

Elam, S. M., "Collective Bargaining and Strikes or Professional Negotiations and Sanctions?" *Phi Delta Kappan*, vol. 44 (October 1962), pp. 1–11.

———, "Who's Ahead, and Why: The NEA-AFT Rivalry," *Phi Delta Kappan*, vol. 46 (September 1964), pp. 12–15.

Elsbree, Willard S., and Reutter, E. Edmund, Jr., *Staff Personnel in the Public Schools*, Englewood Cliffs, N.J.: Prentice-Hall, Inc., 1954.

Evans, John C., *Utah School Crisis of 1963*, Salt Lake City: Utah Education Association, 1963.

———, "Utah Teachers Pin Hope on New Strategy," *Phi Delta Kappan*, vol. 46 (September 1964), p. 16.

Evans, T. H., "Let's Look at the Causes for the Professional Collective Bargaining Group," *Journal of Engineering Education*, vol. 44 (March 1954), pp. 389–391.

Exton, Elaine, "Are Local School Boards on the Way Out?" *American School Board Journal*, vol. 148 (April 1964), pp. 19–20, 84–85.

———, "NEA Blueprint for Professional Negotiations," *American School Board Journal*, vol. 147 (September 1963), pp. 35–37.

———, "Pros and Cons of Sanctions Invoked by Utah's Public School Teachers," *American School Board Journal*, vol. 147 (July 1963), pp. 35–37, 41.

———, "Teachers' Groups Challenge Lay School Board Control," *American School Board Journal*, vol. 147 (August 1963), pp. 28–29, 32.

"Facts About Norwalk," *NEA Journal*, vol. 35 (November 1946), p. 533.

Fewkes, J. W., "Dawn of a New Era for Teachers: Chicago Teachers Union," *American Teacher Magazine*, vol. 48 (October 1963), pp. 13–14.

Fitzpatrick, J. L., "Milwaukee Vocational Story: Milwaukee Vocational Teachers Union," *American Teacher Magazine*, vol. 48 (October 1963), pp. 11–12.

Fordyce, Wellington G., "Historical Background of American Teacher Unions," *American School Board Journal*, vol. 112 (May 1946), pp. 43–44.

———, "Teachers' Unions and Labor's Weapons," *American School Board Journal*, vol. 113 (September 1946), pp. 31–33.

"Foundations for a Profession," *American Teacher Magazine*, vol. 41 (December 1956), pp. 9–10.

Garber, Lee O., "Are Union Shop Contracts for Teachers Legal?" *Nation's Schools*, vol. 61 (February 1958), pp. 70–71.

———, "Supreme Court of Montana Rules Against Teachers' Union," *Nation's Schools*, vol. 64 (September 1959), pp. 57–58.

———, "When Your Teachers Want to Select a Bargaining Agent," *Nation's Schools*, vol. 70 (July 1962), pp. 62–63.

Godine, Morton R., *The Labor Problem in the Public Service: A Study in Political Pluralism*, Cambridge, Mass.: Harvard University Press, 1951.

Gregg, R. T., and Koyen, R. A., "Teachers Associations, Organizations, and Unions," *Review of Educational Research*, vol. 19 (June 1949), pp. 260–264.

Groff, P. J., "Teacher Organizations and School Desegregation," *School and Society*, vol. 90 (December 15, 1962), pp. 441–442.

Hamilton, Robert R., and Reutter, E. Edmund, Jr., *Legal Aspects of School Board Operation*, New York: Bureau of Publications, Teachers College, Columbia University, 1958.

Harrison, G. M., "Procedures in Collective Bargaining," *American Teacher Magazine*, vol. 42 (October 1957), pp. 5–6.

Hechinger, Fred, "The Story Behind the Strike," *Saturday Review*, vol. 45 (May 19, 1962), pp. 54, 56, 78.

Hipp, Frederick L., "Advancing the Welfare of Members: Urban Associations," *NEA Journal*, vol. 53 (January 1964), pp. 19–20.

Hodgkinson, Harold L., "Teacher Strikes: Fourteen Years in Retrospect." (Study of a Case Involving the Condon-Wadlin Act in New York) in *Educational Decisions: A Casebook*, Englewood Cliffs, N.J.: Prentice-Hall, Inc. 1963, pp. 84–90.

"Inside the Teachers Union," *American School and University*, vol. 36 (November 1963), pp. 42–46, 49.

"Investigation of a School Controversy in Polson," *Montana Education*, vol. 27 (May 1951), pp. 7–12.

Jacobs, Paul, *State of the Unions*, New York: Atheneum Publishers, 1963.

Kennan, Richard B., "Professional Sanctions: Where, When and How?" *NEA Journal*, vol. 52 (December 1963), pp. 37–38.

Kleeman, Richard P., "Has This District Found a Substitute for Bargaining?" *School Management*, vol. 8 (February 1964), pp. 59–61.

Kochman, P., "Teacher Organizations on Strikes," *Phi Delta Kappan*, vol. 28 (April 1947), pp. 353–354.

Koerner, James D., *The Miseducation of American Teachers*, Boston: Houghton Mifflin Company, 1963.

Kratzman, Arthur, "The Alberta Teachers Association," *Administrator's Notebook*, vol. 12, Chicago: Midwest Administrators Center, University of Chicago, October 1963. 4 pp.

———, "The Alberta Teachers' Association—A Vision Vindicated," *Phi Delta Kappan*, vol. 45 (March 1964), pp. 288–292.

Kruger, D. H., "Professional Negotiations: Toward Quality Education," *Michigan Education Journal*, vol. 41 (April 1964), pp. 30–31.

Kuenzli, I. R., "It Is Professional To Join the Union," *American Teacher Magazine*, vol. 35 (April 1951), p. 4.

Lerner, Max, *America as a Civilization: Life and Thought in the United States Today*. New York: Simon and Schuster, Inc., 1957.

———, "A Way Out of Our Strike Dilemma," *Look*, vol. 25 (October 12, 1961), pp. 84, 86–90.

Lieberman, Myron, *Education as a Profession*, Englewood Cliffs, N.J.: Prentice-Hall, Inc., 1956.

———, "Some Reflections on Teachers Organizations," *Education Forum*, vol. 24 (November 1959), pp. 71–76.

———, "Teachers Choose a Union," *The Nation*, vol. 193 (December 2, 1961), pp. 443–447, 460.

———, "Teachers Strikes: An Analysis of the Issues," *Harvard Educational Review*, vol. 26 (Winter 1956), pp. 39–70.

———, "The Battle for New York City's Teachers," *Phi Delta Kappan*, vol. 43 (October 1961), pp . 2–8.

———, *The Future of Public Education*, Chicago: University of Chicago Press, 1960.

———, and Moskow, Michael, *Collective Negotiation in Public Education*, Chicago: Rand McNally & Company, 1966.

Lindsey, Margaret, ed., *New Horizons for the Teaching Profession*, Washington, D.C.: National Commission on Teacher Education and Professional Standards, National Education Association, 1961.

"Local Associations Build Professional Strength," (symposium) *NEA Journal*, vol. 53 (February 1964), pp. 18–32.

Martin, Harold H., "Has Success Spoiled Big Labor?" *Saturday Evening Post*, vol. 235 (December 8, 1962), pp. 75–79.

Megel, Carl, "The AFT Reply: Which Organization Gets Results?" *Phi Delta Kappan*, vol. 46 (September 1964), pp. 19–21.

———, "Can A Case Be Made for Teacher Unions?" *Nation's Schools*, vol. 73 (February 1964), p. 51.

———, "Teacher Union Leader Views School Problems," *Teachers College Record*, vol. 59 (January 1958), pp. 26–31.

———, "Union Pattern in Teachers' Organizations," *Teachers College Record*, vol. 63 (November 1961), pp. 115–120.

Michigan Education Association, Professional Negotiation Committee, "Procedure for Negotiation," *Michigan Education Journal*, vol. 41 (November 1963), pp. 6–8.

"Most Teachers Will Not Join Unions, Administrators Believe—and Hope," (opinion poll) *Nation's Schools*, vol. 69 (May 1962), p. 81.

National Education Association, *NEA Handbook,* 1965–66, Washington, D.C.: the Association, 1966. (This handbook is issued annually.)

National Education Association, American Association of School Administrators, *Education Administration in a Changing Community*, Thirty-seventh Yearbook, Washington, D.C.: American Association of School Administrators, 1959.

———, *Roles, Responsibilities, Relationships of the School Board, Superintendent and Staff*, Washington, D.C.: American Association of School Administrators, 1963.

School Administrators view Professional Negotiations. Washington D.C.: The American Association of School Administrators, 1966, 58 pp.

National Education Association, Department of Classroom Teachers, *Classroom Teachers Speak on Professional Negotiation*, Washington, D.C.: the Association, 1963.

———, *Conditions of Work for Quality Teachers*, Washington, D.C.: the Association, 1959.

National Education Association, National Commission on Professional Rights and Responsibilities, *Guidelines for Professional Sanctions*, Washington, D.C.: the Commission, 1963.

———, *Report of an Investigation. Cleveland, Ohio: When a Board of Education Fails to Fulfill Its Proper Responsibilities*, Washington, D.C.: the Commission, June 1964.

———, *Report of an Investigation. North College Hill, Ohio: An Example of Some Effects of Board of Education Interference with Sound Administration of Public Education*, Washington, D.C.: the Commission, 1947.

———, *Report of an Investigation. Utah: A State-wide Study of School Conditions*, Washington, D.C.: the Commission, March 1964.

———, *Report of an Investigation. Waterbury, Connecticut: A Study of the Inhibiting Effect of Political Control on the Quality of Education*, Washington, D.C.: the Commission, May 1963.

———, *Report of an Investigation. West Haven, Connecticut: A Study of Community Inaction*, Washington, D.C.: the Commission, September 1959.

National Education Association, Office of Professional Development and Welfare, *Guidelines for Professional Negotiation*, Washington, D.C.: the Association, 1963. (Revised in 1964 and 1966.)

———, *Professional Negotiation: Selected Statements of School Board, Administrator, Teacher Relationships*, rev. ed., Washington, D.C.: the Association, 1966.

National Education Association, Research Division, *Professional Negotiation with School Boards: A Legal Analysis and Review*, Washington, D.C.: the Association, January 1962.

———, "Collective Bargaining," *The Teacher and the Law*, Research Monograph 1959–M3, Washington, D.C.: the Association, 1959. Part IV, pp. 87–90.

———, "Teachers and Collective Bargaining," *Research Bulletin*, vol. 36 (April 1958), pp. 46–49.

National Education Association and Washington Education Association, *Report of the NEA-WEA Investigation Committee on Kelso, Washington*, Washington, D.C.: National Education Association, June 1950.

Neary, H. James, "American Trade Union Membership in 1962," *Monthly Labor Review*, vol. 87 (May 1964), pp. 501–507.

Nelson, M. L., "Minneapolis Story," *American Teacher Magazine*, vol. 41 (April 1957), pp. 11–12.

Newton, R., and Lee, Betty Jean, "Denver Achieves Professional Negotiations," *NEA Journal*, vol. 52 (February 1963), pp. 14–16.

Nolte, M. Chester, and Linn, John P., "Political and Personal Rights of Teachers," *School Law for Teachers*, Danville, Ill.: Interstate Printers and Publishers, Inc., 1963. Chapter 7, pp. 167–201.

Oakes, R. C., "Should Teachers Strike? An Unanswered Question," *Journal of Educational Sociology*, vol. 33 (March 1960), pp. 339–344.

Petro, Sylvester, *The Kingsport Strike*. New Rocheile, New York: The Aslington House, 1967.

Porter, R. G., "Collective Bargaining for Teachers," *American Teacher Magazine*, vol. 45 (February 1961), pp. 9–10+.

Raskin, A. H., "The Big Strike: A Thing of the Past?" *Saturday Review*, vol. 46 (November 16, 1963), pp. 20–22, 91.

Redefer, Frederick L., "The Morale of Teachers," *Research Memo 1963–18*, Washington, D.C.: National Education Association, Research Division, August 1963.

Remmlein, Madaline K., "Collective Bargaining," *School Law*, 2nd ed., Danville, Ill.: Interstate Printers and Publishers, Inc., 1962. Chapter 5, pp. 85–96.

Rhodes, Eric, "New York City Teacher Election," *NEA Journal*, vol. 51 (February 1962), pp. 21–22.

Rich, J. M., "Civil Disobedience and Teacher Strikes," *Phi Delta Kappan*, vol. 45 (December 1963), pp. 151–154.

Riordan, M. E., "Operation Bandwagon in Detroit: Detroit Federation of Teachers," *American Teacher Magazine*, vol. 48 (October 1963), pp. 15–16.

Scanlon, John, "Strikes, Sanctions, and the Schools," *Saturday Review*, vol. 46 (October 19, 1963), pp. 51–55, 70–74.

Schaub, D. W., "Focus on Professional Negotiations," *Ohio Schools*, vol. 41 (March 1963), pp. 12–13.

Schiff, Albert, *A Study and Evaluation of Teachers' Strikes in the United States*, doctoral dissertation, Department of Education, Wayne State University, 1952. Ann Arbor, Mich.: University Microfilms, Inc., 1962.

———, "Teachers' Strikes in the United States," *Phi Delta Kappan*, vol. 34 (January 1953), pp. 133–135.

Seitz, Reynolds C., "School Boards and Teacher Unions," *American School Board Journal*, vol. 141 (August 1960), pp. 11–13, 38.

Selden, David, "American Federation of Teachers," *School Management*, vol. 8 (February 1964), pp. 56–58, 61–62, 102.

———, "Class Size and the New York Contract," *Phi Delta Kappan*, vol. 47 (March 1964), pp. 283–287.

———, "Needed: More Teacher Strikes," *Phi Delta Kappan*,

———, "Why the AFT Maintains its AFL-CIO Affiliation," *Phi Delta Kappan*, vol. 47 (February 1966), pp. 298–300.

Shanker, A., "N.Y.C. Local 2 in Negotiations: Six-Way Program," *American Teacher Magazine*, vol. 46 (February 1962), p. 16.

Shoben, E. J., "When Teachers Strike," *Teachers College Record*, vol. 65 (November 1963), pp. 164–167.

"Should Teachers Strike? No! Negotiation with Boards? Yes!" (opinion poll) *Nation's Schools*, vol. 66 (October 1960), p. 79.

Smith, F. M., "Teachers Unions vs. the Professional Association," *School and Society*, vol. 90 (December 15, 1962), pp. 439–440.

Stahl, O. Glenn, *Public Personnel Administration*, 5th ed., New York: Harper & Row, Publishers, 1962.

Starie, J. H., and Spatafora, J., "Union or Professional Membership: A Matter of Philosophy and Program," *NEA Journal*, vol. 51 (March 1962), pp. 80–81.

Stecker, F. G., "How the A.F. of T. Began," *American Teacher Magazine*, vol. 41 (April 1957), pp. 13–14.

Steffensen, James P., *Teachers Negotiate with their School Boards*, United States Department of Health, Education, and Welfare, Office of Education, Bulletin 1964, No. 40. Washington, D.C.: Government Printing Office, 1964.

Stinnett, T. M., "Professional Negotiation, Collective Bargaining, Sanctions, and Strikes," *Bulletin of the National Association of Secondary-School Principals*, vol. 48 (April 1964), pp. 93–105.

Stinnett, T. M., and Huggett, Albert J., *Professional Problems of Teachers*, 2nd ed. New York: The Macmillan Company, 1963.

Stinnett, T. M., Kleinmann, Jack H., and Ware, Martha L., *Professional Negotiation in Public Education*, New York: The Macmillan Company, 1966.

Sultan, Paul E., *The Disenchanted Unionist*, New York: Harper & Row, Publishers, 1963.

"Teachers' Right to Strike," *School and Society*, vol. 92 (March 7, 1964), pp. 93–94.

Thorne, Irene, *Collective Negotiation: A Survey and Analysis of Teacher Group College Negotiation Contracts with School Boards* (unpublished doctoral dissertation), New York: Teachers College, Columbia University, 1961.

Ware, Martha L., "Professional Negotiation," *NEA Journal*, vol. 51, (November 1962), pp. 28–30.

West, Allan M., "Professional Negotiations or Collective Bargaining?" *National Elementary Principal*, vol. 42 (February 1963), pp. 20–25.

———, "Victory in Milwaukee: The NEA Tackles Urban Problems," *Phi Delta Kappan*, vol. 45 (March 1964), pp. 293–296.

Widick, B. J., *Labor Today: The Triumphs and Failures of Unionism in the U.S.*, Boston: Houghton Mifflin Company, 1964.

Wildman, Wesley A., "Collective Action by Public School Teachers," *Administrator's Notebook*, vol. 11, Chicago: Midwest Administration Center, University of Chicago (February 1963). 4 pp.

Wildman, Wesley A., and Perry, Charles R., "Group Conflict and School Organization: An Analysis and a Warning," *Phi Delta Kappan*, vol. 47 (January 1966), pp. 244–251.

Winick, C., "When Teachers Strike," *Teachers College Record*, vol. 64 (April 1963), pp. 593–604.

Woodring, Paul, "The New York Teachers' Strike," *Saturday Review*, vol. 45 (May 19, 1962), pp. 51–52.

INDEX OF NAMES

SUBJECT INDEX

Date Due

FEB 8 '74	FEB 8 '74		
3-21-74			
AUG 1 0 1975			
DEC 12 '77			
DEC 1 3 1982			
NOV 2 4 1997			

BRODART CAT. NO. 23 233 PRINTED IN U.S.A.